music in secondary schools

MUSIC IN SECONDARY SCHOOLS

Ira C. Singleton

Allyn and Bacon, Inc. Boston

First printing: April 1963
Second printing: February 1965

Library of Congress Catalog Card Number: 63-12716

preface

This is a methods book. It deals with music teaching in the junior and senior high schools—general music and other music classes, choral music, and instrumental music. Written as a textbook for college and university courses, it offers detailed and practical information to help solve the specific problems of daily teaching for both beginning and experienced teachers.

Because successful teaching does not depend on method alone, this book also discusses many related topics: curriculum, teachers' schedules, supervision and administration, characteristics of adolescence, philosophies and problems of music education. It is appropriate reading for undergraduate and graduate students, school administrators, and parents interested in the nature of music education and the manner in which music teachers achieve their goals in the public schools.

The first two chapters are introductory, describing existing music programs, the historical development of music education, and the characteristics of the secondary-school pupil. Chapters 3–6 deal with the pressing problems of general music and similar required or elective classes designed to give to all students a broad acquaintance with their music heritage. Chapters 7–9 discuss the problems of teaching music through choral activities; Chapters 10–12, the teaching of music through the instrumental program. Chapter 13 is both a conclusion and a bridge to further study; it re-states the current problems of music education and suggests concepts from which a personal philosophy can be developed.

It is generally agreed that there is no one best method for teaching music. A teaching procedure quite inappropriate for one class may be an outstanding success in another. These differences are inevitable. Successful teaching considers many elements—the teacher's background, interests and personality, the pupil's knowledge, attitude and response, the school's curriculum, facilities and location. It is therefore unwise to prescribe one set of teaching procedures for all situations. Yet it is essential that every teacher be informed of the procedures used successfully by other teachers in other situations. This is the intent of this book: to present specific methods practices from which each teacher can develop the procedures best suited to his teaching, his pupils, and his school environment.

Ira C. Singleton

acknowledgments

The author is grateful to the following individuals for their coöperation during the preparation of this book.

Dr. Irvin Cooper, School of Music, The Florida State University, Tallahassee, Florida, for information concerning vocal teaching.

Mr. Damon D. Holton, Director of Music, Norristown, Pennsylvania, for suggestions concerning instrumental teaching.

Dr. James E. Richards, Head, Music Department, East Texas State College, Commerce, Texas, for many valuable suggestions concerning choral teaching.

Dr. Robert L. Garretson, University of Cincinnati, Cincinnati, Ohio, for reading the manuscript and offering numerous suggestions for its improvement.

Vera Freid of the Cincinnati Public Schools, Dr. James E. Richards of East Texas State College, and R. Stanwood Weeks of the Philip Lesly Company for assistance in securing photographs.

The author is indebted to these publishers for permission to refer to copyrighted materials.

Abrahams Magazine Service, Inc., New York, N.Y.
Allyn and Bacon, Inc., Boston, Mass.
American Journal of Psychology, Austin, Texas.
Carl Fischer, Inc., New York, N.Y.
Holt, Rinehart and Winston, Inc., New York, N.Y.
The Macmillan Company, New York, N.Y.
Music Educators National Conference, Washington, D.C.
National Education Association, Washington, D.C.
Prentice-Hall, Inc., Englewood Cliffs, N.J.
Theodore Presser Company, Bryn Mawr, Pennsylvania.

Schmitt, Hall and McCreary Company, Minneapolis, Minn.
Summy-Birchard Company, Evanston, Illinois.
United States Office of Education, Washington, D.C.

Thanks are due to many other individuals—teachers, friends, and colleagues—whose influence helped in one way or another to shape the opinions of the author. Many of these associations are years in the past and the specific ideas they contributed are no longer identifiable. The author wishes to express his heartfelt gratitude, nevertheless, to all these people without whose help, direct or indirect, this book would not have been possible.

contents

PREFACE v

ACKNOWLEDGMENTS vii

PART ONE: MUSIC EDUCATION TODAY

1: patterns in music education 3

SCHOOLS AND THEIR MUSIC PROGRAMS · THE PAST AND ITS PIONEERS ·

2: pupils in music education 25

KNOWING THE PUPIL · THE IMPORTANCE OF ADOLESCENCE · MUSIC PLAYS ITS PART ·

PART TWO: THE GENERAL MUSIC CLASS

3: the nature of general music 39

GENERAL MUSIC IN THE SCHOOL PROGRAM · PUPILS AND THEIR DIFFERENCES · PUPIL NEEDS AND TEACHING GOALS · ASPECTS AND ACTIVITIES OF GENERAL MUSIC · THE TEACHER OF GENERAL MUSIC ·

4: singing in the general music class 58

GUIDING THE ADOLESCENT SINGER · EXPANDING THE REPERTOIRE · MUSICAL GROWTH THROUGH SINGING · THE SINGING WAY TO MUSIC UNDERSTANDING ·

5: listening in the general music class 94

THE IMPORTANCE OF LISTENING ACTIVITIES · THE PUPIL AND HIS PROGRESS · EXPANDING THE LISTENING REPERTOIRE · THE LISTENING WAY TO MUSICAL UNDERSTANDING ·

6: planning for progress 126

THE MANY-SIDED PROGRAM · PLANNING FOR THE GENERAL MUSIC CLASS · THE TOTAL PATTERN OF GENERAL MUSIC ·

PART THREE: THE VOCAL PROGRAM

7: choral organizations and activities 167

ORGANIZING CHORAL GROUPS · UTILIZING ADOLESCENT VOICES · ADMINISTRATIVE CONSIDERATIONS ·

8: the choral rehearsal 207

THE PHYSICAL ASPECT · THE TONAL ASPECT · THE TEACHING ASPECT · PLANNING THE REHEARSAL ·

9: choral performance 248

THE GOALS OF CHORAL PERFORMANCE · THE VARIETY OF CONCERT OPPORTUNITIES · ARRANGING THE CONCERT CALENDAR · BUILDING THE CONCERT PROGRAM · USING CONCERT SHOWMANSHIP ·

PART FOUR: THE INSTRUMENTAL PROGRAM

10: establishing the program 273

RECRUITING NEW MEMBERS · INSTRUCTING THE BEGINNERS ·

11: teaching advanced players 320

PERFORMING GROUPS · SPECIAL CLASSES · GROUP INSTRUCTION AND PERFORMANCE ·

12: administering the program 356

PROPERTY MANAGEMENT · HUMAN RELATIONS ·

PART FIVE: A PHILOSOPHY OF MUSIC EDUCATION

13: looking to the future 385

QUESTIONS IN MUSIC EDUCATION · DEVELOPING A POINT OF VIEW ·

BIBLIOGRAPHY 396

part one: Music Education Today

1: patterns in music education

What will I be asked to teach? What will be my schedule? Whether he is new to the field of teaching or a veteran of twenty years' experience, the teacher with a new position in prospect often asks these questions. They indicate that the music-education curriculum is not standardized and that the teacher's duties in one community can be quite different from those in another.

Music has enjoyed steady growth in popularity during the past few decades. More and more people are turning to music for the unique pleasures it can give. Record-of-the-month clubs are becoming increasingly popular, high fidelity and stereophonic sound systems are being purchased in increasing numbers, and there are encouraging signs of a resurgence of interest in the live performances of the concert hall and operatic stage.

Much of this is reflected in the music courses and activities offered by the public schools. Where there is more interest there are more courses; where there is interest in listening to music there are courses in music appreciation; where there is interest in performing there are courses in piano, voice, and instruments. Public interests and tastes exert influence upon educational programs, and education in turn influences the public and its tastes. If the forces of music education do their work effectively, interest in music will continue to grow and levels of taste will continue to rise.

SCHOOLS AND THEIR MUSIC PROGRAMS

The patterns of music education are influenced by the general structure of the school system. As we survey our schools, we see three principal types: (1) the elementary school in which most children explore the same subject-matter areas, often under the guidance of only one classroom teacher; (2) the junior high school in which there is opportunity for pupils to explore a wider range of subject areas under the guidance of teachers skilled in one or several subjects; (3) the senior high school in which the pupil may choose courses directly related to his intended vocation under expert teachers who specialize in one subject area. Music education is carried on within this framework. It is an integral part of the structure and conforms to the established design of the total educational program.

Music in the Elementary School

In the elementary school, music occupies a relatively important place in the daily activities of the classroom. Younger children respond quickly and easily to music; many of the attitudes and skills they must develop can be approached through music; many teachers of these younger children find music easy to teach at this level. It is productive in terms of child development and brightens the days for both teachers and pupils. In the elementary school, music can be regarded as a required subject in that it is offered to every child regularly as a part of daily classroom activities. Included in this required session are singing, rhythmic activities, listening, creative activities, and work with simple rhythm and melody instruments. Where time and facilities permit, this program is sometimes supplemented with special activities for children who are particularly interested or gifted —choruses and other singing groups, piano classes, instrumental lessons, bands and orchestras.

The required portion of the music program is taught by the classroom teacher, the music specialist, or by both. If taught by the classroom teacher, music work can be planned flexibly for any portion of the school day, the teacher's thorough knowledge of each child can be used to best advantage, and music can be interwoven easily with work in other subject areas through the unit-of-study approach. If music is taught by a specialist, there are obvious advantages in the teacher's higher degree of music training and skill, wider acquaintance with music literature and materials, and in the higher levels of skill which can be developed by the pupils.

If music teaching is reserved for the music specialist, scheduling becomes a major problem. The fortunate music teacher has a music room in the elementary-school building. It is equipped with song books appropriate for the various grades, phonograph and records, rhythm instruments, and other necessary equipment. The less fortunate teacher has no music room and must go from class to class, often with little more than a pitch pipe and as many song books as can be carried under one arm. In either case, the scheduling of music lessons is difficult and the time available for music may seem less than adequate. The teacher who walks from room to room sometimes sees each group of children only once each week for as little as twenty minutes; the teacher fortunate enough to have a music room fares somewhat better, seeing each group one or more times each week in the music room for whatever length of time is permitted by scheduling arrangements. Neither arrangement, however, permits music to be offered when most appropriate to children's needs and interests or with the flexibility possible when music teaching is carried on by the classroom teacher.

In some instances, the question of whether music should be taught in the elementary school by the classroom teacher or by a music specialist is decided solely in terms of the school budget. The special music teacher is sometimes thought of as a luxury and is the last of the additions to the school program when increases in funds are slow to materialize. There are valid reasons for asking the classroom teacher to take an active part in this aspect of the child's development, and there are equally valid reasons for seeking the highly developed skills and special training of the music teacher. This problem is one music education must face and solve. To give the child strong music foundations during his years in the elementary school, it is important to find a way to combine the advantages offered by the classroom teacher and the music specialist.

Music in the Junior High School

The junior high school of today is a community of active, adolescent boys and girls learning to live with their peers and to meet the responsibilities soon to come in adult life. They are guided by teachers thoroughly trained in both subject matter and human relationships. Many of these teachers, often those who are most successful, develop a feeling of dedication to teaching at this level. The junior-high-school age is a critical one. The service performed by a capable teacher can be a major factor in shaping the future character of the pupil.

The curriculum of the junior high school is shaped to meet adolescent needs and interests. A variety of subjects is offered. The pupil continues the studies basic to his general education while surveying new and specialized areas he may explore more thoroughly during later school years. Clubs, activities, and student organizations begin to assume importance—partly because they offer further opportunity to explore areas of special interest, partly because the adolescent is by nature active and interested in joining such groups. Each subject is taught by a specially prepared teacher in rooms equipped for the purpose, such as science laboratories, food service rooms, and industrial arts shops.

To utilize teachers and facilities to greatest advantage, classes move from room to room throughout the school day, beginning and ending each day in homerooms organized to serve administrative purposes. To facilitate instruction, pupils are separated into groups according to age, ability, interest, or need, and the make-up of any one group may change from period to period as the pupils go successively to English, physical education, science, and industrial arts.

Because of its variety of curricular and extra-curricular offerings, and because of the freedom it offers in movement from room to room and group to group, the junior high school can be either a new and disturbing experience for pupils accustomed to the relative stability of the elementary school or a stimulating and challenging new world. Junior high schools and their pupils are unique, and it is this unique quality that provides teachers with both challenge and opportunity.

Although music is regarded as one of the special subjects, along with art, physical education, and others, it fits readily into the junior-high-school pattern of service to adolescent needs. It provides extra-curricular, elective performing groups which offer release to the volatile emotions of adolescence and experience in a type of coöperative effort not duplicated in other school activities. Through general music classes, it builds upon foundations laid in the elementary school and seeks to bring to every pupil new experiences in the perception of musical beauty and new or improved music skills. For some pupils, it is during the junior-high-school years that interest is first shown in a music vocation; for others, junior-high-school music activities are the beginning of life-long avocational enjoyment. Because it is the only required music class and the only means of reaching all pupils, the general music class is rightly regarded as the foundation of the junior-high-school music program.

Elective music activities in the junior high school include both instrumental and vocal performing groups. Mixed choruses, boys' glee clubs, and girls' glee clubs are common, with smaller ensembles such as trios and quartets being developed as needed. In the instrumental area, bands, orchestras, and smaller instrumental ensembles are all desirable, although the band dominates the instrumental scene and the orchestra is often either small and unbalanced or nonexistent.

Best results are obtained with performing groups if the directors are specialists in their fields. Vocal performing groups and general music classes are normally under the direction of a specialist in vocal music, instrumental groups under an instrumental specialist. The vocal specialist, teaching a large number of general music classes and directing the vocal groups and classes, usually finds that teaching duties in any one junior high school are sufficient to provide a full schedule. The instrumental specialist sometimes finds that his schedule is only partly filled by instrumental teaching in any one junior high school. If such is the case, he may spend his extra time in the elementary schools from which his junior-high-school instrumentalists come. This arrangement permits the teacher to offer instrumental training to younger pupils, to supervise their progress for several years before they reach the junior high school, and to raise the performing level of his junior-high-school groups.

In addition to these regular music classes and performing groups, there are numerous special junior-high-school functions in which music plays an important part and which can be regarded as important to the school music program. School assemblies, meetings of parent-teacher organizations, dramatic productions, and annual shows regularly utilize the services of music teachers and their students. Music clubs are a natural addition to the music program and to the extensive array of clubs offered by the junior high school to serve special adolescent interests.

Although music is a special subject, it reaches every pupil in the school and provides experiences unlike those offered by any other school activity. The music teacher in the junior high school is a particularly important member of the school music staff. Though he receives less public acclaim than high-school teachers whose bands and choruses appear in frequent concerts, win contests, and appear at football games, the junior-high-school music teacher has unlimited opportunities to develop interests and skills without which high-school music programs would make only limited progress.

Music in the Senior High School

The senior high school is the culmination of today's system of public education. Although we are becoming increasingly aware of the desirability of junior colleges and general colleges, the senior high school has not yet been replaced as the terminal phase of the public-school system. The function of the high school is two-fold: it strives to round out and complete the education furnished by the public schools, and it strives to prepare each student for the life he will lead upon completion of his public-school education.

For some, the high school offers courses prerequisite to study at the college level. For others, it provides an introduction to specific vocations for which college training is not required. For all, it provides a core of basic subjects to develop the knowledges and understandings believed necessary in our society. As a result, today's high school offers a variety of courses, from English, sciences, and social studies through foreign languages and fine arts to homemaking, industrial arts, and driver training. Subjects considered necessary to all make up the required core. To supplement the required core, each student elects courses to meet college entrance requirements, to prepare for a vocation, or to explore fields dictated by his own interests.

Another very important phase of the high-school program is that which includes the various non-academic activities. Student-government organizations play an important role in shaping and administering certain school policies and activities, giving students valuable experience in self-government. Other student organizations govern school social life, plan and administer dances, manage ticket sales, and conduct much other extra-curricular business. A diversified array of clubs serves almost every interest from photography and sculpture to hunting and fishing. School newspapers, magazines, and yearbooks provide outlets for literary talent. Extensive sports programs offer something for every student. Although these organizations and activities are extra-curricular, they perform important functions in the school program. Through them students begin to learn about human relationships, independent thinking, self-discipline, and administration of personal and business affairs. For students only one step removed from adult life, these extra-curricular activities provide a foretaste of adult responsibility and minister to the desire for adult independence.

In both its curricular and extra-curricular aspects, the high school is influenced by its environment and by public opinion and criticism. The demands of a technological society, the effects of a national or local way of life, the presence or absence of employment opportunities—these and many other environmental factors exert subtle pressures upon the school program. Less subtle pressures are exerted by public opinion and criticism. Because parents are deeply interested in the welfare of their children, and because children spend so much time in schools and can be shaped in mind and character by the educational process, the school system is the object of constant public scrutiny. On the national level, magazines and newspapers editorialize about the merits or deficiencies of the educational process. On the local level, school boards, parent-teacher organizations, and the average citizen tend to evaluate their schools periodically and voice opinions freely. In many respects this sustained public evaluation contributes to the health and well-being of the schools. It makes self-evaluation almost mandatory and requires that schools and teachers define their philosophies, goals, and methods.

The high-school teacher is one who must fit into the pattern of curricular and extra-curricular activities. He must be a capable teacher thoroughly versed in his subject and able to discuss it intelligently with students, their parents, and alert community groups. The high-school teacher has scholarly interests and is widely read and learned in his field. He is able to work with mature students on an intellectual plane, ready to lead those who are particularly interested or gifted in a detailed examination of subject matter beyond the limits of normal classroom discussion. He is interested in phases of student development not directly related to his teaching in the classroom, often serving as faculty adviser to extra-curricular activities. Finally, he must have sufficient professional breadth to present the case for his subject or for the school to intelligent lay audiences.

The music program in the high school serves somewhat different purposes from those of the elementary or junior high school. It is rarely placed in the category of the required subjects, being offered instead as an elective to those whose talent or interest prompts them to continue with music. In its classroom phases, it is one of the fine arts, taught with the purpose of developing deeper appreciations and expanded areas of enjoyment. As activities, the various performing groups often serve social purposes similar to those of other student organizations. For some students, the performing groups serve as vocational training. For the school as a whole, performing groups lend interest and color to football games, annual shows, assembly programs, and other school events. Not least important among the functions of the high-school music program is the fact that it has great public-relations value. It offers to parents and the rest of the community evidence of the achievements of students while furnishing enjoyable entertainment often of near-professional quality.

To achieve these objectives, the high-school music curriculum has developed into a many-faceted program. Because it is not common practice to require any basic core of music courses, the program in one high school may be quite different from that in another. A great variety of music courses is possible and almost every type may be found in today's high schools. For students who turn to music chiefly for listening pleasure, there are courses in general music, music appreciation, music history and literature. For those who like to sing and hope to achieve membership in choral groups, there are sight singing and voice classes. For instrumentalists whose interests range beyond participation in performing groups, instrumental teachers sometimes establish courses in music theory, arranging or orchestration, composition, or even conducting. Of these, general music, voice class, and music theory are probably most common, but every one of these courses has been offered at the high-school level.

In the area of instrumental performance, band, orchestra, dance band, and smaller ensembles are common. Choir, chorus, glee club, madrigal groups, and other small ensembles are among the vocal organizations. In addition to these groups, many directors organize classes in which students are prepared for membership in the more selective performing groups. These may include beginning, intermediate, and advanced instrument classes as well as their vocal counterparts. All of these organizations and classes tend to attract talented or accomplished students, especially those who may choose to follow music actively as a vocation or hobby. For those not interested in performing groups, there is little beyond the general music or music appreciation course. The high-school music program also includes a large number of special, extra-curricular activities which sometimes overshadow regularly scheduled classes. The football band, annual variety show or operetta, contests and festivals, school concerts, assemblies, and out-of-school appearances of many kinds make heavy demands on students and teachers. The better the school music program, the more quickly do community organizations find that a telephone call to the high-school choral or instrumental director will suffice to secure well-performed and enjoyable music for their meetings.

Although there are good reasons for offering a variety of music activities in the high school, the difficulties of scheduling create problems for both music teachers and administrators. Music is a special subject and can not take scheduling precedence over English, social studies and other basic subjects. Music classes are likely to be either very large, such as the band and glee club, or very small and specialized, such as those in music theory and arranging. In either case, it is difficult to find a time during the school day when these groups can meet without disrupting the total school schedule. Members of performing groups, especially, come from all strata of the school population rather than from any one class. A band rehearsal might draw one or more students from every room in the school. There are conflicts even within the music department in that outstanding instrumentalists are frequently the most capable readers of vocal music; thus choral and instrumental directors prefer to schedule rehearsals of their large performing groups at different times during the school day. Suggestions for scheduling will be presented later in the book.

Music classes other than performing groups are treated much like classes in other special subjects. Many are placed in the portion of the school day occupied by physical education and art, sharing the same period each day on a rotating basis. The specialized music groups, such as voice class and music theory, sometimes meet only once each week. General music and music appreciation also meet once each week unless local policy permits them to meet more often.

In the high school, more so than at any other level, teaching duties demand the abilities of specialists in vocal and instrumental music. Glee clubs, choirs, and madrigal groups require the guidance of a capable singer who plays the piano with facility. The vocal teacher often offers the courses in general music and music appreciation for the general student, as well as voice and sight singing classes, when they are offered, for talented and interested students. Instrumental groups require the attention of specialists; a brass or woodwind player for the band, and a string player for the orchestra, although in smaller school systems one teacher may be responsible for the entire instrumental program. In addition to performing groups and instrument classes, the instrumentalist often teaches such classes, when offered, as music theory and orchestration.

Although the prime requisite in each instance is ability and knowledge in either the vocal or instrumental field, the successful teacher has other attributes almost equally important. The director of performing groups must be a capable conductor, able to work with large groups of young people and before audiences of all kinds. Because the success of many music events depends upon the efficiency with which they are organized, the teacher must be systematic, farsighted, and able to plan for all the aspects and eventualities of public performance—including not only program printing and contingents of ushers, but misplaced oboe reeds, laryngitis, and sprained ankles as well. Finally, because the music teacher is much more frequently in the public eye than are many other teachers, he should be able to meet people easily and to talk intelligently about music and his professional field of education.

One other responsibility often rests with the high-school music teacher.

The community large enough to need several music teachers, or one music teacher and a number of elementary-school classroom teachers, finds it desirable to designate a music supervisor. In most cases this is a high-school teacher and in many, it is the high-school instrumental teacher, unless the community is large enough to require a full-time supervisor. The supervisor oversees the total music program of the community, consulting with other teachers about the sequence of music instruction through all schools and grades, needed materials and equipment, methods of instruction, and other pertinent matters. The supervisor serves as consultant to other teachers, a source of information and advice when needed, and on occasion establishes in-service training programs for the classroom teachers of the elementary schools or for all the music teachers of the local staff. With or without this added responsibility, the high-school music teacher occupies a position of paramount importance in the school music program and finds ample outlet for all his energies and abilities.

Teachers and Their Schedules

Within the general framework of music courses and activities, the schedules of individual teachers differ widely and the possibilities for a variety of scheduling arrangements are legion. Some teachers work in one building only, while others divide their time between two or more buildings. In the latter case, the several buildings may include an elementary school and a junior high school, or a junior high school and a senior high school. Some teachers are occupied in either the vocal or the instrumental area exclusively, while others occupy positions in which the two are combined. Other variations in schedules result from school policies and philosophies having to do with teacher load and required music sequences, or from student needs and interests which cause courses to be added or dropped from year to year.

There is, therefore, no such thing as an average or typical schedule followed by large numbers of music teachers in similar positions; almost every teacher finds that his schedule is different in some way from those of other teachers. This is true even in large, metropolitan school systems where there may be a number of high schools, all with identical complements of vocal and instrumental teachers and all governed by similar school policies. There are factors common to many music programs, however, which cause similarities in scheduling patterns for basic courses.

Table 1 is a sample schedule showing the daily routine of a teacher in junior-high-school vocal music. The teacher's day extends from about

TABLE 1. SCHEDULE OF VOCAL-MUSIC TEACHER IN THE JUNIOR HIGH SCHOOL.

Period	*Monday*	*Tuesday*	*Wednesday*	*Thursday*	*Friday*
8:45 9:00	Homeroom	Homeroom	Homeroom	Homeroom	Homeroom
9:00 9:50	Free	Boys' Glee Club	Mixed Chorus	Girls' Glee Club	Mixed Chorus
9:50 10:40	General Music (7A)	General Music (7B)	General Music (7A)	General Music (7B)	Free
10:40 11:30	General Music (8A)	Free	General Music (8A)	Free	Ensemble Coaching
12:30 1:20	General Music (7C)	General Music (7E)	General Music (7C)	General Music (7E)	School Assembly
1:20 2:10	Free	General Music (9B)	General Music (9A)	General Music (9B)	General Music (9A)
2:10 3:00	General Music (7D)	General Music (8B)	General Music (7D)	General Music (8B)	Music Club

8:30 A.M. to 4:00 P.M. It includes six class periods each fifty minutes long, sometimes a brief homeroom period, a lunch hour, and an hour or more at the end of the school day for class preparation, clerical work, or giving special assistance to individual students or groups. In this school, general music meets twice each week, is required of all pupils in the seventh grade, and must be elected for another full year during either eighth or ninth grade. This policy provides a relatively large number of general music classes but permits the teacher to organize three singing groups, meeting once or twice each week, as well as a music club. During weekly school assemblies, the teacher may sit on the stage with the principal, student chairman, and guests, and direct the patriotic and other songs which are a regular part of the program. Free periods are included in many teachers' schedules as a matter of school policy to provide time for necessary class preparation and clerical work. The music teacher finds them useful for special rehearsals of small vocal ensembles or sections of the glee clubs. Although extra responsibilities are not usually apparent in schedules, the junior-high-school vocal teacher finds that much additional time is devoted to preparation for school shows and concert programs, parent-teacher meetings, extra rehearsals, and other duties.

The schedule of the junior-high-school instrumental teacher, Table 2, follows the same pattern of periods and times as that of the vocal teacher. This instrumental teacher is not charged with a homeroom group but finds his time prior to morning band rehearsal always filled; minor instrument repairs, work in the music library, or students who come to him with questions or for assistance consume all the time he can spare.

TABLE 2. SCHEDULE OF INSTRUMENTAL-MUSIC TEACHER IN THE JUNIOR HIGH SCHOOL.

Period	*Monday*	*Tuesday*	*Wednesday*	*Thursday*	*Friday*
8:45 9:00					
9:00 9:50	Senior Band	Senior Band	Senior Band	Senior Band	Senior Band
9:50 10:40	Junior Orchestra	Free	Junior Orchestra	Free	Junior Orchestra
10:40 11:30	Beginning Winds	Beginning Winds	Beginning Winds	Beginning Winds	Beginning Winds
12:30 1:20	Free	Free	Free	Ensembles	School Assembly
1:20 2:10	Beginning Strings	Beginning Strings	Beginning Strings	Beginning Strings	Beginning Strings
2:10 3:00	Senior Orchestra	Junior Band	Senior Orchestra	Junior Band	Senior Orchestra

This junior high school maintains a relatively extensive instrumental program. The excellence of the high-school band and orchestra is due partly to the thorough foundations laid in the junior-high-school classes and ensembles. The high-school program, in its turn, stimulates desire among younger pupils to enter the junior-high-school instrumental classes. Three instrument classes, including senior band, beginning winds, and beginning strings, are scheduled five times each week. This simplifies scheduling, permits the award of credit, and provides time for the sustained and concentrated work which helps these younger players make rapid progress. Junior and senior orchestras meet only three times each week and class time is devoted principally to ensemble playing. The string players in these groups are encouraged to study with private teachers, and the wind and percussion players are given additional class instruction twice each week in junior band. Thus, most of the junior-high-school players receive the equivalent of five hours of instruction each week and all are encouraged to pursue private study with instrumental teachers of the community.

One period each week is set aside for rehearsals of smaller ensembles and free periods are utilized when extra ensemble time is necessary. Additional time can be arranged for rehearsal of the senior band, when necessary, by beginning at 8:45 A.M., during the homeroom period, or even at 8:30 A.M. or earlier before the start of the school day. Senior orchestra rehearsals can be extended to 3:30 P.M. or later without conflicting with other scheduled school activities. Senior band and senior orchestra play during school assemblies on a rotating schedule and at various other school functions. To find time for the extra help he wants to give to outstanding individuals and ensembles, the instrumental teacher uses the time before and after school and during the lunch hour. Often, this extra time is needed to prepare the special music requested by school organizations, parent-teacher groups, service clubs, and other community associations.

For the vocal teacher in the high school, the teaching day shown in Table 3 extends from about 8:15 A.M. to 4:30 P.M. Classes are scheduled during six periods, each one hour in length. There is a brief homeroom period immediately before classes begin in the morning, a lunch hour, and an hour or more reserved after school for extra duties of various kinds.

In this high school, the vocal teacher is occupied principally with the several performing groups. General music classes require a relatively small portion of the schedule because the subject is elective and these high-school students choose other courses necessary for college or vocational preparation. To extend the span of the general music classes for those who wish to continue, a sequence of two years of work is offered, centered around listening and the literature and history of music. Because certain extra duties are shared by the entire faculty, the vocal teacher is assigned to three study halls each week as well as to occasional periods of cafeteria supervision.

Major performing groups include a senior choir, varying from sixty to one hundred mixed voices, and the madrigal singers, a small, select group with high standards of performance. Each of these groups is scheduled for daily rehearsals, permitting concentrated study and the development of a large repertoire to meet frequent performance demands. Two glee clubs, one for boys and one for girls, meet only three times each week. The glee clubs serve as training groups for the senior choir, are made up of from thirty to eighty voices each, chiefly sophomores and juniors, and are called on for fewer performances.

TABLE 3. SCHEDULE OF VOCAL-MUSIC TEACHER IN THE SENIOR HIGH SCHOOL.

Period	*Monday*	*Tuesday*	*Wednesday*	*Thursday*	*Friday*
8:30 9:30	Senior Choir	Senior Choir	Senior Choir	Senior Choir	Senior Choir
9:30 10:30	Study Hall	General Music	Study Hall	General Music	Study Hall
10:30 11:30	Boys' Glee Club	Voice Class	Boys' Glee Club	Voice Class	Boys' Glee Club
12:30 1:30	Free	Free	Free	Free	Free
1:30 2:30	Girls' Glee Club	Music Lit. & Hist.	Girls' Glee Club	Music Lit. & Hist.	Girls' Glee Club
2:30 3:30	Madrigal Singers	Madrigal Singers	Madrigal Singers	Madrigal Singers	Madrigal Singers

The voice class is a special course inaugurated at the request of the vocal teacher. It serves students with particularly strong interests and abilities in vocal music, especially those who can not be accepted into the madrigal singers because of the limitations placed on the size of the group. In this class, the vocal teacher works with individual voices, explores solo literature, and develops a variety of small vocal ensembles. From it, the teacher can draw soloists and ensembles as needed for inclusion in concerts presented by the senior choir and madrigal singers and can fulfill performance requests from community sources.

Although extra duties vary from month to month, the vocal teacher devotes much time before and after school to preparation for such things as local and state festivals, Christmas and spring concerts, annual music shows, and other special events. In addition, the vocal teacher is regarded by the community as an authority on matters pertaining to singing, directs a church choir, and is called upon frequently by service and other clubs to lead community singing or to speak on some music topic.

The high-school instrumental teacher, like the vocal teacher, spends most of his time with performing groups. The busiest of these is the band, with football games in the fall, regular concerts throughout the year, and contests and festivals in the spring. Because of its full schedule, the band meets five times each week as shown in Table 4 and often extends its rehearsals into after-school hours. During football season, at least one afternoon each week is devoted to marching practice at the athletic field. One period each day is set aside for ensembles, each ensemble usually meeting only once during the week to improve and extend its repertoire.

TABLE 4. SCHEDULE OF INSTRUMENTAL-MUSIC TEACHER IN THE SENIOR HIGH SCHOOL.

Period	*Monday*	*Tuesday*	*Wednesday*	*Thursday*	*Friday*
8:30 9:30	Junior Band	Dance Band	Junior Band	Dance Band	Junior Band
9:30 10:30	Technique Class	Free	Technique Class	Free	Technique Class
10:30 11:30	Orchestra	Music Theory	Orchestra	Music Theory	Orchestra
12:30 1:30	Ensembles	Ensembles	Ensembles	Ensembles	Ensembles
1:30 2:30	Free	Coaching Soloists	Free	Coaching Soloists	Free
2:30 3:30	Band	Band	Band	Band	Band

The junior band meets three times each week and is made up chiefly of sophomores who have not yet advanced to the level of the senior band. For a portion of each period the group is treated as an instrumental class studying graded exercises to improve technique and raise the level of general music ability. The balance of each period is devoted to practicing band literature. The technique class also meets three times each week, is made up chiefly of stringed instruments, and serves somewhat the same function as a junior orchestra, studying both technique and ensemble playing.

Both the dance band and the music theory class meet for two hours each week. Each is a special activity organized at the request of the instrumental teacher for the benefit of band and orchestral players whose interests and abilities are not completely served by the regular performing groups. The dance band is especially attractive to advanced instrumentalists interested in jazz and popular music. It gives them opportunity to learn the jazz idiom, to improve reading ability, to develop feeling for ensemble playing, and to experiment with arranging. The music theory class is open to any student with the requisite knowledge of music notation and the ability to play the piano or some other instrument, and is devoted chiefly to ear training and the study of harmony. In addition to his work during the school day with scheduled classes, the instrumental teacher finds much to occupy his time after school, including rehearsals of large groups and small ensembles and special assistance for individual instrumentalists.

These schedules show what might be expected in four different school situations. Although they can not be called average or typical, they are indicative of the patterns followed by vocal and instrumental teachers in many secondary schools. Music teachers are among the busiest members of the school faculty. Although their work may seem more glamorous than that of teachers of academic subjects, music teachers can usually expect to spend more time in extra-curricular and out-of-school activities. Vocal and instrumental teachers are often well known in the community and active in community music affairs. They are sought out by parents and others for advice about subjects ranging from the desirability of private study for children to the necessity for tuning the family piano. They are constantly in the public eye and their many responsibilities add to the challenge and opportunity of their professional lives.

THE PAST AND ITS PIONEERS

As we survey school music programs existing today in communities throughout the country, it is apparent that many of them are highly developed, offer a variety of challenging courses and activities, and achieve noteworthy success with performing groups. Yet, public-school music education is relatively young. Its beginnings are only slightly more than one hundred years in the past and much of its progress has been made during the past fifty years.

The Beginnings of Public Education

The American educational system is much older than public-school music education. The Boston Latin School for boys was founded in 1635, to offer college preparation in Latin and Greek, and a Massachusetts law of 1647 provided for additional schools of the same type. These were called Latin Grammar Schools and were intended for older boys of what would now be called secondary-school age. Almost one hundred years later, in 1743, Benjamin Franklin drew up a plan for an improved type of school, an "academy," in which the curriculum would be expanded to include mathematics, science, and history as well as Latin and Greek. An academy of this type was established in Philadelphia in 1751, marking the beginning of a new movement. The academies increased in popularity until they outnumbered the original Latin schools and continued to be popular throughout most of the nineteenth century. Both academies and Latin schools were private institutions, forerunners of our present educational system, but not yet committed to the principle of public education.

A milestone in public education was marked by the establishment of the Boston English Classical School for boys in 1821. This was a true public school. It was followed quickly by the establishment of a similar school for girls in Worcester, Massachusetts, and by provisions in Massachusetts law for public high schools open to both boys and girls. As such schools became popular and more numerous, teachers likewise increased in number and began to turn their attention to professional responsibilities, inaugurating national teachers' conventions from which developed, in 1857, the National Education Association.

Toward the end of the century, in 1892, increasing professional concern with the nature and purpose of the high schools resulted in the formation of the Committee of Ten to examine the high-school curriculum. The committee submitted its report two years later. Though strongly influenced by committee members from various colleges, it concluded that the high school might well provide preparation for life as well as for college.

Junior high schools appeared in Columbus, Ohio, and Berkley, California in 1909–1910 and were officially sanctioned by the National Education Association in 1918. The junior high school was proposed as a means of ministering to the unique needs and interests of adolescents. Through a variety of courses and activities, it was to provide for individual differences, special abilities and interests, vocational exploration, and the development of proper social attitudes and behavior.

Also in 1918, and closely related to the concept of the junior high school, a National Education Association commission formulated the "Cardinal Principles of Secondary Education." [1] These principles, regarded as objectives to be achieved by pupils through public education, included (1) health, (2) command of fundamental processes, (3) worthy home

[1] *Cardinal Principles of Secondary Education,* A Report of the Commission on the Reorganization of Secondary Education, Appointed by the National Education Association. Department of the Interior, Bureau of Education Bulletin No. 35. Washington, D.C.: Government Printing Office, 1918, pp. 10–11.

membership, (4) vocation, (5) citizenship, (6) worthy use of leisure, and (7) ethical character. As an indication of later developments in educational thinking, a report published in 1938 by the Educational Policies Commission of the National Education Association stated the purpose of education to be centered around objectives of (1) self-realization, (2) human relationships, (3) economic efficiency, and (4) civic responsibility.[2] In both of these comparatively recent statements of educational objectives, there is implicit acceptance of the benefits which can be derived from effective programs of music education.

Vocal Music

Perhaps because of the influence of the singing schools, in existence since at least the early eighteenth century, the first developments in public-school music were chiefly in the area of vocal music. Lowell Mason experimented with the teaching of vocal music in the Hawes School in South Boston in 1837, the same year that music was introduced in the schools of Buffalo, New York. The following year the Boston school board voted to hire a teacher of vocal music for the various public schools in the city. During the next few years, between 1840 and 1852, music was introduced in many other cities—Pittsburgh, Louisville, Washington, D.C., Cincinnati, Chicago, Cleveland, San Francisco, St. Louis, Philadelphia, and New York. At this point, music had gained a strong foothold in the public grammar schools, but had not found its way into the elementary schools or the public high schools. It remained for Luther Whiting Mason to introduce music in the primary grades of the Cincinnati schools in 1857. Seven years later, in 1864, Mason was in Boston organizing an elementary-school music program there. This was followed by the introduction of music into a Boston high school in 1869 and provisions for music in all Boston high schools in 1872.

Despite this seemingly rapid progress, it was reported in 1886 by the United States Commissioner of Education that music was being taught regularly in fewer than 250 school systems. Perhaps this was the turning point. During the next three years the number of schools employing music teachers increased by one third. By 1899 the high school in Cambridge, Massachusetts, had expanded its music curriculum to include harmony, counterpoint, and melody writing.

[2] *The Purposes of Education in American Democracy,* Educational Policies Commission, National Education Association of the United States and the Association of School Administrators. Washington, D.C.: 1938, p. 47.

A further step was taken by the New England Education League during its 1902 conference devoted to the secondary-school music curriculum. This group recommended a music program extending through all four high-school years and including five hours of music each week, a program endorsed by the National Education Association and the Music Teachers National Association in 1904. Additional endorsement of public-school music was offered by the College Entrance Board for New England and the Middle States Association through a 1906 decision to include music in the list of subjects granted college entrance credit.

Perhaps as a result of these advancements, a music committee was among those organized by the National Education Association in 1912 to study the entire process of secondary education. The 1913 report of this committee suggested a program including ensemble singing, chorus practice, music appreciation, harmony, orchestra, and credit for applied music studied under private teachers.[3]

Instrumental Music

Prior to World War I, instrumental music appears to have played only an incidental role in music education. School orchestras were formed in a few cities between 1890 and 1900, including Wichita, Kansas, Richmond and Indianapolis, Indiana, and Hartford and New London, Connecticut. These instrumental groups were informal organizations rather than products of established instrumental programs.

Los Angeles began an organized program of instrumental music by forming an orchestral department for the public schools in 1910. Violin classes were formed in the Boston public schools a year later. Other cities followed these examples until, in 1915, a number were able to show considerable progress, including Joliet, Illinois, with the beginnings of a band program, Kansas City with forty orchestras in elementary schools, and Oakland, California, with twenty-nine orchestras and an equal number of bands, all in elementary schools.[4] An outstanding example of the growing importance of instrumental music was the appointment in 1918 of Joseph E. Maddy to the position of Supervisor of Instrumental Music in Rochester, New York, possibly the first such position in any public school system.

[3] Peter W. Dykema, and Karl W. Gehrkens, *The Teaching and Administration of High School Music*. Boston: C. C. Birchard and Company, 1941, p. 6.

[4] Theodore F. Normann, *Instrumental Music in the Public Schools*. Philadelphia: Oliver Ditson Company, 1939, p. 14.

During its infancy, public school instrumental music was concerned chiefly with the development of orchestras. Bands were few in number. They did not become a factor in instrumental music programs until after 1920, possibly because of the interest stimulated by military bands during World War I and the large number of men who utilized their military-band training by teaching in the public schools after their release from military service. Further stimulation was provided by instrument manufacturers who sponsored band contests, the first national contest being held in Chicago in 1923, the first state contests in 1924. These contests aroused interest among music educators who saw their inherent possibilities for stimulating the expansion of instrumental music. As a result, a national school band contest was sponsored in 1926 by the Committee on Instrumental Affairs of the Music Supervisors National Conference.

In the same year, the first National High School Orchestra played in Detroit for the Music Supervisors National Conference. This group of 246 youthful players representing 34 states prompted much favorable comment. In the following year a similar orchestra played in Dallas, Texas, for a meeting of the National Education Association. The favorable impression on this important organization may have been another turning point, for instrumental music developed rapidly during the years that followed. The National Music Camp was founded at Interlochen, Michigan, in 1928. The first national school orchestra contest was held in 1929 in Mason City, Iowa. State band contests grew until, in 1932, contests in which 1050 bands participated were held in 44 states.[5]

In the next ten years, to the beginning of World War II, instrumental music continued its growth until many communities boasted a high-school band, an organized program of instrument classes or lessons in the elementary school, junior-high-school classes and ensembles, and a varied and active high-school instrumental program. Instrumental music had at this time reached a stage of advanced development, a status which has not been markedly changed in the ensuing years.

Professional Organizations and Publications

Early in the history of public-school music education, teachers began to recognize the benefits offered by professional organizations. The desire to raise the level of pupils' music achievement and the search for better ways

[5] Gerald R. Prescott, and Lawrence W. Chidester, *Getting Results with School Bands.* Minneapolis, Minn.: Paul A. Schmitt Music Company, 1938, p. 9. Used by permission of Schmitt, Hall & McCreary Company.

of teaching prompted the formation of associations and conferences dedicated to the service of school music programs. The Music Teachers National Association was formed in 1876. Though it was composed chiefly of private music teachers, the broad interests of this group in every phase of music teaching focused attention on the problems of school music as well as on those of the conservatory and the private teacher.

A group of music teachers from public schools successfully petitioned the National Education Association to establish a music division in 1884. This group, an integral part of a national organization dealing almost exclusively with public education, conducted meetings for the discussion of a variety of topics germane to public-school music. In the same year, a summer school for public-school music supervisors was held in Lexington, Massachusetts, under the direction of the author of a series of music books for use in the public schools. This was the first of many such professional gatherings sponsored by publishers for teachers. The culmination of the movement toward professional organizations was the formation of the Music Supervisors National Conference. Although the first national meeting was held in 1907, the name was not adopted until 1910 during a conference in Cincinnati.

Further developments followed in rapid succession. The Eastern Supervisors Conference met for the first time in 1917, starting a trend which resulted in the formation of six large sectional conferences, each serving a convenient geographical area. The National Conference trebled its membership in the few years immediately following World War I, from 1919 to 1922. An instrumental committee began its work within the Music Supervisors National Conference in 1922. In the following year, a committee of the Music Teachers National Association interested in public school music investigated state requirements concerning the training of public-school music teachers. The National School Band Association was formed in 1926 and changed its name to the National School Band and Orchestra Association following the first national orchestra contest in 1929. Three years later, this group separated to form two distinct organizations, one dealing with band matters, the other with problems of orchestral teaching. In 1934, the Music Supervisors National Conference changed its name to the Music Educators National Conference, a significant change indicating the rise of a new concept of the function of the music teacher in the public schools.

Such developments continued, resulting in a hierarchy of associations and conferences serving almost every level of music teaching and every geographical division, including a national conference, sectional conferences serving a number of states, state associations, and district organizations serving a number of counties or municipalities. In this wide array of professional organizations, music education has at its disposal the machinery to deal effectively and efficiently with pertinent problems of almost any kind, and it is probable that the future will bring important developments in this area of coöperative effort.

Closely allied to the rise of professional organizations was the appearance of various professional periodicals, some published by commercial houses, others by the professional organizations themselves. The monthly publication *School Music Journal* appeared in 1885, published in Boston, but did not endure for more than a few years. *School Music* and *School Music Monthly* were initiated in 1900 and merged two years later. Books of proceedings were published on an annual basis by the Music Teachers National Conference in 1912. The *Music Supervisors Journal* was established in 1914 as the official organ of the National Conference, changing its name to *Music Educators Journal* in 1934. These publications, plus the official organs of the various state music-education associations and the periodicals published commercially, offered the music teacher a wealth of timely and valuable information concerning teaching materials and methods, supplies and equipment, philosophies and trends without which many of the advances of recent years might have been much more difficult to achieve.

The patterns of music education in the United States today are rooted in the successes of the past. The history of music education is relatively short. The vocal-music program is only a little more than one hundred years old, the instrumental program began as recently as our own century, and large forward strides have been made since World War I. Music education today finds its way into almost every community and every school, achieving results of astonishing quality and providing a strong foundation for the gradually increasing music interests of the adult population. With this heritage of achievements wrought by pioneers in music education, today's music teacher can be not only proud of his profession, but strengthened in his determination to push even further toward the goal of music education—a society in which every individual is able to turn to music for the unique and deep satisfactions it can give.

2: *pupils in music education*

In the secondary school, including both the junior- and senior-high-school levels, music teaching must take adolescence into consideration. Because of the nature of adolescence, the secondary-school pupil is especially responsive to music, receptive to its rhythms, sympathetic to its moods and emotions, and interested in its technical devices. Yet experience proves that the adolescent pupil does not respond readily unless class activities, teaching methods, and materials are appropriate to his nature and interests. For effective teaching, it is important to know both the individual pupil and the nature of adolescence.

The teacher of music must be aware of the psychological characteristics of his pupils and sensitive to their reactions to the infinite varieties of music. It is not enough simply to teach music; it is essential that the teacher of music be a student of human nature as well.

KNOWING THE PUPIL

As the new teacher meets his classes for the first time, particularly those of junior-high-school level, he is struck by the wide differences in appearance and other characteristics among the pupils of each group. There are obvious inequalities in size, physical development, maturity, emotional stability, and intellectual alertness and power. Although pupils may be grouped within narrow age limits, in any one class there may be adolescents, pre-adolescents, and post-adolescents. In classes grouped according to ability, there will be differences in physical and emotional maturity. In classes grouped according to interest, there will be differences of every kind, including differences in degrees of interest. Although we are accustomed to thinking of people as individuals, fully aware that each personality is unique, the new teacher often does not understand that music classes can not be homogenized and that best results are achieved when each pupil is regarded as a distinct individual reacting in his own way to the subject matter, the teacher, and the other members of his class.

It is at this age that boys and girls become peculiarly conscious of each other and of the differences between sexes. They become interested in each other as boys and girls. They are no longer children given to the uninhibited associations of play, but young people at the brink of an adulthood which seems sometimes an abyss of uncertainty, sometimes a pinnacle of freedom and independence.

One factor emphasized by the activities of the music class is the changing voice of the boy. It is often the object of strong interest for both boys and girls, a source of concern and embarrassment to the boys, and a phenomenon which must be treated with insight and skill by the music teacher. For the younger boy, it is one of the first, unnerving symptoms of his changing status. For the older boy, the new and virile voice is proudly displayed as evidence of manhood. For the teacher, the changing voice presents both problems and opportunity. The teacher can never be certain at what point the voice will begin to change; there are individual differences here as pronounced as any in adolescent development. According to Ramsey,[1] more boys experience voice change at the age of thirteen than at any other. The curve of frequency peaks at this point drops to lower but approximately equal levels at the ages of twelve and fourteen, and diminishes through the ages of eleven and fifteen. Although the teacher can expect a large number of changing voices in the eighth and ninth grades, there is also the possibility they will appear in the seventh and tenth, and, on occasion, as early as the sixth and as late as the eleventh grades. As a result, the boys in any one class may have voices in every stage of development, from the unchanged voice of the child through the changing voice of the adolescent to the changed voice of the adult.

Junior-high-school pupils, especially, may seem to reverse their personalities from day to day, or even from hour to hour, undergoing complete changes of mood or character. In many respects, the junior-high-school pupil is a paradox, successively exhibiting contradictory traits which are

[1] Glenn V. Ramsey, "The Sexual Development of Boys," *American Journal of Psychology*, 1943, LVI, No. 2, p. 217.

deep and real despite their seeming incompatibility. At one moment shy and retiring, the junior-high-school pupil a moment later may be a brash exhibitionist. He may give an impression of being aggressively strong-willed and yet be completely lacking in self-confidence. His lack of self-confidence may be sufficiently strong to make him fearful of class recitation and willing to undergo punishment rather than speak before the group. According to Garrison,[2] this fear is more pronounced among boys than girls, perhaps because of the boy's reluctance to expose his changing and uncontrollable voice.

On occasion, the junior-high-school pupil will seem unfeeling and completely impervious to any emotion; at other times, he will be acutely sensitive and even reduced to tears by ridicule or censure. He may seem intensely curious, interested, eager to learn and ask questions, or he may appear blasé and sophisticated, knowing everything and interested in nothing. He will at times resent authority to a point of physical violence; at other times, he will be completely submissive and seek authoritative approval for his most inconsequential acts. In either case, he will need and desire the discipline of rules imposed by superior authority, becoming confused and insecure without them.

Despite their paradoxical natures, junior- and senior-high-school pupils have varied and absorbing interests and respond enthusiastically to effective teaching. At this stage of development, the young person develops markedly increased abilities to think in abstract terms, to deal effectively with generalizations, to utilize symbols in thinking, and to be sensitive to quality.[3] He is often strongly interested in creative activity and enjoys a degree of facility in creative expression, perhaps due in part to the active imagination common to adolescence. Boys especially, and girls to a somewhat lesser degree, find pleasure in constructive and manipulative activities; the boys interested in making things in the school shops, building radios, and tinkering with automobiles, the girls interested in cooking and sewing.

Because of these characteristics, there is wide opportunity for the teacher to stimulate productive work and to foster learning, exploiting a potential that probably is developed to its fullest extent in comparatively rare instances. An important factor of which the teacher must be aware, however, is the adolescent's aversion to drill, or to any monotony, unless there is immediate and practical benefit.[4] If the adolescent's intellectual

[2] Karl C. Garrison, *Psychology of Adolescence,* 5th ed. Englewood Cliffs, New Jersey: Prentice-Hall, Inc., 1956, p. 104. Adapted by permission.

[3] Arthur T. Jersild, *The Psychology of Adolescence.* New York: The Macmillan Company, 1957, p. 76.

[4] Luella Cole, *Psychology of Adolescence,* 5th ed. New York: Holt, Rinehart and Winston, Inc., 1959, p. 626.

curiosity can be aroused and sustained through activities compatible with his nature, there are rewarding and almost unlimited possibilities of worthwhile achievement in secondary-school teaching.

A negative factor, important to both pupils and teachers, is the abrupt change encountered by the pupil when he first enters the secondary school. Whether he enters the seventh grade in a three-year junior high school or the ninth grade in a four-year senior high school, the pupil is often confronted for the first time by a pattern completely different from that of the elementary school. The experience can be disturbing enough to reduce markedly the effectiveness of his class work.

In the secondary school, perhaps for the first time and certainly to a greater extent than in the elementary school, the pupil is forced by his schedule to move from one room to another for almost every period of the school day. He meets a different teacher for every subject and may see some special teachers only once each week. He encounters a much wider diversity of school subjects, some of which he may be free to elect or refuse, as he wishes. Finally, due to the necessity for revising class groupings for special and elective subjects, he may be denied the comfort of associating constantly with the same group of friends and classmates.

For pupils accustomed to the relative stability of the elementary-school curriculum and scheduling, this constant moving and mixing may destroy the feelings of security developed in the elementary school. It offers new freedoms in choice of subject, in action, and in speech to which the pupil is unaccustomed. It may create feelings of insecurity especially pertinent to the work of the music teacher who often meets classes less frequently than teachers of other subjects and is consequently less acquainted with individual class members. The difficulty of adjusting to these new circumstances may be partly responsible for the deterioration of pupil morale and decline of interest in school work, observed by Jersild,[5] as pupils advance from the elementary school through the junior high school to the senior high school. Whatever the causes, these changes in pupil attitude do occur, developing in some instances into passive or active hostility, and are problems that must be considered by the teacher.

There are good reasons for examining the backgrounds of pupils new to the music class in the secondary school. Those in any one class may have a variety of school backgrounds, having arrived at the high school from a number of elementary or junior high schools in which music programs were radically different. There will be pronounced individual differences in music knowledge and skill as well as differences in attitudes toward

[5] Arthur T. Jersild, *The Psychology of Adolescence*, New York: The Macmillan Company, 1957, p. 281.

music itself. These differences, coupled with those of physical development, maturity, emotional stability, and intellectual capacity, make it mandatory for the music teacher to study each individual as carefully as time permits, adjusting teaching materials and methods to every class and providing for individual differences within the class. For these reasons, also, elective groups chosen by interested and able pupils may function at superior levels, while required music classes are held to much lower levels by pupils deficient in knowledge, skill, and interest.

Where general music classes are concerned, the music teacher can well bear in mind that the music instruction provided here may be the last available to many pupils. General music is rarely required beyond the junior-high-school level; elective music classes and activities, although attractive to interested pupils, are often crowded out of full schedules in which required subjects must take precedence. The music teacher, therefore, may regard these classes as terminal for many pupils, accepting the challenge and the opportunity they hold for developing music interests.

THE IMPORTANCE OF ADOLESCENCE

Many of the problems of music education in the secondary school become easier to solve if we thoroughly understand the nature of adolescence and keep its needs constantly in mind. According to Cole, "The main business of the adolescent is to stop being one."[6] This statement may be the key to a better understanding of pupils of the junior and senior high school. Secondary-school pupils are young adults in many respects, perhaps not yet fully matured, but aware of the approach of adulthood, nevertheless. The adolescent is fully convinced that he is an adult even though he may realize that he is not yet in full command of adult powers. He likes to feel that he is independent, free of authority, permitted to make his own decisions and work for his own benefit. Although he is in need of the security of established rules and patterns of conduct, he is prone to resent and rebel against what he considers interference in his personal affairs. This is adolescent nature, a nature of infinite variety and constant change, but one which constantly grows closer to adult maturity.

Physically, the adolescent undergoes rapid and radical changes. There is a material increase in height and weight immediately prior to pubescence. A source of embarrassment to the adolescent is that his arms and legs seem

[6] Luella Cole, *Psychology of Adolescence*, 5th ed. New York: Holt, Rinehart and Winston, Inc., 1959, p. 9.

to grow faster than his torso, making him appear clumsy and causing his clothes to become too small while they are still new. He will seem poorly coördinated, prone to tripping over furniture, unable to master simple dance steps, and completely inept in physical games and sports. He may seem to be chronically fatigued, always lethargic, and with a pronounced distaste for active games.

Paradoxically, the adolescent also shows gains in bodily agility and muscular control. He may be less agile and adept during the period in which his extremities grow most rapidly, but thereafter his development progresses even more swiftly. He may give the impression of having limitless sources of energy. His coördination improves, he begins to move with ease and grace, and he develops interest in activities that display physical prowess.

The adolescent often becomes deeply concerned about his own appearance. Because of obvious changes in bodily proportions among boys and girls, and the appearance of facial hair and the changing voice among boys, the adolescent can not ignore the physical changes taking place in his own body. The adolescent may take pride in this evidence of approaching adulthood, or may be ashamed of the unfamiliar aspects of his developing physical nature. In either case, the changes arouse his curiosity about both his own and the opposite sex.

Equally significant changes occur in the adolescent's emotional nature with differences among individuals wide enough to make generalization extremely difficult. The adolescent is subject to moods, vacillating between depression and elation in unpredictable patterns and without apparent cause. The emotions are highly volatile. They lack the stability imposed by adult experience and control and tend to be intense and disturbing. Fear, anxiety, and frustration are created by the adolescent's awareness of physical and other changes and by the realization that adulthood is soon to offer an entirely new set of experiences. Joy, excitement, and pride are created by new freedoms and the awareness of hitherto unsuspected powers. The adolescent's emotions are closely related to what he thinks and experiences, and manifest themselves in observable physical reactions. Of importance to the teacher is the knowledge that such emotions demand expression and can create deep-seated personality deviations if repressed. The emotions are responsible for many of the patterns of adolescent behavior, including some that are objectionable in the classroom. They can be responsible also for noteworthy achievement if channeled in desirable directions.

Equally important to the teacher is the fact that adolescent interests are stimulated by the imagination and the emotions.[7] If he is presented with subject matter in which there is adventure, romance, or imaginative stimulation, or if otherwise mundane subject matter is approached in an imaginative way, the adolescent often develops the interest that makes rapid and effective learning possible.

Adolescent pupils are different; they differ from adults and children, from each other, and each may differ in his own emotional characteristics from day to day. In some circumstances, the adolescent may be capable of mature, adult behavior; in others, he may lapse into childish inconsistency. He is a creature of emotions that demand outlet. He is moved by uncertainties, fears, and anxieties similar to but more intense than those of the adult, and can be stimulated to extremes of behavior by the pressures and tensions of his emotions.

Among the most important factors in adolescent behavior is the desire to be accepted by the crowd, gang, or clique. Many adolescent drives and fears are social in nature and arise from factors having to do with social status. According to Garrison,[8] the desire to conform to standards established by his peers stands out above almost every characteristic at this stage of the adolescent's development. He wants to be well-liked, respected, and popular among others of his own age and status. He will follow the crowd in matters of dress, speech, and conduct. He may flout adult authority rather than deviate from the patterns established by his associates. He chooses friends on the basis of gang standards rather than according to compatibility with his own tastes and interests, finding in this way a kind of support not provided by his adult associates. He may be especially sensitive to factors of social class, family wealth, and background and adhere even more closely to ties that bind him to his own social group. Closely allied to this need for social support and approval is the adolescent's tendency to select and imitate a hero, often adopting the idols chosen by his group rather than selecting his own.

Because of the infinite variety of adolescent natures, and the improbability of finding a common denominator among large numbers of young people with varying interests, adolescent cliques are often small in number and any large group of adolescents often includes a number of smaller cliques. Each may distinguish itself from the others by adopting some unique form of dress, speech, or conduct, extreme by adult standards but

[7] Luella Cole, *Psychology of Adolescence*, 5th ed. New York: Holt, Rinehart and Winston, Inc., 1959, p. 627.

[8] Karl C. Garrison, *Psychology of Adolescence*, 5th ed. Englewood Cliffs, New Jersey: Prentice-Hall, Inc., 1956, pp. 116–17. Adapted by permission.

necessary for the adolescent to establish his identity as a member of the clique. Here, too, is an opportunity for the teacher to turn the interests of entire groups of pupils to worthy heroes, and to influence cliques by attracting their leaders.

Intellectually, adolescence is a stage in which the pupil should be especially susceptible to education. The adolescent is intensely curious and eager to find causes for both natural phenomena and social conditions; he wants to know why things happen. At this age, among boys especially, there may be a strong interest in science leading to experiments in chemistry, the construction of electronic equipment, or expert knowledge of internal combustion engines. On the other hand, the adolescent may be impatient with school subjects or with teaching methods that do not seem logical or practical. He will have little interest in memorization, preferring to learn through understanding, and will be impatient with the drill needed to learn unrelated facts. Adolescent interests are strong and varied. Once interest is aroused in a subject, the adolescent sometimes follows it with more determination and singleness of purpose than is mustered by an adult. If he encounters difficulty in school subjects, it may be because he has so many and such varied interests that there are too many claims on his time and energy.

Adolescents enjoy work that demands quick thinking and cleverness. Such work may be of great interest to pupils even though it seems to have no immediate or practical application, because it provides exercise for the mind and the developing powers of abstract thinking. Religion is another avenue of adolescent interest,[9] along with other sources of ideas concerning man and his destiny. Although the adolescent may either possess an intense interest in religion or rebel against it, the combination of intellectual curiosity with romantic imagination makes philosophy an intriguing subject.

The adolescent, then, is a curious mixture of youth and maturity, developing rapidly through various phases of physical and intellectual growth and exhibiting many and sometimes conflicting facets of character and conduct. Each is a distinct individual, does not fit readily into any generalized pattern, and requires individual attention and understanding from the teacher. He is inclined to be introspective, subject to fluctuations of mood and emotion, and finds it difficult to explain his inner feelings to others, adults in particular. Deprived of sympathy and understanding, he can become withdrawn and recalcitrant. Given appropriate attention and motivation, he can develop intense interests and display a large ca-

[9] Arthur T. Jersild, *The Psychology of Adolescence*. New York: The Macmillan Company, 1957, p. 331.

pacity for learning. Because of his unique make-up, the adolescent may be among the most difficult teaching problems in the public schools, but he is also the pupil who can respond wholeheartedly to effective teaching, providing deep satisfactions to the teacher interested in leading youth to new knowledge and insight.

MUSIC PLAYS ITS PART

Because it is not in the same category as English, social studies, science, and other core subjects, music is usually regarded as a special subject in the curriculum of the secondary school. It is also "special" in that it provides unique experiences difficult to duplicate in other subject areas and in that it arouses particularly strong interests in many students. Because music is often regarded as an activity rather than a subject, it capitalizes upon the adolescent's interest in the unusual and upon his natural tendency to join clubs and other special groups.

Music activities, especially the elective classes and performing organizations, provide opportunities for membership in distinctive groups attractive for the same reasons as the gang, crowd, or clique. They are both elective and selective, implying that their members possess certain unique qualifications or skills. They are worthy and respected, regularly presenting programs applauded by adults and other pupils alike. They furnish a firm basis for feelings of security, for recognition, and approbation of accomplishment. As social groups, they widen each pupil's circle of acquaintances, at the same time providing for the common interests and coöperative effort that help develop acquaintances into meaningful friendships. Membership in music groups cuts across boundaries of social class, wealth, and family background. Music talent is not restricted to any one social group. It is common to find that leadership patterns in music organizations are somewhat different from those of other school activities. The music organizations often serve as social levelers. They provide for a beneficial mixing of pupils who might otherwise remain aloof. They weaken the influence of cliques and gangs. They provide opportunity for boys and girls to work together toward common ends. Instrumental music, in particular, places boys and girls side by side, de-emphasizing the natural and growing differences between the sexes.

In performing organizations, perhaps for the first time, pupils can begin to see the need for group discipline. Although the performing group is completely dependent upon the skills of its members, so too is each member dependent upon the efforts of all the others. Each individual comes quickly to the realization that his own work is inconsequential unless it meshes precisely with the work of others and that the only possibility for satisfying performance is in the subordination of personal desires to group goals. Out of this realization comes personal discipline and willingness to coöperate, growing from within each pupil rather than being enforced by the teacher. In few other school activities is there the possibility for building this kind of social responsibility and demonstrating it in such convincing ways.

Music is equally useful as a means of building self-confidence in adolescent pupils. Adolescents often make rapid progress when learning to play a music instrument, particularly if interest is aroused through membership in a band or orchestra during the early stages of instruction. The increase in skill coupled with utilization of the skill in ensemble playing is evidence that the pupil is achieving mastery, that he can do something well, and that he is worthy of the esteem of others. Through performance before audiences, he develops poise and self-assurance that carry over into his social activities, overcoming the natural shyness engendered by the uncertainties of his age. Because his achievements are recognized by his peers and by adults, he develops a feeling of security nourished by pride in his accomplishments and the popularity he enjoys because of them. In performing groups he finds himself in positions of responsibility, accepting his share of work and of credit. Through these experiences, the adolescent moves closer to the stability and confidence he should feel as an adult, learning to control himself and his emotions, and developing an assurance that improves his social conduct.

In the area of physical development, music plays a less obvious but important role in aiding the adolescent gain control of his growing body. Studies have shown that certain types of physical activity can be sustained for longer periods when accompanied by music. The rhythmic flow of music tends to guide muscular activity into rhythmic patterns and to provide a basis for efficient timing. The adolescent, whose lengthening bones present new problems of leverage, and whose growing muscles create new difficulties of control, appears clumsy and uncoördinated until he learns how to use these new physical powers. According to Cole,[10] boys develop bodily agility and muscular control rapidly in later adolescence, but show little or no improvement, or even a decrease in agility and control, for a short period during early adolescence. Girls also show improvement in control and agility, make smoother progress than boys, but do not reach the

[10] Luella Cole, *Psychology of Adolescence*, 5th ed. New York: Holt, Rinehart and Winston, Inc., 1959, p. 49.

boys' high degree of physical proficiency. For both boys and girls, music provides rhythmic activities such as folk dancing, conducting, and other forms of patterned bodily movement. These activities, performed in music classes to the accompaniment of rhythmic music, offer controlled physical exercise and opportunity to practice coördinated physical movement.

Instrumental music ministers to the smaller muscles and helps satisfy the adolescent's manipulative desire. Junior-high-school instrumentalists especially, and those of the senior high school to a lesser degree, show strong interest in the development of finger dexterity. Although they may be completely disinterested in questions of tone quality, phrasing, and expressiveness, they will often spend hours practicing technique, racing through scales and arpeggios with reckless abandon. This is the manipulative instinct which finds productive outlet in instrumental music, providing needed exercise for the smaller muscles and practice in coördinated finger movement.

Through vocal music, the adolescent learns about the changing voice and develops facility in its use. Vocal and general music classes furnish opportunity to discuss the problem and classes sometimes become deeply interested in following the progress of boys passing through voice change. The boys can be aided in many ways. They can be prepared for the approaching change before its symptoms appear and can work toward vocal flexibility and control through singing activities once the change begins.

The religious and spiritual interests of the adolescent are among the most difficult to express. Music is closely related to them, partly because it calls up subtle shades of feeling and emotion and conveys meanings too nebulous to be captured in speech. Music is an outlet for the spiritual strivings of the adolescent and brings him closer to the spiritual world that interests and moves him. It furnishes a medium for expressing emotion and relieving emotional tension, providing the emotional catharsis believed necessary by ancient Greek philosophers for the health of the human mind and character. If emotional pressures can be reduced through vicarious musical expression, and if emotional stability can be fostered through controlled emotional exercise, music can perform a vital service in ministering to the intensely emotional nature of the adolescent. It supplies a medium for expressing the ineffable, for saying things the adolescent is unable to put into words, and expressing feelings he might otherwise be reluctant to expose to his friends or to adults.

Music satisfies the aesthetic need which is in everyone to some degree and which may be especially acute among adolescents. It satisfies the hunger for beauty in a subtle way, can be interpreted by the individual to suit his tastes or mood, and can be enjoyed inwardly and privately without ostentation or embarrassment. Through choral singing, music offers a unique aesthetic experience not provided by any other art, the experience of reacting *en masse* to beauty while producing it with the most sensitive of all instruments. It is a highly moving and intensely personal form of creative expression which touches responsive chords in adolescent nature.

For the intellectual aspect of adolescent development, music is a subject which can and does stimulate intense interest. The theory and techniques of music supply ample material for the adolescent's interest in intellectual exercise and cleverness. Properly approached, such studies as harmony, music form, and acoustics are understandable to adolescents and serve to introduce them to a facet of music which is intellectually challenging and serves to deepen understanding and appreciation. The rewards of music performance can be sufficiently attractive to overcome the adolescent's aversion for drill and memorization, and the creative aspect of music expression is an antidote for the tedium of drill.

Music serves individuality and thrives on individual differences. In music activities there can and should be room for every degree of talent. Vocal and instrumental groups need both leaders and followers, soloists and accompanists. Music classes offer something for those who like to sing, those who listen, those who are well coördinated, and those whose talents are mechanical rather than artistic. Music has been influential in redeeming the pupil who might otherwise have withdrawn from school due to academic or social difficulties, holding his interest and enabling him to achieve success, first in music and then in other areas. Finally, music activities can be used to counteract the lowering of morale and interest among the school population as a whole, making assembly programs and football games more colorful and enjoyable, presenting concerts and shows for the entire student body, and creating outlets for many pupils with talents for leadership.

Music is an integral part of the secondary-school curriculum. It is possible to exaggerate its usefulness, of course, but it is equally easy to overlook the many useful ends it serves in the education of the adolescent. In one way or another, music plays a part in almost every aspect of adolescent development. It ministers to social, spiritual, physical, and intellectual needs. It opens avenues to self-confidence, emotional stability, and maturity of character. It can do all these things if it is taught with skill and insight into the nature and needs of the pupil, and with due regard for the special conditions of adolescence.

part two:
The General Music Class

3: *the nature of general music*

The term "general music" is used by music educators to designate music courses of many kinds within the school music program. In some schools, the general music class is a course in music appreciation. In others, it is a class devoted primarily to singing. In still others, it is a preparatory class developing skill and knowledge for membership in selective choral groups. More common, however, is the general music class that combines singing, listening, and other activities in a varied but unified program of music instruction. In this latter form, general music offers a broad survey of the field of music, continuing the music work of the elementary school and providing an introduction to the music courses and activities of the secondary school. Although it is sometimes the most demanding of the subjects taught by music teachers, it is the heart of the school music program and the class that most nearly realizes the aim of music education to provide music for every pupil.

GENERAL MUSIC IN THE SCHOOL PROGRAM

General music classes designed to offer a broad survey of the entire field of music may differ from each other both in basic concept and in minor details. The age, grade, and music background of the pupils in the class influence the manner in which it is taught, the subject matter it includes, and the level of maturity to which it can aspire. The philosophy of the music teacher or of the school system may affect the objectives of the course. Even such minor, mechanical details as the size and shape of the music room, the availability of equipment such as pianos and phonographs, and the amount of class time permitted by the schedule can cause major differences from one class to another.

One of the more important factors causing these differences is the level at which the course is offered, whether in the junior high school or the senior high school. Most frequently, general music is offered in the junior high school and is required of all pupils for one or more years. It is then regarded as a continuation of the music program of the elementary school, is similar to it in content and procedure, but strives for higher levels of achievement. Less frequently, general music is offered in the high school and is elective rather than required, reaching only those who choose to take it.

In this respect general music reflects a characteristic progression of music subjects from required to elective status through the public schools. In the elementary school, virtually every music activity in the school program is required. All children participate and none are excluded because of lack of ability or training. In the senior high school, conversely, all music activities are likely to be elective and many are closed to those who do not have the requisite ability or training. The junior high school is a mid-point in the progression in that it usually offers both required and elective courses and activities. This progression from required to elective status, and from a large mass of pupils to a relatively small group of talented performers, is a matter which merits study by music educators. If it is felt that music should reach all pupils and should continue through the entire span of public education, it is possible the general music class should be included in more high-school music programs.

Scheduling

There are many possibilities for scheduling the general music class. In one junior high school it may be required for three years; in another it may be required for only one year. It may meet five times each week, three times each week, or only once. If it is required of all pupils for as many as three years, it may meet infrequently, perhaps once each week. If it is required for only one year it may be scheduled more frequently. Each class meeting normally lasts from forty to sixty minutes, although double periods of up to two hours are possible, and, in some respects, desirable. In the senior high school, the same variation in number of meetings is possible, although the elective status of the general music class at this level often limits its length to one year or even one semester and its frequency to one, two, or three meetings each week.

The arrangement that permits only one meeting each week is undesirable. With so little time available, both teachers and pupils are severely handicapped. It is difficult for the teacher to treat the varied aspects of music in a comprehensive and coherent manner. It is equally difficult for pupils to follow the progress of the course and to become familiar with its subject matter. For many reasons, it would be desirable to arrange scheduling so that general music classes could meet five times each week, reducing the total length of the course to one-half year if necessary. Although there are valid reasons for continuing music study through a longer period, the benefits of daily meetings would outweigh the disadvantages of the shortened span of the course. Scheduling would be simplified, especially if other special subjects could be arranged in the same pattern. The class could be more productive in terms of learning and pupil achievement. The teacher's task would be simpler and more satisfying, offering greater benefits to the pupil, the music program, and the school as a whole.

Class Size

General music classes may be equally diverse in size. The most desirable class is one of perhaps thirty pupils, large enough to encourage group discussion and permit satisfying group singing, yet small enough to permit the teacher to become well acquainted with individual students. Nevertheless, circumstances sometimes cause classes to include as few as fifteen students or as many as one hundred.

The Meeting Place

Some classes meet in a regular classroom equipped with desks or writing-arm chairs, but with special music equipment, such as a piano, phonograph, and music books. Other classes meet in a specially designed music room or rehearsal hall. Still others may be forced, by the lack of pianos or other facilities, to meet in a large auditorium, in a gymnasium, or even behind stage curtains while another class is in progress in the auditorium itself. In any case, it is desirable that the room provide chairs that can be rearranged as necessary and permit comfortable writing, a piano that is in tune and of suitable quality, and a phonograph that reproduces sound accurately.

Ability Grouping

For certain subject areas, it is common to group pupils according to ability. This is true not only in academic subjects, but in music performing groups as well due to their selective nature and the needs of performance. Although general music classes do not need to be selective, and should not be if they are to fulfill their purpose, there are certain advantages in the type of selectivity known as ability grouping.

Criteria for grouping can be academic, musical, or a combination of both. If criteria are the same as those used for academic subjects, each group will include pupils of similar learning aptitude but different degrees of music ability. If criteria are musical, each group will contain pupils with similar degrees of music talent. Neither plan, of course, eliminates individual differences within the group, but ability groupings of both types offer opportunities for effective teaching. Musical groupings create "advanced" classes in which the talented are not retarded in their progress by those with less interest or talent, and other "slow" classes in which materials and activities can be adjusted to pupils of lower interest and ability. In groupings according to learning ability, slow learners tend to react favorably to folk and fun songs and there can be emphasis upon enjoyable unison singing with less stress upon music reading and singing in parts. Rapid learners tend to be more sensitive to the beauties of art songs and to make greater progress in reading and part singing.

Credit

The general music class, both in the junior high school and the senior high school, should and usually does receive academic credit. Full credit is merited when the class meets every day and when class assignments require outside work. Laboratory credit—half credit—is appropriate when work is confined to the class period and there are no or few outside assignments.

To justify the award of credit, it is reasonable that the general music class meet the same requirements and set the same standards as those applied to other courses. In academic courses, it is customary to administer frequent examinations, sufficiently objective in nature to permit the award of marks and to provide proof of pupil progress. Notebooks or workbooks are often prescribed and serve as records of pupil achievement. Independent projects pursued outside of class are utilized also, consisting of assigned readings, written reports, or other outside work. In addition to justifying the award of credit, the examinations, notebooks, projects, and other such requirements stimulate learning, permit assigned tasks to be varied in accordance with individual differences, and are highly desirable as instructional devices.

It is for the lack of such class requirements that some general music classes have been criticized and regarded by administrators and other teachers as courses devoted to recreation rather than to the attainment of solid goals of learning and development. Although music classes are unique in that they must win pupils to music through interest and enjoyment, rather than compel them to master stated quantities of subject matter, those who look critically at music education are justified in questioning the worth of these classes unless they set well-defined requirements and standards.

PUPILS AND THEIR DIFFERENCES

The general music class is conceived as a means of developing music interest and skill among large numbers of pupils. It is an outlet for the music interests of those who are unable to participate in bands, orchestras, or glee clubs, and for pupils who do belong to performing groups but want further class instruction as well. It is also for those who have had few opportunities to learn about music or develop its skills prior to the general music class.

Not all pupils show the same degree of interest in the work of the general music class. The pupils who have little interest submit themselves to music only because it is required in the junior high school, because their choice of electives is limited, because the electives they might prefer conflict with required courses, or because they regard the music class as one that requires little work. The general music class, therefore, is often a mixture of diverse interests and abilities, including pupils who have extensive music backgrounds and respond eagerly to class instruction, others who suffer silently through classes in which they have no interest, and still others who on occasion rebel against their assigned tasks.

Elementary-school Influences

One reason for these differences is that pupils in the general music class may be the products of a number of different elementary schools and reflect the differences in their music programs. It is common to find that teachers of general music in the junior high school are critical of the work done by music teachers in the elementary school. They remark that children who enter their classes from the elementary school are unable to read music, are unable to sing in tune, are disinterested in singing and in music in general, and know little of the factual data associated with music learning. Such teachers are equally prone to overlook those children, of whom there are many, who read music with relative facility, enjoy singing, sing in tune and with pleasant quality, and have acquired a reasonable store of music learning.

Before forming conclusions about the results achieved by music programs in elementary schools, it is well to remember their characteristics and objectives. The nature of the elementary-school music program is such that children are not taught with the sole purpose of developing high levels of skill and knowledge. To the contrary, music in the elementary school is designed to offer a broad background of experience in music. It serves as a basis for pleasurable participation and the development of rather general understandings. The teaching procedures and activities of the elementary school are different from those of the secondary school. With certain exceptions, their chief purpose is to encourage participation, self-confidence, and self-expression. Finally, the child may be disturbed by the changes he experiences as he moves from the elementary to the secondary school. The approach of adolescence, the change in his school environment and its routines, and the change in teachers affects the child's body, mind, and emotions. They may even cause him to retrogress for a brief period at the beginning of his first year in the secondary school.

It is true, nevertheless, that pupil differences do exist in the general music class as a direct result of the disparity among elementary-school music programs, and that these differences add to the difficulties of the teacher in planning and carrying out an effective teaching program.

Home and Family Influences

In the general music class, it is common to find a variety of tastes, preferences, and prejudices concerning music. There are wide differences in home and family background, such that almost every set of parents will have different attitudes toward music. Pupils are affected by these attitudes as well as by the tastes and preferences of their older brothers and sisters. They tend to respond to the music heard or accepted in their homes, rejecting that with which they are unfamiliar. Because of the social connotations of popular music, and the very fact that it is popular, adolescent boys and girls accept it unthinkingly and deprecate serious music simply because it is not part of the social life of groups of their own age. There are marked differences in taste even among those who prefer serious to popular music. Further differences in taste are caused by previous music training or the lack of it. Some pupils will have studied the piano or other instruments prior to entering the general music class. Others will have had the benefit of dancing schools, children's concerts, or membership in church-sponsored singing groups. Still others will have had none of these advantages and little or no contact with music prior to the general music class.

PUPIL NEEDS AND TEACHING GOALS

As a result of the many differences among pupils in the general music class, the teacher must be prepared to meet a variety of pupil needs. For a few pupils, general music is a stepping stone to other, more advanced music activities in school and a professional career or avocational interest in later life. For these, general music can properly strive to develop consuming interest, the will to progress, and the foundations for music skills. For a larger number of pupils, general music is the last formal music instruction, a terminal point beyond which the pupil will not progress unless his interest is firmly established. Most students will become consumers of music, if the general music class does its work well, but will have little talent, opportunity, or desire to be performers. They will be the audiences who listen to music, who purchase concert tickets and phonograph records, who react to and help determine the music quality of radio and television programs.

A few pupils may find their way into church choirs and other community singing groups as adults, but even they remain essentially consumers rather than producers of music. It is appropriate that general music give them sufficient skill for the enjoyment of choral singing and the ability to perform reasonably well, but not to the exclusion of objectives more significant to their function as consumers of music.

In any case, general music is often the foundation for future music activities. The success of the class determines the extent to which music becomes part of pupils' future lives. If general music fails, pupils leave school unable to realize the benefits of music; if it is successful, large numbers of pupils develop deep music interests and continue to expand the scope of their appreciation through the years that follow.

Enjoyment

The basic objective of almost every music class and activity in the school program is one of providing a basis for the enjoyment of music, an enjoyment which will continue to expand and deepen and which will endure beyond the years the pupil spends in the public schools. Whether we use the term enjoyment, pleasure, satisfaction, or appreciation, the essential meaning is the same. Music is an art that satisfies elemental needs in human nature and prompts in all men certain unique and pleasurable responses. It is the capacity to find this unique pleasure that general music strives to develop.

Other objectives, although they are important and serve to guide the work of the general music class, are useful chiefly in that they aid the teacher or the pupil in attaining the principal objective, that of enjoyment. This principal objective is significant to the teacher for two important reasons. It is the cornerstone of the entire philosophy of music education, guiding the teacher's thought and action concerning the larger problems of music teaching and the general goals of the music class, and it is a criterion by which every teaching procedure and every choice of music may be judged.

Interest

Closely related to enjoyment are interest, experience, and taste. It is the objective of the general music class to create interest if none exists, to sustain that which already exists, and to progress toward intensified interest strong enough to live after formal instruction has stopped. Such interest aids, and is perhaps essential to, the music learning the general music class hopes to achieve. Because of the variety of interests natural to pupils in general music, it is important that the class offer wide experience including many different types of music. Because we are prone to accept that with which we are familiar, this experience should include much and repeated contact with enjoyable and worthy music appropriate to the interests and tastes of the pupils concerned. None of the music chosen should violate the canons of good taste and much of it should be selected with a view to raising the levels of taste of the members of the class.

Taste is a faculty about which there can be much debate. It is difficult to define. It is affected by obscure attitudes, emotions, knowledge, and experience. It is intensely personal and subjective. Although it is difficult to arrive at a formula for teaching good taste, it is the responsibility of music education to be sensitive to the problem and to search for effective means of developing powers of discernment and discrimination. Pertinent to the work of the general music class is the probability that the development of discriminating taste is aided by frequent contact with that which is good and by knowledge of the criteria by which the good is judged. Taste is influenced by experience; taste and experience help to direct interest; taste, experience, and interest are directly related to enjoyment; all four of these factors are important to the objectives of the general music class and its content and activities.

Exploration

The general music class has as one of its objectives the exploration of music literature. For some pupils, this may be the first conscious contact with great music; for others, it may be the last opportunity to sample in any systematic way the limitless varieties of music. Thus it is the duty of the music teacher to guide pupils in a survey of the vast resources of music literature. We sometimes think of education as a chore, a set of imposed tasks which must be completed before the student embarks on the more real and rewarding pursuits of later life. Where the arts are concerned, however, we can regard education as the agency that opens the eyes of youth to boundless vistas of beauty and artistic truth, with the firm conviction that acquaintance with the arts is a right that should not be denied.

General music can extend the scope of the pupil's music experience, both as a performer and as a listener. It can build familiarity with desirable music, increase the pupil's knowledge of the musical art, and help him understand the greatness of music through something no more complex than the exploration of its literature.

Appreciation

It is a purpose of the general music class to help pupils realize that music is an art, the embodiment in beautiful and stirring form of some of man's greatest thoughts and aspirations. It is both a language, in that it has the power to communicate feelings and emotions, and an extension of language in that it expresses shades of feeling beyond the descriptive power of words for all but poets. It is like language in that it progresses in time, unlike the relatively static arts of architecture, sculpture, and painting. It is like language also in that its effects are cumulative, changing and growing as themes, forms, and harmonic rhythms unfold and are pitted against each other. As a language, it is peculiarly suited to the expression of man's innermost feelings, many of which are never expressed, not because they do not exist, but because man is incapable of finding words to express them. It is because music has this expressive power, and because the expression itself is beautiful, that music is an art. It is for these reasons that music is part of man's cultural heritage. Great music, in company with enduring works of literature and the other arts, is one of the gifts offered to the young by past generations, priceless, yet entirely free. Music education, including the general music class, can help youth appreciate the value of this gift.

Participation

Objectives such as those described above can be achieved only if pupils participate actively in the work of the general music class. The process of listening to music, for example, would seem to be a passive one in which the listener sits quiety in the presence of music. The listener who actually hears music, however, is inwardly active, exercising the mind, the emotions, and even the muscles to follow and respond to the music. Similarly, if general music is to foster enjoyment and learning, it must encourage pupils to participate. This is true not only where inward response is concerned but, as well, in the sense that pupils must be led to attitudes of interest and coöperation in class work. Without such participation it is difficult to develop the skills music demands or to create a class atmosphere conducive to music progress.

Developing Skills

The skills of music are many, but chief among them is the aural skill. Music is an aural art and must be heard clearly to be understood and appreciated. The listener develops the ability to focus aural attention upon tones and rhythms, following their progress, recognizing their characteristics, and perceiving their relationships. Young people as well as adults develop the ability to block out or ignore unwelcome and meaningless sounds, practicing this negative skill daily in the presence of the many distracting noises around them. Music teaching strives to reverse this trend, cultivating the ability to hear sounds and be sensitive to their characteristics.

Next in importance is the vocal skill. The human voice is not only the most sensitive and personal of all music instruments; it is also the universal instrument, the one most natural and convenient to each member of the general music class. It is the means through which each pupil can achieve performing satisfaction and feel living contact with music. It is the one avenue along which almost every pupil could progress toward active membership in a performing group during adult life. The development of singing skill is properly an objective of the general music class, particularly in that pupils in the class are either in or near the stage of voice change. If the general music class guides vocal development and supervises vocal practice during this crucial period, it preserves vocal ability and interest for later school years and adult life.

Other skills include the muscular ability to respond to and produce rhythms, the intellectual ability to understand the structure of music, the ability to recognize music symbols and use them in both reading and writing, and the ability to play instruments. All of these skills are useful and each of them can be developed through the activities of the general music class. It is proper that the general music class develop a degree of skill in music reading and other relatively technical areas, but this skill is undoubtedly of less importance to the music progress of the majority of pupils than the aural and vocal skills basic to music listening and appreciation.

Other Goals

Among the goals of general music that apply to only a few pupils or are not necessarily musical in nature are (1) the discovery of talented pupils not identified through other music classes and activities, (2) training pupils to work coöperatively with others, and (3) correlating music with other school subjects.

In general music classes, there may be pupils who have had no previous training or experience, who show little interest in the music activities of the secondary school, but who have outstanding music potentials. The disparity between interest and talent is perhaps more common at the junior-high-school level than at any other due to the tendency among adolescent boys to reject music in favor of more active and manly pursuits. These individuals can be identified in the general music class and stimulated to develop their music abilities.

The benefits of coöperative effort can be demonstrated effectively through music activities, particularly those of a choral nature because of the necessity for unanimity in group singing. Although this objective is not basically musical, and is taught through many other activities in the school program, the effects of coöperation or its absence in music performance are so convincingly apparent that it is often opportune and beneficial to discuss the subject in general music classes.

In addition to being an objective, correlation can be a boon to the teacher of music. If taught so that environmental relationships are apparent, music is often more readily accepted by the pupil and becomes more meaningful. Music can play a part in the teaching of other subjects, particularly social studies and literature, by giving pupils a broader view of the social and cultural temper of other countries and ages and by adding variety and interest. It is the responsibility of the music teacher to take the initiative in suggesting possible ways in which music can be used and to coöperate with other members of the school staff in carrying out correlated studies.

In summary, these are the objectives of the general music class, important in relation to the needs and interests of adolescent pupils.

1. To provide a basis for the lasting enjoyment of music.
2. To develop and sustain interest in music.
3. To develop discriminating musical taste.
4. To explore the rich literature of the musical art.
5. To foster appreciation of the expressive, artistic, and cultural aspects of music.
6. To encourage participation in class and other music activities.
7. To develop music skills, especially those essential to listening and singing.
8. To discover latent music talent.
9. To help pupils reach an understanding of democratic procedures and their values.
10. To demonstrate the relationships between music and other subjects and utilize them for effective teaching.

One of the distinctive challenges of music education is inherent in its objectives. To a large degree, the objectives of music education deal with attitudes and concepts which are almost indefinable. The beauty of music is intensely real, yet despite centuries of discussion philosophers are not unanimously agreed on its definition. Man's responses to music are equally real but equally indefinable, made up of ideas and feelings which defy description. Man himself is a creature of infinite variation; each individual is different from every other and displays different characteristics in each stage of his development. Thus music education deals with a series of variable and intangible factors. It must press forward toward goals that are nebulous, along paths only dimly apparent, often guided only by intuitive principles. Yet the values of these goals are universally accepted and eminently worthy. It is the responsibility of music education to strive for their attainment.

ASPECTS AND ACTIVITIES OF GENERAL MUSIC

Singing and Listening

To achieve its many objectives, general music turns to a variety of activities and studies. The major portion of class time is usually occupied by two principal activities, singing and listening. Group singing is most common. Ensembles such as quartets and trios have their place and occasional solo selections are included if there are suitable voices among the members of the class. Both unison and part singing are desirable, though neither is relied on exclusively. Songs are of many types, chosen to fit the interests of the class but with due regard for musical quality. Singing activities form the basis of general music even though problems arise in some classes due to the presence of the changing voice, making it difficult to find song materials all can sing. Singing necessitates the alert participation of each individual, providing close and personal contact with the music material, and is a convenient means of exploring diverse areas of music literature.

Music listening, although it is less active than singing and requires more teacher ingenuity to bring about attentive participation, is equally appropriate as a basis for general music. It offers limitless opportunities for exploring enjoyable music of many kinds. It is essential to the general music class in that it presents music performed at a high level of excellence, a level the general music class can not attain in its own performance or hear in the programs presented by special music groups of the school. It is an introduction to the type of music enjoyment open to all adults regardless of their technical training, a more convenient source of adult satisfaction than either vocal or instrumental performance. Through music listening, general music extends the pupil's knowledge of music literature, provides a basis for the development of music taste, and actually teaches such things as the history of music, the elements of music theory, and the significance of music in man's historical, social, and cultural progress. Both singing and listening offer these teaching opportunities, permitting the teacher to present many of the relatively technical aspects of music in meaningful context, making them significant in relation to the music heard or sung, and placing them within each pupil's personal experience.

Voice Training

Closely related to these activities of the general music class are certain aspects of voice training. To enjoy fully the experience of choral singing, pupils must be able to sing easily and well. General music strives to develop pleasing tone quality, clear diction, interpretive sensitivity, proper breathing habits, and other essentials to good singing. The procedure is not that of the voice studio, but one that encourages the gradual development of singing skills through example, suggestion, and the performance of song literature that induces good singing habits.

Learning about Instruments

A knowledge of orchestral instruments is a desirable part of the pupil's general information, permitting him to listen more intelligently to orchestral music. In the general music class, it is appropriate to show the instruments, to demonstrate the manner in which each produces tone, and to discuss the principles and mechanisms that produce various pitches. Pupils are often interested in exploring the instruments for themselves, experimenting with whatever instruments can be made available. From the standpoint of listening, it is especially important that pupils become acquainted with the distinctive tone qualities and the ways in which they are used expressively in instrumental music. The discussion of acoustical principles is a natural outcome of instrumental exploration and leads to further discussion of such subjects as high fidelity or stereophonic sound systems and the importance of physical science in music theory and practice. Here, too, is subject matter suited to the natural interests of the adolescent, offering an indirect but effective means of arousing music interest.

Rhythmic Activities

Rhythmic activities and the playing of simple instruments are as appropriate in the general music class as they are in the elementary school. Rhythm is the element of music to which many people respond most easily. It is often the source of the first response and is an element which can and perhaps should be felt rather than understood. It involves the muscles more than the mind or the voice and response often occurs automatically without instruction or experience. Rhythm is an essential element of music, as necessary to a Mozart symphony as to the primitive surgings of a Stravinsky ballet, and one which must be felt by the listener if he is to know the immediacy of music's appeal.

Of particular importance is the fact that adolescents are especially responsive to rhythm. Their expanding physical resources make muscular and manipulative exercise necessary and natural, and their impulse to physical expression finds satisfying outlet in rhythmic music activities. These include all the responses to music that require physical movement, from folk dancing through clapping, tapping, and conducting to the use of percussion and other instruments. The rhythm instruments associated with Latin-American dance music are especially useful. Adolescent imagination is stimulated by their exotic flavor and adolescents enjoy practicing the movement required to play them as well as the exhilaration of the dances they accompany.

Music Theory

Ear training and certain aspects of what is usually called music theory are productive areas for study in the general music class. Ear training directly benefits both singing and listening. It leads to accurate concepts of the interval and rhythm patterns encountered in vocal music, aids music reading, and helps develop sensitivity to intonation. For the listener, aural skill is based upon the ability to hear, recognize, and understand melodic, harmonic, and rhythmic patterns. The acute perception of these factors in music structure and style leads to heightened music enjoyment. Music theory, although a study in itself, is closely related to ear training. It is important to the general music class because of its contributions to aural skill and understanding rather than for the disciplines of its study. Aural recognition is aided by understanding as well as by experience, and the study of music theory provides both. Under the heading of music theory, the teacher examines meter, rhythm patterns, intervals, tonality, scales and chords, notes and rests. The teacher applies this learning in the aural analysis that accompanies music listening, the visual analysis we call music reading, and in creative activities of a level appropriate to the ability of the class. Properly integrated with other activities of the general music class, ear training and music theory lose their forbiddingly technical character and make valuable contributions to the musical growth of the pupil.

Other Phases of Class Work

A number of other studies and activities are equally suited to the general music class, but normally are of less importance in the total program than the activities described in the preceding paragraphs. Music history makes a contribution, although historical study is undertaken only if it aids music understanding and enjoyment and if it helps make music of the past come to life in the present. A general acquaintance with the history of music is a natural but incidental result of the survey of music literature. The usual practice in the general music class is to use historical information when and if it is helpful in stimulating interest or increasing understanding, but to avoid historical study for its own sake.

Library assignments and written reports fall in the same category as music history. They are called into use when beneficial to music progress but are in general disfavor when used simply to provide occupation for idle hours or to furnish a non-musical basis for awarding marks. The use of audio-visual aids is worthy of mention also among the activities of the general music class, including projected slides and filmstrips as well as the usual phonograph records and actual music instruments. Experience in many fields has proved the effectiveness of visual aids in teaching. Particularly for those who have little knowledge of music, the sound film with its combination of visual image, narrative, and music serves as an exciting introduction to new aspects of music study.

Of even greater potential for stimulating interest are invited, guest performers. To teen-agers especially, music emanating from a phonograph is something from the past, worthy of being preserved for posterity, perhaps, but far removed from the living world of today. For them, there can be no comparison between the recorded music of Pablo Casals and the opportunity to see a cellist who sits among them. For this reason it is highly desirable that the teacher search out every opportunity to provide live music played by visiting performers.

Equally stimulating is the field trip that permits pupils to gain first-hand knowledge of community or school resources. Almost every community offers something to make a field trip rewarding. Churches, music stores, radio or television stations, instrument factories, professional or amateur concerts, all are desirable field-trip destinations. The schools, too, offer surprising opportunities for seeing music in action if the teacher will but search them out. The rehearsal hall in which another teacher is working with a band, orchestra, or chorus can be a stimulating place to visit, especially if the conductor of the performing group can be persuaded to use a few minutes of his rehearsal time to explain and demonstrate the instruments or voices in the group and to demonstrate their use in a few brief passages from the music being studied.

The following headings summarize the separate activities and studies of the general music class.

1. Singing activities
2. Listening activities
3. Rhythmic activities
4. Ear training
5. Music theory
6. Music history
7. Voice training
8. Orchestral instruments
9. Acoustics and the science of music

These topics are discussed separately in the preceding paragraphs and in later chapters. It should be emphasized, however, that it is rare for any one of them to be pursued separately, to the exclusion of the others. Even if the general music class concentrates its effort either in the singing or the listening area, creating the impression that it is in one case a singing class and in the other a "music appreciation" class, the other topics are studied also. The singing or listening program serves as an approach to other activities, a framework within which they all have a logical place.

THE TEACHER OF GENERAL MUSIC

The teacher of general music must be a particularly skillful and understanding person, well equipped to work toward the goals of the general music class, to stimulate interest in pupils with different attitudes toward music, and to present music in such a way that it is attractive and enjoyable to adolescents.

Among the most important of the skills requisite to this kind of teaching is the ability to play the piano. Too often, the general music class falls to teachers trained primarily as singers or in the field of instrumental music—thorough musicians, perhaps, and capable performers in their own media, but not at home at the keyboard. In the general music class, keyboard facility is a necessity. The teacher must be able to accompany songs, providing through pianistic accompaniments sufficient musical interest to balance the deficiencies likely to exist in vocal music performed by untrained adolescent singers. In the area of listening activities, the teacher uses the keyboard to illustrate themes, harmonies, and rhythms, reproducing at the keyboard the effects of music performed by full orchestra, on occasion reading from the orchestral score.

Rhythmic activities, ear training, music theory, and almost every other music activity pursued in the general music class benefit from the use of the piano. The piano is the only instrument with a wide range of powers and potentials, able to translate almost any music score into sound, providing the flexibility and the intimacy required in the classroom. Adolescent pupils often seem to find more pleasure in listening to the piano than to any other instrument. Their frequent requests for piano selections played by the teacher should not be ignored. Without pianistic ability the teacher of general music is severely handicapped; with the ability to play the piano fluently and musically, the teacher's work is immeasurably easier and far more successful.

Because singing activities play an important part in many general music classes, the teacher is required to have some degree of vocal ability. It is not necessary that the teacher of general music have the extensive training required of the concert soloist—the fully developed, resonant tone of the professional singer is sometimes actually detrimental to the work of the general music class—but it is necessary that the teacher be able to sing easily and pleasantly and without hesitation or embarrassment. Adolescents and other singers learn by imitation; their tone quality and singing habits reflect what they hear and it is important that the teacher of music set an example worthy of imitation. When songs are being taught, whether they are unison or part-songs, the teacher has many opportunities to demonstrate desirable interpretations of parts if he is vocally capable of doing so. The piano is at best a poor substitute for the voice in teaching vocal literature. There is far less use for the teacher's vocal skill in the teaching of music literature, rhythms, and other non-vocal aspects of music, but the teacher who has vocal ability finds it surprisingly useful in many phases of class work.

The teacher of general music needs extensive music background, including knowledge, understanding, and appreciation of music of many types, from many historical periods, and for many performance media. To survey the literature of music and search for examples appealing to the tastes within the class, the teacher relies on broad knowledge of music history. It is necessary, too, that the teacher draw on detailed and technical knowledge of the music being studied. Music must be understood to be appreciated, and understanding is based on knowledge of such technical factors as the treatment of theme, the progression of harmony and the architecture of form. These elements often provide a means for stimulating interest in music which would not otherwise be appealing to pupils. It is futile to talk of beauty in such instances, but it is often interesting and usually productive of music learning to note craftsmanship and historical mutations in style. The teacher also needs tolerance, the ability to accept and use music that appeals to pupils but may not agree with the teacher's more highly refined tastes. Equipped with both knowledge and tolerance, the teacher finds it easier to accept and understand the initial levels of pupil enjoyment and to guide progress from them to higher levels of taste and appreciation.

The teacher needs certain other qualities not musical in nature. These include a sincere interest in pupils and their progress, a knowledge of pupils and their characteristics and attitudes, and an understanding of the total school program and its objectives. The processes of teaching are influenced both by the music and by the pupils being taught; to consider one and ignore the other is to place barriers in the path of music progress. Thus the teacher of general music needs many qualifications, both musical and otherwise, to meet the demands of what may be the most important position in public-school music.

4: singing in the general music class

Singing is an essential part of the general music class. All of its larger objectives can be achieved through the performance of vocal music and some can be achieved more easily through singing than through any other music activity. When planning singing lessons, the teacher gives special thought to the following goals and the manner in which they can be approached in each class period: to encourage participation, foster enjoyment, develop singing ability, explore music literature, and teach music knowledge.

GUIDING THE ADOLESCENT SINGER

The adolescent experiences many changes in his physical, mental, and emotional make-up during the years when he stands on the threshold of maturity. For the teacher of general music, and for the pupil in the music class, the change in vocal characteristics is perhaps the most significant. If voice-change is understood and dealt with properly, the entire singing program benefits.

The Adolescent Voice

Before puberty, the voices of boys and girls are much alike. During preschool years, the vocal mechanism grows rapidly in size as do other bones and muscles of the body. The rate of this growth decreases during the years of the elementary school, but there is continued growth in strength. At some point in adolescence, however, there begins a new process. The boy's voice changes radically and becomes the voice of a man, completely unlike the voice of a child. Girls' voices undergo change also, but without either the obvious symptoms or the noticeable consequences of the change that affects boys.

VOICE-CHANGE AMONG BOYS. Prior to voice-change, boys sing with a quality often called "flute-like" in a range essentially that of the treble staff. The tone is light, pure, and clear, possessing tonal beauty which for centuries has given boys' voices places of prominence in church music. When adolescence arrives, the beauty and flexibility of the child's voice disappears. The voice sometimes becomes unmanageable without warning so that boys who sing well one day may be quite unable to sing the next. In general, however, the approach of voice-change is gradual rather than abrupt, heralded by certain observable symptoms. The beginning of voice-change appears at almost any grade from the sixth to the ninth, but seems to affect a larger number of boys during the eighth grade than during any other.

Among the advance symptoms shown by boys is rapid increase in body size, a better index of approaching voice-change than chronological age. Facial characteristics begin to change. The nose and lips begin their mutation from child-like roundness and softness to the distinctly chiseled features of the adult. Facial hair appears and the "Adam's apple" begins to be apparent. Signs of change are noted in the speaking voice. It loses its childish, piping quality and begins to grow heavier and thicker.

As the voice of the boy begins to change, the first symptom observable in the singing voice is often a thickening of quality. The voice will seem heavier and more difficult to manage, losing some of its easy flexibility. There may be some reduction in the compass of the voice also, the upper tones becoming strained and shrill or perhaps no longer attainable.

The next definable stage is what has been called "alto-tenor," a term invented to describe the changing voice of the boy during a period in which it retains the alto quality of the changing voice but approaches the range of the adult tenor. At this point, the voice is usually lower in register and perhaps further reduced in compass. It often sounds husky and strained, as though the tone is being produced with great difficulty. It may "break," slipping from bass to treble without warning and causing great embarrassment to the boy. Some boys of this category are able to sing only within a very narrow compass, perhaps in the interval of a third or a fourth near or immediately below middle C. Other boys may have two distinctly separate voices, one of lower register approaching that of the adult male and one of higher register similar to the unchanged voice of the boy.

A third stage is often called "bass." This is a term used for the changed voice of the adolescent, despite the fact that the adolescent voice is far removed in quality and range from the bass voice of the fully matured male. The adolescent bass voice is often limited in compass, perhaps to an octave or less. It sounds husky and raucous and shows signs of strain when attempting to produce pitches near the upper limit of its compass. It is limited in flexibility, is hard to manage, and may continue to "break" in both singing and speaking.

Finally, the voice passes into a stage approaching mature development. It may drop further into the register of the male baritone or bass or may revert to tenor. It improves in quality, losing much of the huskiness of the changing voice, and is more settled and easier to control.

Although it is useful in understanding the boy's changing voice to describe the four stages discussed above, it must be remembered that each voice has its own characteristics and its own unique sequence of qualities during change. The process of change is one of mutation, rather than one of a series of well-defined steps. Some voices do seem to pass through these separate categories. Others change gradually and almost imperceptibly from unchanged treble to changed bass, rarely showing huskiness or strain, rarely breaking, and with little reduction of voice compass during the gradual descent in register.

The boys who experience most difficulty are often those who have had too little singing experience or those who have been encouraged to resist voice-change to preserve an attractive "boy-soprano" voice. If gradual and easy change occurs in too few cases, it is possible the fault lies with teachers and directors rather than with the boy voice. There are physical reasons for voice-change, of course, among them an increase of approximately one third in the size of the voice mechanism, and it is natural that the adolescent boy should find his new vocal powers unfamiliar and difficult to control. We believe with increasing certainty, nevertheless, that boys can continue to sing during voice-change without strain, discomfort, or injury to the voice, reaching vocal maturity without losing the skill or the pleasure of singing.

VOICE-CHANGE AMONG GIRLS. The unchanged voice of the girl, like that of the boy, lies more or less within the treble staff and is clear and sweet in quality. It changes during adolescence, but without the obvious symptoms or the pronounced lowering of register of the voice of the boy. Where girls are concerned, the noticeable difference between the voice of the child and that of the woman is one of maturity. The mature voice has power and a richness of quality absent from the child voice, but in many instances shows only minor differences in register and compass. It is the absence of well-defined symptoms that makes it difficult to detect vocal problems among girls. The principal symptom is one of quality, the tone losing its purity and becoming husky or breathy. Some may sound strained or weak, the higher pitches sounding as though they are produced with effort, and there may be a pronounced preference for lower parts.

Many girls find the voice difficult to control at this stage, to such an extent that they sing out of tune even when pitches are within comfortable range. This is a matter that merits special attention. The problems experienced by the boy are so apparent that he is aware of his difficulty and either sings in tune, if he can, or remains silent. Girls tend to be less aware of their difficulties and to continue singing, apparently insensitive to matters of intonation. It may be partly for this reason that there seem to be more out-of-tune singers among girls than among boys during late adolescence.

In the general music class, the problem of the changing voice deserves the constant attention of the teacher. Adolescent voices are immature and unsettled, undergoing rapid and constant change. Despite their growth in size and strength, vocal mechanisms at this stage of development tire easily. The fatigue resulting from improper use of the voice can cause adolescent singers to develop faulty singing habits. The voice is difficult to control and a source of embarrassment when it responds in unexpected ways and leaps from one register to another. Embarrassment is intensified by the adolescent's normal reluctance to appear inadequate and can cause boys, especially, to withdraw completely from singing activities.

It is important that the teacher of general music be especially alert to factors that cause vocal difficulty. It is well to avoid heavy singing that tends to force the voice down into the throat or chest. It is important to avoid music that forces the young voice to strain for higher tones, an effort that encourages the inexperienced singer in his natural inclination to lift his chin and tighten his throat. It is desirable to exercise good judgment in assigning voices to alto or other low parts. There are few true altos of public-school age, and it is as harmful to force the immature voice downward as it is to force it to sing pitches at the upper limit of its compass.

Possibly the best solution to such problems is frequent voice testing. If the teacher makes it a practice to check voice development frequently, noting both the compass of the voice and the range in which tones can be produced most easily, singers can be assigned to parts that encourage rather than hinder smooth vocal development.

Attitudes Toward Singing

It is important for the teacher to understand the nature and problems of the adolescent voice and equally important that the adolescent himself understand and accept voice mutation. If the pupil can be led to an awareness of the approaching change in his voice, and an interest in the progress of the change, he is more likely to accept it and to continue singing while learning to control his new vocal instrument. The responsibility for this guidance rests with the teacher, and guidance in this instance includes both explanation of the change and proper utilization of the voice during the change period.

The first step in explaining the change to adolescents is one of pointing out that it happens to everyone, all boys and all girls, and is a normal part of becoming an adult. It is a result of normal body development, desirable in that it is evidence of the achievement of maturity. One can not change human nature, or speed or halt its progress. Neither should one fear the progress of vocal development or be ashamed of or embarrassed by it. To the contrary, voice-change permits the exploration of excitingly different varieties of vocal literature and leads to new pleasure in singing. All of this can and should be explained to adolescents.

It is important that the class as a group does not ridicule the few boys whose voices first show signs of breaking, and equally important that the first "breaks" heard in the classroom are not signals for laughter. To prevent ridicule and merriment, it is well for the teacher to be alert for the first symptoms of voice-change, the tonal heaviness and thickening that are not apparent to the members of the class, and begin discussing voice-change immediately. Healthy curiosity and interest are desirable attitudes. They can be developed to the extent that pupils themselves become interested in their progress, request voice tests whenever they feel their voices have changed, and become sympathetic toward those with the greatest vocal difficulties.

To give pupils a clearer understanding of the change, and to capture their interest, it is desirable to demonstrate the physical laws involved. The teacher might arrange to borrow a violin and cello or double bass, using them to demonstrate the effects upon pitch and tone quality of string diameter, length, and tension. A less musical but perhaps more interesting procedure would be to borrow from the physics teacher the equipment he uses to demonstrate these same laws. If no such equipment is available, pupils can examine the strings of the piano, noting that the long, heavy strings produce low pitches and that the short, slender strings produce higher pitches. The simplest procedure, and one with which the pupils might experiment for themselves, is one in which rubber bands of various sizes and thicknesses are simply stretched between the fingers and plucked, producing pitches determined by length, thickness, and tension.

The second step in helping pupils through the period of voice-change is one of encouragement. Muscles of all types retain strength and flexibility if they are used. The singing voice, too, must be given reasonable amounts of exercise if it is to progress smoothly toward maturity. Adolescent pupils should continue to sing while their voices are changing, with due regard to limitations of range and endurance. Although the voice should not be strained, neither should it be idle. It is no more reasonable to believe adolescents should give up singing during voice-change than to believe they should stop speaking.

Pupils may be naturally reluctant to sing during this awkward phase, but it is the duty of the teacher to offer encouragement and to insure success. It is in the latter respect that voice testing is especially important. To prevent the negative effects of embarrassing inadequacy, and the harmful effects of attempting to sing pitches too high or too low, the teacher tests voices frequently, assigning them to parts they can sing easily or adjusting class singing to fit the capabilities of the singers. If the teacher leads pupils to understand their voices and to use them with pleasure and success, voice-change is a less disturbing experience and classroom vocal activities are more satisfying to all.

Adolescent Voice Ranges

Although it is necessary for practical purposes to define the voice ranges of adolescent singers and to group them in categories, each voice is unique in quality and range. It is erroneous to think of voices as being all alike, or to assume that voices can be separated into a few groups of identical range and quality. For the purposes of the general music class and of singing activities in general, it is necessary to arrive at a satisfactory criterion for grouping similar voices so the parts assigned will be within the vocal compass of each singer in the group. This is especially difficult to accomplish where adolescents are concerned because of the relatively narrow compass of some voices and the frequency with which vocal ranges change.

REGISTER AND COMPASS. As an indication of the marked change in register occurring in boys' voices, and the relatively minor change in girls' voices, Example 1 shows the differences between ranges of adult men and women and those of boys and girls at the age of ten, prior to voice-change. These data from Jersild and Bienstock[1] include information concerning the pitches produced by children younger than ten years of age, both boys and girls. The extremes of range shown include all pitches the tested individuals were able to produce, including those of the man's falsetto voice, and are pitches produced alone rather than in the context of a song or some other vocal line. The ranges shown, therefore, are not necessarily those throughout which the test subjects were able to sing easily and well. Pitches at the high and low extremes may have been beyond comfortable singing compass, of faulty tone quality, and produced with extreme vocal strain. The data tend to show that (1) the voices of boys and girls expand similarly in compass until they reach approximately nine years of age, (2) the voices of boys and girls begin to show slight differences in range at age ten or soon thereafter, (3) the compass of girls' voices expands downward, but not upward, as the voice matures, (4) the voices of boys drop approximately one octave during voice-change.

FREQUENTLY USED TERMS. The literature dealing with adolescent voices uses a variety of terms to identify ranges and qualities. The differences of opinion among various authors testify to the difficulty of establishing categories suitable for all voices. Example 2 summarizes these terms. Some are normal to vocal literature written for mature voices; others are appropriate only to changing voices.

The problem of range is a complex one. It is possible to describe their variety more completely by increasing the number of range classifications, but this increase in categories does little to solve the teacher's problem of using adolescent voices in the song material available. What, then, is the teacher to do? The principal objective is to find a place for every voice in the singing activities of the class. To accomplish this, the teacher must test each voice to discover its range limitations, must examine the available song literature to discover its range demands, and on the basis of this information must assign voices to parts each can sing without discomfort.

DEMANDS OF SONG LITERATURE. As an indication of what the teacher may meet in analyzing song literature, Example 3 summarizes the findings of

[1] Arthur T. Jersild, and Sylvia F. Bienstock, "A Study of the Development of Children's Ability to Sing," *Journal of Educational Psychology*, 1934, XXV, No. 7, p. 491.

EXAMPLE 1. VOICE RANGES OF CHILDREN AND ADULTS. PITCHES NOT IN PARENTHESES WERE PRODUCED BY 50 PER CENT, PITCHES IN PARENTHESES BY 48–50 PER CENT OF TOTAL INDIVIDUALS TESTED. RANGE FOR MEN INCLUDES THE FALSETTO.

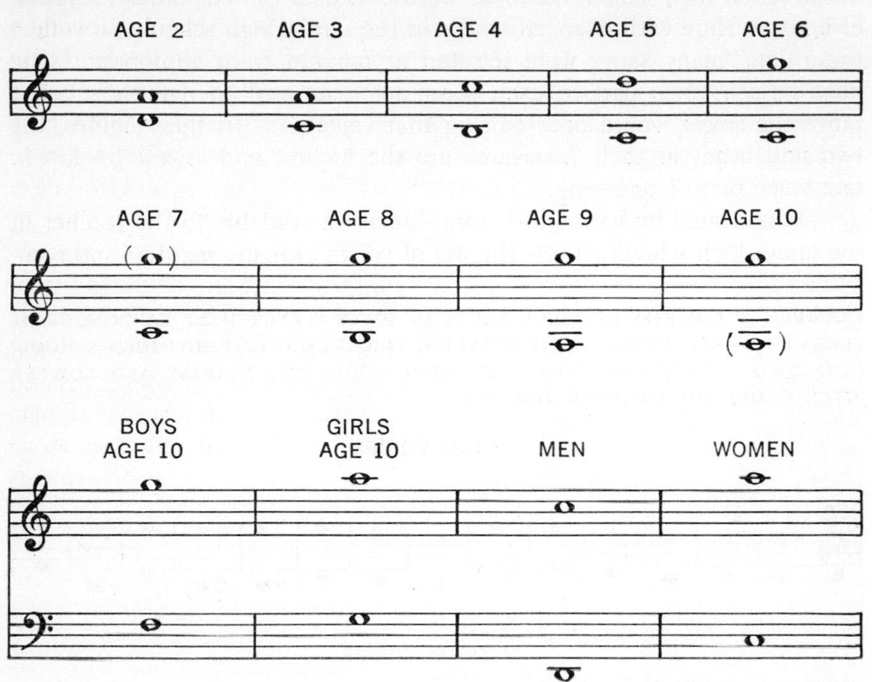

EXAMPLE 2. CLASSIFICATIONS AND RANGES CITED IN VARIOUS TEXTS TO DESCRIBE THE VARIETY OF ADOLESCENT VOICES.

a random sampling of song materials intended for use with changing voices in the junior high school; Example 4 presents data from a similar sampling of books for use with changed voices in the senior high school. To collect these data, many songs were selected at random from appropriate song books. Each voice part in each song was examined to determine what range the singer would need to sing that voice part. In these figures, the two note-heads in each "measure" are the highest and lowest pitches in one voice part of one song.

As indicated by Example 3, song literature available to the teacher in the junior high school permits the use of voices of many registers and com-

EXAMPLE 3. COMPASS OF VOICE PARTS IN SONGS SELECTED AT RANDOM FROM BOOKS INTENDED FOR USE WITH CHANGING VOICES IN THE JUNIOR HIGH SCHOOL. (THE TWO NOTE-HEADS IN EACH MEASURE SHOW THE HIGHEST AND LOWEST PITCH IN ONE VOICE-PART OF ONE SONG.)

passes. Unison songs and parts for higher treble voices offer compasses of from less than one octave to as much as a twelfth, occasionally rising to two-line G or descending to small B-flat.[2] Parts for medium voices may vary from a fourth to an octave or more in compass, with two-line D and small A as their upper and lower extremes. Lower voices of both boys and girls may be assigned to parts of from a fourth to a tenth in compass, descending as far as small G. Boys with changing voices may be assigned to parts as narrow in compass as a fourth or fifth and rarely more than an octave, all centered around middle C. Boys with changed voices may be assigned to "bass" parts of from a fifth to a tenth in compass, but rarely descending further than great A. In this variety of ranges and registers there is something suitable for voices in almost every stage of voice-change.

The literature for changed voices, as indicated by Example 4, is more

[2] Pitches are referred to here as being in the great octave, small octave, one-line octave or two-line octave, these octaves beginning, respectively, two octaves below middle C, one octave below middle C, at middle C, and one octave above middle C.

EXAMPLE 4. COMPASS OF VOICE PARTS IN SONGS SELECTED AT RANDOM FROM BOOKS INTENDED FOR USE WITH CHANGED VOICES IN THE HIGH SCHOOL. (THE TWO NOTE-HEADS IN EACH MEASURE SHOW THE HIGHEST AND LOWEST PITCH IN ONE VOICE-PART OF ONE SONG.)

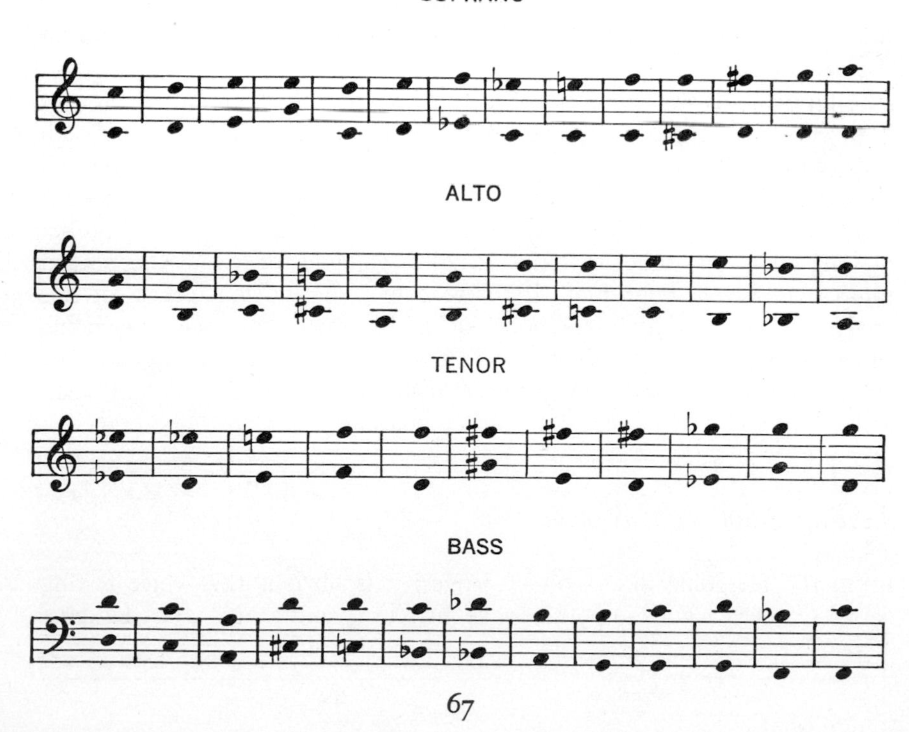

demanding. Here there are fewer songs in which the compass of voice parts is an octave or less. Sopranos, altos, tenors, and basses are assumed to have developed the ability to sing through a compass of a twelfth or more, the separate parts approaching the difficulty of those intended for mature, trained voices. There are some arrangements in which each part remains within an octave, but it would be extremely difficult to find enough literature of this sort to meet the demands of the general music class. As a general rule, it is easier to find appropriate song literature in books intended for use with changing voices.

A WORKABLE SOLUTION. To use adolescent voices properly, the teacher of general music begins by testing voices. In testing, it is the teacher's objective to discover the register and compass of each voice and to establish a relatively small number of range categories for grouping all the voices of the class. To facilitate the assignment of parts, the compass of each category should be narrow enough to permit all voices in the group to sing throughout the entire compass without strain, and each category should be wide enough in compass to include enough voices for satisfactory singing of parts in the song literature. This is an ideal which is sometimes difficult to achieve. Each class is different from the others and the voices in any one class change in register and compass with dismaying rapidity. The alternative of asking pupils to refrain from singing when their voices are not equal to the demands of the literature tends to defeat the purpose of the general music class.

The second step is to examine the available song literature. Here it is the teacher's objective to determine the compass of each song or each vocal part, and to select those suitable for the range categories established through voice testing. Although this can be a time-consuming process, it is made easier by the teacher's experience and by the fact that the number of song books and other materials usually available for use in the general music class is relatively small. If the teacher keeps written records of this analysis, in a card index, notebook, or on the fly-leaf of each song book, showing the page numbers of songs suitable for each vocal category, the list of appropriate materials grows month by month and year by year, ultimately ending the need for further analysis.

Testing Adolescent Voices

From the foregoing discussion of ranges, it is obvious that voice testing is one of the teacher's important responsibilities and that it must be done carefully and accurately. The voice test must be appropriate to the nature and objectives of the general music class. The aim is to nurture voices, not to force them into what the teacher believes to be proper choral balance. Choral balance is desirable, but the welfare of each voice is of paramount importance and choral balance is sacrificed if individual voice characteristics do not permit a balance of choral parts.

In the general music class it is appropriate to depart from the usual concept of the voice test as a means of determining quality rather than range. Where professional singers or trained choral groups are concerned, it is proper to classify voices on the basis of voice quality to insure, for example, that alto parts are sung with alto quality. Where adolescent singers are concerned, it is more important that changing voices be assigned to parts they can sing comfortably than that any one voice part be homogeneous in quality. The voice test, therefore, is a means of determining register and compass, vocal quality being of secondary importance until the voices of the group have matured sufficiently to sing standard voice parts without difficulty.

Because adolescent voices change rapidly, voice tests are given on a regular basis at least twice each year, more often when the progress of voice-change in the class warrants further testing. In addition to the regular testing of entire groups, individual voices are re-tested whenever it becomes difficult for the pupil to sing with the group to which he has been assigned.

To test large groups efficiently, it is necessary to establish a test procedure, to describe it briefly to the class before testing is begun, and to adhere to the established procedure in all subsequent tests. This makes the task much easier for the teacher, facilitates quick but accurate testing of large numbers of voices, helps avoid embarrassment for pupils reluctant to display their changing voices, and contributes materially to class discipline and control. In some respects, voice testing is the cornerstone of singing activities in the general music class. Correct voice classification protects adolescent voices, permits progress in the vocal work of the class, and is conducive to the success in singing which encourages interest and participation.

TESTING INDIVIDUALS. The most accurate voice-testing procedure is one in which each voice is heard individually and sufficient time is allotted to permit complete exploration of each pupil's vocal capabilities. In some few instances, the teacher may be able to arrange individual tests before or after school or during free periods. Once pupils of the general music class have become accustomed to the teacher, to each other, and to voice-testing procedures, it may be feasible in some classes to conduct individual voice tests during class time. If so, it is desirable to move the piano to the rear of the room, turning it so the back of the pupil being tested is to the backs of those in their seats and so the teacher at the piano can see the class as well as the pupil being tested. In addition, it is necessary that all pupils in the room be given assigned work, preferably of a written nature, to engage their attention during the testing period.

In view of the adolescent's normal reluctance to sing alone, it is not advisable to attempt individual testing until each class is well under control and until each pupil understands the necessity for voice testing and is curious about his own vocal progress. On the whole, individual testing requires experience in class management on the part of the teacher and well-developed coöperative attitudes on the part of pupils. It is to be avoided by the inexperienced teacher or by any teacher who has not won the complete coöperation of the class.

TESTING SMALL GROUPS. A procedure somewhat less accurate, but more appropriate to the general music class, is one in which voices are tested in small groups. In this procedure, from four to six pupils gather at the piano at one time, singing as a group except when the teacher finds it necessary to ask individuals to sing alone, briefly, to check accurately some factor of register or compass. In this procedure, as in the previous one, every effort is made to insure privacy for those being tested and to establish circumstances favorable to class control. The piano can be moved to the rear of the room or turned so pupils being tested do not face those at their seats. Pupils at their seats need assigned work as well as the visual attention of the teacher.

The first step in determining vocal register is to listen to the speaking voice of each pupil. Boys, especially, show the effects of voice-change in their speaking voices. The teacher can often make accurate preliminary judgments from listening to the boy give his name or answer a routine question. This is done prior to voice testing, if possible, so the teacher may have some general basis for selecting voices of similar register to make up each test group.

To begin testing, the teacher plays a familiar song, asking the pupils of the group to sing with the piano. The best songs for this purpose are those of limited melodic compass, based on relatively simple harmonic patterns, and well known to all members of the class. The first phrase of "America," for example, requires pupils to sing only through the narrow compass of a diminished fifth, can be transposed easily by the teacher into a number of different keys, and is well known to all pupils. Because the melody is familiar and easy to sing, pupils begin singing with little hesitation. By transposing this melodic fragment into different keys the teacher can explore the upper and lower limits of voices being tested.

If the teacher is not content with the information obtained through the use of a familiar song or melodic fragment, it is possible to use short scale passages. These provide a better measure of the upper and lower extremes of the voices, need extend only through the compass of a fourth or fifth, and should be sung by the group to the accompaniment of an interesting harmonic pattern. The short scale patterns and their harmonic accompaniments, like the melodic fragment, can be transposed by the teacher as needed to extend the span of the test, probing further and further into the extremes of vocal range.

In this process, it is important that the entire group of pupils being tested sing together, that they sing always with the support of the piano, and that the piano accompaniment be appealing to adolescent tastes. The teacher, face to face with only a small group of pupils, is able to hear each of the voices in the group as they sing together, noting the pitch at which any voice stops singing or begins to show signs of strain. The pupils in the group, even boys in the most awkward stage of voice-change, feel relatively at ease among others with similar vocal characteristics. They are never asked to sing without the piano and seldom without the vocal support of the balance of the group, are asked to sing only familiar passages of narrow compass, and may even find the testing enjoyable if the teacher shows imagination in creating attractive piano accompaniments.

When testing voices, it is almost inevitable that the teacher will discover one or more pupils who have difficulty finding the pitch at which the other members of the group begin singing. For these changing voices of limited range, the teacher begins by finding a pitch that can be sung, then expands the range from that point to determine how far above and how far below the first pitch the pupil can sing. Here, even more than in other parts of the test, the teacher provides support for the uncertain singer through piano accompaniment and the singing of the other members of the group. Adolescents who have this singing difficulty usually respond better when tested among a group of friends. They are more in need of support than the accomplished singers, and far more in need of the teacher's close attention, careful testing, and correct voice-part assignment.

TESTING LARGE GROUPS. In some general music classes even the foregoing method of group testing is impractical because of pupil attitudes and problems of class control. In others it is desirable to test voices during the first few meetings of the class, before the teacher has had time to stimulate interest in singing or to win class support and coöperation. Here there is need for a means of testing voices quickly without drawing special attention to any one singer or even to a small group of pupils who must sing while the major portion of the class is silent.

One such process [3] is intended for use in the junior high school. It assumes that voices of adolescent girls are more or less uniform in range and that most girls can sing either first or second soprano parts. This implies that girls' voices need not be tested and that the teacher's first duty is to identify unchanged, changing, and changed voices among the boys.

To test the boys' voices, the teacher first asks all boys to sing "Old Folks at Home" in the key of B-flat, identifying as "baritones" all those able to sing it in the lower octave. These changed voices are then instructed to remain silent as the rest of the boys sing "Old Folks at Home" again in the key of G-flat. In this key, the boys able to sing in the upper octave are unchanged voices (sopranos) and the balance are changing voices (cambiata). Although this procedure does not permit the teacher to test voices carefully or accurately, it has obvious merit in that it solves the problem of initial voice classification without placing any pupil in the focus of class attention.

SEATING. After voices have been tested the teacher seats the class according to voice classifications, placing like voices together in any seating plan that facilitates singing activities. Two general rules govern this seating: (1) place uncertain singers near the piano so they may take full advantage of its support; (2) place boys near the teacher so their natural exuberance may be more easily controlled. If these two rules are followed, girls are seated toward the rear of the room, higher voices toward one side and lower voices toward the other. Boys with unchanged voices sit immediately in front of the girls, similarly separated in terms of higher and lower voices. Boys with changing voices sit toward the front of the room, grouped in seats closest to the piano. Boys with changed voices are seated near the piano also, and toward the front of the room, grouped next to the boys with changing voices.

If there are pupils of any voice classification who find it difficult to match pitches, it is usually helpful to surround each of them with experienced singers. In some instances, boys' attitudes improve when they are separated from each other and interspersed among the girls, but in general, they seem to be more at ease in the music class when seated together.

[3] Irvin Cooper, *Letters to Pat Concerning Junior High School Vocal Problems.* New York: Carl Fischer, Inc., 1953, pp. 19–20.

EXPANDING THE REPERTOIRE

The topics discussed thus far are important in that they aid the teacher in the work of enlarging the song repertoire of the general music class. The enlarged song repertoire is important because it provides a basis for much other music progress. Broad acquaintance with song literature and the ability to sing many songs well are objectives guiding the teacher's daily work in the classroom.

During initial class meetings, the teacher relies on songs already known to the pupils. These will be unison songs for the most part, although there may be among them songs to which harmony parts can be improvised easily. Class singing begins with these familiar songs even though the first few classes seem more like campfire songfests than meetings devoted to the serious study of music. The vigorous, rollicking nature of some songs, and the quiet beauty of others, appeals to adolescent natures, encourages pupils to participate in the singing, and provides a fitting introduction to the work of the class. Piano accompaniments are used to bolster the singing and, with due regard for good taste, to hide its flaws. The songs should be varied in type, mood, and text, offering something to appeal to every variety of taste among the pupils of the class.

Teaching Unison Songs

Unison songs form an important part of vocal literature and are a necessary part of the song repertoire of the general music class. They can be taught more quickly and easily than part-songs, permit the entire class to sing as one group, and often stimulate participation more spirited than do part-songs. Suitable material includes songs of almost every type—fun songs, patriotic and devotional songs, popular and art songs, and excerpts from operas and operettas.

Songs can be taught by rote, more appropriately perhaps than through music reading, although most teachers continue to hope that pupils will develop reading skills and strive for gradual improvement of reading ability. Through songs taught principally by rote, pupils of the general music class can experience musical beauty which would be denied to them if their singing were limited to songs they could read. Similarly, because unison songs are taught more easily by rote than are part-songs, it is through them that general music classes, composed largely of pupils without reading facility, can most conveniently explore vocal literature.

Rote learning is based on imitation and repetition. A unison song taught this way in the general music class is presented by the teacher through any available medium—voice, piano, or phonograph recording—so that pupils may hear and imitate a worthy model. The song is then heard by the pupils again and again, until they have become sufficiently familiar with the song to perform it without the support of the teacher. If necessary for memorization, the song is sung repeatedly until pupils are thoroughly familiar with it and can sing it unaided.

Because pupils of the general music class are able to read song texts from books in their hands, however, they need learn by rote only the melody and its interpretation. Although they may not be able to read music notation with proficiency, they can sense from the music score the general configuration of the melody, using the music as an aid to memory when attempting to recall and sing the song. With older pupils, therefore, songs are rarely taught entirely by rote. The teacher takes advantage of whatever language-reading skills the pupils have and encourages them to expand their knowledge of music notation.

Because pupils learn through imitation, the teacher presents each new song artistically. The quality of performance offered by a phonograph recording is highly desirable, although it is improbable that suitable recordings will be available as frequently as the teacher would wish. In most instances, the teacher presents the song by singing it or by playing it at the piano. Each presentation is regarded as a performance, the teacher adopting the artist's careful attitude toward accuracy of rendition, tone quality, phrasing and interpretation, pronunciation and diction. In doing so, the teacher sets a performance example that ultimately is reflected in the singing of the class.

Each repeated hearing of the song has definite teaching purpose. Before each hearing, class attention is directed to one specific element of the song—its meaning, mood, form, rhythm, harmonic, or melodic characteristics. Pupils are asked to listen for this element or to observe it in the music score as they hear the song. They can be asked to respond to each element, conducting the meter, clapping or tapping the rhythm, humming the melody softly, or raising their hands at each recurrence of the phrase. In this way the teacher emphasizes a different aspect of the music at each hearing, directing pupil attention to each aspect in succession as the song is being learned.

The rote process is not only a manner of teaching songs, but a means of teaching other aspects of music as well. Songs are cast in music forms, are based on harmonic progressions, include rhythmic and melodic patterns, and utilize music notation. Each such element offers opportunities for developing knowledge applicable to all music as well as to the song being studied. To conserve interest, the teacher extends the work with any one song over several class meetings, shifting class attention to a different music activity before interest begins to wane. To provide a feeling of achievement, the class begins singing quickly, relying on the piano accompaniment to provide help where needed. Minor inaccuracies are remedied through later hearings and, if necessary, difficult rhythmic or melodic patterns are removed from the context of the song for intense drill.

Through this process, rote learning becomes a succession of experiences, each one different from the last. Songs are learned through exploration of their various elements. Much incidental but meaningful music knowledge is acquired and the songs themselves retain their interest for, and are sung more musically by, the pupils of the class.

Teaching Part-Songs

Choral music is unique in its power to give the singer an experience of shared beauty provided by no other art. Even at the level of the general music class, where vocal music sung in parts is usually far removed in character and effect from the choral sonorities produced by trained singers, choral singing offers the pupil an experience both aesthetic and educational. Adolescents enjoy the sensation of choral singing for the sheer pleasure of producing and being part of the choral sound. They like to harmonize, have fun doing it spontaneously at parties, and often display a surprising facility in improvising added parts to songs they know.

From the standpoint of the general music class, part-songs open doors to many new varieties of vocal literature, developing skills useful in exploring other areas of music. Songs containing parts for voices of many different registers and compasses are essential in the general music class if pupils with unchanged, changing, and changed voices are to be drawn into the singing; if part songs are not used, many pupils are unable to sing with the rest of the class and must remain silent. Part-songs, therefore, are both necessary and desirable in the work of the general music class, contributing to the pupils' enjoyment, permitting them to participate, and providing useful avenues to music learning.

PREPARATORY EXPERIENCES. Before actual part-singing is begun, other types of singing prepare pupils for the new experiences and requirements of choral music. Some pupils new to the general music class will have had no experience in part-singing in the elementary school or elsewhere. Others, taught to sing harmony parts in the elementary school, find their new voices and the new music so different from their experience that they are no more sure of themselves than the totally inexperienced.

One preparatory step is the singing of unison songs for basses alone, for changing voices alone, or for lower treble voices alone. Boys in particular tend to take pride in the lowered register of their voices. They welcome the opportunity to display it, perhaps as a symbol of approaching manhood, if they have opportunity to sing with a group of boys their own age. Unison songs in bass range for these boys, and unison songs in appropriate ranges for each of the other voice classifications, help demonstrate that each type of voice has its own peculiar quality and is a valued contributor to choral tone. By including unison songs in which each voice classification sings as a group, while other members of the class listen, the teacher counteracts the tendency of pupils to feel that voice-change is an undesirable aberration excluding them from the singing activities of the class.

As further preparation for part-singing, the teacher can turn to a number of song types and singing activities—rounds, simultaneous or combined songs, descants, dialogue songs, chants, harmonized endings, improvised thirds and sixths, the singing of chord roots and choral backgrounds—many of which have merit and some of which have serious disadvantages.

Rounds are desirable in that they require pupils to learn only one melody, in that each part is of equal importance, and in that they can be sung by either similar or dissimilar voices. They are undesirable, however, in that they are contrapuntal rather than harmonic and tend to be competitive rather than coöperative. They encourage pupils to ignore the effect of the combined voices while singing loudly to hold their own parts.

Combined songs, such as "There's a Long, Long Trail a-Winding" and "Keep the Home Fires Burning," are those that can be sung by two different groups at the same time, combining to create a more or less pleasing harmonic and melodic effect. Singing exercises of this sort are usually enjoyed by the participants, but the value of the experience as preparation for part-singing is questionable. The competitive spirit is stimulated far more strongly by combined songs than by rounds and the results often are completely unmusical.

Descants may be used to good effect, except that they tend to be contrapuntal in nature, difficult to learn, and difficult to sing. The song with descant serves a purpose similar to that of the round, but is more complex than the round due to the necessity for learning and singing two distinct melodies. The descant is most successful with inexperienced singers when it is made up of easy intervals and notes of long duration, permitting the singers to listen for the harmonic interplay of voices without losing the continuity of their own parts.

Of more practical value in the general music class are the easier singing activities that can be learned quickly and without intense drill, can be sung easily by adolescent voices, are themselves musically satisfying, and offer experiences characteristic of part-singing. First among such activities is the conversation song in which the text includes the words of two or more characters who converse with each other. After the song is learned, the teacher divides the class into two or more groups and assigns each group a role. Through performing the roles, alternately singing and remaining silent, pupils gain vocal independence and assurance, learning to think of themselves as divided into parts rather than as one large singing group. A similar procedure can be followed with many familiar songs, the teacher signaling various groups to sing alone on successive phrases in the same manner that a conductor cues the entrance of parts or sections. This encourages singers to remain alert and, what is more important, to develop ability for tone-thinking during the phrases in which they are silent.

Second among the easier singing activities is the chant, a recurring musical pattern often consisting of only one or two pitches and words, providing a suitable vocal accompaniment to a familiar song. Chants of various levels of difficulty can be devised by the teacher or created by the class for most rounds and for many songs. The experience of singing a chant is close to that of part-singing, requires vocal independence as well as feeling for ensemble, and is usually enjoyed by boys who can sing the chant successfully in a register appropriate to their changing voices.

Harmonized endings are a further extension of part-singing ability, can be devised easily by the teacher, and taught quickly by rote. They are particularly effective when they consist of only two or three chords, the last being sustained until it is perfectly in tune and the class senses the beauty of the choral harmony. One of the natural ways for adolescents to learn to sing in parts is through improvising harmony in thirds and sixths. They do this spontaneously at parties and can be successful with little or no assistance from the teacher or piano, being guided solely by aural, harmonic intuition.

DEVELOPING HARMONIC FEELING. Preliminary experiences which emphasize chord qualities and harmonic progression are among the most valuable in the development of part-singing ability. Among them is the singing of chord roots as an accompaniment to a familiar song, especially useful for boys with changed voices but equally appropriate for the class as a whole. The teacher selects a song already familiar to the class and based on only two or three chords. The two or three chord roots may be learned by the class through a brief rote process, may be notated on the board in the appropriate staff, or may be played at the piano as the bass of a rhythmic accompaniment. These pitches can be sung as an added part, by boys with changed voices as the remainder of the class sings the melody, by both changed and unchanged voices as half the class sings the melody, or by the entire class as the teacher plays the song at the piano. After a few such experiences, many classes are able to find correct bass notes for songs of only two or three chords without teacher guidance, relying solely on harmonic sense.

Of similarly harmonic nature is the experience of singing chordal backgrounds to familiar songs. As a first step, the class learns to sing a simple harmonic progression, I-V-I or I-IV-I-V-I, in three or four parts depending upon the number of voice classifications in the group. The chord progression can be derived from previous experience with the autoharp or other chord instruments, presented in conjunction with a discussion of the structure and quality of the various chords, or taught quickly by rote or through board notation. Adolescents enjoy singing these progressions and participating in the choral effect despite the fact they are not applied to or derived from a song. Once pupils have learned to sing such a progression and feel the quality of the chords, they can sing or hum attractive chordal backgrounds to familiar songs played at the piano, performed by a vocal or instrumental soloist, or sung by a portion of the class.

The value in these singing activities is that they develop a feeling for part-singing. Pupils learn to sense the harmonies, develop sensitivity to intonation and blend, and learn to listen for the effect of their own part in combination with others. Many classes find this approach to part-singing enjoyable and musically satisfying, far more conducive to enthusiastic acceptance of part-songs than the drill-like study of parts.

TEACHING TWO-PART SONGS. As an initial step in the teaching of actual part-music, it is logical to begin with songs in only two parts. This is appropriate in classes composed of unchanged voices only, but is equally successful in classes including bass and tenor voices. If possible, the teacher utilizes songs already familiar to the class, perhaps those learned as unison songs to which a pleasing harmony part can be added.

The teacher first provides an opportunity for the class to hear and feel the harmony (*chords*) using the piano or autoharp to emphasize the harmonic texture. The class then sings the melody and simultaneously hears the harmony *part*, played or sung by the teacher, while observing the notation of the parts in the score. After this introduction, several capable singers join the teacher in singing the added part as the balance of the class sings the melody. The teacher then plays or sings the melody as the entire class sings the added part, using the music score as a guide, after which the class should be able to sing the two-part song with little assistance from the teacher. This rote process is suitable for classes with little reading facility and can be revised as necessary to take advantage of existing reading skill.

TEACHING THREE- AND FOUR-PART SONGS. As the class progresses to songs in three or four parts, the teacher continues to present added parts through a rote-like procedure. Here, too, the first songs are harmonically and melodically simple, already familiar to the class as unison songs. The teacher first helps the class develop a feeling for the harmonic basis of the song and then progresses naturally to teaching the bass part, perhaps by teaching the entire class to sing the chord roots. The song can then be performed in two parts, its harmonic character emphasized by the presence of the bass part. In three-part songs, the upper and lower treble parts often form a duet, permitting the lower treble (alto) part to be taught quickly due to pupils' prior experience in learning two-part songs. The developed harmonic sense and the presence of melody and bass help many pupils sing inner parts virtually "by ear."

Other songs can be learned quickly by referring to harmonic progressions and chordal backgrounds previously sung by the class, the teacher identifying in the score the places in which the movement of parts is different from that of the parts already learned or improvised. In all such teaching it is essential that pupils be encouraged to develop aural sense and to follow the notation of the score, using it as a guide to the movement of parts. Easy songs studied during early attempts at part-singing can be learned quickly by rote, but the more difficult songs to which the class should progress require a degree of both aural sense and reading facility. Without them, song-learning is a tedious process which destroys much of the pleasure the pupils might derive from performing music in the choral style.

GUIDING PRINCIPLES. During the study of part-songs, the teacher is guided by several principles. Changing voices are difficult to control and do not easily negotiate rapid passages or awkward intervals. Young singers are most successful in part-songs which are slow in tempo or require only small degrees of flexibility, not only because such songs are appropriate to adolescent vocal powers but because they permit the development of harmonic sense as well. Many voices are narrow in compass during voice change, requiring that the teacher be alert for parts that exceed the compass. Conversely, some voices may benefit from the attempt to sing parts that help expand vocal compass. Melodic parts are of greatest interest and some pupils excluded from melodic singing are prone to lose interest.

To maintain interest, especially among boys with changing and changed voices, the teacher chooses many songs in which the lower parts carry the melody. Boys with changed voices are simultaneously learning the capabilities of a new vocal instrument, learning to sing a new part, and reading from a new clef. In addition to singing easy and familiar melodies, these boys should be given much experience in singing chord roots. Bass parts consisting of chord roots are often easier for them to sing, develop the harmonic sense which makes part-singing easier, and provide a fitting introduction to the parts they will sing after their voices have matured. For all pupils, the combination of problems of voice-change with those of learning to sing in choral style leads to difficulty and is conducive to disinterest and antipathy. It is therefore important that the teacher be content with slow and steady progress and make every attempt to understand pupil problems and sustain pupil interest.

MUSICAL GROWTH THROUGH SINGING

Singing is enjoyable for its own sake and worthy of a place in general music for that reason alone, but it also provides a way to increase music skill and knowledge. Vocal and reading skills, knowledge of music literature, history and theory—all serve to intensify the unique pleasures of music. The singing activity of the general music class is one of many means to these ends, especially desirable in that pupils who learn through singing have personal contact with the music being studied, gaining and applying their knowledge in a meaningful and practical way.

Improving Vocal Skill

The human voice is the most sensitive and responsive of all music instruments. It offers the singer personal contact with music and extraordinary satisfaction in its performance. For this reason, and because the capable singer experiences pleasures denied those who sing less well, the teacher strives to improve the singing of pupils in the general music class. In the areas of tone quality, intonation, breathing, diction, interpretation, and ensemble singing there is work that can be done, necessary to the progress of class singing and useful to pupils in later life. For the teacher, however, there is a guiding principle: all such work must contribute to the immediate enjoyment and interest of the class and must not be permitted to transform general music into a species of voice class. Voice-training procedures must grow out of and be applied to the vocal literature being studied, with principal emphasis upon singing rather than vocal development. This is due not only to the nature and objectives of the class, but also to the fact that adolescent voices are not ready for intensive vocal training and may suffer harm when forced beyond reasonable limits of endurance.

TONE QUALITY. Tone quality is perhaps the most important single factor in singing. To some extent, it is governed by the physical characteristics of the singer and the individual vocal mechanism, characteristics which establish limits to the possibilities of vocal development. Few individuals develop their voices sufficiently to be halted by these limits; there is in almost every voice an undeveloped potential providing ample opportunity for improvement.

Of paramount importance is the development by each singer of habits of listening. The pupil must be constantly alert to the sound of his own voice, developing an aural concept of good tone quality and the ability to judge the degree to which his own voice matches that concept. To develop an aural concept of good tone, the pupil must hear examples worthy of imitation. The teacher must sing pleasingly, being aware that pupils imitate this model when learning songs in class. Other imitable models may be found in soloists and ensembles selected from the class, from other classes or school performing groups, or in visiting artists who perform in school assemblies or the classroom. Visitors may be either vocal or instrumental performers, the violin, flute, and other orchestral instruments providing excellent examples of resonant, singing tone.

Carefully selected phonograph records offer opportunities to hear good tone and are especially convenient for classroom use. The teacher acquires recordings of good quality, plays them through a sound system of suitable fidelity, and gives them proper care. Nothing is less conducive to good tone quality, or to interest, than recordings that are old, worn, and scratched. Pupils are influenced by everything they hear, including the tone of recordings and the quality of the teacher's speaking voice. They progress more rapidly when reminded constantly by the sounds in their daily experience of the beauty and expressive powers of good tone.

Because tone quality is influenced by an aural concept, the teacher is guided by the belief that good tone is determined largely by mental factors. Tone is produced by physical means, of course, and its quality is influenced by the manner in which physical powers are used, but young singers unable to control the physical mechanism of voice production often develop undesirable singing habits if their attention is directed to the physical aspects of singing. Their chances for vocal progress are much improved if attention is directed away from the voice mechanism to ideas conducive to good tone.

The manner of shaping and singing vowels influences tone quality and can be practiced without undue emphasis of the physical aspects of tone production. Song texts may be read aloud in the manner of choral speaking to focus attention upon vowel sounds as well as other elements of enunciation, and rapid songs of tongue-twisting character may be sung to improve articulation.

BREATH CONTROL AND SUPPORT. Breathing is important to tone quality and can be improved without recourse to breathing exercises. Much can be done to improve breath control if the teacher makes it a practice to call attention to matters of phrasing and dynamics and habitually to present new songs artistically. Although there is merit in exercises and drills to develop breath control, they are less appropriate to the general music class than the lessons and practice inherent in the vocal literature being studied. Good breathing can be encouraged by proper room ventilation and singing posture. Breath support can be induced by the use of full tone and attention to dynamics. On the whole, it is best for the teacher to assume that proper breathing is natural to pupils and to avoid exercises that seek to train or develop the breathing apparatus.

RESONANCE. Resonance is an important factor in tone quality and can be developed through singing songs, through judicious exploration of upper and lower areas of vocal compass in songs, and through reasonable use of both soft and full tone, also in songs. These things can be done without recourse to vocalises and exercises. Soft humming often helps create the feeling that the voice resonates in the upper portion of the face, as does the practice of singing songs on sustained vowels rather than with words. Some teachers prefer the vowel sounds of OH or OOH for such practice, whereas others prefer UH, EH, or AH. Each of these may be successful, depending upon the manner in which the teacher presents the concept and the readiness with which the class responds, provided the vowel sound centers the tone near the bridge of the nose and can be produced without tenseness in the throat, jaw, or tongue.

THE OUT-OF-TUNE SINGER. Of concern to teachers in the secondary school is the pupil who finds it difficult to sing in tune or to match pitch. Every effort is made to aid these pupils during their years in the lower grades, but the teacher of general music can expect to find some who did not learn to sing in the earlier grades as well as others who develop singing difficulties due to voice-change after they arrive in the general music class. There are two principal causes for this singing problem: psychological or emotional blocks created by earlier failures in singing or by ridicule of first singing attempts; lack of singing experience or practice. Rarely, if ever, does the teacher find a pupil whose difficulty stems from an irremediable, physical deformity; the teacher can safely assume that every pupil can be taught to sing in tune.

The teacher's best procedure in working with uncertain singers is based on understanding and encouragement. In some cases it is possible to offer private assistance through encouraging the pupil to discuss the problem and to accept the teacher's help during free periods or after school. In no case should the pupil be further embarrassed by being forced to display his inadequacy before the other members of the class. If the teacher can arrange time for private assistance, patience and perseverance will be rewarded with slow but gratifying progress in the ability to discriminate among and match pitches and a gradual widening of vocal compass. The teacher first finds a pitch the pupil can sing, then helps him extend his vocal range by striving to match pitches further and further from the first through procedures similar to those useful with younger children.

In class, the pupil is seated with the group whose part includes his vocal range, preferably close to the piano, but surrounded, wherever he sits, by other pupils who sing well and with good intonation. The teacher tries to give him a feeling of achievement and success, helping him excel at playing the autoharp, or conducting, perhaps appointing him to a responsible duty not necessarily of a musical nature. Instruments played by the pupil, the autoharp, song bells or piano, can be of great help in bringing the uncertain singer into close contact with pitches he produces himself and can hear close at hand. For the pupil who is reluctant to accept private assistance, the teacher provides the same sort of encouragement in class as that offered to the coöperative pupil, avoiding situations that embarrass him but contriving circumstances to build assurance and the will to progress.

LEARNING THROUGH SINGING. Each of the separate elements of vocal skill can be improved through the singing activities of the general music class. Singing, however, is a coördinated effort in which each element functions in combination with the others. Breath support, tone production, and resonance, for example, are interdependent in singing and equally important to it. The act of singing not only depends upon their confluence, it may also suffer from analysis which separates its elements and attempts to develop each one independently. Too much emphasis on one aspect of singing destroys the coördinated effect, especially where the adolescent singer is concerned, developing undesirable vocal habits by causing the singer to concentrate on one element at the expense of others.

It is usually unwise to devote time in general music classes to vocal exercises of the type practiced by the professional singer. Exercises and drills, if they are necessary, arise naturally out of the song literature being studied. Other exercises, not related to the songs under study, are used as infrequently as possible and then only when their direct relationship to an existing vocal problem can be made apparent. This is particularly important when dealing with adolescents who want to know why things are done. When drill arises out of materials being studied, its purpose and application are apparent, but when unrelated drill is pursued as a matter of class routine pupils lose interest.

Teaching Music Reading

The question of music reading has been a source of debate among music educators for decades. There have been those who felt that developing reading ability ought to be the chief objective of the vocal program in the public schools. Others felt that the drills and exercises used to develop reading ability served chiefly to destroy interest and eliminated them in favor of a program devoted almost exclusively to the singing of songs. Still others decry the drudgery of reading drill but seek to achieve reading skill through other methods.

Those who would reduce emphasis upon music reading question its value for the pupils who enter general music classes, few of whom need or use the ability to read music in later life. Only a relatively small number participate in church choirs or community singing groups as adults, and even in such groups there are places for singers who do not read music with facility. Artistic music can sometimes be sensed, sung intuitively without the need for accurate translation of every detail of the music score, and that which can not be sensed can be learned quickly through imitation and repetition. The need for accurate interpretation of music notation at first sight may be of less consequence than the need for large numbers of people who are interested in music and enjoy participation in singing. In the face of such arguments, some persons conclude that music reading is not of paramount importance in the general music class and that minimum time, if any, should be devoted to it.

It is also pertinent, however, to compare the value of the two seemingly opposed approaches to music interest, through participation and enjoyment or through knowledge and skill. Maximum interest and enjoyment come to those who possess knowledge. Music education can not reach its goal of building for every pupil a foundation of lasting interest in music by refusing to teach its techniques. It is knowledge that opens the door to understanding, whether for the professional musician or the interested amateur; it is skill that makes participation possible and rewarding. Although interest, enjoyment, and participation are the principal objectives of the general music class, the extent of their development is limited by the absence of knowledge and skill. Music reading is such a skill, the important factor in music literacy, and a prerequisite to full participation in choral singing. If the interdependence of interest and knowledge is accepted, the problem becomes one of pursuing both objectives simultaneously so that each reinforces the other. The conclusion as it bears upon the general music class, is that singing activities can be the source of improvement in music reading and that skill in music reading contributes to the improvement of singing activities.

ANALYZING THE SKILL. Before attempting to teach music reading, the teacher analyzes the skill itself to formulate a plan of teaching. When reading, the singer first sees the symbol and recalls it as having meaning based on past experience; in rare instances, perhaps never, can the singer interpret a totally new symbol having no connection with previous experience. The singer then "images" the sound indicated by the symbol; he forms it in the mind by associating it with a tonal or rhythmic pattern in the repertoire of sounds familiar to him through singing or listening. Finally, the singer uses the voice to reproduce the pattern already clearly formed in the mind, the aural sense judging the correctness of the reproduced sound and prompting its adjustment if necessary.

Thus the skill of reading requires knowledge of symbols, a repertoire of tonal and rhythmic patterns, tonal imagery or tone thinking, vocal ability to produce tones accurate in pitch and duration, and aural ability to discriminate between like and unlike tonal patterns. With this analysis, the teacher is ready to plan the activities that lead to skill in music reading, striving to develop each skill both separately and in conjunction with others. No area of music knowledge or skill exists in isolation; each depends on and benefits from the others. The act of music reading does not in practice separate itself into a series of well-defined and independent steps; it is an almost instantaneous reaction in which all separate acts occur so quickly as to appear simultaneous.

BUILDING A READING VOCABULARY. An early step in the development of reading ability is the establishment of a repertoire of tonal and rhythmic patterns similar to the vocabulary essential in literary reading. These patterns exist in all the music sung, heard, or discussed and can be added to the tonal vocabulary without intensive drill in unrelated study of scales, intervals, and rhythms. They must be pointed out and are retained more easily if their structure is understood and can be related to other knowledge. The sound of the patterns is learned and retained more effectively if the aural impression is reinforced with visual and physical sensations.

The teacher directs attention to patterns in the vocal literature being studied and notes the manner in which visual symbols reflect the characteristics of each tonal pattern. To develop physical understanding the class sings each pattern, conducts or taps those that are rhythmic in nature, and devises a physical response to those characterized by pitch differences. Pupils can play pitch patterns at the keyboard or using simple instruments and can draw graph-like pictures of each pattern at the board or in the air by picturing the rise and fall of the melodic pattern with their hands. Through singing the pattern, seeing its notation, and reproducing it through physical movement the pupil gains a multiple impression deeper and more memorable than the relatively fleeting impression provided by singing alone. At the same time, the pupil becomes acquainted with the symbol and attaches to it all the meaning of the aural and physical sensations. Both symbol and tonal pattern are impressed upon the memory in a manner that associates one with the other.

Through such procedures, adjusted as necessary to fit the age and ability of the pupils in the class, the teacher begins to build pupils' repertoire, establishing a foundation for music reading. This process is less systematic and less intense than one which teaches music reading through a graded series of drills and exercises, but it has merit in that it need not destroy pupil interest, is directly related to other general music activities, and can result in gradual but marked increase in reading skill.

FIRST STEPS IN READING. The first associations are made between sound and symbol when pupils hold and watch the music they perform. Although much of the literature sung in the general music class is learned by rote, pupils use song books, referring to them for the words of songs and becoming familiar with the appearance of notation even though they do not actually read it. Because the notation is at hand, it is convenient to encourage pupils to use it as an aid to memory while learning each new song or recalling the melodies of songs learned during previous lessons. The general appearance of the notation indicates the ascending or descending movement of the melody, its use of scale or interval patterns, and the recurrence of phrases.

By directing attention to specific portions of songs being sung, the teacher emphasizes the notation for tonal patterns already in the pupil's repertoire and expands the repertoire by noting new patterns as they occur. As a new song is learned, the patterns it contains are identified and imaged so the pupils may apply their knowledge to reading portions of the notation. As the pupils' repertoire grows they are encouraged to use more and more of these patterns, making a gradual transition from rote learning to reading. When the need arises, patterns are removed from the song context for discussion or analysis, for comparison with other patterns, or for use in drill related to the song being studied.

Drill is a natural outcome of the process. Its need is apparent when it becomes necessary to practice a difficult or unfamiliar tonal or rhythmic pattern, to review a series of related patterns, or to explore the differences among closely related patterns. It is probable that no melodic interval or rhythmic pattern is completely learned until it is isolated from the song in which it is first learned, can be produced in drill context, and produced again in the unfamiliar surroundings of one or more new songs. It is also probable that skill in music reading develops only through extended practice in a process that continues to confront the pupil with new material, encouraging him to apply his reading ability again and again, strengthening and expanding it as each new song is added to his experience.

To encourage the development of reading ability, the teacher focuses attention on some aspect of notation during every lesson. Some teachers turn to the "mystery tune," notating a familiar melody on the board for every class and asking pupils to study it until they discover the name of the song. Other devices are of less interest, perhaps, but may be applied to songs being learned. Pupils can be taught to recognize phrases, at first because they coincide with units of thought in song texts, later by being alert to the sound of the phrase and the symbols which indicate the pause of the cadence. This leads naturally to learning that phrases recur or are repeated, and to detecting recurrence through both the ear and the eye. Next, there is the repeated phrase which differs slightly from its counterpart, creating the question and answer effect of the antecedent and consequent. Finally, there is music form, a structure created from phrases, cadences, recurrence, and variation, all of which can be used to help the pupil hear and read music.

In a slightly more technical vein, pupils can learn about scales and chords through meeting them in the songs they study. Introduced in a song, the scale or chord becomes part of the pupil's singing experience. Removed from the song for analysis and discussion, it becomes meaningful and memorable as a music element which is understood. Met and recognized in the context of a new song, it becomes another familiar pattern in the reading repertoire.

In any or all of these ways, training in music reading can be made a part of every singing lesson. No class period and no song need pass by without making its contribution to reading skill. Music reading need never become drudgery; it can be simply another aspect of music, challenging, interesting, and valued for its contribution to the improvement of singing. Even the drill necessary to learning fundamentals can be interesting and enjoyable, as challenging as playground exercises in skill and dexterity.

The intensity with which reading skill is pursued is a matter of the teacher's discretion; the thoroughness with which reading skills are learned depends upon the teacher's planning and ingenuity. Music reading can be undertaken as a major project, the sequence of reading skills to be learned determining the selection of song materials, or music reading can be regarded as incidental to class singing, the skill developing more slowly as favorite songs each make their contribution to the reading repertoire. In either case, music-reading skill is derived from vocal literature sung in class. The learning necessary to the skill is meaningful in terms of song literature and can be applied immediately to familiar and new songs. The process itself can be enjoyable in that it is centered upon enjoyable singing and is flexible enough to follow the interests and desires of the class. Pursued in this manner, the development of reading skill is an appropriate goal of the general music class, leading to greater success and deeper satisfactions in singing.

Achieving Musical Understanding

It is enjoyable to sing music, or to play it or listen to it, and it is a noteworthy achievement for many pupils simply to develop the skill necessary for the group singing of the general music class. There is more to music, however, than mere singing, playing, or listening. Deeper satisfactions come to those who understand the music they perform, perceiving the relationships inherent in its structure. There is further benefit in that the development of understanding tends to improve performance, increasing the performer's sensitivity to the more subtle shades of music meaning and causing him to be attentive to artistic rendition. Such understanding is beneficial to the pupils of the general music class and its development a more worthy objective than performing ability.

Understanding grows out of knowledge and is nourished by familiarity and sympathy. In music, the knowledge which breeds understanding is acquired through the study of music theory. This study, music theory, has negative connotations for many professional and amateur musicians. It is associated with formal music training. It is remembered by some as an unpleasant and unmusical experience, a disciplinary study necessary to music training but not necessarily conducive to personal satisfaction. To the layman, there is something distasteful and frightening about the technical aspects of music. He would like to play or sing "by ear," or listen in completely relaxed comfort, but instinctively withdraws at the first mention of a subject he thinks will tax his patience or his intellect. He knows nothing about the theoretical aspects of music and fears their technicalities. He is quite content with the knowledge he possesses and with his own tastes and prejudices.

Despite these attitudes, there is a positive and important aspect of theory as it bears upon the music pleasures of both professionals and laymen. Music theory is not an isolated study pursued solely for disciplinary reasons or to develop specialized techniques. It is inherent in all music of every age, an important factor in its make-up and in its effect upon the performer and listener. Knowledge of music theory is essential to music understanding, aids music performance, deepens enjoyment for the listener, and is an important component in aesthetic experience. A basic understanding of the theoretical aspects of music can be transmitted to the pupil through singing and other activities of the general music class. There is no need for him to withdraw from singing activities because he is confronted with facts concerning the structure and content of music he sings; to the contrary, learning these facts serves to sharpen his perception and increase his interest.

MUSIC FORM. A concept of music form is among the first of the theoretical learnings derived from experience with song literature. Form is the architecture of music, the broad, structural outline of music composition. Form has to do with the relationships in which beauty resides and which, when perceived, create feelings of pleasure in the performer and the listener. Songs lend themselves easily to the discovery of formal elements. Early in their singing experience, pupils can observe that phrases repeat and recur and that musically satisfying patterns can be constructed from only two or three phrases. In songs of more complex structure, a larger number of different phrases, often of related design, succeed each other in patterns appealing to the mind of the listener and calling forth appropriate emotional response.

The teacher turns naturally to music form for help in teaching new songs. Pupils are quick to see the repetition and recurrence which permit them to sing entire songs after having learned only two or three short phrases. Through only a small extension of this process, the teacher transforms these initial observations into knowledge of and sensitivity to music form. Pupils review songs they know, discovering their phrase patterns through examining the notation and by listening for the music design as they sing. They determine the form of new songs before attempting to sing them as an integral part of the song-learning process. Through singing, they develop understanding of the basic principles of music form and knowledge of the simpler forms found in song literature. Once this is accomplished, the teacher proceeds to a discussion of reasons for the existence of the various forms. Pupils are asked to note the manner in which one song differs from another in structure and to search for reasons for this difference in the text of the song, its emotional content or mood, its descriptive or narrative qualities, or in some other aspect of its nature or purpose. The song forms can be compared with those of poetry, architecture, or those of the other arts, indicating that form is in all things and serves universal purposes. Concurrently, the knowledge of form is applied to other music activities as an aid to learning and understanding.

For the more detailed study of form, and to achieve clearer understanding of even the simplest forms, it is necessary that the pupil be familiar with certain rudimentary factors in the language of music. Form is rhythmic in nature and grows out of the accumulation of rhythm patterns created by notes of different duration. Form is equally dependent upon tonality, scales, and intervals, the raw materials from which melody is constructed and which give to each melody its own peculiar configuration. Form is closely related to harmonic rhythm and chord relationships, the divisions of form marked by cadences which are strongly harmonic in nature.

To perceive and understand form, therefore, the pupil must be conversant with matters of meter and rhythm, scale and interval, harmony and cadence. This knowledge can be derived from song literature and, like other music knowledge, serves to aid performance and heighten appreciation.

RHYTHM. Rhythm is the element to which many pupils respond first. It is proper for the teacher to encourage rhythmic response by asking pupils to conduct meter and tap or clap rhythm patterns while learning new songs, and to clarify rhythmic understanding by developing familiarity with the symbols through which rhythm is notated.

MELODIC STRUCTURE. Tonality, scales, and intervals are inherent in all songs and can be learned from them. The important functions of the tonal center and the leading or more active tones of the scale are apparent in melody and need only be identified for the singer to be of use to him in singing. Knowledge of scale structure and the characteristics of various intervals can be developed if the teacher directs attention to their use in song literature and helps pupils explore their descriptive and mood-producing qualities. By defining these melodic elements and focusing attention upon them both in song literature and in other contexts, the teacher helps the pupil understand and remember their characteristics, enabling him to apply this knowledge in other music activities. The knowledge of scales and intervals is then applied in the exploration of harmony, leading to a clearer understanding of form and of the language of music.

HARMONIC STRUCTURE. In the area of harmony, the teacher has a wealth of material significant to music understanding and of potential interest to pupils because of the pleasure they find in experimenting with harmonies while singing. A logical starting point is the emotional or affective qualities of the chords themselves. Pupils hear and feel the qualities of major, minor, augmented, and diminished chords, and the relationship of tonic, dominant, and subdominant, in the songs they sing. The teacher helps them by calling attention to one or more chords in a song being studied, encouraging pupils to discuss its effect upon mood and its relationship to the words of the text.

To gain a clearer concept of the quality of each chord, the pupils can sing sustained triads out of song context. To accomplish this, the teacher divides the class into three parts, assigns the pitches of a major triad, signals the class to begin singing, then signals pupils singing the third of the triad to lower their pitch the distance of a semitone to form a minor triad, and finally raises the third to its original level to return to the major triad. Similarly, the root and third can be lowered a semitone to create an augmented triad and the third and fifth can be lowered to create a diminished triad.

With this preliminary experience to stimulate curiosity, it is a natural step to examine the structure of the chords and their relationships to tonality and scale. Tonic, dominant, and subdominant can be explored in the same manner, the principal factor here being the effect of tension or repose created by each chord. From this beginning, the teacher proceeds to chord progression, noting the chord patterns in familiar songs, especially those which use only the three primary chords, using this knowledge in singing sustained harmony "by ear," and applying it to the learning of new songs in which the harmonies are sung either as chords or in arpeggiated form to furnish melodic pattern. In some classes, the learning might progress to experiences with chords having added ninths, elevenths, and thirteenths, such as those in the idiom of popular music, or to the harmonic practices of contemporary composers. Even cursory examination of the most rudimentary aspects of harmony arouses interest, improves the singing of the class, and results in deeper insight into the nature of music.

TRAINING THE EAR. All of these elements of music must be heard. Form, tonality, scale and interval, rhythm and meter, harmony and cadence—all have meaning and must be identified by performer and listener alike if music is to be understood and appreciated. Applied to the general music class, this means that the pupil must be trained to hear as well as to know and to understand. Knowledge helps him focus attention upon the element to be heard by describing its characteristics and defining its nature, but knowledge alone is not sufficient for hearing. Hearing, in the musical sense, includes recognition and identification, the ability to remember and recall, and the ability to reproduce in the mind. This ability, reinforced by knowledge of the elements of the language and art of music, is the basis of music understanding.

THE SINGING WAY TO MUSIC UNDERSTANDING

Conceived as a means of approach to the art of music, the singing of the general music class is more than an enjoyable activity. It is pleasurable experience, of course, because favorable pupil attitudes toward the work of general music forms the cornerstone of all the music progress it can hope to achieve. But singing must be a profitable experience as well, resulting in a steady increase in music knowledge and skill.

As a prerequisite to the successful guidance of singing activities, the teacher must understand pupils and the problems peculiar to their age, striving continually to increase this understanding particularly as it pertains to adolescent voices and their progress toward maturity. The teacher begins the work of the general music class by striving to capture the interest and enthusiasm, and win the coöperation of every pupil in the class. A first step may be singing familiar and well-liked songs for the sheer enjoyment of participation. As quickly as possible, the teacher tests voices, classifying them and selecting song literature to avoid singing difficulties which might destroy interest and limit participation. Concurrently, the class explores song literature, learning unison and part-songs of many types and building a repertoire of worthy music which can be sung with pleasure.

As new songs are learned and familiar songs are reviewed, the teacher grasps every opportunity to improve the singing of the class, to help pupils use notation as an aid to singing, and to grow toward music understanding through increased knowledge and wider experience. All of these activities are inseparably bound together. Each element of music is related to the others, and each gain in music knowledge facilitates music progress. Singing is of value for itself, but of equal value as a means of teaching the various skills and knowledges of music. Progress is slow, perhaps, because the nature of the general music class does not permit the sacrifice of interest and enjoyment for intensive, disciplined study. Great progress can be made, nevertheless, if full advantage is taken of the opportunities provided by song literature for effective teaching. More important, the integrated learnings are meaningful, derived from and applied to the pupils' own singing experience. In this way, the singing activities of the general music class serve the true purpose of the music program of the public schools, bringing every pupil closer to the unique pleasures of music.

5: listening in the general music class

The term "listening activities" is used to denote those phases of the work of general music pertaining directly to the development of music appreciation and centered upon the act of listening to music performed by others. In practice, not all general music classes give an important place to music listening. As indicated in Chapter 4, some classes are devoted primarily to exploring vocal literature and developing singing skills. This is not in accord with the purpose of general music. General music is expected to achieve its objectives through a variety of activities, including both singing and listening. Listening, in the sense that it promotes the ability to hear, understand, and appreciate music of worthy quality, is essential.

THE IMPORTANCE OF LISTENING ACTIVITIES

Because no aspect of music can be fully understood without being heard, listening is an integral part of every music activity. It is essential to singing and to the playing of music instruments. The relatively intellectual study of music theory is meaningless unless related to the sounds of music.

Listening is also a separate activity, important as it applies to the enjoyment and appreciation of music. Although every music activity and every branch of music study makes its contribution to music appreciation, it is listening that provides the final application and test of appreciative powers.

The Nature of Music Appreciation

The term "appreciation" as applied to music and the other arts has a number of shades of meaning. Basically, there is an implication of appraisal, of recognition of worth, of the exercise of knowledge and judgment to evaluate correctly a work of art. This suggests the need for delicacy of sense perception—the sensitive awareness of artistic worth created not so much by separate technical factors as by their confluence and proper relationship. The term "appreciation" further implies the derivation of aesthetic satisfaction from the perception of artistic worth, a pleasurable warmth of feeling resulting from critical admiration based on knowledge of and emotional sensitivity to the expressive medium of the art. In terms of academic discipline, the term applies to a course of study dealing with aesthetic values and seeking to raise the level of aesthetic judgment and satisfaction. Related to music education, "music appreciation" refers to the development of a unique type of enjoyment—based on knowledge and understanding, requiring perception, recognition, and response—and to the studies that tend to increase critical powers and sensitivity to musical worth.

In contemporary society, there is a need for this sort of appreciation. We are deluged with music at every turn in our daily lives. Music finds its way into virtually every home through radio, television, or the phonograph. A radio is now an accepted part of the family automobile. Shopping centers, professional offices, manufacturing plants, restaurants, and places of amusement provide a steady flow of music through public address systems. At home or away from it, at work or at play, even while traveling from one to the other, music is inescapable. Unfortunately, much of this music is not worthy of or conducive to higher levels of appreciation. Nevertheless, there is today a continuing growth of interest in music of many kinds.

This increased interest in music may be due to the changing patterns of American social life. The tendency for decades has been to shorten the work-week and increase the time available for recreation and pleasure. There has been a more or less steady trend upward in income making it possible for more and more families to enjoy what were once regarded as life's luxuries. Paradoxically, there seems to be an increase in life's tempo and tension. We are geared to higher speeds and larger areas of travel, increased pressures of social and recreational activity, and subtle compulsions to crowd still more activity into every available hour. As a result, many adults have more time, more money, and more need for music.

Adolescents are not immune to these influences. They, too, feel the need for social activity and respond to social pressures, perhaps more strongly than adults, giving music an important place in their social activities. More important, adolescence is an impressionable age, forming opinions and attitudes which may endure and influence reactions throughout adult life.

Music appreciation is therefore an important part of the music education program. It is of immediate value to adolescents and can continue to serve them in later life. It is important to the maintenance of cultural standards and the preservation of our cultural heritage, and is essential to the growth of music discrimination in society as a whole. Listening is for everyone, and it is the duty of music education to assure that listening is guided by discriminating tastes.

The Goals of Listening Activities

ENJOYMENT. The first concern of the teacher of general music is the development in every pupil of the capacity to enjoy a variety of music experiences. This objective is pertinent to every aspect of the work of the general music class, but especially important where listening activities are concerned.

PERCEPTION. Closely related to the capacity for finding pleasure in music is the ability to listen intently and to hear its elements. Aural attention is essential; the faculties of the listener must be focused on the music consciously, searching for tonal relationships and attempting to recognize their characteristics. The teacher's task is made difficult by the fact that in his normal, daily routine the pupil learns to shut himself off from many sounds, ignoring those that are distracting. To respond to music in an appreciative manner, however, he must learn to listen to it, not in the way he hears recorded music in the shopping center, but in an intense and concentrated process that blocks out other sounds and thoughts.

It is true that few listeners sustain this concentrated attention through extended periods of listening; confirmed music lovers, professional musicians, and music critics alike are subject to fluctuations in the degree of attentiveness to music. The competent listener is aware of these fluctuations and periodically re-directs his attention to the music, especially during portions of greatest significance to critical evaluation or aesthetic response. For the pupil in the general music class, it is necessary to develop the ability and stimulate the desire to use aural skills in following the progress of music. Not only must the pupil learn to listen, he must develop the ability to listen intelligently as well. To do so, he must possess knowledge of the elements of music, using this knowledge to identify and understand the musical sounds he hears. Aural skill is the listener's tool, a prime requisite to the enjoyment of music. For the teacher of general music, the development of aural perception ranks high in the list of goals sought through listening activities.

KNOWLEDGE AND SKILL. An important objective deals with teaching the fundamentals of music through listening activities. These fundamentals include the elements of music theory, the skills related to music reading, and the skill of singing. We believe that knowledge and skill permit the listener to fathom more easily the deeper meanings of music. They help him climb to higher levels of appreciation. Without knowledge and skill, the listener is susceptible to the warmth of tone color and the physical pleasures of rhythm, but has little hope of achieving aesthetic perception. With knowledge, the listener can control his musical destiny, understanding music and its effects, discriminating between the worthy and the less worthy, and finding enduring satisfaction.

For most pupils, it is in the area of listening rather than performance that outlet is found for music interests during later years, and it is desirable that pupils be shown the benefits of knowledge and skill in terms of increased appreciation. We know that concrete music knowledge can be taught through listening and that listening activities conducted without definite purpose permit the decrease of class interest. It is therefore important that listening activities have purpose and that the teacher of general music strive to teach through each such experience something of the language or skill of music.

GENERAL INFORMATION. The teacher also numbers among the objectives of listening activities the exploration of music literature, the acquisition of information concerning the historical progress and cultural environment of music, the correlation of music study with other subjects, and the development of familiarity with the music resources of the community. Music literature is a broad field, embracing a long historical span, many performing media, many music styles and forms, and a limitless variety of music types. The general music class surveys this extensive panorama to acquaint pupils with the vastness of music resources, to give them perspective in their view of music development, to develop tolerance for music not of their own time and culture, and to demonstrate the many opportunities for finding pleasure in music.

The history of music need not be a tedious study of dates, names, and places; it can and should be a matter of becoming acquainted with information that injects life into music, interesting in itself and for the added enjoyment it gives to music listening. Music is neither intellectually abstract nor socially isolated. It grows out of people and their hopes, dreams, and ambitions. It is influenced by the temperament, personality, and daily experiences of the composers who create it. It is part of society and related to developments in manners, customs, politics, science, the other arts, and many other areas of human endeavor.

General music strives to introduce pupils to opportunities for participating in or listening to music in their own community. In addition to the music fare available in the home through radio, television, and the phonograph, there are music programs offered by churches, by groups which sponsor concert series, by private teachers who present their students in recital, by many different school organizations, and by other agencies peculiar to each community. Attendance at such concerts does much to stimulate interest in music, giving the listener experience with living music far more vital than that produced mechanically in the classroom.

DISCRIMINATION AND TASTE. Related to all the other objectives of the work in listening is the goal of developing discriminating taste. It is difficult to define "good taste" in music or in any other art. The Latin phrase *de gustibus non est disputandem,* "of taste there is no disputing," indicates that the question of taste is almost as old as civilization itself and that each individual is privileged to develop his own tastes and follow his own preferences. To permit this freedom to become license would be to destroy all standards, nullify criteria of artistic worth, and eliminate the need for self-improvement; preference would then become an excuse for ignorance.

Knowing that tastes differ from era to era and from society to society, we also realize there are standards of taste accepted in our own time and society. They are established by the concurring opinions of those who exercise enlightened judgment developed through knowledge and experience; they are based on the correct appraisal of such factors in works of art as craftsmanship, technical perfection, and expressive content. We know also that taste can be developed, that individuals can raise themselves to higher levels of taste, ultimately turning away from the less worthy to that which offers deeper and more lasting satisfaction.

To encourage the improvement of taste, the teacher gives pupils wider acquaintance and frequent contact with worthy music as well as increased knowledge of the components of musical art. Through wide acquaintance the pupil is able to make comparisons and form opinions of the relative values of different music works. Through frequent contact with music of accepted quality, he begins to know and accept it, to grow accustomed to the subtleties of its effects, and to perceive its enduring quality. Through increased knowledge he begins to understand music, recognizing its materials and becoming conscious of their appropriate use in the music he hears.

In the general music class, the teacher has an opportunity to lead the multitudes, to develop discriminating tastes among large numbers of pupils who in adult life form the audiences which accept or reject musical offerings. It is within the teacher's province to determine whether music is for them a source of momentary and superficial pleasure or a source of deep intellectual, emotional, and spiritual satisfaction.

In summary, the objectives of listening activities for pupils in the general music class are as follows:

1. To develop the capacity for enjoying many different types of music experience.
2. To increase the ability to focus aural attention upon music and to perceive the elements which combine to create its beauty.
3. To teach the fundamentals of music language and skill.
4. To explore the vast resources of music literature.
5. To impart knowledge of music's historical progress and social relationships.
6. To show and utilize the relation of music to other school subjects.
7. To encourage use of community resources.
8. To develop discriminating music tastes.

THE PUPIL AND HIS PROGRESS

When planning listening activities the teacher takes into consideration the factors which determine pupil response and progress: age and maturity, previous music training or background, and the possibility for supplementary music experiences. Pupil tastes are equally worthy of consideration. They determine the level at which listening activities must begin and indicate the amount of progress the teacher can hope to achieve. All of these factors bear upon the manner in which pupils respond to music. The pupil is the subject and the object of music teaching; the first requirement for effective teaching is that of understanding his reactions to the subject being taught.

The Response to Music

PHYSICAL RESPONSE. There are many ways in which individuals react to music. The pupil in the general music class may respond in any one manner or in all of them simultaneously. First, there is the physical response. In the presence of music, the physiological mechanism of the human body responds to the tone and rhythm perceived through the aural sense. There may be a change in the pulse rate, a similar change in respiration, an effect upon the digestive tract, and a change in the factors that create feelings of fatigue. These inner reactions are for the most part of an involuntary nature; the listener can not control them and usually is not aware that they are taking place. They are of undoubted importance to the listener's feelings about music, but of less significance to the teacher than other reactions of which the listener may be conscious and that can be observed and either stimulated or repressed by other influences.

The important physical response is to rhythm. Some listeners respond to music by tapping a foot, nodding the head, or making some other obvious physical gesture. Others who show no outward sign of physical response may contract a small muscle of the arm or leg in the rhythm of the music. Rhythm is basic to all music and is physical in nature. It can be felt first and best through the movement of muscles and perceived only dimly and ineffectually through the intellect or the emotions. The uninitiated listener's first response to music is often the physical response to rhythm. Because rhythm is basic to music, is physical in nature, and may prompt the listener's first reaction, the physical response should be encouraged rather than repressed. In this respect, there is a negative value in concert attendance. Concert etiquette requires that the listener remain still, restraining impulses to physical movement that might disturb others in the audience. In the classroom it is possible to lift some of this restraint, permitting the pupil to succumb to his natural empathy for rhythm and bringing him closer to the enjoyment of music.

EMOTIONAL RESPONSE. Another means of response to music is through the emotions. The physical response already alluded to can be conducive of emotion, producing excitement, exhilaration, and a feeling of well-being. The listener reacts emotionally not only to rhythm, but to tone qualities and colors, to the contrasts of harmonic tension and repose, to the configurations of melody, and to the unfolding of music structure. He may react consciously to some specific element in the music or may feel its emotional effect while being totally unaware of the cause. As evidence, there is the popular notion that minor modes are sad and major ones happy, and the frequent statements of people who say they like a particular music selection because it makes them feel gay or because it is attractively somber. Emotions produced by music are sometimes strong, gripping, and dramatic. More frequently they are less intense, creating a mildness of feeling identified as mood. For the most part, these moods are pleasant, relished by the listener and sought by him in music again and again.

Because it can not express specific thoughts or depict particular scenes, music permits the listener to form his own mental image of its meaning and to apply it to his own experience. Music is thus very personal and has the power to recall for the listener experiences which may have distinctly emotional connotations. In recalling them, the listener savors past emotions without feeling their full power or the pain of their immediacy. All of this is natural and proper. Music is an expressive art. It sprang into existence in response to man's need for an emotional outlet. It expresses emotions too subtle to be described by words and strikes responsive chords in listeners who may remain unmoved in the presence of art works of other kinds.

Adolescents especially are subject to the emotional effects of music. Their tendencies toward emotional reaction, their emotional instability, and their fondness for romantic daydreams make them particularly susceptible to music's emotional stimuli. In the general music class, the teacher may expect emotional response to music of all kinds, especially that heard during listening activities because it is of better quality than music produced by the pupils themselves. The teacher plans listening activities to take full advantage of pupils' emotional response, utilizing it to win attention and interest and to create the warmth of feeling toward music that could not be created through other types of response. This reaction, like the physical response to rhythm, is among the first to be felt by the uninitiated listener and is a useful tool in the hands of a resourceful teacher.

IMAGINATIVE RESPONSE. Closely related to the emotional response is that which depends upon imaginative associations. Many listeners give themselves up to flights of fancy prompted by the music they hear. The thoughts that pass through the listener's mind are stimulated by the music—perhaps because the listener associates certain tonal patterns with past experiences or with the moods they produced—but tend to be highly imaginative and not necessarily related to the music. Thus it is that some listeners see in music the procession of clouds along a far horizon or a sailing vessel buffeted by stormy seas, finding in these imaginings a pleasure dependent upon music but not especially musical in nature. For them, music is pleasant because it induces pleasant thoughts.

This, too, is one of the ways adolescents respond to music. They tend to be imaginative, prone to flights of fancy that project them into the adult world, permit them to indulge inwardly in hero worship and vicarious heroic exploits, or provide a means of exploring distant and romantic places. In a sense, this is a very creative response to music, made possible by the listener's facile imagination and his powers of imagery. The imaginative response makes it possible for some listeners to discuss the music that appeals to them. They would be able to say nothing about music if their comments were restricted to matters of rhythm, theme, harmony, and form, but they can speak with animation and conviction about the mental images prompted by music.

Although there is only a tenuous relation between music and this kind of imagination, and only limited progress is possible toward deeper understanding of music through imaginative associations, they are useful to the teacher because they provide another means of approach to music interest and enjoyment. In general music classes especially, composed of adolescent pupils who have little music knowledge and skill but who are capable of emotional and imaginative response, music that elicits these responses may be the teacher's best means of awakening class interest.

INTELLECTUAL RESPONSE. A less common response, but a more significant one from the teacher's point of view, is that which involves the intellect rather than the muscles, emotions, or imagination. The intellect responds to tone qualities, colors, patterns of pitches and rhythms, and to the progress of music structure. The mind thinks about what it hears. It recognizes familiar patterns of sound and distinguishes among those that may be similar but not alike. It summarizes the progress of music development, remembering the first tones of a theme and adding those that follow, constructing a mental picture of the total pattern.

This is the intellectual response, a reaction of a somewhat higher order than the physical, emotional, or imaginative. It is based on knowledge in that the listener must have a repertoire of familiar tone patterns to recognize them and their variants, and in that the listener must have further knowledge of music's techniques and materials to interpret what he hears.

Response of an intensely intellectual nature is reserved for those who have broad backgrounds of music knowledge. Almost every listener utilizes intellectual processes in his response to music. At one level or another, he recognizes, distinguishes, summarizes, and projects. But it is desirable that he progress to higher levels of intellectual response. The response to music form, for example, requires first the ability to recognize elements from which form is created—phrase and melody, harmony and cadence. To recognize these the listener must first be able to recognize such things as intervals and harmonic colors. Although the listener may find a degree of pleasure in music through only minimum intellectual response, he progresses toward greater pleasure of an aesthetic nature as he learns to know and to respond to more and more of music's intellectual materials.

AESTHETIC RESPONSE. The highest level of response is the aesthetic. It is one that perceives and reacts to beauty, utilizing and combining all other responses but transcending them in its power to give the listener unique and unforgettable music experience. It is appreciation in its true sense, including sensitivity to and correct appraisal of music values and creating a satisfying warmth of approval in their recognition. The aesthetic response captures the complete attention of the listener; it perceives meaning in the music without reference to any extra-musical association. It is not self-conscious; it causes the listener to forget himself and his personal emotions, avoiding trains of thought that cause him to ignore the music itself.

The aesthetic response is emotional but abstract. Other emotions are related to personal experiences and are strong because the cause of the emotion is of direct consequence to the individual; aesthetic emotion is impersonal and not directly related to the pains and pleasures of past or projected experience. It is a source of pleasure emotional in nature but selfless and enduring rather than personal and transitory. It includes empathy, a kind of sympathy felt for works of art rather than for the feelings of others, causing the listener to become one with the music and attuned to its nuances. Aesthetic response is stimulated by the perception of relationships in musical art. It is sensitive to subtleties as well as to powerful dramatic effects. It can be stimulated by the sheer beauty of tone, by any of the elements of music, or by all of them combined. It discriminates among different types and styles of music and requires sensitivity to pitch, timbre, intensity, duration, rhythm, form, consonance, and dissonance.

Even though this much can be said to describe aesthetic response and its causes, it is still essentially indefinable, a question subject to much debate, and as difficult to explain as beauty itself. We agree, nevertheless, that it is a highly desirable response and offers the deepest and most lasting satisfactions to be found in music. It is not necessary that the listener feel only aesthetic response or that aesthetic response be sustained through the entire duration of any period of listening. Like other unique experiences, the ultimate in aesthetic response occurs infrequently. For the teacher of general music, aesthetic response stands as a peak the pupils may some day scale if they develop the requisite interest and skills. It is not something the teacher can create for or teach to pupils, but it is an experience for which they can be prepared through the listening activities of the general music class. Like music appreciation and perhaps identical with it, aesthetic response may be regarded as the principal objective of music education in the public schools.

TYPES OF LISTENER. The listener's concept of music pleasure may be related to the sensuous feelings created by musical sounds or to the intellectual satisfactions felt when music is perceived and understood. He may be a "listener," focusing careful and sustained attention on the music, or a "hearer" who submits to the effects of music without making any attempt to understand or be attentive. He may be an active participant who responds visibly to music and is impelled to talk about his reactions, or a quiet auditor who shows no outward sign of attention or response.

The type of response experienced by each pupil depends upon a number of factors. His physical, mental, and emotional maturity may influence his response to various types of music. His previous experience at home or in school may condition his reaction. His music knowledge, aptitude, and sensitivity may aid or impede his understanding. His interests, determined by his nature, influenced by his friends, or aroused by the teacher, may encourage or deter his response. Although there may be pupils who seem immune to music and resist listening activities, there is not one who is unable to feel some response.

Learning through Listening

In music as in many other studies, we believe the pupil who tries to learn will gain more than one who does not. Similarly, we believe that the teacher who strives to impart knowledge and develop skills encourages pupil progress to a greater degree than the teacher who makes no such effort. These statements would seem to need no defense, but in the area of music appreciation the need for effort on the part of both teachers and pupils is not as obvious as in other studies. Because music is enjoyable and because almost everyone develops enjoyment for music of one kind or another, it is easy to assume that pupils will learn to like music if they are given opportunity to hear it; even if they do not like it upon first hearing, they will be unable to resist its pleasures if only they can be persuaded to hear it again and again.

Through such lines of thought, the teacher is led to the conclusion that actual teaching is unnecessary when it deals with music appreciation. Music classes become a series of listening periods in which phonograph records are played one after another with only minimum comment, few requirements being established for pupils except quiet attendance. Such a procedure is of little more merit in music teaching than it would be in any other subject. Enjoyment comes to those who know and understand, as well as to those who have experience; knowledge comes to those who try to learn.

To be effective, the guidance of listening activities in the general music class requires that the teacher strive to teach something of the language and skills of music and that pupils be motivated to learn. Not only is this important to the development of appreciation, it is in accord with the general pattern of music study. Each of the areas of music learning can be approached individually and in conjunction with others; each separate skill can and should be developed through a number of different activities. The general music class is an opportunity for both listening to worthy music and learning through listening.

Music that appeals first and calls forth the lower orders of physical, emotional, and imaginative response tends to lose its power over the listener as it becomes more familiar. If interest is to be sustained, the listener must progress toward higher orders of music and higher levels of response.

By adhering to this procedure, the teacher gradually builds a fund of music knowledge for each pupil. As each new understanding is achieved, it opens doors to other understandings and provides foundations for them. As this fund of knowledge grows, the pupil continues to refer to it as he hears new music, being rewarded by recognition of more and more of music's structural materials. He becomes sensitive to more of the facets of music and more sensitive to its deeper meanings. He makes progress because he learns through listening, because the teacher guides his experience and stimulates him to learn. This is the intent of listening activities. They are a means to music progress, adjusted to the pupil's level but utilized as tools for teaching as well as sources of listening pleasure.

EXPANDING THE LISTENING REPERTOIRE

General music, conceived as a means of acquainting pupils with the music of our cultural heritage, seeks to broaden this acquaintance by enlarging the repertoire of music to which pupils can listen with pleasure. There are additional and perhaps more important reasons, however, for seeking to broaden pupils' listening experience. Interest is stimulated by the new and the different; sustained interest depends on a reasonable mixture of the new with the familiar. The teacher presents new music to discover the preferences of the class as a whole. The class surveys a variety of music styles and media seeking contrasts and comparisons as well as the interest that variety provides. It explores music to develop familiarity with the literature and to provide many opportunities for learning about music.

What to Include

Because of the vastness of the literature of music, the teacher's first problem is one of selection. Criteria for the selection of music depend upon the teacher's knowledge of pupil background and the extent to which community resources offer opportunities for becoming acquainted with music literature. If pupils have had neither training in music nor contact with it in their homes, and if there is a lack of music activity in the community, the teacher turns to the standard repertory of music that is generally well known and has popular appeal. If pupils have had either training or contact with music, the teacher omits certain of the more popular works, including others that arouse pupil curiosity because of their newness or their contrast to music that is familiar. The selection depends also upon the teacher's approach to listening activities. The approach might be through the pupils' natural interest in popular music, through rhythmic response to music, through the relationships between singing and listening activities in the class, or through other interests or activities, each of which would require the selection of music suitable for that approach.

FOLLOWING PERSONAL PREFERENCES. In selecting music, the teacher is wary of following pupil preferences, choosing music to serve the purposes of instruction rather than music having no other usefulness except to pamper the tastes of the pupils. Adolescents are quick to express their preferences, to show pleasure in what they like and to express their opinions of what they do not like. When the class responds favorably to one music selection, the teacher is inclined to go on with other music of the same type, following pupils in a search for pleasure rather than leading them to music knowledge and appreciation. It is essential to select music pupils can learn to enjoy, of course, but this music must provide opportunity for learning as well as for immediate listening pleasure.

Similarly, the teacher must be wary of following his own tastes. It is improbable that pupils with little knowledge or experience will be interested in music that appeals to the teacher's tastes, cultivated through years of study and guided by strong interests. In dealing with a subject as indefinable and personal in its appeal as music, it is inevitable that there should be differences of opinion concerning the types of music that might appeal to the tastes of the general music class. Moreover, it is probable that each general music class will show interests different from other classes. The teacher can therefore assume it will be necessary to explore the tastes of each class by experimenting with different types of music, being guided by a knowledge of the music that has immediate and popular appeal and beginning with selections that produce physical, emotional, or associative response.

DEVELOPING A CHECKLIST. As a guide in the selection of music, the teacher examines the various ways in which music is classified, developing a checklist of selections, including each of the possible categories, and insuring that the list does not omit any type of music useful in stimulating class interest. As a beginning, there are categories based on the history of music, media or performance, music style, large and small music forms, and levels of popularity and response. In terms of history and style, there is music from the renaissance, baroque, classic, romantic, modern, and other periods. There are categories containing descriptive, programmatic, dramatic, and nationalistic music as well as pure or absolute music not intended to represent anything beyond the tonal beauty of music itself. Under performing media there is music for voices and music for instruments, including literature for large ensembles, smaller ensembles, and solo performers, for orchestra, band, and keyboard instruments. The categories under form are numerous. In instrumental music there are the symphony, concerto, suite, quartet, sonata, theme with variations, tone poem, overture, ballet, and smaller dance forms. In vocal music there are the opera, oratorio, cantata, operetta, anthems, chorales, and others. Where appeal and response are concerned, the teacher might consider such categories as popular songs, folk songs and art songs, musical comedy, light opera, oratorio and opera, dance orchestra, military band, solo concerto, and concerted symphonic music.

By considering some such checklist of music types and styles, the teacher discovers opportunities for arousing class interest, being reminded of particular selections that have strong appeal. The checklist is a useful guide for the teacher in planning lessons that survey music literature in accordance with the objectives of the general music class. It would be virtually impossible and perhaps undesirable to include all the possible categories while surveying music literature, but it is proper to select from the categories music that indicates the wide range of music types and styles.

VOCAL MUSIC. In compiling a selected list of music for listening activities the teacher avoids undue concentration on any one type of music. Many listeners, especially those who purchase phonograph records, turn principally to instrumental music and neglect both the large choral works and shorter choral selections. Choral music is worthy for itself and for the special interest it holds for pupils because of the unique appeal of combined voices. Choral music lends itself readily to class activities in which pupils sing excerpts from music presented in listening periods, permitting closer contact with the music and aiding learning.

Art songs and other literature for solo voice should be included in the listening repertoire also. Because of their expressive nature, they illustrate an aspect of music sometimes not clearly apparent in instrumental selections. The teacher may influence the quality of the singing of the class by providing models of tone quality worthy of imitation by the pupils. For the general music class, such songs should be performed in English. There are obvious reasons for retaining the original language of art songs and operatic excerpts, of course, but the controversy concerning translations may well be reserved for works presented on the concert or operatic stage. When songs are presented to young listeners, it is important that the texts be intelligible so the listener may understand the literary meaning of the song and the manner in which the music describes and reinforces it.

USING THE UNUSUAL. The class list should include music in both the ancient and modern idioms. Many of the well-known and popular works, those that appeal most quickly to young listeners, are from the nineteenth or late eighteenth century. Music from other periods should not be overlooked, because even untrained listeners are often deeply impressed by the unfamiliar sounds of sixteenth and seventeenth century works and by the dramatic dissonances of contemporary compositions. Organ and harpsichord music should be included as well as compositions for smaller ensembles such as the woodwind quintet, string quartet, percussion ensemble, and brass choir. It is neither necessary nor desirable to restrict listening to music for full orchestra despite the natural tendency to select music from the standard orchestra repertoire. Finally, it is often advantageous to include some popular music and excerpts from operettas and musical comedies.

Although the teacher may feel the works of the masters are more worthy of class study, there is much that students can learn from lighter music, especially if it appeals to their tastes or to their lively interest in the world of today. This is not to imply that class study should be devoted solely to the types mentioned here or that other music should be slighted. To the contrary, a listening list suitable for the general music class will probably be composed chiefly of well-known works from the standard repertoire with less familiar music added to provide variety. Judicious use of the less familiar helps sustain interest and may help the teacher utilize class interests in stimulating musical growth.

Where to Start

The most important portion of the listening program is that in which pupils are introduced to the activities of the class. First experiences form lasting attitudes and should be calculated to arouse interest and enjoyment. In planning these first experiences, the teacher provides a basis for future successes by heeding the tastes of the class and by remembering the ways in which untrained listeners respond to music they meet for the first time. It is important that the teacher try to discover class tastes quickly and that first lessons be based on the teacher's past experience and best judgment, utilizing music appealing to adolescent listeners. The teacher can select music conducive to physical, emotional, or associative response, being guided by what is known of the psychological effects produced by music in various listeners. When estimating tastes, the teacher is guided by what is known of the nature of adolescence and the probable attitudes and interests of adolescent pupils.

POPULAR MUSIC. Music of a popular nature often seems a desirable starting point. Adolescents hear a great deal of popular music, seem to accept and enjoy it, and often express a desire to hear it in the general music class. The teacher often discovers, however, that adolescents are attracted by the term "popular" rather than by the music itself. Popular music may serve as a point of departure provided the teacher plans class listening with as much care as would be devoted to any other type of music, devising ways to hold class attention and using the music as a source of learning.

Selections from current musical comedies and operettas may be included in the popular category and are useful as first listening experiences. Adolescents sometimes show strong interest in this type of music and like to listen to it, especially if class work can be related to presentations of community theaters or to popular shows being discussed by their parents and friends.

In general, however, the teacher is apt to find that popular music of any kind, even if it is enthusiastically received when first introduced, does not hold the interest of the class and creates difficulties in making the transition from popular to more serious music. Although there is no good reason for excluding all popular music from the general music class, it must be used with discretion and with definite teaching purpose rather than as a source of entertainment. Used judiciously, it can arouse strong interest and establish class attitudes favorable to further listening.

MUSIC OF LASTING VALUE. In view of the objectives of general music, the teacher is better advised to turn to music of lasting value, choosing from the resources of serious music works that represent popular taste and have obvious appeal. Folk music often meets these requirements, being strongly rhythmic in nature, offering distinctive and memorable melodies, and being simple in structure. Certain selections from ballet music have similar qualities, are relatively familiar, and have the added advantage of stimulating discussion of such things as plot and historical setting. Descriptive or programmatic music is often well received because it appeals to the imagination and expresses definite moods in telling its story. It provides extra-musical ideas to capture pupil attention and offers many opportunities for discussing the characteristics of the music as they relate to programmatic events.

Music played by military bands proves of interest to some classes, the stirring sonorities of brass and woodwind instruments stimulating pupil imagination, the vigorous movement of marches in particular and band music in general appealing to pupils' rhythmic sense. Music played by relatively unusual instruments in small ensembles or alone—woodwind quintet, harpsichord or organ, for example—tends to arouse curiosity and leads to discussion of the instruments and their mechanical or acoustical characteristics, subjects appealing to adolescent interests.

PARTICIPATION. The teacher searches for music that stimulates pupils to participate actively in the listening lesson. Participation may take the form of discussion prompted by pupils' curiosity about some unusual factor in the music, by pupils' past experience that relates in some way to the music heard, or by relationships between the music and other subjects. Participation may be a matter of response to the music, reacting physically to its rhythms, singing its themes, or following its form. Finally, participation may be a matter of intent listening or intellectual activity prompted by music that contains unusual tonal effects or raises questions about the nature of music itself, instruments and their use, or extramusical connotations. In planning first lessons, the teacher also seeks to include variety, presenting music of different types and for different performing media, avoiding routine in either music materials or teaching procedures.

Choosing a Theme

The first stage in planning a series of listening lessons is one of choosing a central topic to which each of the various lessons can be related. The central theme provides for the coherency of a number of different lessons and permits logical progression from one to another, providing a feeling of achievement and of progress toward a defined goal. In choosing a central theme, it is desirable to select a topic of natural interest to pupils. If pupils are interested in the topic itself, their interest can be transferred to the related music.

This is the "unit" plan of teaching discussed in Chapter 6; work in which subject matter is grouped in large blocks, all of the work in any one block being pertinent to the central theme of the unit. Rather than being an arbitrary grouping in which a series of separate topics is arranged to fill a stated number of class meetings, the unit consists of any number of related studies that grow naturally out of the central theme and are closely related to each other. The unit plan is used successfully in the teaching of many subjects, but is especially useful in the area of music listening. Because the succession of listening lessons depends on many factors other than logical progress through the history of music, and because the selection of material may be determined by such unpredictable factors as pupil taste and response, a series of listening lessons is more likely to seem aimless than a series of lessons in, for example, history or mathematics. The teacher of music can use the unit plan to advantage, selecting a unit theme as the first step in planning and providing for the treatment of every phase of music learning within the course of the unit.

Selecting the Music

To present music to the class, the teacher relies most often on recordings but is alert to the possibilities of introducing pupils to live music in actual performance. For pupils in the general music class, recordings are at best a poor performance medium. Not only are they of comparatively little interest, they are inadequate substitutes for living music in the same way that photographs are inadequate substitutes for the experience of seeing the Grand Canyon or Niagara Falls.

Although general music classes may see live performances infrequently because of the difficulty of making schedule arrangements, there are many opportunities for hearing live music. As suggested in Chapter 3, the teacher utilizes them as often as possible. There may be pupils in general music who can perform for their classmates, or parents and other adults of the community who can be invited to the classroom as visiting performers. There may be soloists or small ensembles from school choral and instrumental groups as well as regularly scheduled rehearsal periods that can be visited with little inconvenience.

SCHOOL AND COMMUNITY RESOURCES. The teacher of general music can obtain a number of visiting performers simply by asking the directors of high-school choral and instrumental groups. The high-school instrumental director, for example, may be searching for performing opportunities for soloists and ensembles preparing for concerts. He may welcome the opportunity to send his groups to the general music class or to a junior-high-school building for an assembly program. If his performance schedule permits, he might open a band or orchestra rehearsal to the general music class, arranging to demonstrate instruments and techniques and to play music appropriate for the visiting pupils.

Similarly appropriate listening opportunities are offered by most communities. There are church choirs and community choral groups, recitals arranged by private teachers for their pupils, and community bands and orchestras. A particularly interesting visit would be to one of the community churches to examine the organ. The teacher might persuade the church organist to play a few appropriate selections, to explain the mechanism of the organ, and to give pupils an unforgettable experience by permitting them to stand among the pipes as the organ is played, hearing the rushing of the wind and the clacking of valves and levers mixed with the tones of the pipes.

USING RECORDINGS. Although recordings are far less interesting to pupils than live music heard in actual performance, they have important advantages in addition to the convenience with which they can be used in class. The quality of performance is normally far superior to that of school or community groups or guests who visit the classroom. They offer music accurate in pitch and tempo, performed with sensitive artistry.

Tone quality, aside from distortions created by inadequate reproducing equipment, is more pleasing. Recordings permit the presentation of music otherwise unobtainable, make it possible to hear a variety of performing media, and bring outstanding artists to the classroom.

Because recordings are the most convenient source of music and may be the only means of presenting much of the music needed for teaching purposes, the teacher does everything possible to make this music seem alive to the class. A fund of interesting anecdotes and curious facts is useful to the teacher for this purpose. Such uninteresting chores as learning to spell composers' names and recite the dates of their life spans can be replaced with discussions that explore the human qualities of the composer and the significance of his music for today's listeners. The teacher encourages concentration upon the music itself rather than upon the historical facts surrounding it, guiding pupils in exploring the elements of theme, rhythm, harmony, and orchestration.

CHOOSING RECORDINGS. Much of the success of listening lessons depends upon the care with which the teacher selects recordings. The first requirement for any recording is that it produce beautiful tone. Music is an art of tone; its appeal to the listener is a tonal appeal. To rely on recordings that are old, worn, and covered with dust is to destroy almost every possibility of enjoyment. Although it is obvious that music presented in the classroom should be tonally attractive, the teacher who is able to find only one old recording of a selection needed for a lesson is prone to overlook its poor quality. For the same reason, the teacher secures the finest of sound-reproducing systems for use in the classroom and takes the best care of both recordings and equipment. No matter how great the music, it is worthless in the classroom if its tonal beauties are obscured by imperfections in reproduction.

Next in importance are the factors of rhythm and melody. Adolescent pupils respond naturally to the rhythmic aspects of music. The teacher selects music that has rhythmic vitality and in which the rhythm is sufficiently apparent and regular to be followed easily by the untrained listener. Melody is another element to which most people respond easily, an essential inducement to attention for many. The pupil without experience in listening finds it difficult to give sustained attention to music for more than short periods. He finds it doubly difficulty if the music does not contain a recognizable element of progress, some succession of pitches, rhythms, or tone qualities that is repeated, recurs, or develops. For the untrained listener, melodic progression is far easier to follow than progressions of harmonic colors or elements of music form.

Further desirable requirements are that the music create a distinct mood or that it be descriptive in style. Because pupils can be expected to respond emotionally or imaginatively to music, the music they hear should call forth these responses. Music that clearly defines a mood or vividly describes a scene or story is understood and enjoyed by young listeners; music that appeals to the intellect or the higher orders of aesthetic response, although it is sometimes well received because of its indefinable artistic appeal, can be used sparingly or reserved for later experiences.

Finally, the teacher selects music of reasonable length. Untrained listeners have short attention spans, especially for recorded music that does not provide the added visual interest of the live performance. Unless the teacher provides an activity to maintain attention or re-direct it to the music at regular intervals, it is best to choose short selections that encourage pupils to listen intently for short periods of time.

In the listening lesson it is the music that is important and the music that must make its appeal to the pupil; no amount of planning or extra-musical activities can compensate for music to which pupils do not respond. It is essential that the teacher choose wisely, calling on all resources of teaching experience, music background, and knowledge of pupil attitudes to aid in the selection of music that will be listened to with interest and enjoyment.

Challenging the Mind

For pupils to learn while listening it is necessary that they give music their attention by listening to it intently. This is one of the teacher's first responsibilities—to engage and sustain attention by stimulating interest and by planning teaching procedures that focus attention on the music.

USING MENTAL POWERS. The secret of listening is mental activity. Although the listener may respond physically or emotionally while in the presence of music, he has not actually listened to it until his mental capacities have been used in some way to direct his response or to seek an understanding of what he hears. Music is a means of communication. It should be listened to in the same way one reads and assimilates a book or hears and comprehends speech.

As in listening to speech, the hearer directs his attention to certain sounds, blocking other sounds and extraneous ideas from his consciousness. He listens to each sound and follows the succession of sounds in time. As each sound reaches the listener, he attempts to recognize it and its meaning. He follows the succession of sounds and adds the meaning of each new one to those that preceded it. In doing so, he remembers the sounds already heard, making an effort to recall and understand the total pattern created by their succession. The listener also projects himself into the future, using the pattern of sounds already heard to help him imagine additional sounds to complete or extend the pattern.

Thus the listener must hear, recognize, recall, and imagine. He listens in a mentally active way in an effort to understand what he hears. It is possible to bask passively in the sounds of music as in the warmth of the sun, but this is neither hearing nor listening. Passive listening does not lead to learning.

USEFUL DEVICES. Because listening should be an active, mental process, the teacher plans listening activities in such a way that pupils have something to listen for in almost every music selection, the exception being the cases in which the class listens purely for enjoyment or review to music already familiar. Active listening normally occurs when the teacher presents elements of the music before it is heard in its entirety, asks questions that can be answered only after attentive listening, or provides for activities that accompany the music and must be timed to it.

Pupils may be asked to imagine a plot or succession of events appropriate to the character of the music, a scene the music seems to describe, or a mood it creates. They may be asked to choose a color, a design, or a picture suggested by the emotional or other characteristics of the music. On occasion, pupils may be motivated to listen by the knowledge that they will be asked to draw a picture or cartoon or write a paragraph or brief story based on the music. An exercise of this type is approached in a creative spirit, of course, rather than as a disciplinary measure. Pupils may be asked to listen with pencil and paper, listing adjectives to describe the music they hear, or to choose from a list of adjectives on the board those that best describe the music. Specific themes, rhythms, harmonies, or instruments may be heard in the music. The teacher can suggest that pupils raise their hands as they hear the element of interest, or the pupils may follow themes notated on the board as the music progresses.

The attempt to associate similar things or distinguish between those that are dissimilar encourages attentive listening. The teacher can present two recordings in quick succession, asking that pupils compare the mood of two different selections, the qualities of two voices, tempos, instrumentations, harmonic styles, and so forth. The attempt at comparison might involve one recording and two paintings, one poem and two recordings, or any such combination from which pupils can select the two works most nearly alike. Pupils may be asked to use the music as a clue to the temperament or personality of the composer, to the nation or region it represents, or to the scene or event it describes. As for activity during listening, pupils may play rhythm patterns from the music using rhythm instruments, conduct, sing themes, or in some other way take active part in the performance.

None of these devices is used for itself alone or solely to engage the attention of the pupils; each has a musical purpose and helps pupils gain a degree of music insight. Some of them encourage pupils to become sensitive to the many moods of music. Others emphasize music style, music's descriptive qualities, or teach something about the characteristics of music and the elements of musical language. Still others encourage pupils to be creative and to express their reactions to music in an articulate way. Each device, therefore, is used with a double purpose. It helps engage and sustain attention while teaching something about music as well.

Guiding Learning

Another stage in planning listening lessons is one of providing for the development of skills, music knowledge, and discriminating taste. A prerequisite is that the teacher accept the desirability of "learning through listening." Unless the teacher is guided by this philosophy, listening lessons descend to the level of entertainment and do not result in music growth for pupils in the class.

TEACHING THE MATERIALS OF MUSIC. There are many things to be learned through listening, including specific facts about the structure and materials of music. These facts have to do with music itself and contribute directly to the pupil's knowledge and understanding. They are the elements of music that can be discovered in the score. Included among them are facts concerning rhythm, melody, harmony, form, notation, and instruments.

In the area of rhythm there are tempo, meter, note values, and rhythm patterns. Pupils should know the intellectual aspect of these rhythmic elements and feel and respond to them physically as well. In the area of melodic structure there are phrases, intervals, scales, keys, and modes, all coupled with the rhythmic factors essential to melodic design. Pupils should learn to follow melodic lines, to recognize the factors that give each melody its distinctive characteristics, and to be sensitive to the differences created by variations in melodic structure. Harmony deals with chords and their structure, with tension and repose, with the succession of chords, and with the important factors of key and cadence. In this area of music, pupils can acquire knowledge about the technical elements of harmony and develop aural feeling for harmonic color and progression. Where form is concerned there are the short song forms, the larger symphonic forms, and such terms as symphony, concerto, suite, oratorio, and opera, to name but a few. The general music class builds a vocabulary of these terms for each pupil in addition to giving him a basic understanding of the principles of structure.

Through listening, the pupil gains familiarity with the families of instruments and with voice qualities, learning to recognize them by identifying tone colors, becoming familiar with the appearance, register, and principles of tone production of instruments and with the qualities and classifications of human voices. Through such studies, pupils also become familiar with music notation, including key and meter signatures, clefs, the staff, and the system of notating pitch and rhythm. Concurrently, there is opportunity to develop skills in both singing and music reading. Acquired knowledge of the technical facts of music is applied in music reading; each new concept of tone color, each new experience in hearing desirable tone quality, and each attempt to match desirable tone with the singing voice leads to the improvement of singing.

RELATED KNOWLEDGE AND SKILL. Among the learnings of a less specific nature are those that have to do with attitudes toward music, concepts of its function, and the skills of listening. Pupils should develop sensitivity to the moods of music and to its expressive function. They begin to learn about music style and the characteristics of music from different historical periods. They become aware of relationships between music and the cultures in which it is created. They acquire a vocabulary of both musical and non-musical terms to permit discussion of the music they hear. They develop favorable attitudes toward music, including the ability to enjoy music of many types and the willingness to listen without prejudice to unfamiliar music. Finally, it is the objective of music education to teach pupils to evaluate the music they hear, exercising good taste in the selection of music for their own listening pleasure.

SELECTING THE GOALS. In establishing a learning goal for each listening experience the teacher has ample opportunity for challenging pupils of every age or grade and every level of ability and background. Lessons planned for younger, inexperienced listeners deal with the simplest rudiments of music and are discussed in non-technical language; for older and more advanced listeners, lessons explore the technical aspects of music structure and the relatively abstract ideas concerning music beauty and style.

The teacher selects specific items from the score, basing learning activities on the items selected. For classes of beginning listeners, the materials appropriate include elements of rhythm, melody, and harmony that can be easily recognized and understood and that elicit immediate physical or emotional response. For classes with music knowledge and listening experience, appropriate materials are those that utilize existing knowledge, prompt further learning, and elicit higher orders of response. The teacher is guided also by knowledge of pupils' age and maturity, selecting subject matter and learning activities appropriate to pre-adolescent pupils in the seventh grade or the young adults who elect music as seniors in high school.

BUILDING ON PAST EXPERIENCE. In planning a series of listening lessons, the teacher selects a sequence of music materials for study. He begins with simple learnings for which there are no prerequisites of knowledge or experience, building on these first experiences during succeeding lessons to develop further music knowledge. A series of such lessons, planned with full awareness of pupils' interests, attitudes, and abilities and with specific goals based on each successive listening experience, results in the accumulation of a large body of meaningful knowledge concerning music.

THE ACTIVITY APPROACH. To carry out this philosophy, the teacher identifies the music learning that can be acquired through each music work and then plans class activities that help pupils master this learning. The term "activities" is used advisedly. Music is an active art. The listener participates in the music he hears. The student learns best when he seeks knowledge through some sort of active participation in the music. The fact that music is among the most personal of the arts implies that the pupil must respond if he is to learn; he can not develop musically if he remains passive and does not actually experience what is taught. Adolescent pupils respond better to procedures that permit them to be active than to those that restrict or prohibit activity.

If listening lessons are to be productive of music learning and appreciative powers, it is necessary to avoid procedures in which a major portion of class time is occupied by lectures. One wins pupils to music with experiences, not with words. Although the teacher can not step completely aside to let music do its work unaided, neither should the teacher stand in the way of music and its message. The lecture is a poor substitute for music as a conveyor of subtle moods, and lectures about the technical details of music are unsatisfactory as a means of creating music response. They tend to be of little benefit unless they are closely related to existing knowledge and are supplemented by actual experience with the factors being discussed. Intellectual knowledge contributes to appreciation, but such knowledge is best acquired through actual experience with music. It is for these reasons that the teacher plans in terms of activities. The natures of the pupil and of the subject demand that learning be an active process.

ACTIVITY DEVICES. In the area of rhythm, pupils learn about meter and tempo by conducting portions of the music heard in class. They learn note values and rhythm by clapping, tapping, or singing rhythm patterns selected from the music and placed on the board. When appropriate, they use simple percussion instruments to duplicate rhythm patterns from the music or to improvise new ones suitable to its character. In doing so, they respond physically to rhythm, learning to feel it through muscular activity and discussing the intellectual factors of notation and mathematical relationships only as needed to guide physical response.

In the area of melody, pupils sing selected themes from the music, developing feeling for phrase lines, intervals, and tonality. Themes are notated on the board for visual reference and as a basis for discussion of melodic structure. These melodies may be played by pupils, using simple melody instruments or the piano keyboard. Discussion may be conducted to clarify pupils' understanding of intervals, scales, and other factors in melodic structure, the discussion being meaningful in proportion to its relationship to the pupils' experience in actually singing or playing the melodic example.

Similar procedures are used to investigate music's harmonic characteristics. Whenever possible, single chords or harmonic progressions are lifted out of their context in the music, placed on the board, and played or sung by the pupils. In some instances, these harmonic progressions lend themselves to part-singing, being read from the board or sung as an accompaniment to a portion of the music played on the phonograph. The quality or color of single chords may be experienced in this way also, the pupils first singing a major triad and then shifting one or two pitches to create a minor, diminished, or augmented triad, or extending the triad by adding pitches to form chords with sevenths or ninths. Pupils achieve understanding of the qualities of tension and repose and develop feeling for cadence by singing chord progressions with a neutral syllable, or by improvising simple chord progressions to accompany themes from the listening lesson. Chord instruments such as the autoharp, guitar, ukulele, or piano are used to duplicate or create the chord progression, reinforce the singing, and provide another means of hearing and feeling harmonic color. Notated on the board in an arrangement appropriate to the voices in the class, the chord progression can be examined and discussed in relation to the music heard and to pupils' experience in singing and playing.

To become acquainted with music structure, pupils diagram less complex forms as they listen to music played on the phonograph or analyze melodies notated on the board. In other instances they simply note the recurrence of themes as they listen by raising hands each time the theme reappears. They sing themes to experience vocally the effect of theme recurrence or the small changes that impel the phrase to move ahead in one instance and give it finality in another. Through singing they compare themes and forms from the listening lesson with those they have met previously in vocal music. Here as in other class activities the visual, vocal, and aural impressions are supplemented with discussion to increase understanding, the emphasis being placed upon experiencing form rather than talking about it.

To gain familiarity with orchestral instruments, pupils combine the visual impression of seeing the instruments or pictures, the aural impressions received from hearing them played on a recording or in live performance, and the intellectual understanding arrived at through discussion. In so far as possible, this involves activity rather than passive listening. Instruments can be played and demonstrated by capable members of the class. Pupils may experiment with certain instruments, attempting to produce tone or manipulate the instrumental mechanism. The class may define the tone of each instrument by discussing its quality and searching for descriptive terms, ultimately listening to recordings to identify by sound alone the instruments they have discussed.

To teach notation through listening, the teacher places themes, harmonies, and rhythm patterns on the board, each example drawn from the music of the listening lesson. As pupils refer to these examples to examine factors of rhythm, melody, harmony, or form, they gain familiarity with the appearance of music notation, learn the meaning of various symbols, and gain skill in interpreting them. Although music-reading skill is not the principal goal of these activities, comments by the teacher, discussion of the symbols and their meanings, and occasional brief drill with difficult patterns help pupils make progress in reading ability. Similarly, general music classes improve singing abilities through the activities of the listening lessons. Through singing many themes, rhythms, and harmonies, increasing the ability to interpret notation symbols, developing sensitivity to pitch, interval, and melodic flow, learning to feel harmonic colors and progressions, and through developing sensitivity to tone quality, pupils build the skills and concepts that help them sing better.

LEARNING THROUGH DISCUSSION. In each of these specific areas of music learning there is need for discussion as well as participation in music experiences. The type of discussion needed is that in which pupils express their opinions, ask questions, and suggest answers. A lecture delivered by the teacher, or a recitation of historical and other facts by pupils, does not constitute discussion. A discussion is a means of exploring, expressing, reasoning about, and debating both facts and opinions. It is guided but not monopolized by the teacher, who must resist temptation to supply answers pupils can discover for themselves. Pupils are encouraged to express themselves, to describe music and its effects, to state their reactions, and, most important, to search for reasons for their preferences and explanations of music's effects.

Through these discussions and through the study of the elements of music, the teacher helps pupils build a vocabulary for music discussion. Pupils tend to be inarticulate when asked to express their feelings about music, partly because music projects meanings too subtle to be expressed in words and partly because pupils do not have at their command terms that express the finer shades of feeling created by music. By helping pupils build a suitable vocabulary the teacher opens for them new opportunities for discussing music and for defining music concepts. Some discussions may deal with the techniques of music, others with the effects of music upon the listener, still others with the relatively abstract, philosophical ideas of aesthetics and musical beauty. All of them contribute to the music development of the pupil and are important to the listening activities of the general music class.

Retaining Music Knowledge

Nothing of what has been said about maintaining interest or providing for active participation in class work should be interpreted as excluding concentrated study of subject matter in the general music class. For pupils to gain lasting benefit from their work in music they must achieve goals, gain knowledge, and develop attitudes and skills. Insuring retention of newly acquired music knowledge through appropriate teaching procedures is one of the goals of planning listening activities.

RE-TEACHING AND REVIEW. It is desirable that music heard in class be remembered, that the pupil recognize it on subsequent hearings, and that the survey of music literature provide residual knowledge of music of different styles and periods. Although general music classes often permit less time for listening than the teacher thinks necessary, there is time to provide for repeated hearings of works studied in class. Each additional hearing should be purposeful, though there is benefit to be derived from incidental hearings arranged for no purpose other than renewed acquaintance.

If listening experiences are used as a basis for music learning, one selection may be used in several lessons as a means of studying different elements of music, perhaps to show the difference between major and minor modes in one lesson and to illustrate metrical rhythm in another. Such purposeful hearings do much to create a lasting impression on the listener. Incidental hearings are useful also during the portions of music classes that might otherwise be wasted. In some instances it is possible to play recordings between classes as pupils are entering or leaving the room. In others, there are portions of the class during which complete silence is not required while pupils are writing, reading, or distributing materials and will not be disturbed by music played at reasonable volume. In some schools the public address system provides opportunities for playing worthwhile music during the lunch hour or before or after school. In still other instances, music heard in class serves to review or preview works performed by school or community groups or music presented on radio and television programs.

Each of these devices for providing multiple hearings is useful to the teacher in helping pupils remember the music they hear. Equally useful are the teaching devices that permit pupils to experience music in different ways, to perceive it through different senses, or to see different facets of its structure. The visual impressions created when pupils see excerpts notated on the board help them remember the music studied. The vocal experience of singing themes or harmonies, the muscular experience of responding to rhythms, and the intellectual experience of analyzing theme recurrence or other aspects of the music leave similarly lasting impressions. Each helps the pupil learn and remember.

THE VALUE OF UNDERSTANDING. Understanding is important to both learning and memory. Pupils learn more quickly if they understand the facts they are attempting to learn, seeing the logic of their sequence and relationships. The teacher strives to provide knowledge and experience that lead to understanding. Although pupils in the general music class have no direct need for technical knowledge of music, they are encouraged to learn certain of music's technical data. They learn the language of music so that in their listening they may perceive more clearly, recognizing the elements of music and attaching proper labels to aid thinking and remembering. This is the value of music theory for the listener; it gives him the tools essential to thinking about music, sharpens perception, and makes music intelligible.

Similarly, the teacher develops pupils' ability to understand basic but broader aspects of music. Pupils benefit from the physical understanding of rhythm, the emotional understanding of melody and harmony, the imaginative and associative understanding of the moods and expressive content of the total musical fabric. Pupils gain these understandings through actual participation in the music and through feeling its effects in a direct and personal way. Once these deeper understandings are achieved, the pupil is better equipped to listen intelligently and to develop enduring interest in the musical art.

THE NEED FOR PROGRESS. It is especially important that pupils be able to see evidence of progress and achievement. In the general music class it is not probable that pupils will have textbooks to read, that they will examine the history of music in a systematic survey that begins with early music and progresses to that which is contemporary, or that they will be able to see clearly a pattern as logical and as well organized as those followed by many other school subjects. The nature of the general music class requires that it be completely flexible in its choice of subject matter, following pupil interests and selecting from a variety of materials as occasion demands. In the absence of a clearly discernible pattern of progress, it is natural that the pupil should regard the work of the class as aimless and that he should have little feeling of achievement after participating in a number of seemingly unrelated lessons. It is therefore important that the teacher provide evidence of progress to encourage the class to persevere in its interest and effort.

A first step is the selection of a unit topic. The pupil is apt to remember the completion of a number of units, these larger blocks of learning making a deeper impression than single lessons not noticeably related to each other or to a central theme.

Some teachers require that pupils keep notebooks as evidence of achievement. The notebook is a desirable tool if it serves a real purpose and is more than a scrapbook or a repository for tedious exercises in copying. It can be a means of recording significant information meaningful to the pupil and useful for reference, review, and study. It can be a listening diary in which the pupil expresses his reactions to the music he hears. In rare instances, the notebook might even contain manuscript pages on which the pupil records important music themes in correct notation for reference and review.

Also useful as a record of progress is a list of the music works heard and studied in class. The list might be posted on a classroom bulletin board and added to as the class studies each new composition. For a more colorful record, the teacher hangs record jackets in a conspicuous place, adding a new jacket for each recording heard, or selects a committee to collect interesting pictures and hang an appropriate one for each new music selection. If pupils keep notebooks, each keeps his own list of music studied as a personal record of achievement. In some classes it may be feasible to require regular listening outside of class, either by assigning specific radio and television programs or concert performances or by establishing the requirement that each pupil listen to a minimum number of minutes of serious music each week. In either case, the teacher stipulates that each pupil prepare a weekly listening report on single sheets of notebook paper, on small filing cards, or in a listening notebook. The report is of necessity brief, listing only such facts as composer, title, performing medium, date and time of performance rather than describing the music in essay form. It is examined periodically by the teacher and is further evidence of achievement for the pupil.

THE LISTENING WAY TO MUSICAL UNDERSTANDING

Listening activities are included in the work of the general music class because of the important contributions they make to its objectives. Properly conducted, listening activities lead to music appreciation in its best and most desirable sense. Like true appreciation, they have to do with interest and enjoyment, with sensitive perception and critical evaluation, and with discriminating taste. The ability to respond to beauty in an appreciative way is becoming increasingly necessary in today's society and it is the function of general music to give to every pupil a foundation of knowledge and understanding on which to build expanding powers of appreciative response. With these powers the pupil can in later years turn to music as an antidote to social tensions as well as to satisfy the spiritual hunger for beauty. The general music class has many goals, but all are subordinate to, and exist because they aid in achieving, the goal of paramount importance—the development of appreciation.

There are many ways in which the listener may respond to music; his reactions may be physical, emotional, imaginative, associative, intellectual, aesthetic, or a complex mixture of several of these responses. The pupil in the general music class may feel any or all of them but is more likely to respond to physical and emotional stimulants than to those that are intellectual or aesthetic. The teacher considers the factor of response when planning class work to expand pupils' listening repertoire, including a variety of music to elicit a variety of responses. The class surveys the many periods of music history, the variety of performing media, the variations of music form and style, and the wealth of available music literature. In planning, the teacher selects specific music works for class study with full knowledge of pupils' interests and abilities and with due regard for their natural tastes and preferences, turning first to music that has immediate appeal.

The teacher of general music thinks always in terms of interest and enjoyment but avoids any tendency to sacrifice goals of learning to class procedures that are entertaining rather than instructive. To the contrary, the teacher strives to make each activity productive, teaching specific facts about music and developing favorable attitudes toward music. Listening activities are used to teach every phase of music knowledge and skill, including music literature, history and theory, and the skills of listening, singing, and playing. Such knowledge is taught not for its own value alone, but for the contributions it makes to enjoyment and appreciation. Taught in this way, listening activities are a worthy part of general music instruction. They contribute to clearly defined educational goals, deal with the mastery of specific subject matter, and contribute to the musical growth of pupils in the class.

6: *planning for progress*

General music is the heart of the program of music in the public schools and the phase of music teaching most nearly in accord with the broad objectives of music education. It establishes no prerequisites and welcomes all pupils regardless of ability, training, or previous music experience.

The first objective, therefore, is to find a means of reaching every pupil in the class. In planning, the teacher bends every effort toward arousing and maintaining interest and providing some species of music enjoyment for every pupil. In doing so, the teacher accepts the basic assumptions that music is meaningless unless it satisfies through some variety of pleasurable response and that pupils can have no reason for learning about music unless the learning leads them to a higher level of appreciation.

The teacher also accepts the assumption that advancement to higher levels of response is impossible without advancement in knowledge and experience. Thus a second objective is one of providing a broad background of music experience, offering something for every level of taste, establishing a broad foundation for music learning, and opening many avenues to future musical growth. Closely allied to these objectives is the development of skills that make participation possible, permitting the pupil to come closer to the true spirit of music through singing, playing, reading, and hearing.

THE MANY-SIDED PROGRAM

As indicated in earlier chapters, some general music classes are centered on vocal music, devoting the major portion of class time to singing and the exploration of vocal literature. Others focus attention on recorded music, devoting class time principally to listening and to discussion and study based on music heard in class. It is probable that emphasis on vocal music is most common among general music classes of junior-high-school level and that emphasis on listening is most common at the high-school level.

It is natural that classes should be different from one another and that each class should follow its own course to study the phase of music that results in the greatest progress. The danger, however, is that in following such preferences the class will move toward a pattern of study that concentrates on one phase of music to the exclusion of the other, and it is improper to exclude either aspect of music from the general music class.

Best results are normally achieved by the general music class that combines singing and listening with many other music activities. These other activities are important to the success of the general music program. It is through them the pupil clarifies his musical understandings and gains insight to make music experience rewarding. Without them, singing and listening seem purposeless and unproductive, occupying class time without promoting noteworthy musical growth. It is therefore important that the general music program be many-sided, made up of singing, listening, and a number of other aspects of music activity.

The Rhythmic Aspect

Through rhythmic activity, the teacher encourages pupils to listen intently to music, hearing the sounds of rhythm in order to adjust movements to their tempo and patterns. This kind of listening, especially meaningful because it bears directly on the pupil's action and serves as a guide when his attention is focused and sustained, is far more significant than that which asks him to identify elements having little or no relationship to his personal actions.

It is true that there are limits beyond which some pupils may not be able to pass in developing facility in coördinated movement, and that there are wide individual differences in aptitude for certain kinds of dexterous physical movement. It is also true that most pupils have some degree of aptitude for coördinated movement, often including potentials undeveloped through other activities. Younger adolescents in particular derive concrete benefit from rhythmic music activity because of the new problems of leverage and control created by growing bones and muscles and because musical rhythm helps them guide and pattern their movements.

The objective of rhythmic activity is one of teaching pupils to feel and understand aspects of musical rhythm. Pupils can learn to feel tempo and meter, to respond to them, to recognize many different kinds of meter and rhythm, and to understand them through physical response. They can learn rhythm patterns and note values by duplicating what they hear, by creating new patterns, and by using physical movement in deciphering the symbols of music notation. In all cases, they learn rhythm not so much by thinking and talking about it as by participating in it and developing a feeling for it.

Rhythmic activities are any activities in which physical movement is patterned, following some understandable sequence, and in which the movement is adjusted to fit metrical rhythm. In the general music class, the metrical rhythm is normally provided by some sort of musical accompaniment, but it can come from any source of rhythmic sounds—a drum, the ticking of a clock, or the sounds of machinery. A natural starting point in the general music class is the action song, such as "Alouette" or "Johnny Schmoker," in which the class makes rhythmic gestures to reflect both the words and the rhythmic spirit of the song. These are "fun" songs. They are useful in the general music class as devices to create interest and enthusiasm, as introductions to rhythmic movement, and as means of teaching certain of the elements of music.

FOLK DANCING. Equally enjoyable but far more ambitious are the many varieties of dancing. Folk and square dances, dances from early periods of history such as the gavotte and minuet, Latin-American and other social dances have all been used by teachers of general music to good effect. They are fun to do, they are especially attractive to adolescents because of their social connotations, and they call for use of the entire body in large, free movements that must be rhythmically coördinated.

There are deterrents, however, to the use of dances in the general music class. First, there is the limitation of space. Dancing requires either a large music room in which desks and chairs can be pushed aside or that the class be moved to a gymnasium or other spacious area. Second, there is the limitation of time. Dancing can not normally be included in a music lesson as an activity that will occupy only a portion of the class time; it is more likely to occupy a complete lesson hour or several hours in succession. Many teachers are unwilling to take this much class time away from other music activities, suggesting instead that folk and square dance clubs be formed for the noon hour or after school. A third limitation has to do with the teacher's temperament, attitude, and ability. The teacher must know and be able to execute the dance steps, and this is a neglected area in the preparation of music teachers. More important, the teacher must be willing to demonstrate the steps with enthusiasm. This too is something for which many music teachers are not prepared either by temperament or training. For these reasons and because it would be improper to convert the general music class into an extended period of dance instruction, this kind of rhythmic activity is included infrequently by some teachers and not at all by others. It is useful, however, for the teachers to seek the coöperation of the physical education teacher and to have a dance repertoire to turn to when a particular dance is directly related to the music work at hand.

CONDUCTING. The most useful and directly pertinent rhythmic activities are musical in nature and closely related to the music being studied. These include the various kinds of muscular responses that interpret or accurately reflect musical rhythm. Conducting is a means of showing, feeling, and interpreting metrical rhythm. Pupils can learn the several basic conducting patterns without difficulty, differentiating in this way among two-, three-, and four-part meter. They can conduct as they learn and review song material, improving both their original reading of the notation and their subsequent interpretation of its spirit. They can also conduct certain of the music selections presented during listening lessons, learning about meter and tempo and developing feeling for the rhythmic vitality of the music. Student conductors may be selected to direct the singing of the class. Conducting of this type should not require that the pupil mechanically follow the tempo of an accompaniment played forcefully by the teacher at the piano. To the contrary, it should permit the conductor to experiment with variations in tempo, with rubato, and with starting and stopping the singing of the group, requiring and testing the altertness of both singers and accompanist. Although many pupils may be unable to gain the flexibility and assurance necessary to independence in conducting, the few who do acquire the skill challenge the attention of the class and the experience is likely to be a source of considerable enjoyment as well as music training.

MUSCULAR RESPONSE. Similarly musical in nature are the rhythmic activities that depend on accurate muscular response to note values. The most common devices require movement of the hands and arms to clap, tap a pencil, or to play rhythm patterns with two hands. General music classes often enjoy activities of this type, especially those that require coördination and challenge pupils' dexterity. These rhythmic activities are useful in both the singing and listening portions of a lesson. Pupils who tap or clap rhythm patterns while learning a song remember them longer than pupils who simply imitate the piano or the teacher's voice. The activity directs attention to the notes and to their rhythmic meaning, translates the notes into physical movement the pupil can sense clearly, and defines the rhythm with more accuracy than would be possible with the voice. In addition to serving as teaching devices, clapping and tapping may be used to provide rhythmic accompaniment for songs. This is the area in which two-handed drumming is most useful, permitting pupils to invent rhythm patterns appropriate to the music but of a level of difficulty to be both playable and challenging. Pupils can also clap, tap, or drum rhythm patterns from the listening lesson, learning the rhythm, discovering something to listen for in the music, and coming closer to complete understanding of it.

CHORAL SPEECH. Less obviously rhythmic in nature, but valuable in the general music class, are the rhythmic sounds produced with the organs of speech. Choral speaking is rhythmic in nature and helps pupils feel the rhythmic flow of song texts. It is valuable as a tool in teaching both unison and part-songs and in discovering the rhythmic characteristics of poetry and prose. To focus attention on the rhythm of songs being learned, the teacher can ask the class to recite the rhythm using neutral syllables such as "ta ta" or "bum bum." The class may recite rhythm only, using a speaking tone, or practice rhythm and pitch simultaneously by singing the song with a neutral but rhythmic syllable.

In the listening phase of the lesson pupils use neutral syllables in much the same way to learn rhythm patterns from the music they hear in class. Such music can be the source of many rhythm patterns through which pupils can learn the effects of dotted notes, rapid notes such as sixteenths and thirty-seconds, syncopation, and other rhythms they do not often encounter in vocal music. They gain personal experience with orchestral music by reciting the basic rhythm of the score—the final movement of Mozart's "Haffner" Symphony, for example, consists of: Dee dit dit dit dit; dit dit dit dit dit dit; deedleedleedleedl deedleedleedleedl deedleedleedleedl dit. The use of spoken rhythms also permits pupils to use their hands to conduct or clap the meter, producing rhythm and meter simultaneously.

RHYTHM INSTRUMENTS. Other possibilities for rhythmic activity involve the use of rhythm instruments. This too is an activity often thought of as the exclusive province of lower grades due to the popularity of the rhythm band. Although such instruments as jingle clogs and pat-a-cakes are hardly appropriate for use in the general music class, other percussion instruments may be well received, especially if identified by their correct orchestral names and if their orchestral use is discussed and demonstrated. Older pupils are particularly enthusiastic about Latin-American instruments such as bongo and conga drums, maracas, guiro, claves, and castanets. They are usually interested in experimenting with orchestral percussion devices such as the whip, sleigh bells, and tambourines as well as the orchestral snare drum and cymbals. For use in the general music class, the teacher acquires these instruments in the large, orchestral size rather than the smaller sizes used in the elementary school and rejects every instrument that does not produce satisfactory, musical tone. The first requisite is that percussion instruments look and sound like music instruments. The second is that pupils be taught to play them musically, the teacher demonstrating correct playing techniques and taking immediate steps to correct impressions that percussion instruments must be pounded in an excess of enthusiasm.

To introduce the instruments, it is usually desirable to present them one or two at a time rather than to distribute one to every member of the class. The latter procedure results in pandemonium and immediately destroys any possibility for producing artistic musical effects. By introducing instruments singly, the teacher arouses interest in their construction and use and demonstrates the manner in which each is played. Each instrument is then used singly in class and played by a number of pupils in turn to provide an accompaniment to a song or to duplicate rhythm patterns from the music of the listening lesson. After a number of instruments have been introduced from the same family, there may be opportunities to create a percussion ensemble to provide song or dance accompaniments or to join the orchestral forces presented through a recording.

The instruments can be used in conjunction with almost every other rhythmic activity to enhance the effect and define rhythms clearly. They help pupils feel tempo and meter and learn note values and rhythm patterns. They may be used to stimulate creative work in which pupils devise their own rhythms. They may be used to accompany any form of rhythmic movement, with action and fun songs, to stimulate interest in procedures that require clapping, tapping, or drumming, and in conjunction with choral speaking and the recitation of rhythms. In some respects, instruments are the basis for the most productive of the rhythmic activities; they define rhythms clearly and help pupils feel them through muscular response more accurately than through most other forms of physical movement.

The Aural Aspect

Ear training begins with the child's first music experiences in the elementary school and continues during his membership in music classes through the junior and senior high schools. It is one of the objectives of teachers who direct bands, orchestras, and glee clubs as well as those who teach general music and other classes. It is important in the general music class because of the purpose of the class and the type of pupil involved. The interested and able pupils who belong to performing groups have natural incentives to improve aural perception; the rehearsals and performances in which they participate provide repeated opportunities for practicing aural skills. Pupils come to the general music class, on the other hand, with neither interest nor skill. Unless the teacher provides for it through thoughtful planning they have little incentive to develop listening skill and little opportunity to practice.

ANALYZING THE AURAL SKILL. This skill, important to the appreciation of music, is much like the reading skill except that the sequence of steps is reversed. The pupil must first hear the musical sounds, being aware of all of them and perceiving each one clearly. He must then be able to form a mental image of the sound, singing it inwardly or producing it in his imagination. Simultaneously, he associates it with concepts already established in his listening repertoire, noting whether he has heard it before or noting the respects in which it differs from the patterns of tone he knows. Finally, he visualizes a symbol for the sound, also from his repertoire, providing something concrete the mind can remember and manipulate.

As pointed out in the chapter dealing with listening, this process is similar to that followed by the listener when reading a book or listening to speech. He consciously directs careful and sustained attention to the music, recognizes each pattern of sound, follows the tonal patterns as they succeed each other in time, retains in his memory what has passed, imagines what has not yet been heard, and exercises intellectual powers to interpret the pattern created by the succession of musical sounds. This is the listening skill. It requires aural discrimination, knowledge of music, and the ability to think in the musical language. It is an alert and attentive process far different from passive hearing and is developed through intensive study and practice.

IMAGING SOUNDS. A first step in developing the pupil's ability to hear is one of training him to remember musical sounds and to "image" them in his mind. To demonstrate the nature of this sort of imagery the teacher might begin by asking pupils to imagine other sensations. Pupils can imagine visual sensations by closing their eyes and seeing inwardly a scene, building, or place they all know. They can feel tactile sensations by closing their eyes and imagining that they are holding a peach, a golf ball, or a quantity of sand. They can try to imagine the gustatory sensation of drinking chocolate milk or orange juice or the olfactory sensation of sniffing anything from gardenias to frying onions.

The next step is to ask pupils to close their eyes and imagine that they are hearing a familiar song. As an experiment in imaging songs, the teacher might give the starting pitch for a well-known song such as "America," conduct the meter as the class sings the song mentally and without accompaniment, occasionally signaling the class to sing one pitch aloud. If the teacher's directions are clear and the class focuses its attention on the song, the pupils will all sing the same pitch at the same time.

The goal of these procedures is one of training pupils to be attentive to the music they hear, to remember patterns of pitch and rhythm after only one or two hearings, to image the sounds mentally and produce them vocally. The skill can be practiced and tested constantly during the teaching of songs and in the course of listening activities by asking pupils to sing phrases and rhythms after only one hearing, the pupils singing the themes as part of this learning procedure rather than as exercises in ear training or solfège.

IDENTIFYING SOUNDS. Another approach to aural skill is that of directing pupils' attention to specific elements of the music they hear, asking questions that encourage them to exercise aural discrimination. For beginning classes with little knowledge the questions deal with the simplest and most obvious factors—the difference between high and low pitch, loud and soft tone, fast and slow tempo, sustained or percussive effects, and differences in tone quality among instruments or voices. Classes with more knowledge identify ascending and descending scale passages, melodic patterns that progress by step or by leap, phrase endings, and the repetition or recurrence of phrases or other tonal patterns. More advanced classes identify chord colors, cadence harmonies, specific intervals, subtle differences in tone quality or the effects of orchestration, and other more advanced music factors that require both knowledge and acute perception. In this way, ear training becomes a part of almost every music activity. It is an essential part of the process of teaching songs and can be incorporated into listening and rhythmic activities. It can be an incidental activity that develops aural skill gradually without interrupting other class work and without becoming a matter of tedious drill.

Of further benefit to the development of aural discrimination are knowledge and experience. To perceive, identify, understand, and remember the sounds of music, the pupil must have a repertoire of music knowledge from which to select labels for the sounds he hears. This is the area of music theory, but it is applied theory in that it is used by the pupil as he thinks about music. Musical sounds are intelligible only as they can be related to existing knowledge in the same way that the sounds of a foreign language have meaning only as they refer to vocabulary already familiar to the hearer. Thus there is ample reason for the teacher to think of ear training in terms of the pupil's knowledge of music theory, providing opportunities for him to hear and identify what he knows and for new experiences to increase his vocabulary of music knowledge.

PLAYING "BY EAR." With a basic knowledge of some of the rudiments of music structure, the pupil is better equipped not only to hear music, but to produce music "by ear" as well. This too is of value in the general music class for the practice it gives in applying aural skill. Pupils should be encouraged to try to do things by ear and given many opportunities to improve through practice. They can improvise bass and other harmony parts to songs, improvise choral backgrounds composed of simple harmonies, and make up their own harmonizations for cadences and endings of songs they know. If instruments are available, they can learn to play the autoharp by ear, feeling the need for chord changes rather than reading chord names from music, and can practice playing melodies by ear using recorders, song bells, or the piano. During listening lessons they can analyze selected harmonic passages by ear.

APPLYING AURAL SKILL. The final step is one of applying the knowledge gained through aural perception. After the pupil has learned to distinguish elements of melody, rhythm, harmony, and form he is encouraged to use his knowledge in every phase of music activity. He can use it in music reading, learning to associate items in his aural repertoire with the symbols of notation and developing ability to hear sounds inwardly as he reads the symbols. During listening, he can identify the various tonal patterns he hears and search for reasons for their presence in the music. The class can discuss the effect of harmonies, rhythms, and melodic configurations upon the mood of the music or the effect it creates for the listener. Pupils can note the descriptive qualities of tonal patterns and the degree to which each is appropriate in specific programmatic works. The class can use aural skills in rhythmic activities, listening closely to rhythm patterns to understand, follow, and duplicate them. They may be able to use powers of imaging sounds in creative work, mentally conceiving tonal patterns before singing, playing, or writing them. Most important, they are encouraged to utilize aural perception in gaining a clearer understanding of the expressive and aesthetic qualities of music. This is the importance of ear training. It is meaningless if it is treated as an abstract skill valuable only for intellectual discipline, but it is of immediate and practical value if it contribues to the enjoyment and appreciation of music.

The Theoretical Aspect

Music theory deals with music itself and with its nature. In the general music class especially, it should not be a series of exercises in intellectual discipline or in learning rules about music. Music theory is significant in the general music class only as it aids the listener, helping him enjoy, understand, and appreciate worthy music. It is meaningful only as it is applied, helping the listener to perceive tonal patterns and combinations, to understand them and to respond to them in an intelligent way. In planning work in the area of music theory, the teacher considers the needs of pupils, being guided by a knowledge of what the pupil needs immediately and what will be of use to him in the future.

This is not to imply that music theory in the general music class should avoid investigation of the technical aspects of music. The teacher accepts the fact that pupils are able to learn music theory and that they must learn in order to become intelligent, appreciative listeners. Musicianship requires knowledge, and feeling is more acute when it is based on understanding. One learns to listen by hearing a great deal of music, by striving constantly to focus attention upon the music being heard, and by accumulating an ever-increasing store of knowledge about the nature and variety of musical sounds. It is the latter that makes music intelligible; it is knowledge that directs the focus of attention and permits the listener to sustain perceptive attention while hearing large quantities of music.

It is not music theory that discourages pupil interest, but the manner of teaching it. If it is taught in the general music class from the listener's point of view and functionally applied to other areas of study, it is a source of exciting music discoveries. Music theory can be applied to singing activities, listening activities, rhythmic activities, the study of music literature and history—to every phase of the work in general music. It is highly desirable that the teacher of general music think of music theory in these terms, for the class that teaches music theory teaches music appreciation also.

Music theory has a two-fold objective in that it is concerned both with the intellect and with feelings, striving to increase the pupil's sensitivities in both areas. Through the increase in these powers it builds discriminating tastes. It accepts the necessity for understanding the structure of music and the reasons for music's expressive effects. It increases the pupil's ability to analyze both aurally and visually and tends to improve reading and performing skills. It adjusts its objectives and procedures to pupil needs and avoids any tendency to give undue emphasis to rules not immediately applicable to the listening experience.

Music theory is sometimes thought of as the mathematical aspect of music. The facts of key and meter, scale and chord structure, music form and notation must be learned by the person who wishes to understand music. But this is only a portion of the subject matter of music theory significant to the pupil in the general music class. Ear training is part of music theory and is closely related to the acquisition of knowledge about music structure. Solfège, the skill of reading music for the voice, is music theory and depends on both knowledge and aural ability. Keyboard harmony and the ability to play "by ear" are applications of music theory and are properly included in its study. Laws of science are the foundation for many of the rules of music and serve to explain its effects. Creative work is the application of theoretical knowledge. In short, almost every aspect of music has theoretical components and may rightly be included in the study of music theory.

Although the chief objective of instruction in music theory is a broad one related to music appreciation, the immediate goals of daily teaching have to do with specific knowledge and are selected to guide the planning of each lesson. Music theory requires the exercise of ear, eye, and mind, and it is the daily task of the teacher to develop these faculties both separately and together. Pupils gain new knowledge of some element of music from every class meeting—the feeling of two-quarter meter, the sound of a minor triad, the knowledge of a perfect fifth, the duration of a dotted quarter note, the effect of a plagal cadence, or some other concrete knowledge of music structure. In each lesson, they learn the correct name of the element studied, learn to hear and feel it in music, and develop the ability to recognize and identify it immediately.

This knowledge is applied in each activity of the class, the attention of the pupils being directed to the structural elements of the music they meet while singing, listening, or playing instruments. They are also encouraged to apply their knowledge by referring to it in class discussion, using correct terminology, and in any reading they may do by recognizing and understanding the terms learned in class. The teacher helps pupils apply their knowledge in music reading, the knowledge gained through music theory aiding them in imaging sounds as they see notation. The teacher's goal is to plan each lesson to achieve all these ends, choosing a fact to be learned, choosing music for singing, listening, and playing in which it can be studied initially and observed in a variety of settings, devising class procedures that help pupils hear, feel, and understand it.

In planning lessons, the teacher thinks in terms of the activities that foster learning. First, there is aural analysis. During both singing and listening, pupils are asked to listen for specific intervals, scale lines, rhythm patterns, chord colors, and so forth, responding in some suitable way when they recognize the item they are studying. The goal of listening may be to recognize elements as simple as the leap of an octave in a melodic line or as complex as a rondo form in symphonic music.

Second, there is visual analysis. Pupils are given every opportunity to read the symbols for tone and rhythm patterns they learn, analyzing and reading the new songs, following and singing excerpts from listening lessons notated on the board, and playing instruments. On rare occasions there may be opportunities for transposition when songs are beyond the range of voices in the class or in awkward keys for the instruments at hand.

Third, there is performing activity that permits the pupil to experience what he learns through direct, personal contact with music. The music that contains the element to be studied is performed through singing and the use of keyboard and other instruments. Excerpts from the listening lesson are sung, and excerpts from the song lesson are heard and played. In advanced classes where pupils do outside work in melody writing, harmonization, or composition, their work is performed in class. The performing activity is especially important; it is the only way for pupils to experience what they learn in music theory and it is the most productive application of their knowledge.

Other activities include writing original music, dictation, and outside assignments. These are not especially appropriate for the general music class but are used by the teacher to serve a special purpose. Each activity is preceded, accompanied, or followed by suitable explanation, illustration, and discussion through which the teacher gives meaning and purpose to the activity.

The basic principle of music theory for pupils in general music is that it must be functional, directly related to other music work and applied to every possible phase of class activity. Pupils sing and play chords and harmonic progressions, using them to accompany songs vocally and using the keyboard or the autoharp when possible. They apply the lessons learned about melodic structure, intervals, and scales in reading music and in understanding what they hear. They make similar use of knowledge concerning rhythm, music form, and every other aspect of music theory, referring to it constantly to develop the musicianship that refines perception and response.

Conversely, both teacher and pupils apply musicianship to the study of music theory. Excerpts and exercises used in class should be played or sung with artistic finesse. If original work is done by pupils, it is regarded as an opportunity for creative expression, carefully done and respectfully performed. Even exercises in solfège, if they must be done, should be treated as musical examples rather than as routine exercises. This requires that the work in music theory be based on music of artistic beauty and that the teacher avoid dull, unmusical exercises contrived to illustrate a point with little regard for musical effect. If the study of music theory is based on music selected for singing and listening activities, this problem will rarely arise. Because there is so much music available from which to choose, and because each selection normally contains enough material for numerous lessons devoted to theory, there is no need for the teacher to accept unworthy material.

PLANNING FOR THE GENERAL MUSIC CLASS

Careful planning is one of the teacher's most important responsibilities. No amount of music knowledge and background, performing ability, enthusiasm, or personal magnetism is an effective substitute. It is planning, or the lack of it, that most frequently determines the extent of a teacher's success. This is especially true where beginning teachers are concerned and for those of experience who find themselves in new positions. For the beginning teacher, careful planning compensates to some degree for lack of experience, helping initial class meetings progress smoothly until the teacher becomes acquainted with pupils and the school environment.

Preliminary Considerations

CORRELATION. A broad area of general planning has to do with the correlation of music with other studies discussed briefly in Chapter 3. All music grows out of a cultural and social environment and is influenced by political movements, social movements, advances in scientific and other knowledge. If the music itself is not directly related to any stylistic, social, or political movement, the composer and his attitudes can not help but be shaped by environmental influences that are then reflected in his music.

The teacher is aware of these relationships and in planning searches for opportunities to make them clear to pupils. In the general music class especially, this information does much to make music interesting and to give it living vitality even though it comes from what is in the pupil's point of view the dead past. The teacher seeks ways to show pupils the manner in which each music selection grew out of social needs or was shaped by them, was influenced by political events, was affected by manners, customs, and dress, or is similar in style and general character to the work of other creative artists of the same historical period.

A more common concept of correlation refers to the practice of relating music study to other subjects in the school curriculum through active coöperation with other teachers. Pertinent social and political influences may be discovered in the topics discussed in history classes. Relationships to literature may be identified through the work of English classes. Physics and mathematics classes may deal with subjects pertinent to the acoustics of music or the mathematical principles that govern the function of music instruments. Coöperation is possible with foreign language classes, physical education classes, and other curricular areas, each area of correlation offering its own advantages to the study of music.

A first step toward correlation is the regular interchange of ideas between music teachers and those in other subject fields. Through either scheduled meetings or informal conversation the music teacher gathers information about the work of other classes and their plans for future scheduling of topics or work units. If the other teachers have had no previous opportunity to utilize music in their work, the music teacher takes the initiative by volunteering to include related materials in the work of the general music class, furnishing any needed information about the music to the other teachers as background for their class discussions. Once the pattern of coöperation is established, the music teacher selects materials or schedules topics to coincide with related work in other classes. Teachers of other subjects reciprocate by providing time for discussion of the topics that apply to the work in music.

Ideally, coöperation that begins with the interchange of ideas among teachers develops into an all-embracing unit of work involving the participation of many members of the school staff. In such a program all classes center their work around a common theme selected and planned by a committee or jointly by all the teachers concerned. Each teacher plans class work in terms of the topic and schedule selected by the planning committee. The work of all classes culminates in a major activity such as an exhibit, assembly program, or play presented for parents and the community at large. Although correlation is possible on this ambitious scale, it is improbable that the teacher of music will encounter it frequently due to limitations imposed by time and the necessity for covering required materials in classes of an academic nature.

On a smaller scale, the teacher of general music enlists the coöperation of other teachers in arranging related work on specific topics during convenient and shorter periods. Sixteenth century English music might be planned for the period during which another teacher is presenting a Shakespearean play, or the physics teachers might present the laws of vibrating strings at the same time the music teacher is presenting orchestral instruments. Even if there is no direct relationship between the music taught and the specific materials of the other class it is usually possible for the music teacher to select materials related in some general way to the work in another subject. This kind of correlation is practical and convenient, stimulating interest and effective learning in both classes without interrupting the work of either. In the event it is impossible for other teachers to take part in a correlated approach to subject matter, it is still possible and desirable for the teacher of general music to follow the principles of correlation in planning music work, utilizing the subject matter of history, geography, literature, and other subjects in class discussion when it aids music learning.

Although it is desirable to correlate the work in general music with the work of other school departments, there are negative factors to which the music teacher should be sensitive. It is essential that material presented in the general music class be of high caliber and that inferior music be rejected regardless of its pertinence to the work in other subjects. It is well for the music teacher to be wary of projects not musical in nature. A correlated program dealing with South America, for example, might prompt pupils to construct Latin-American percussion instruments. This is a worthwhile activity and one likely to stimulate interest, but it is ill-advised if it converts general music classes into periods devoted to carpentry and painting. Finally, there is the factor of time. Correlation is a time-consuming process. It requires periods of discussion for the interchange of ideas, meetings devoted to the broader aspects of planning, and extra hours of planning for individual lessons. It requires that portions of class time usually devoted to music instruction be freed for presentation of related but non-musical information. If the process of correlation introduces too many of these factors and permits them to grow beyond reasonable proportions it defeats its purpose. Regardless of the obvious benefits of the correlated approach, it is not desirable unless it improves the effectiveness of teaching and leads to increased musical growth.

UNIT PLANNING. Closely related to the correlated approach is the principle of the unit of study discussed briefly in Chapter 5. The unit plan of teaching is especially desirable in the general music class in that it ties a series of lessons together. This is particularly important where scheduling arrangements permit general music classes to meet only once each week. Under such a schedule it is difficult to maintain the thread of continuity through a series of lessons. If the unit plan is used, the central topic provides continuity for several weeks, a month, or even an entire term. Even if the unit plan encompasses a shorter span of time, the unit scheme and the manner of thinking it implies may be beneficial, improving the structure of single lessons and increasing their potentials for stimulating interest and learning.

UNITS FOR YOUNG LISTENERS. Subjects suitable for use as unit topics are numerous, but special consideration is merited by those likely to appeal to young listeners. *Music Instruments by Sight and Sound* is a topic of general interest to adolescent pupils. It permits members of the class to demonstrate instruments of their own and permits the teacher to bring instruments to class for demonstration and display. This procedure captures the attention of pupils who are intrigued by the instruments and the opportunity to examine them closely, to handle them, and even to experiment with playing some that are easier to manipulate. There are many possibilities for selecting music that illustrates the tone of each instrument and its characteristic passages, as well as for introducing such related subjects as the acoustical principles of music instruments, the related ranges and tone qualities of human voices, the music effects created by composers of different historical periods through various instrumental combinations, and the use of instruments to represent characters and portray moods in descriptive music.

A closely related topic is *Music and the Science of Sound.* Adolescent pupils, boys in particular, tend to be interested in the mechanical and scientific aspects of the world about them. Here, too, are many opportunities for the teacher to generate interest in music and to extend interest in the scientific aspects of sound to the examination of many different facets of music. The acoustical properties of instruments is an obviously related subject, but the development of harmony and various styles of music composition are subjects equally appropriate.

In the popular vein, resourceful teachers build interesting units upon questions such as *Where Do Tunes Come From?* There are many examples of "popular" songs derived from "classical" music, of folk songs woven into major orchestral and choral works, and of worthy themes used again and again by composers of different historical periods. In addition, there are examples of radio and television theme music derived from standard symphonic literature. In a unit of this type, the opportunity to play tune detective may intrigue certain classes. In the course of the unit, pupils can learn much about music literature. They compare the use of music materials by different composers, discuss the degree to which themes are appropriate to the words of popular songs and to the spirit of television shows for which they are used, and learn about the language of music through examining the changes in form, harmony, rhythm, and melodic pattern required when music is adapted for different uses.

POPULAR MUSIC THROUGH THE AGES is a topic similarly useful to the teacher who wishes to begin with music pupils know and enjoy. Starting with popular songs of the day, it can progress to music from the current stage, music of the more enduring operettas, Viennese waltzes, selections from the operatic repertoire, dance music of the seventeenth and eighteenth centuries, and so on to limits determined only by teacher ingenuity and class interest. It leads to discussion of the factors that make music popular and memorable, the short life span of some popular music, and the characteristics of art music.

For classes with minimum background, a unit such as *Rhythm in Music* permits the teacher to utilize pupils' first and most natural music response. It leads to use of the exotic percussion instruments such as bongo drums, maracas, and claves. It can include music of almost any type, including popular and Latin-American dance music, marches played by military band, the symphonies of Mozart, the vitally rhythmic works of Stravinsky, even choral music in markedly rhythmic style. It provides ample opportunity for physical response to music through rhythmic activity and can be used to motivate learning of music notation.

Equally rhythmic in its materials and activities would be a unit such as *Music for Dancing.* This unit also could begin with popular music, progressing through folk dancing to dance music of other ages, to ballet music, and to the older dance forms included in orchestral suites. As rhythmic activity, it could include folk dancing and the use of percussion instruments to provide dance rhythms. It leads to a survey of music history and the many dance forms found in orchestral music of each epoch as well as to discussion of the social and other environmental factors that influenced the development of the dance and its music. Both of these units, because they examine the rhythmic element that is close to the heart of music, and because they offer a wealth of materials to which pupils respond easily, can be of great service to the teacher in developing class interest.

Also appropriate for classes of comparatively little music background are units based upon music's power to call forth imaginative or associational response. A central theme such as *Music Tells a Story* paves the way for lessons devoted to works that express literary ideas, either by following the narrative closely and attempting to depict specific characters and events or by turning away from the narrative to present only its general mood. In music of this type, there are possibilities for correlation with the study of literature and for allusion in general music to literary works not examined in any other class. There are opportunities for discussing the moods portrayed by music and the techniques of composition and orchestration used to create these moods. The study can delve into the language of music, examining factors as rudimentary as the differences between major and minor modes or as advanced as the techniques of the twelve-tone system. Music examples can be selected from almost any period in music history and in many performing media.

Similarly, such units as *Pictures in Music* can include descriptive and programmatic music, surveying the entire range of music history. Opportunities for correlation exist not only between music and literature, but between music and painting, sculpture, and architecture as well. There are, for example, interesting possibilities for comparing two paintings dissimilar in style with two music examples that exhibit the same stylistic differences. In all units of this type, there is strong appeal to pupils' imaginative powers.

STUDY UNITS. For more advanced classes, units dealing with music form, with themes, scales and intervals, or with harmony and its effect upon music style can be planned in a manner appropriate to the class level of knowledge and interest. Units including music of specific nations, regions, or peoples provide for close correlation with the work of social studies and other classes. Units can be adjusted to many levels of class ability, age, and grade, exploring the technical aspects of music or avoiding technical difficulties to concentrate on pupil interest and response. The class activities included in unit planning may be restricted to listening only or may be expanded to include singing, rhythmic activities, creative work, ear training, and playing instruments.

One difficulty is that the unit plan offers so many opportunities for engaging pupil interest through correlations and varied activities that the teacher may lose sight of the basic purpose of the unit. The unit that leads to constructing home-made instruments, drawing pictures, making costumes, presenting oral reports about foreign countries, and other such extra-musical activities—and drastically reduces the time devoted to music to make them possible—becomes something other than a music unit and is not appropriate to the general music class.

COÖPERATIVE PLANNING. In choosing a unit topic there is reason for heeding pupil interests and seeking pupil opinions in coöperative planning. Although the teacher is qualified by training and experience to select topics appropriate for each class, the variety of pupil attitudes is such that each class may require a different approach that can not be selected until pupil interests have been explored. The teacher who refuses the benefits of coöperative planning and relies solely on personal judgment may be influenced by personal tastes and follow a course directed by his own interest rather than by class needs. Not only is it helpful to the teacher to be aware of pupil interests, but it is the nature of the adolescent pupil to desire participation in planning class work.

This is not to imply that pupils should direct the work of the class. It is the teacher's role to direct; pupils have neither the knowledge nor the judgment to insure their own music progress. Instead, the teacher explores class interests through discussions during initial class meetings, plans class activities to demonstrate the need for or arouse interest in music progress, and introduces materials to stimulate curiosity about various aspects of music literature. In doing so, the teacher guides the class to questions that can be answered through a unit of music work. The procedure demands imagination, diplomacy, and skill in directing discussion. It requires that the class first develop favorable attitudes toward music and a high regard for the ability and sincerity of the teacher.

It may not be practical to plan coöperatively in some classes until the teacher has been able to win class support through many class meetings, although it is possible that the discussion of music's meaning and purpose during the first meeting will permit the coöperative selection of the first unit of music work. It is the teacher's role to guide the class and to be prepared to suggest areas of interesting and rewarding unit study, preparing these suggestions in advance as the first step in planning listening activities.

VISUAL AIDS. Another preliminary consideration has to do with the use of visual aids, particularly desirable for pupils who have not developed skill in listening. Because music is an aural art and most pupils do not come to the music class with well-developed powers of aural perception, many general music classes are virtually immune to the materials they are expected to absorb. As an aid to hearing, or as a temporary substitute for it, the teacher turns to visual materials to hold attention and interest until pupils develop aural sensitivity. Visual aids can be of almost any variety—music instruments, pictures, slides, filmstrips, sound films, and so forth. It is particularly useful to bring to the classroom the music instruments to be discussed or heard through recordings, and to invite a performer to demonstrate the instrument concerned. Too often, the sounds heard by pupils as they listen to recordings are completely divorced from the instruments themselves and have little meaning until the pupils can associate them with visual impressions of the instruments and their players. Similarly, music performed by either choral or instrumental groups makes deeper impressions when it is heard in conjunction with a motion-picture film. Operatic selections, for example, may be of great interest to pupils if presented through the medium of the sound film.

The teacher surveys available visual aids as a preliminary step in planning, examining the resources of school libraries and visual aids departments, community libraries, and other sources. Local resources may be sufficient to warrant planning an entire unit in terms of the visual aids available. Here, too, there are negative factors. A significant amount of extra time is required to survey materials, to arrange for the use of projectors, screens, and other equipment, and to assemble and operate them in the classroom. Further, the teacher may find that visual aids, especially films and filmstrips, are not designed to focus attention on the specific items to be taught and that time can be used more efficiently if the teacher plans class activities in terms of the immediate teaching objective.

OTHER CONSIDERATIONS. Further preliminary considerations have to do with the broader aspects of pupil response. Adolescent characteristics and interests, class maturity, and background determine the general level and pattern of lessons being planned. The presence or absence of changing voices and the level of vocal skill determine the type of singing activity to be planned. Pupil tastes and levels of response influence the materials and procedures of the listening lesson.

In practice, there are so many variables in the teaching equation that no one teacher follows precisely the practices found successful by any other. Each community, each school environment, and each classroom exerts its own influence on class procedure. Each group of pupils is different from every other. Every teacher has his own characteristics of temperament, personality, attitudes, knowledge, and skill. The factors pertinent to the relationships between one teacher and one class vary from day to day or even from hour to hour. As a result, each teaching situation is unique and the teacher plans each lesson with all possible consideration for the multitude of variables that influence class reaction. Once the teacher has analyzed the general factors peculiar to his own situation, he is ready to plan the format of individual lessons to achieve best results.

The Planning Process

SELECTING GOALS. The first step in planning a lesson requires that the teacher define the material to be covered and the learning to be achieved. One area of definition is that of selecting specific goals for each lesson. The larger objectives of music education, those that deal with appreciation, enjoyment, and attitude, guide the teacher's work in a general way; the goals useful in the day-to-day work of the classroom deal with specific elements of music knowledge and define results which can be achieved during one class meeting. Appropiate goals include specific learnings such as feeling the effect of a dotted quarter note, learning to distinguish between two-part and three-part meter, learning to hear and sing the interval of a major third, or learning to recognize major and minor modes.

In a series of lessons with goals such as these, the teacher is aware of the sequence of learnings, basing each new goal upon the knowledge acquired in preceding lessons. The goals for each lesson are related to the central theme of the unit, to the other subjects with which music is being correlated, and to any other factor that bears on the work in music. This restricts the choice of objectives to some extent, requiring that the teacher refrain from attempting to teach material pupils are not ready to understand or material not pertinent to the larger subject at hand, but even with these restrictions the teacher has a great deal of latitude in selecting the goals for each lesson.

SELECTING MATERIALS. As the teacher selects the music knowledge to be taught, he simultaneously considers means of demonstrating it through song and listening materials. For this phase of planning it is desirable that the teacher have a broad knowledge of music literature and that school resources include a number of song books and a comprehensive library of recordings. The teacher searches through his recollections of music he has heard, analyzed, or performed, tentatively choosing those that contain the music element he wishes to teach, then examining song books and recordings to see whether the music is available for presentation to the class. As an alternative, the teacher may begin by surveying available song and listening materials, tentatively choosing selections that contain the music element to be taught and then examining each selection to determine its suitability for the lesson. In doing so, the teacher decides whether each selection is related to the central theme of the unit, whether it is appropriate to the interests of the class, and whether it is suitable to pupils' levels of response and appreciation.

Where song materials are concerned, the teacher considers pupils' vocal abilities, the presence of changing voices, and the variety of voice classifications in the group. He may find it necessary to select either unison or part-songs and may wish to select songs that contribute to the development of singing or reading ability. Song texts must be considered because of their relation to unit topics or their significance to adolescent pupils. Finally, the song literature selected should be worthwhile for its musical qualities, should contribute to pupils' expanding acquaintance with music literature, and should stimulate the desire to participate. Similar criteria are applied to listening materials. In terms of future plans for class work and pupils' past experience, do the music works selected provide a variety of experience, do they expand pupils' listening repertoire, and do they encourage pupils to be perceptive and to develop discriminating tastes?

ANALYZING THE MUSIC. A third aspect of this first phase of planning requires careful analysis of the music selected. Each selection is examined carefully to determine whether it contains the music knowledge to be taught and whether this element of the music is sufficiently clear to be readily apparent to the class. It should lend itself to aural and visual analysis and to some manner of performance. It should be appropriate for use in some teaching device or classroom procedure. For this aspect of planning, *it is essential that the teacher use the score.* Songs are played and sung by the teacher and analyzed both aurally and from the score. Recorded music is played so the teacher may judge its probable impression upon the class, to estimate pupil reaction, and to note whether pupils are likely to hear the element they are to learn about. The teacher listens with score in hand and uses the score as a basis for analysis of the music. In the process of examining both song and listening materials, the teacher times each selection in order to know how much class time will be occupied by the music and how much will remain for other work, as well as to judge whether the music is commensurate with pupil attention spans.

SELECTING TEACHING DEVICES. The next stage of planning requires selection of teaching devices or activities. We know it is not usually sufficient simply to present music knowledge to pupils through lecture or explanation. To learn effectively and to understand what they learn, pupils must make the new knowledge part of themselves by performing it or by participating in it in some other way. The teacher searches for a teaching device or class activity that permits pupils to learn through personal contact with the music and with the element to be learned. Devices must be appropriate to the music selected and to the interests and nature of the pupils. They emphasize the element being taught and permit pupils to experience it in a meaningful and memorable way.

BEGINNING THE LESSON. The critical period includes the few minutes during which pupils enter the room, take their seats, and look to the teacher to begin the work of the lesson. If the teacher calls the roll, makes announcements, and distributes materials, pupils divert their attention to other things until the teacher is ready to call them back to the work at hand. If the teacher takes advantage of the first few minutes, by doing something to arouse curiosity related to the work of the lesson, the lesson will begin and progress smoothly. For this reason the teacher gives careful thought to the possibilities for showing an object of interest, playing a unique music selection, asking a stimulating question, or in some other way challenging pupils as soon as they are in the room. This, too, is a teaching device and must be calculated in terms of pupil interests, unit topics, music materials, lesson goals, and other such factors.

For a lesson dealing with music instruments, a display of several instruments arranged on a table at the front of the room might be suitable. For a lesson dealing with the science of sound a similar display of equipment from the physics laboratory is indicated. If the lesson is about keyboard instruments the classroom piano might be turned to face the class with front panels removed to expose the strings and hammer mechanism, or the teacher might begin dismantling the piano, without comment, as soon as the class is in the room. For lessons devoted to descriptive or programmatic music a large picture placed on an easel or projected on a screen might capture the attention of the class, or the teacher might begin with a dramatic reading of the story or poem on which the music is based. For other lessons, the teacher might simply write a provocative statement or question on the board, ask a stimulating question of the class, begin playing the piano or a recording without comment, or use unusual articles as "props" to arouse curiosity. In short, it is entirely proper and quite desirable that the teacher display showmanship in utilizing the dramatic potentials of music materials. Although it is improbable that the teacher will be able to devise a dramatic opening for every lesson, a procedure that arouses immediate curiosity provides an auspicious beginning.

INTRODUCING THE MUSIC. In a similar manner, the teacher provides motivation for listening. A field trip to a public concert or school band rehearsal, for example, might be suitable motivation for an entire unit of work, but each music selection presented during the unit might benefit from further motivation as it is presented in class.

The teacher displays articles of interest related to the music or invites pupils to bring related instruments, souvenirs, or other objects for display and discussion. Pictures, stories, and poems are presented before the music is heard, including motion picture films, filmstrips, and slides. The teacher asks questions of the class to promote discussion of the music or factors related to it, or tells an interesting anecdote about the music, its composer, or some pertinent personal experience.

In a more musical vein, the teacher arouses interest in a particular music selection by presenting certain of its musical materials before the selection is heard in its entirety. Themes notated on the board and sung or examined by the class become familiar and are listened for as the music is heard, providing satisfaction as they are recognized. Other elements of the music such as rhythm patterns, harmonic progressions, forms, and orchestration characteristics are examined and discussed to stimulate curiosity about the music and make it seem familiar at first hearing.

SUSTAINING ATTENTION. Due to the short attention span of young listeners and to the necessity for hearing the continuity of musical patterns, the teacher strives to sustain interest throughout the entire duration of music heard in class. Two provisions are necessary: that all possible distractions be eliminated, and that pupils be given something to listen for as the music progresses.

A common distraction results from the tendency of some teachers to talk during the playing of recordings. If the teacher is vitally interested in the music being presented and wants to make certain that pupils hear elements important to the lesson, it is easy to fall into the habit of pointing them out and making explanatory comments as the music progresses. This is a practice to be avoided; pupils can not be expected to follow the music and the teacher's comments simultaneously. The teacher adopts the attitude of quiet attention expected of pupils, refrains from walking about the room or shuffling books or papers, perhaps even retiring to the rear of the room or out of the pupils' line of vision.

Other aural distractions may be reduced by lowering windows and closing doors. Some teachers eliminate visual distractions by asking pupils to listen with eyes closed. The exception to these rules is the case in which the teacher asks the pupils to follow something written on the board—lists of words, notes concerning sequences of themes, forms, characters, or incidents, or the themes themselves—to make notes at their seats as they listen, or to make some physical response to the music.

PLANNING THE ACTIVITY SEQUENCE. A final step in planning requires that the teacher visualize the sequence of activities and adjust it as necessary to maintain class interest and achieve effective learning. In many lessons there will be singing, listening, rhythmic activity, discussion, and other types of class activity. These are interspersed so there is variety in the lesson, so periods of quiet listening are brief and relieved by active participation, and so the sequence of activities leads to the acquisition of knowledge. Many lessons include an opening activity, a series of varied activities to explore, experience, and define the music element being studied, and a culminating activity in which the new knowledge is applied or experienced. In some respects, the lesson is similar to a concert program, the teacher presenting music to an audience of pupils and being sensitive to the sequence of events in the same way a conductor is sensitive to the sequence of works when planning a concert program. Similar factors of interest, enjoyment, and appreciation are involved. The teacher who regards a class as an audience to be captured is more successful than one who regards a class as a captive audience.

PRINCIPLES OF PLANNING. When planning lessons in this way it is well to keep five principles in mind.

1. The "approach" to each lesson should be a device to capture attention and arouse curiosity at the beginning of the lesson.
2. The lesson should provide many opportunities for pupil "participation" in the work of the class and in the music itself, permitting pupils to feel direct, personal contact with the music, and taking full advantage

of the adolescent's natural interest in procedures of an active nature.

3. The lesson should be conceived in terms of class "activity" in which pupils learn about music by performing it, talking about it, or in some other way acquiring knowledge and understanding actively.
4. The lesson should include "variety" to maintain interest, to provide for limitations of pupil attention span, and to offer a number of different experiences leading to understanding of the music.
5. The teacher should consider the "tempo" of the lesson as it is related to the amount of time consumed by each activity, the speed with which pupils absorb ideas, and the efficiency with which the teacher utilizes allotted class time.

The teacher calculates pupil reaction to each class activity and each music selection. He visualizes the progress of the lesson in terms of the sequence of activities and the probable responses of the pupils, foreseeing what is likely to occur and planning for each eventuality in such a way that the class is led to the desired response. To do so, the teacher draws on every resource of knowledge and experience pertaining to pupils, their natures and interests, music and its characteristics, and the manner in which music affects the listener. This is the area of planning in which the teacher exercises judgment and creative imagination to pre-determine the success and effectiveness of each lesson.

THE WRITTEN PLAN. As a record of the planning and as a guide for the teacher during the lesson, it is necessary to prepare written lesson plans. They may be in either detailed or skeleton form, depending upon whether the teacher wishes to preserve them for future reference and whether the teacher has sufficient experience to present effective lessons with only a few terse notes as reference.

Many teachers would like to have time to write detailed lesson descriptions several pages in length, including observations concerning the effectiveness of the lesson as a whole and its various aspects and activities. A plan of this sort is too detailed to be practical for use in the classroom but provides a comprehensive record for reference. At the other extreme are the teachers who habitually begin class with nothing more than a few page numbers jotted on a small slip of paper. This is not a lesson plan; it is virtually useless for future reference and is an unsatisfactory teaching guide even for those with extensive teaching experience. Between these extremes is the lesson plan that may occupy only a 3″ x 5″ card or a page of significant notes, but serves effectively to guide the teacher during the class period and as a satisfactory record for reference. Such a plan is needed, although it is not necessary that it be elaborate or detailed. It should be referred to by the teacher during the lesson as a "cue sheet" or reminder of the sequence of activities and as a source of needed information.

TIMING. In writing the plan, it is desirable to estimate the amount of time consumed by each activity, to note this estimate in the lesson plan, and to make every effort to adhere to estimated time allotments. Although the teacher's estimates are rarely precisely accurate, they are essential if planned material is to be covered in the fixed number of minutes allotted each music class. In addition, the practice of timing music selections and estimating the time required for class activities prevents the teacher from over-taxing pupil attention spans. As a guide for reference during class, it is useful for the teacher to place estimated times in a column at the edge of the lesson-plan page, referring to them and the clock periodically to adjust the tempo of the lesson so it may be brought to a timely but unhurried conclusion at the end of the lesson period.

QUESTIONS AND ANSWERS. Another desirable element of the lesson plan often omitted by the beginning teacher is the leading question and its desired answer. The teacher uses questions to initiate discussion and to direct it into desired channels. Discussions usually do not start spontaneously, but they can be started by the teacher through adroit questions. Similarly, the teacher uses questions to prompt pupils to contribute information. Adolescent pupils have large stores of information and it is probable that in the general music class there will be one or several pupils who can tell the class pertinent facts about music, its composers, history, and performance. If so, it is better that pupils contribute the information and it is desirable that the teacher acquire the habit of asking questions rather than delivering fact-filled lectures.

Whether it is being used to initiate discussion or elicit information, it is important that the question be phrased carefully to produce the desired response and that the desired answer be noted in the teacher's lesson plan. The difference, for example, between "How many of you have heard Tchaikovsky's *Romeo and Juliet?*" and "What do you know about *Romeo and Juliet?*" could be sufficient to disrupt an entire lesson. Thus the teacher may find it useful to include important questions in the lesson plan, estimating the time to be devoted to discussing their answers and noting any answers necessary to introduce subsequent phases of the lesson.

ACTIVITY DESCRIPTIONS. A third element of the lesson plan includes brief descriptions of any special activities or procedures. "Class clap rhythm of notes in first two measures," for example, would remind the teacher of a means of helping pupils feel the syncopation of the first movement of the Debussy quartet for strings.

REFERENCE INFORMATION. Finally, the lesson plan includes any needed reference information—page numbers in song books, names of recordings used, items of information that must be announced or explained to the class. All this information is noted in outline form, detailed enough to be meaningful to the teacher, but concise enough to be read at a glance in the course of the lesson.

The process of planning a lesson, then, follows these steps, each of which is expanded or reduced to an extent appropriate to the nature of the lesson and the amount of the teacher's experience.

1. Consider the factors that exert general influence on the lesson being planned, such as correlation, unit topic, pupil background and ability, pupil attitudes and interests, and the availability of audio-visual teaching aids and other special equipment. Keep these factors in mind as criteria against which to judge the suitability of the materials and procedures for inclusion in the lesson.
2. Select as a specific goal for the lesson a concrete fact of music knowledge, skill, or understanding; choose song and listening materials to illustrate the fact to be learned; analyze the music to make certain of its usefulness, and in search of teaching ideas.
3. Determine teaching devices and class activities appropriate to the maturity, interests, and background of the class through which pupils can experience the fact to be learned by participating in class activity and in the music itself.
4. Search for a means of arousing pupil curiosity and interest at the beginning of the lesson, a teaching device related to the subject matter of the lesson which directs class attention toward the activities to follow.
5. Visualize the sequence of class activities observing the principles of (a) approach, (b) participation, (c) activity, (d) variety, and (e) tempo, judging probable class reactions and re-arranging class procedure to sustain interest and to achieve the desired goal.
6. Write the lesson plan, including estimates of alloted time, leading questions and answers, notes concerning special activities, and necessary information for reference.

With a carefully prepared plan to give direction to the lesson, the teacher gains freedom in conducting the class. The plan is not followed slavishly and does not restrict the work of the teacher; it is a tentative course of action explored by teacher and class together, the plan giving the teacher confidence and a reservoir of carefully considered procedures from which to draw as necessary.

It is often necessary and wise to deviate from planned procedures. Class attitude at the beginning of the lesson may dictate a change of activity. Pupil questions and discussion may disclose areas of special interest the teacher can use to advantage. The speed with which pupils absorb material may prompt the teacher to omit planned portions of the lesson or to expand other portions when it is apparent that pupils have not achieved mastery of the material. The teacher must be prepared to nourish every spark of interest as soon as it appears and to follow the lead of class response. Sensitivity to class reaction plays a large part in successful teaching and the rigid lesson plan that prevents the teacher from adjusting class work to pupil reaction prevents effective teaching. Nevertheless, carefully prepared lesson plans are essential to good teaching.

Planning a Lesson

To observe the manner in which planning principles are used in building an actual lesson, let us assume that Mr. Smith is preparing for his general music class composed of pupils of the ninth grade. Most of these boys and girls are fourteen years of age. A number of the boys have changed voices and can sing comfortably in the octave between great B-flat and small B-flat, but a few are still in the awkward period of voice change and sing most comfortably in a narrow compass centered around middle C. All pupils have had the benefit of music instruction in the elementary school but, because of school policy concerning the scheduling of music classes, did not have music instruction in the seventh or eighth grades. For this reason, Mr. Smith decided at the beginning of the year to review the music knowledge his class might have acquired in the elementary school, adjusting the intensity of study to the needs of the class. Although there is no detailed plan for correlation of music with other school subjects, Mr. Smith tries to coöperate with the teachers of social studies who are currently discussing United States history and government and the United Nations and world affairs. For this purpose, he chooses what he considers a flexible unit topic dealing with "Folk and Work Songs Around the World."

In choosing a specific goal for the approaching lesson, Mr. Smith recalls that his class seems to be sensitive to the effects of music but shows little knowledge of its structure. In addition, the class shows special interest in the exotic flavor of a European folk song learned during a recent lesson. Mr. Smith therefore chooses tentatively to explore the difference between major and minor modes in his next lesson, hoping to utilize existing class interest and to lay a foundation for a more detailed examination of this area of music theory in subsequent lessons. As he searches through available materials, he quickly selects "The Volga Boatmen," a song learned a few weeks ago, as an example of the minor mode. For contrast, he next searches for a folk or work song in the major mode. He first chooses "I've Been Working on the Railroad," then discards it because of the major mediant harmony in the twelfth measure of the chorus and decides instead to include "Blow the Man Down." He now has two songs the class can sing easily and with pleasure, both of which are likely to appeal to ninth-grade interests and both of which can be harmonized with two or three primary chords.

As listening material, Mr. Smith hopes to find a music selection that includes both major and minor modes and presents them clearly so they can be recognized by the class. After considerable thought, Mr. Smith recalls rather dimly a piano piece he remembers as "Turkish Rondo." He looks for the title in several reference books without success, then begins to leaf through volumes of piano music. At last he comes to the Mozart Piano Sonata in A major, K. 331, the third movement of which is marked *Allegretto, Alla turca.* At first glance, this movement seems an ideal choice. It is exotic in flavor and consists of a series of sections alternating between major and minor modes. He locates a recording of the sonata and listens to this movement, then realizing that the pianistic style might not be of interest to his class. He next turns to the popular Mozart symphonies and selects the *Menuetto* of the "Symphony in G minor," K. 550. The movement is intensely rhythmic in nature, contains several singable themes, and provides contrast in that the minuet is in G minor and the trio in G major. Upon playing the recording, Mr. Smith approves its general effect and notes that it is three and one-half minutes in length. In search of an approach to the lesson, Mr. Smith decides to look for pictures that can be projected on a screen or otherwise shown to the class to illustrate differences in mood. The art teacher suggests El Greco's "View of Toledo" and another landscape by Monet or any of the impressionists. After looking through the art teacher's files, Mr. Smith finds "View of Toledo" and selects a painting by Monet titled "The Seine Near Argenteuil." The El Greco is dark and somber, the Monet bright and sunny, and Mr. Smith decides they will provide a suitable introduction to the subject of mood and color in music. Mr. Smith now feels he has the materials he needs—two songs of contrasting mode, a selection for listening that presents both major and minor mode, and two paintings that offer a contrast in mood due to color and style.

To develop feeling for the difference between major and minor modes, Mr. Smith thinks pupils should be given opportunity to discuss their reactions to the sounds of the music and that they should participate in and produce the music themselves.

He is now ready to think of the sequence of events in the lesson. First, he will challenge the pupils by asking them to define "mood." He will then show the two paintings and ask pupils to describe the mood of each and to suggest reasons for their effect upon the viewer. Second, the class will sing the two songs and discuss their effect upon the singer as well as the music characteristics that produce these effects. To feel the harmony more clearly, the class will then sing simplified harmonic progressions, I-IV-I-V-I, in both major and minor modes, the progressions notated on the board in three-part, SAB arrangement. Returning to the songs, the teacher will select six pupils to sing the melody of each song as the rest of the class sings a sustained, harmonic background. Pupils will conduct as they sing the songs with sustained choral accompaniment to feel the rhythm of each song and to help achieve uniformity of tempo and ensemble. Following this experience, the class will discuss major and minor modes, the teacher leading the discussion to the specific difference between major and minor harmonies. To apply this knowledge, the class will listen to the Mozart selection and then summarize the material of the lesson in discussion.

With these thoughts in mind, Mr. Smith writes his lesson plan in a form that will permit him to refer to it as he conducts the lesson. It occupies one sheet of paper and is in brief, outline form, with estimated elapsed time noted in the left margin.

00 Write "mood" on board.
Question: What does this word mean? (state of mind or feeling)
Question: What words do we know that describe different moods? (List terms on board: gay, sad, somber, angry, thoughtful, etc.)

05 Here are two paintings: "View of Toledo" by El Greco and "The Seine Near Argenteuil" by Monet.
Question: Are they different in mood?
Question: Which word from the board describes each?
Question: What quality in the painting creates these moods? (color)
Question: What was the mood of the song "Volga Boatmen" we sang recently?

10 As you sing "Volga Boatmen," try to discover why it creates this mood. (Page 96. Sing song in unison with piano accompaniment.)
Question: Why is it sad? (words, slow tempo.)
Sing "Blow the Man Down," page 43, in unison with piano accompaniment.

18 *Question:* What makes this song seem gay and boisterous? (words, rhythm)
There is another element in music—harmonic color.
Sing the harmony written on the board. (F major. I-IV-I-V-I. SAB)
Now sing the same harmony, changing *Mi* to *Me* and *La* to *Le* where I have added flats.
Question: Is there a change in mood?

28 We can use these harmonies to accompany songs. Sing eight measures of "Volga Boatmen" using tonic and subdominant only and "Blow the Man Down" using tonic and dominant only. Sextet sing melody; others sing chords indicated by teacher at board. All conduct.

35 *Question:* Does anyone know the musical names for these two moods? (Major and minor. Note difference of spelling and meaning between "mood" and "mode.")

40 Now we will hear music played by full orchestra containing both major and minor modes. Close your eyes to listen and raise your hand when you hear a change from minor to major or major to minor. (Play Mozart's Symphony in G minor, Movement III.)

45 *Question:* What was the order of modes? (Minor, Major, Minor.)
Question: Is the minor mode always sad?
Question: How could you summarize what we have learned about mood in paintings and in music?

With this plan to guide him, Mr. Smith is prepared to teach his class. He may deviate from it as he feels the pulse of class reaction, omitting some portions and enlarging on others, but the plan will be at hand to direct his teaching, nevertheless. He is not certain he has estimated time allotments accurately, but he will use his estimates to govern the tempo of his teaching and hope to complete the planned work within the fifty minutes of the lesson period. As he looks back over his experience, he realizes that some lessons planned in much less detail were quite successful and that other lessons he considered very carefully did not arouse interest. Despite these exceptional instances, Mr. Smith has developed feelings of confidence and assurance through planning the lesson in detail, is eager to test it in the general music class, and has every reason to expect the class will find the lesson interesting and will learn from it.

Class Management

Another type of planning has to do with the details of administering the general music class, establishing a system through which the inevitable clerical work and other routine duties of the teacher are accomplished automatically and without encroaching on the time devoted to teaching. It is a type of long-range planning that permits the class to function smoothly in its day-to-day activities, foreseeing the necessity for keeping records, and for becoming thoroughly acquainted with the needs of each pupil. Through such planning the teacher becomes a well-organized individual and creates a favorable teaching situation. This type of planning, as well as that which deals with the sequence of learning activities in each lesson, creates conditions favorable to effective teaching, contributes to the success of the teacher and to effective class control. The teacher who is not well organized spends needless hours in routine administrative work not directly related to teaching; the teacher who establishes a system for such work finds that it progresses smoothly and easily and requires minimum teacher time and effort.

Each school has its own system for gathering administrative information and its own array of forms to record the data collected. The teacher's responsibility is to become acquainted with the requirements of the school and to devise means of fulfilling them efficiently. Two important areas of information are those that deal with pupil attendance and marks. The teacher needs a roll book or attendance record and a book for recording recitation, quiz, and examination grades for each pupil. In addition, the teacher may need to record information concerning voice classification and special music talent or lack of it. In many cases, all this information may be recorded in one roll book; in others, there may be separate forms for recording attendance and marks.

Periodically during the school year it is necessary to transfer some of this information, or a summary of it, to records maintained in the school's central administrative offices or to a report submitted to the parents of each pupil. These tasks are often more complex for the teacher of general music than for teachers of other subjects. The general music teacher sees a larger portion of the school population in heterogeneous classes not always grouped according to age, grade, or academic section. To solve these problems, a first step is to discuss them with other teachers who are familiar with the records and routines of the school. Ask them for information, advice, and assistance; their experience is valuable and they share its benefits freely. Ask about the records and how to keep them. Ask several other teachers to explain the systems they have found most efficient. With this advice, and by considering the ways in which another teacher's system might be revised to meet the requirements of the general music class, the music teacher can develop a suitable plan for maintaining class records and for reacting promptly to requests from the administrative offices. By planning these procedures in advance, the teacher saves times and reduces the load of non-teaching duties.

It is equally desirable to establish a system for dealing with matters pertinent to teaching and the daily routine of the classroom. Establish a file for lesson plans as a record of class progress and for future reference when planning new lessons. Many schools provide for this also. A book in which the teacher notes each day's class work is sometimes filed in one of the school's administrative offices. Because such books normally permit only the briefest descriptions of class work, however, it is useful for the teacher to maintain a personal file for the more detailed lesson plans used in each day's teaching. Other files might be established for notes concerning outstanding song materials, useful recordings, miscellaneous teaching ideas and suggestions, and other information to which the teacher might wish to refer at a later date. Useful equipment includes a supply of 3″ x 5″ or 4″ x 6″ cards and a box in which they can be filed according to an appropriate indexing system. With cards available, the teacher can quickly jot down ideas or notes as they come to his attention and place them in a file where they can be found easily as needed.

The teacher should also search for ways to rid himself of the burdens of routine clerical and other class-management duties. It may be possible to delegate the duties of checking attendance, distributing books or other materials, regulating light, heat, and ventilation. Pupils can be selected as teaching assistants or class monitors and given the responsibility of performing their tasks at every class meeting. This assures that routine tasks will not be overlooked when the teacher becomes intent upon the lesson at hand. It also gives the teacher an opportunity to minister to individual differences, rewarding pupils who are outstanding or providing responsibility and a sense of achievement for those who find few opportunities for success in the music work of the class. In addition, the practice of assigning tasks to class members contributes to class control. It gives pupils something to do immediately upon entering the room, occupies individuals whose exuberant spirits need channeled outlet, and creates an impression of orderliness that emphasizes the need for conforming to the patterns of class routine.

Becoming acquainted with individual pupils and gathering information about their capabilities, limitations, backgrounds, and attitudes is an important teacher function. A first step is to assign a seat to each pupil in each class. This is done at the first class meeting if possible, or as soon thereafter as class membership is sufficiently settled to permit definite seating arrangements. Seating may be changed several times during the course of any one term as voices are tested and classified or for other reasons, but seats are assigned immediately even though voice classifications are not known. The teacher then prepares a seating chart for each class so that a glance at the chart enables the teacher to identify any pupil immediately. The chart is an invaluable aid for checking attendance, for calling upon pupils for recitation, and for helping the teacher learn the names of pupils in each class.

To gain information about each pupil, many teachers prepare a mimeographed questionnaire to be distributed to pupils at the first class meeting. The form may provide space for such information as name, address, telephone number, instrumental lessons and playing experience, singing experience and part sung, membership in church choirs and other music groups, parents' music interests, and other pertinent information. The questionnaires are useful for reference and provide evidence to direct the teacher's special efforts or to explain the pupil's class behavior.

A source of further valuable information is the system of cumulative records maintained by the school to record each pupil's progress through his entire school career. These records are usually filed in a central administrative office and are available to any teacher who needs the information they contain. They show the marks awarded to the pupil in each subject and grade, the results of intelligence and aptitude tests, participation in extra-curricular activities, the comments of previous teachers and notes concerning the pupil's home background. Although the teacher rarely has time for careful study of all the records pertaining to every pupil, a great deal of information is available when special circumstances warrant analysis of any one pupil's progress or behavior. If time permits, the teacher may find that even a cursory survey of cumulative records is rewarding, identifying pupils who have special abilities or interests or who need special treatment in class.

To gather information concerning the specialized work in music, some teachers give music aptitude or achievement tests to each class. This is desirable only if no such tests are shown in the cumulative records or if results of previous tests are old enough to warrant re-testing. These tests help the teacher know individual pupils and estimate the capacity of each class as a whole, identifying those with latent talent or with little potential for music work, and aid the teacher in his work of discovering and developing talent.

There is a further application of this sort of planning of practical value to the teacher in the daily conduct of classes. It is important that the teacher cultivate habits of punctuality and dependability. Classes should begin and end on time. The teacher is ready for every class when it enters the music room. He avoids any tendency to become immersed in clerical duties between classes or to permit administrative work to overflow into the first few minutes of scheduled classes. By planning for such duties in advance, learning how to utilize school records efficiently, delegating routine duties to selected pupils, and by being generally well organized, the teacher creates an efficient class atmosphere that influences the behavior and attitude of music classes. Pupils respond well to a class pattern that moves quickly and smoothly through a planned sequence of activities in which there is little time wasted by inefficient routines. They develop respect for the teacher who has a plan and insists firmly that it be followed. These are the values of efficient class management. It lightens the teacher's load, provides more time for music teaching, contributes to class control, and is conducive to effective music learning.

THE TOTAL PATTERN OF GENERAL MUSIC

The most important factor to be considered when planning the work of the general music class is that it is intended to develop powers of appreciation and enjoyment in all pupils. The general music class springs from the philosophy that music is part of our cultural heritage and that it offers spiritual, intellectual, and emotional benefits to all. General music therefore reaches out to every pupil. It is often required. It seeks to attract large numbers of pupils if it is elective. Because of the philosophy on which it is based, it seeks to win pupils to music, not by coercing them or exploiting their abilities, but by showing them the rewards of musical sensitivity and by giving them knowledge and skill that increase perceptive powers. General music begins with enjoyment but does not stop there; it goes on through study and experience to the higher level of enjoyment we know as appreciation.

The general music class works toward its ends through a variety of class activities and music studies, seeking the well-rounded musical development of each pupil. It includes much singing because the voice is the instrument used most easily by each pupil. Through singing, it gives pupils close, personal contact with music, explores music literature, and teaches music knowledge and skill, paving the way for continued participation in music during later life. It includes much listening because this is the area of music interest open to the largest number of pupils and of greatest permanent value to them. Through listening, it shows the infinite variety of music literature, develops aural and other skills, and lays foundations for a continuing desire to find enjoyment and release in music. In doing so, it further demonstrates the variety of music's appeals and expressive qualities, concentrates its efforts on concrete and meaningful learning, and builds increased musicianship for both performers and listeners. Although each of these activities is a separate and distinct phase of music experience and learning, general music welds all of them into a unified program of class work. Each element of music is learned not for itself alone, but for the contribution it makes to each of the other elements and to increased music understanding. Each element is experienced rather than learned, in order that pupils may feel the effects of music and actually experience the principles they are being taught.

Effective general music programs are achieved through planning. Planning is important to the total pattern of general music work, to the success of each lesson, and to the efficiency and personal assurance of the teacher. It takes into consideration everything that affects the pupil, his attitudes and opinions and his progress in achieving higher levels of response to music. Planning is based upon a foundation of general knowledge concerning the adolescent pupil, the school and home environments, and the nature and effects of music. It deals with broader aspects of music teaching such as long-range goals, correlation with the work of other subjects, and use of the unit-of-study principle. It deals also with certain administrative responsibilities and records, studying them and utilizing them to increase the efficiency of teaching and to lighten the burden of administrative work. A large portion of the teacher's planning is devoted to creating successful, productive lessons. The teacher considers every detail of pupil reaction and response, basing each lesson on existing abilities and needs, foreseeing pupil attitudes toward the materials of the lesson, and calculating activities that cause true learning to occur.

For this task, the teacher of general music must be the possessor of certain professional and personal qualities and must strive for continuing advancement in teaching skill. The teacher needs a broad background of music knowledge and experience and warmly sympathetic understanding of the pupils he teaches. (It is impossible to say which of these is considered first, for the true teacher regards pupils and subject matter as being inseparably related.) The teacher needs a similarly broad background of knowledge concerning the schools and their function and the place of music in the pattern of public education. He must see his work in true perspective, vitally interested in its progress but safe against the biases that arise from narrow points of view and cause distortion of teaching goals and procedures. Finally, the teacher must be a warm and human person, sincerely interested in the welfare of those in his classes. General music deserves the best efforts of the most capable teachers. It is the core of the music program and ultimately could determine the fate of music education in the public schools.

part three:
The Vocal Program

7: choral organizations and activities

Choral singing is among the oldest of man's musical endeavors. The rhythmic chantings of primitive tribes were a form of concerted vocal utterance as was the singing of chants and psalms by the early followers of the Hebrew and Christian faiths. In America, singing schools pre-dated the establishment of public schools and singing groups of one kind or another have been an accepted part of public education ever since.

There are deep-seated reasons for man's impulse toward choral singing. There is in choral music opportunity for expressive utterance and emotional release not found in any other art and not achieved as readily in any other area of music performance. The human voice, the instrument of the singer, is entirely personal. It is used naturally as a means of communication and possesses expressive powers more intense and diverse than those of any other instrument. Its unique advantage is that it permits the singer to produce musical sounds through his own physiological powers, to participate in the music in a direct and personal way, and to feel the effects of the music intimately and clearly.

Choral music has been popular in the public schools for these reasons and others. During recent years especially, the consistently successful choral programs in many schools lend impetus to the development of better and more varied types of choral performance. Schools now sponsor a great variety of performing choral groups. The socially oriented glee club has become a well-trained music organization of near-professional caliber. It has made the transition from extra-curricular status to that of the scheduled class and is often offered for credit. It is perhaps the most easily organized and administered of all the performing groups, offering fewer problems than either orchestra or band. It requires little special equipment and comparatively little financial support when first formed. Its initial performances are usually successful—received with enthusiasm by other pupils, school administrators and parents—even when the music and its performance are artistically less than perfect. Although too few high-school groups strive for excellence commensurate with their capabilities, those who listen to the efforts of the singers tend to accept them warmly and with more tolerance of weaknesses in musicianship than they would display toward the efforts of an instrumental group.

Choral music is popular in the public schools partly because of its ability to stimulate interest in the music program and in the work of the school. A moderately successful choral group quickly arouses interest among the student body and attracts more singers. It makes a favorable impression upon school administrators and can be relied upon to stimulate support of a total music program. It is well received by parents and has great public relations value of benefit to all phases of the school program. Choral organizations permit both singers and audiences to become acquainted with worthy music. They provide for individual differences in talent among pupils. Those who have special talents can be challenged in advanced groups while those of less talent can be encouraged to continue in groups whose activities make fewer demands. Finally, the choral group tends to be social in nature, providing opportunities for pupils to work together toward common ends and to see the results of coöperative social effort.

Although there are public relations values in highly trained choral groups, they serve the same educational ends as all other music activities in the public schools. Their basic goal is one of developing powers of enjoyment and appreciation. They serve every pupil in the school population. Membership is not restricted to pupils with outstanding voices or other special music talent and the abilities of the groups should not be exploited to achieve other than educational ends. Every type of choral organization, whether a selective group for trained singers or an open group for those with little more than interest, is regarded by the teacher as a means of finding enjoyment in music and increasing the abilities that lead to higher levels of appreciation.

The choral program is regarded as an instrument of music education. It rightly provides for the survey of choral literature and for the acquisition of knowledge about music history. It teaches harmony and music theory, understanding of music style, and develops reading and listening skills. It includes singing, listening, and rhythmic activities and is sensitive to the rhythmic, aural, and theoretical aspects of music. In a sense, the choral program is an extension of the general music class. It strives for similar goals but utilizes different means. Its work is concentrated in the area of vocal music; it encourages a higher degree of vocal skill, deals with a higher level of choral music in a more artistic manner, and culminates in performance. Its goals, however, are essentially the same as those of the general music class in that it strives chiefly for the well-rounded musical growth of its participants.

The special opportunities of the choral program have to do with the improvement of vocal skills. The teacher works with tone production to improve tone quality and color. Pupils are encouraged to develop desirable habits of posture and breathing as they apply to singing and to general physical well-being. The various elements of diction and the music skills of accurate hearing and correct interpretation of notation are important to singing. The choral group is not a voice class, but it works toward the goals of the voice class with the realization that this voice training is valuable in developing enjoyment and appreciation.

There are other goals of the choral program that have to do with the social development of the pupil, goals not especially musical in nature that are the common responsibility of every member of the school staff. Through choral activities, pupils develop poise and self-confidence, gaining assurance through performing for audiences. They learn social disciplines by seeing the necessity for coöperation in rehearsals and performances. They gain facility in self-expression by accepting music as an expressive outlet and using it with the assurance developed through performance. The total school program accepts as one of its responsibilities the task of preparing pupils for the general aspects of life in society. It is proper that the music program share the responsibility and make every possible contribution to this aspect of the pupil's education.

There is a paradox in the goals of the choral program that must be understood if the teacher's efforts are to be properly directed. The principal goal is one of enjoyment and appreciation. This would imply a choral program intended primarily to provide enjoyment for the singers. It might lead to rehearsal devoted entirely to "fun" songs, to an absence of productive work, and to emphasis on social activity. Another goal, however, is the acquisition of knowledge and skill. This implies a choral program of a different type in which rehearsals are devoted to concentrated vocal study and to mastery of difficult choral literature. Neither of these extremes is appropriate for the choral program in the public school, but each concept holds something meriting consideration by the choral teacher. Enjoyment is an end, but the acquisition of knowledge and skill is a means to that end. The appreciative enjoyment sought by the teacher for the pupils grows in direct relation to the degree in which the pupil masters vocal abilities and music knowledge.

It is especially important that the choral teacher adopt this point of view because he deals with many pupils who come to him without music training. Whereas the instrumental teacher must teach his pupils certain technical skills before any performance can be presented, it is possible for the choral teacher to establish a choral program without actually teaching pupils very much about music. This is especially unfortunate in that the large number of pupils in the choral program need the benefits of competent teaching if music is to give them anything of lasting value; they are not likely to progress unless the teacher makes a conscious effort to develop music knowledge and skill. The choral teacher, like every other teacher of music, prepares the pupils under his guidance for a lifetime of rewarding music experience by striving to increase their music knowledge, perception, and sensitivity.

ORGANIZING CHORAL GROUPS

Rarely does the choral teacher enter a new position to find that choral activities are organized to his satisfaction. Even if the new teacher is fortunate enough to find a well-organized choral program in existence, to sustain it through succeeding years he must be constantly alert to the necessity for renewing interest.

The first steps in planning have to do with the stimulation of interest and support, recruiting members, establishing the necessary variety of organizations to take care of them, and the scheduling of regular rehearsal periods. This helps the teacher establish the program and permits it to continue to grow once it has been established. Choral groups can not endure in the public schools without a steady flow of new members to replace those who must depart at the end of the senior year, or without regular meetings in which the recruited members can be welded into an effective choral group. The teacher must be aware of these factors to assure the continuance and improvement of the choral program.

Gaining Members and Support

The first step in initiating or revising a program of choral activities usually requires that the teacher secure the approval and support of school administrators. Matters that pertain to the establishment of classes and extra-curricular activities, scheduling school time, the expenditure of school funds, and the utilization of school personnel must have the approval of the school principal and, in many instances, of the superintendent of schools. If there is a supervisor of music, or if other music teachers of the school system are affected, proposed changes should be discussed with them as well. It is the school administrator, however, who gives final approval and whose enthusiastic support can be of great value to the choral teacher.

SEEKING ADMINISTRATIVE SUPPORT. Administrators are especially sensitive to evidence of careful planning and efficient organization. They respond favorably to proposals that have been considered carefully and in which every problem of organization has been examined. The teacher who wishes to suggest a change in the existing pattern of choral activities or the establishment of a new choral group is well advised to plan the presentation of his recommendation in such a way that the details of the proposal are clear to the administrator and so the proposal itself makes an immediate impression of careful organization. It is desirable to put such proposals in writing. The attempt at written description is beneficial to the teacher; it requires that ideas be put in logical order, encourages attention to detail, and clarifies problems of organization. It is also appreciated by the administrator who can retain the written proposal for examination at a convenient time, need not rely on his memory for information gained through informal conversation, and can examine the details in the written proposal in a logical way.

Requests for school time, funds, and equipment should be specific, complete in all details, and considerate of the problems that must be faced by the administrator in approving them. Reasons for the proposed change are stated briefly but clearly. Inadequacies of existing arrangements are pointed out also, but with good judgment concerning the work of other teachers and established school practices. Administrators are also sensitive to the educational benefits of school activities, constantly evaluating the school program to determine whether it produces results commensurate with the function of the school and the broader implications of educational philosophy. It is appropriate that the choral teacher refer to the aims of education and the function of music as a part of the educational program. If there is any tendency for the administrator to regard music teachers as somewhat impractical, immersed in their art, and given to inspirational thinking, it is especially important that proposals emphasize music's contributions to educational aims and the specific ways in which the proposed change will benefit both pupils and the school as a whole.

SCHEDULES AND BUDGETS. Among the important details of such a proposal are those that have to do with scheduling and the school budget. There are so many demands made upon school time that it is sometimes more precious than school funds, but funds too are limited and must be apportioned with due regard for the relative importance of the items for which they are used.

The music teacher has an advantage where scheduling is concerned in that proposed choral groups can begin their work in extra-curricular time. Although in most instances they should ultimately be scheduled as regular school activities during normal class hours, they can prove their worth by developing through rehearsals scheduled before or after school, during the noon recess or in activity periods. The music teacher is fortunate in that choral groups often require less expenditure than instrumental groups both in their initial stages and after the program is established. Music is inexpensive and can be retained for repeated use. The acquisition of robes can be postponed, the pupils simply wearing uniform dress in their first public appearances. Nothing more than a piano is essential as special equipment and the purchase of other desirable items such as risers and a tape recorder can be deferred. Thus it is possible for the music teacher to suggest solutions to scheduling and budget problems or to show that they can be eliminated completely from the first year or more of the group's existence.

PUBLIC RELATIONS VALUE. The administrator may be interested also in the public relations value of a proposed choral group. The school is constantly in the public eye. It must demonstrate its effectiveness to parents and depends upon the public for support through taxation. The administrator is aware of these factors and must consider the impression made upon the public by the various phases of the school program. Although he is unlikely to approve school projects for their public relations value alone, he can not help but be influenced favorably by activities that create good will without sacrificing educational benefits. Performing groups have this advantage. A choral program that serves a large number of pupils, creates favorable impressions upon large numbers of parents, requires only small expenditures of school time and funds, and presents enjoyable programs both in school and throughout the community is a desirable public relations asset.

BUILDING FROM SUCCESS. Administrative support for choral activities also depends upon their past successes. The choral teacher who can point to existing choral organizations with a history of successful performance and worthwhile educational achievement, and who is known to the administrator as one who does effective work, plans carefully, and organizes efficiently, is given the administrator's close attention when a new organization is proposed. Success may be the most potent evidence the teacher can offer. The administrator is reluctant to approve requests supported by the most lucid planning if he feels the teacher may fail to carry out new plans satisfactorily. It is important that the teacher work diligently to improve existing choral organizations before requesting new ones, to make the most of every opportunity for music achievement within the existing framework of the program, and to propose changes infrequently and only when there is no suitable alternative. The teacher who appears in the principal's office regularly with plans for sweeping changes in the entire music program is given a cooler reception at each successive request. The teacher who first works conscientiously with the materials at hand and then goes to the principal with a carefully conceived plan for making minor changes to improve the choral program is more likely to be given adminstrative support.

RECRUITING NEW MEMBERS. The next step in organizing choral activities is one of arousing student interest and recruiting new members. It is important that the first choral group or the first appearance of a new group be successful. To this end, the teacher is justified in selecting new members carefully and in searching for talented pupils as potential members. Although the goal of choral activities is to reach large numbers of pupils, a first appearance that is musically unsatisfactory because of the participation of pupils who lack vocal or other abilities could effectively destroy further interest. Talented pupils can be identified in a number of ways. The cumulative records maintained by the central office of the school may include results of aptitude tests and notes concerning membership in previous vocal or instrumental ensembles. These may be of value even if the information is several years old. The pupil who showed music aptitude and interest in earlier grades, or who performed with instrumental or vocal groups may be a potential leader in choral groups of the senior high school even though he has not been active in the music program for several years.

CONSULTING OTHER TEACHERS. Additional information can be secured from the teachers who know the pupil through general music or other music classes in lower grades. The instrumental teacher in particular may be able to offer useful suggestions concerning pupils who have shown music aptitude and interest. Classroom teachers may be able to make suggestions concerning pupils who might develop into valued members of a choral group. The classroom teacher's more detailed knowledge of the pupil includes information not available through any other source. By making maximum use of all these resources, the choral teacher identifies the pupils who would be most desirable as members of the singing group, discovering those with singing ability, musicianship, and interest. Once the list of prospective members is complete he endeavors to interest them in becoming active in the new choral organization. By using especially able pupils as a nucleus, the teacher can form a choral group destined for success from the moment of its founding.

USING PUBLICITY DEVICES. Further steps in recruiting are largely a matter of suitable publicity and good public relations. The teacher grasps every opportunity to attract the interest of the student body. A bulletin board in the hall adjacent to the choral rehearsal room attracts the attention of pupils who pass it regularly. It can be used to display an attractive photograph of the choral group in robes or other costume, announcements of approaching choral activities, press clippings, cartoons, and posters pertaining to the choral program. Glass cases in the hall, often reserved for athletic trophies, can feature displays of photographs, choir robes, or other objects related to choral activities. The school paper may be used for feature articles concerning the choral program or a regular column devoted to the activities of the glee club and its members. Further publicity of this sort may be available through community newspapers, homeroom bulletin boards, and other media. Through each means, the student body is reminded constantly of the existence of choral activities and invited to participate in an active and desirable program.

RECRUITING THROUGH CONCERTS. To further attract new members, the choral teacher presents performing groups in concerts designed to appeal strongly to the student body. The choral teacher selects music for in-school concert programs to appeal to the majority of pupils in the audience. The music is rehearsed and polished carefully so the performance can be as nearly flawless as possible. The choral group is presented in robes or other uniform costume to appeal to the adolescent's natural interest in distinctive dress. The concert itself is presented with as much showmanship as possible within the limits of good taste. This sustains audience interest and helps the school program compare favorably with television and other performances. A particularly potent stimulus is the annual concert, variety show, or operetta. Similarly, the choral teacher may arouse general interest in choral activities by arranging for the appearance of outside performing groups in school programs—professional singers, community groups, or choral organizations from neighboring schools. By presenting choral groups in this favorable light, and by reminding the student body constantly of available choral activities, the teacher creates an impression that participation in the choral program is an exciting and enjoyable experience, a compelling reason for adolescents to seek membership.

DIRECT RECRUITING. The active recruiting program is a productive means of securing new members. The usual posters, homeroom announcements, and newspaper articles announce the possibility of membership and provide opportunity to describe its most attractive benefits. Further recruiting can be done by members themselves, each being invited to bring a friend. The assistance of other teachers can be solicited in identifying potential individual members or in discussing the topic briefly in homeroom or class meetings. The choral teacher himself can do much to recruit new members, either by talking with desirable candidates or by being generally active in school affairs other than those devoted to music. In all these ways the teacher tries to assure the constant flow of new members without which any choral program must decline in membership and quality. As the program develops and more and more interested pupils apply for membership, choral activities can be diversified through the establishment of additional groups, and one or more of the organizations can become increasingly selective to raise the level of performance, each such improvement increasing the probability of success for the total choral program.

ENLISTING COMMUNITY SUPPORT. The support of parents and other adult members of the community is highly desirable. Parents are impressed by results. Performance, again, is a means of demonstrating results. Parents can be invited to attend school concerts. The choral group can perform for the Parent-Teacher Association, at churches, for service clubs, and other civic groups. The teacher can address the Parent-Teacher Association, discussing the values of the choral program in terms of benefits to the pupils, problems that have been overcome, recent noteworthy progress or performances, and the needs peculiar to the performing group. Demonstrations may serve to stimulate parental interest, the teacher using the performing group or selected pupils to show rehearsal procedures, techniques for improving the singing of the group, or for studying choral literature. This is appropriate for the PTA concert and might even be included in a public concert to increase audience interest and develop public understanding of the activities of the choral group. To sustain parental interest, the teacher can turn to community newspapers, mimeographed bulletins such as a regularly issued "Choral News," and to placards and posters announcing concerts and other special events.

LETTERS AND BULLETINS. Of special merit is the bulletin to parents that keeps them informed of the activities of their children and the requirements imposed by membership in the choral organization. Parents are justified in asking about school activities in which their children participate and the reasons for special requirements and extra demands upon their time. This information should go to the pupil's home as a matter of routine and on a regular basis. Parents should receive it in accurate and detailed form from the teacher through an official channel rather than in incomplete or erroneous versions relayed orally by pupils. The director of any performing group accepts the responsibility of providing either a letter to parents or a regular bulletin in which selected issues contain informative articles. In some instances, where the student must secure parental permission for trips or where he must pay dues, a special letter is provided for signature by the parent and returned to the teacher. In other instances it may be desirable to provide a form to be signed by both student and parent, the form containing statements concerning the responsibilities of choral members and signifying the pupil's willingness to comply with the established requirements. In general, parents might be interested in knowing requirements for admission and membership, regulations concerning participation, dress and attendance, and the planned schedule of performances, particularly as it requires pupil attendance during other than normal school hours.

In some schools, parental interest can be developed through the establishment of a "Parents Association." Such an organization can be of great assistance to the choral teacher and of value in the development of the choral program. Many activities can be discussed, arranged, organized, and cleared with the assistance of interested parents. The association can help in raising funds when necessary, purchasing robes and other equipment, in managing and supervising trips or other out-of-school appearances. An annual banquet for the association, attended by parents, pupils, and teachers and complete with the presentation of awards to outstanding pupils and addresses by student officers and guest speakers, can do much to arouse enthusiasm among both parents and pupils.

The procedures for arousing interest, recruiting members, and gaining support for the program are important to the choral teacher. Regardless of the music talents and teaching skills of the director, the choral program can not achieve maximum success unless it is built upon a foundation of enthusiastic coöperation among all concerned. The ultimate success of a choral group is often determined by the teacher's skill in solving problems outside of the rehearsal room.

The Variety of Performing Organizations

The first organization established in a choral program is often a glee club, but the successful program can develop to include a wide variety of performing groups. There are types based upon different categories of personnel, including those for boys and girls, boys alone, girls alone, and alumni. There may be senior or advanced groups and those which might be regarded as training ensembles. There is the large choral ensemble of perhaps one hundred voices, the smaller and more select group of from sixteen to thirty-two voices, and small ensembles such as the girls' trio and male quartet. There may be groups devoted chiefly to the performance of special types of music, including the madrigal singers, the Bach chorale, the modernaires or the popular songsters. Within this wide array of possibilities the imaginative choral teacher can find something to appeal to every taste and can provide interesting and challenging activity for every degree of vocal and music talent. His first responsibility, however, is to provide for the large number of potential members, including those who may not be capable of performing the more unusual works of choral literature, and his best opportunity for initial success lies in establishing a glee club in which many pupils of normal ability can participate.

There are many types of groups to which the choral director might well give special thought. First, there is the type that separates older from younger pupils. Seniors and juniors sometimes feel they should belong to a distinctive group not open to pupils from lower grades. There are differences between older and younger pupils in voice quality, music ability, and attitude. Thus there is merit in establishing two groups, such as concert choir and mixed chorus, in which materials and procedures can be adjusted to the ages and abilities of the members. A similar differentiation might be justified solely by differences in vocal ability, one group being composed of pupils who have had experience or training, the other being a training group in which the teacher can give special attention to vocal development for younger pupils. The advanced group would then concentrate on the study of choral literature and be called upon for a relatively large number of performances; the training group might be regarded either as a voice class or as a rehearsing group concentrating on vocal technique and would appear in performance less frequently. Through an arrangement such as this, the teacher has an opportunity to develop an outstanding advanced chorus, to give competent vocal training to those who might benefit from it, and to provide adequately for individual differences in ability and interest.

Another area of special organization is that which includes the smaller vocal ensembles such as trios and quartets. These are especially useful as outlets for those who have special talent or exceptionally strong interest in singing. They are valuable as sources of training in musicianship, the members of the small group finding it necessary to be especially alert to the correct and sensitive interpretation of the music they sing and to the unanimity of feeling characteristic of the small ensemble. The ensemble is also of practical use to the teacher as a means of lightening the performance load of the larger group. Trios and quartets can be used to fill the requests of community and school organizations that request special music and can be featured in choral concerts to add variety to the program and make it less taxing for the larger choral group. Finally, there is the alumni chorus open to all who have participated in the choral program of the school. Although the teacher's schedule is invariably crowded and the alumni chorus must rehearse during the teacher's otherwise free hours, it is a means of preventing the waste that occurs when music ability developed during school years goes unused after graduation. The alumni chorus that grows and serves a large number of older singers can be a strong force for stimulating community interest in the choral program of the school.

SENIOR CHORUS. In the senior high school, the mixed chorus is probably the group organized first. It is composed of from fifty to one hundred singers, varying according to the size of the school, the interest of pupils, and the policies of the teacher, and is devoted principally to singing music in four parts in standard SATB arrangements. It sings both accompanied and unaccompanied music. It utilizes accompaniments to aid the singers and because much appealing choral music is accompanied, but turns to unaccompanied music to add variety to its repertoire and to explore the beauties of music for voices alone. It can be called glee club, chorus, or choir.

The term "glee club" often indicates a group in which social factors play a relatively important part. It may be a boys' glee club or girls' glee club with student officers and extra-musical activities. For it, the teacher selects music calculated to capture the interest of young singers not of outstanding ability. The "choir" is often a group with more serious musical purpose, emphasizing musical performance rather than social activity. The term "chorus" sometimes indicates neutral ground, a group to which the teacher hopes to attract pupils interested in the serious study of choral literature and in artistic performance, but which is open to large numbers of pupils and may provide for certain social activities to maintain interest.

Groups such as these arouse strong interest in pupils, are easy to form, and are popular as performing organizations. The glee club or chorus relies chiefly on four-part music because of the natural distribution of voice classifications among high-school pupils and because music of this type offers many opportunities for achieving satisfaction in performance at varying levels of difficulty. It normally includes a large number of singers because its purpose is to serve a large portion of the student body and because the voices of inexperienced singers create a better effect when the group is composed of a reasonably large number of pupils. It admits both boys and girls, partly because choral literature demands voices of both types and partly because the young adults of the high school respond favorably to mixed social activity.

SENIOR MALE CHORUS. To provide for special interest or for an exceptionally large number of interested pupils, there is the male chorus. This organization for boys only includes from thirty to sixty voices and sings standard four-part literature for male chorus. It chooses materials full of rollicking good fellowship, including some of the "barbershop" variety and catering to the virile interests of the singers, but does not overlook the quieter and more serious literature that can be sung to good effect by male voices. Both accompanied and unaccompanied selections are appropriate. The male chorus is sometimes difficult to form, due to the many activities that claim the high-school boy's time and interest, but it can be a very active and popular organization if the teacher exercises good judgment in selecting materials and absorbs the spirit of the all-male singing group.

SENIOR GIRLS' GLEE CLUB. The girls' glee club is entirely different from the male chorus, due to the different quality of girls' voices and to the different nature of girls' interests. It might be made up of from thirty to sixty voices and sings music in three parts, rarely turning to four-part music because of the scarcity of true second altos among girls of high-school age. In other respects it sings standard literature for women's voices, usually accompanied because of the absence of lower pitches from the tonal spectrum of the unaccompanied women's chorus. It is different from the male chorus in that its chief objective is one of exploring the beauties of the large quantity of excellent material intended for women's voices, the emphasis being placed on musical beauty rather than on fellowship. The girls' glee club is in some instances more difficult to form than the male chorus, due to the girls' natural preference for mixed social activity, but it can be developed into a group that creates strong interest because of the unique beauties of the music it performs.

SENIOR CHOIR. For pupils with outstanding talent and strong interest, the teacher can form a choir, sometimes called the "a cappella choir." This is a selective group open only to those who meet strict membership requirements and possess sufficient vocal and music ability to permit high standard of performance. The choir might consist of from thirty to seventy voices, each member carefully chosen because of voice quality and classification, general music ability and sensitivity, interest and dependability. It studies the best examples of choral literature, including both accompanied and unaccompanied music. Its performances are artistically outstanding in terms of tone quality, balance, intonation, and interpretation. A performing group of this type is a rewarding investment of the teacher's time and energy. It is deeply satisfying to both director and singers, provides music of the highest quality for concert audiences, sets an example worthy of emulation by other vocal groups, and is in great demand for performances both in school and in the community. In addition, it is a strong incentive for other pupils who wish to gain membership, stimulating them to preparatory participation in other groups and encouraging them to increase their music skills through study and practice.

An equally desirable group is one of smaller size such as the madrigal singers. It might consist of sixteen voices or some other multiple of the basic four parts, the object being to approach closely the unanimity of the solo quartet without requiring that each voice be of solo caliber. Parts are precisely balanced in both number and intensity, and voices are of carefully matched quality and color. It can explore madrigal literature but should not ignore other worthy music, both accompanied and unaccompanied. Its objective is to develop perfection of ensemble and its performances should be noteworthy events. This group, like the choir, offers many satisfactions and can serve as strong incentive to other singers.

SENIOR ENSEMBLES. The smaller ensembles serve two purposes. They are a natural extension of opportunity for pupils of outstanding ability, but are equally desirable as training groups for those of average ability. Possibilities include the girls' trio, the male quartet, the girls' quartet in the rare instances in which a true second alto is available, and multiples of these groups such as the sextet, octet, or triple trio. They sing standard literature for the most part. The male quartet usually finds it enjoyable to explore the "barbershop" style. For outstanding pupils, these ensembles provide music challenge not found in the activities of the larger groups. The singers must learn to be precise in matters of rhythm, intonation, phrasing, and ensemble. They gain independence and assurance from working together and develop rapidly in musicianship through ensemble practice. For pupils of less ability, ensembles offer the same highly desirable training in musicianship although they depend more heavily upon the teacher's musicianship for guidance. In many respects, the singing of a chorus or choir might be much improved if all its members were organized into ensembles of one sort or another and spent a portion of their time in regular ensemble practice. Although such an arrangement would make impossible demands upon the teacher's time, it is desirable that the choral director form a reasonably large number of ensembles, nevertheless. They stimulate interest, improve musicianship, and are an important part of the choral program.

Possibilities for the organization of choral groups are less varied in the junior high school, principally because the voices of junior-high-school pupils are less well developed and partly because the level of music ability is often lower. Further limitations are imposed by the fact that pupils in the junior high school have less choice of subjects and electives. Because they must take a relatively large number of required subjects it is more difficult to find places in the daily schedule for regular rehearsals of large choral groups. The most common groups are the glee club and chorus. Advanced choirs and smaller selective groups, although possible in some schools, are less common at this level than in the senior high school.

JUNIOR GLEE CLUB. The mixed glee club or chorus is often impractical in the junior high school for two important reasons. The voice of the adolescent boy is so unsettled at this stage that it is difficult for the teacher to form a chorus in which the distribution of parts is stable for more than short periods of time. In addition, boys and girls differ so markedly in their interests and attitudes at junior-high-school age that it is equally difficult to guide activities of the group along paths of common interest.

It is possible, however, for the teacher to surmount these difficulties and create a mixed chorus that captures the interest of both boys and girls and achieves suitably high performance standards. If pupils have discovered the pleasure of singing in the elementary school or in the general music classes of the junior high school, it is much less difficult for the teacher to carry out the necessary voice testing and to work with the group toward mastery of choral material. It is possible to accept the boys who want to sing and to encourage them to request voice tests whenever they feel their voices are not suited to the assigned parts. Girls are often quite willing to sing materials of interest to boys and boys can be persuaded to reciprocate by singing materials of special interest to the girls. When the chorus reaches a stage of development at which its singing is musically satisfying, the singers may find musical beauty more important than the meaning of the text. To be successful in developing a mixed chorus, it is necessary that the teacher possess strong interest in junior-high-school pupils and their progress in music and that he be willing to devote extra time and energy to the project. If the teacher is successful in forming the group and giving it vitality, the musical results are especially satisfying and there is added benefit to the participating pupils in that they are encouraged to continue membership in choral groups through their high-school years.

The mixed chorus in the junior high school might consist of from fifty to eighty voices, large enough so that undeveloped voices have the support of large numbers but small enough for the teacher to control the exuberant spirits of the adolescents in the group. There are numerous possibilities for part distribution, each of which depends upon the voices available and the degree to which boys' voices have changed. In this group, especially, it is vital that the teacher be less concerned with choral balance than with the welfare of each singer. In some instances, music in three treble parts is suitable, boys with unchanged and changing voices being distributed among the high, middle, and low voices. Perhaps the most common distribution is soprano, alto, and bass, the upper part consisting of girls only, the lower part sung by boys with changed voices, and the inner part being assigned to girls with low voices and boys with changing voices. In other situations four-part music is possible. Boys with changed voices are assigned to bass parts, boys with changing voices to tenor parts, and boys with unchanged voices to whichever treble part is suitable.

Here, as in every other choral organization, the pupil is assigned to the part he can sing comfortably, regardless of the effect upon choral balance. The teacher must either achieve choral balance through adjusting the number of members in the group or be content with the imperfect balance that results when all interested pupils are correctly assigned. This same factor determines whether the chorus will sing SSA, SAB, or SATB arrangements. Although it may be undesirable because of differences in tone quality to place a few unchanged boys' voices among the girls who sing soprano, or a few tenor voices among the changing voices assigned to tenor parts, the alternative is to exclude these few pupils from participation in choral activities. If the teacher subscribes to the intent of the choral program, he must provide a place for every pupil with the requisite interest and ability. The principal considerations are the welfare of each voice and the music development of every pupil.

JUNIOR BOYS' CHORUS. The boys' chorus is somewhat more practical than the mixed chorus, but it too offers problems of interest and voice utilization. Boys of junior-high-school age are apt to show little interest in singing, regarding it as an activity appropriate for girls only. For this reason, they may show little interest in a boys' chorus, especially when the organization is new. Interest mounts, however, if the music teacher is skillful in dealing with boys of this age and develops the group to the point where it can present several enjoyable performances in school assemblies, offering selections appropriate to the interests of adolescent boys. Once pupils realize that music for the boys' chorus is vigorous and spirited and that the boys in the chorus find singing enjoyable, especially if there are a few clique leaders among the group, requests for membership rise sharply.

The boys' chorus may include from forty to sixty voices and sing music of almost any variety, the criterion being the availability and distribution of voice parts. In some situations, the presence of unchanged, changing, and changed voices requires the use of four-part music. In others, voice distribution demands three-part music with two treble parts and one for changed voices. In addition, the teacher can explore the possibilities of both two-part and unison singing, including music of this type even when the chorus is capable of singing standard choral literature. The unison or two-part arrangement sometimes offers subjects of more interest to boys than music in more complex arrangements. This group might sing many selections with accompaniment, but the teacher should make a strong effort to prepare at least a few selections of the unaccompanied type characteristic of the male chorus. Boys' voices at this immature stage need the support and assurance provided by an accompaniment and the effect of their singing is enhanced by the musical embellishment of the accompanying part, but the teacher should not overlook the possibility of stimulating interest by including the unaccompanied music reminiscent of the barbershop quartet. In this group, as in the mixed chorus, the teacher must be constantly alert to the necessity for assigning voices to suitable parts, testing voices frequently, and asking that the members of the group request special voice tests whenever they feel an assigned part is beyond comfortable range.

JUNIOR GIRLS' CHORUS. The girls' chorus is often the most popular of the junior-high-school choral groups. Girls of this age show strong interest in singing and other activities open to girls alone. They are more susceptible to poetic and musical beauty than are the boys and have spiritual and romantic interests that find outlet in choral music. There is a great deal of worthy literature available, some of it difficult but much of it within the capabilities of the junior-high-school singer. The group can be large in number, consisting of sixty or more voices. This is due to the thinness of the voice of the adolescent girl and the lack of carrying power in the tone produced by a small group. For the same reasons, and because of the absence of bass and other lower parts for the girls' chorus, it is advisable that the singing be accompanied. Much of the singing should be in two or three parts, although occasional unison songs are effective and lend variety to concert programs. Music in four parts is rarely suitable due to the absence of second-alto voices and even three-part literature contains alto parts too low for many junior-high-school choruses. Although the need for frequent testing of girls' voices is not as apparent as it is where boys are concerned, the teacher is equally careful when assigning parts, re-testing voices frequently and encouraging the girls to ask for special tests as necessary.

JUNIOR ENSEMBLES. Smaller ensembles are less common in the junior high school than in programs for older pupils, but can be used to good effect. Their principal value is one of providing outlet for the pupils with outstanding voices or for pupils with interests than can not be served in one of the larger groups. If there are pupils with outstanding talent, it is possible their voices will not blend well in the large mass of undeveloped voices and that the material sung by the larger group will provide too little challenge. Although they may be valued members of the larger group, important for the leadership they provide and for the manner in which their voices support those with less assurance, the alert teacher provides supplementary experience in smaller ensembles as well. There may also be pupils with special music interests such as the girls who want to form a trio to sing popular songs or provide music for special church functions. The teacher does a service to these pupils in encouraging them to develop their music skills through helping to form the requested ensemble and guiding its rehearsals. Although the teacher may frown on the "popular trio," it is better that it develop under the teacher's guidance and ultimately turn its attention to serious music than that the girls be left to their own devices with nothing to imitate but current fads in popular-song styles. The types of ensemble organized depend on the voices available, and are apt to be composed of girls rather than boys, but they are of sufficient value in the development of music skill and interest to merit the extra time and effort they require of the teacher.

Whether in the junior or senior high school, the performing groups are affected by the same considerations and have the same basic purposes. The types of choral organization formed depend upon the variety of voices available, the degree of pupil interest, and the interest and ingenuity of the teacher. In addition, the teacher's estimate of needed instruction or experience may indicate the desirability of training or other special groups. The aim of the choral program is to provide activities suited to the abilities of all interested pupils and to arouse interest among as many pupils as possible. Although choral groups have distinct entertainment and public relations value, these are not their major objectives and there should be no tendency to exploit the groups in performances of little educational benefit. Like other phases of the music education program, choral activities are conducted so as to contribute to the well-rounded music development of the participating pupils and to the development of foundations for continued interest in performing and listening to worthy music.

Scheduling Choral Activities

One aim of music education during the past several decades has been to achieve curricular status for the larger performing groups. To make this possible, it is necessary that the group conform to certain of the standards established for curricular subjects, including requirements for pupil achievement, evaluation of pupil progress, and systematic study of organized subject matter. It is also necessary that music teachers demonstrate to administrators and the public that performing groups are worthy of curricular status, meeting these requirements and proving through performance and pupil development that their work is rightly a part of the total educational program. If this is done, performing groups can be scheduled during curricular time, reaping many benefits from their status as regular subjects. More important, by keeping such requirements in mind the teacher is reminded of the true function of the choral program and of the necessity for directing the activities of the choral groups toward justifiable educational ends.

If the choral group achieves curricular status, the scheduling arrangements that result are beneficial. The group can meet regularly with minimum conflict with other subjects and extra-curricular activities. Participating pupils are available for every rehearsal; they are not forced to be absent by required school subjects or required to give up hours before and after school. Curricular status often permits more frequent rehearsals than a scheduling arrangement that permits the group to meet only during club or activity periods. It provides for the award of credit, permitting the pupil to allocate school time to music without sacrificing progress toward graduation. This is the goal toward which the choral director should strive: regularly scheduled rehearsals during normal school hours, frequent enough to permit sustained development of choral skills and worthy of graduation credit. Daily rehearsals are highly desirable because they lend continuity to the work and eliminate much of the need for re-teaching subject matter presented during earlier rehearsals. The schedule that permits three rehearsals each week is sometimes satisfactory also, but the chorus that meets only once or twice each week faces the probability that much of the material learned during one rehearsal will be forgotten before the next. Such arrangements are especially desirable in the high school due to the natural tendency to expect higher levels of achievement from high-school choral groups. They are also more practical and easier to achieve due to the greater freedom in electives permitted high-school pupils and the growing tendency among administrators to approve credit status for high-school performing groups.

The time and place of rehearsal is important also, affecting the success of each rehearsal and the progress of the group toward learning and performance goals. It is usually advisable to avoid the hours immediately following both breakfast and lunch. There is good reason to avoid the last hour of the school day also, and perhaps the hour immediately before lunch. At these times pupils tend to be fatigued and restless, not prepared for the intense concentration conducive to productive rehearsal. The ideal rehearsal time, then, is mid-morning or mid-afternoon. Although it is not always possible to achieve this ideal, because scheduling preference must be given to academic subjects that form the core of the curriculum, the advantages of singing and learning readiness are such that the teacher strives to approach it as closely as possible.

Scheduling may also affect the choice of a rehearsal room. For best results, the room should be acoustically satisfactory, large enough to seat the chorus comfortably and to permit the development of choral tone, with unoccupied space sufficient to permit free movement about the room by both pupils and teacher. A piano is essential, as are chairs that permit good singing posture without the interference of desk space or a writing surface. The ideal here is a choral rehearsal room, although a room intended for instrumental groups or an auditorium may be satisfactory. If facilities are limited, the choral teacher may find it necessary to accept a less desirable rehearsal hour in order to use the instrumental rehearsal room or the auditorium, a desirable concession if it eliminates the necessity for conducting choral rehearsals in a room totally unsuited to the singing group.

Despite the desirability of curricular status, there are advantages in scheduling groups during extra-curricular hours. Pupils who participate often feel there is something selective and special about the group that meets before or after school. They apply for membership and sacrifice free hours because they are interested in the work of the group and are willing to meet its requirements. Administrators are favorably impressed by the group that does not disrupt the school schedule by conflicting with basic subjects, but achieves its results in extra-curricular hours by stimulating strong pupil interest. In some instances, the only possibility for meeting a large number of pupils with a variety of responsibilities toward other school subjects and activities is to schedule rehearsals when no other school function is in progress. This applies not only to the hours immediately before and after school, but to evening and weekend rehearsals as well. If there are special occasions on which evening rehearsals are necessary, and if these occasions do not arise too frequently, the teacher may find that pupils accept such an extra rehearsal eagerly and that a great deal can be accomplished in one evening of intense work.

Where there is a pressing need to prepare for performance, it may be helpful for the teacher to arrange sectional rehearsals for one part alone or for some combination of two or more parts. In normal circumstances, sectional rehearsals are not recommended for choral groups. The essence of choral teaching is that each part is presented in relation to the others and that other parts help each pupil feel the necessity for adjusting his own part to agree perfectly with the tonal and rhythmic patterns of the whole. To persist with sectional rehearsals is to lose all the benefits of hearing the other parts and to encourage singers in the undesirable habit of concentrating on their own parts rather than listening to the others. The sectional rehearsal is common among instrumental groups where any one section may form a complete ensemble, but in choral groups, except perhaps those studying works for double chorus, a section withdrawn from the balance of the group loses its identity as a part of the larger pattern and must practice uninteresting and unmusical material in drill-like fashion. For these reasons, sectional rehearsals are not regularly scheduled and rarely occur during the school day. If drill on individual parts is unavoidable, a sectional rehearsal may be an alternative preferable to a teaching procedure that forces three parts to remain idle while one section learns its part through drill. In general, however, the teacher avoids such difficulties by choosing music within the capabilities of the singers.

The arrangement of schedules for meetings of performing groups completes the preliminary steps in establishing a choral program and permits the start of actual teaching. It is essential that these preliminary matters be regarded by the teacher as important, providing solid foundations for the structure of choral activities.

UTILIZING ADOLESCENT VOICES

It is the teacher's most important responsibility to treat adolescent voices with care. Every effort must be made to preserve them, to avoid harming them, and to encourage vocal development. This requires that voices be tested carefully and often in order that the teacher have an accurate concept of their range. Pupils must be assigned to parts they can sing without strain to avoid the development of undesirable singing habits. The teacher must approach the problem of choral balance with caution, being content with imperfect balance if available voices leave no alternative. Seating is a factor in the utilization of voices also, permitting the teacher to place each pupil where his voice can receive maximum support from other voices and the accompanying instrument and helping achieve choral balance even though parts may be numerically unbalanced. By solving these problems intelligently, the teacher encourages pupils to continue their interest in singing activities and creates circumstances favorable to the development of vocal abilities.

Voice Ranges and Classifications

The first fact for the teacher to accept is that each voice is different from every other, a completely personal music instrument whose characteristics are determined by physical, mental, and emotional traits in combinations unique to every individual. Voice ranges and qualities exhibit limitless

TABLE 5. VOICE CLASSIFICATIONS, RANGES, AND CHARACTERISTICS.

Classification	*Range*	*Description*
Soprano	c^1 to a^2	Characterized by brightness of quality and ringing tone
Coloratura soprano	e^1 to f^3	Agile voice suited to execution of coloratura embellishments
Lyric soprano	c^1 to c^3	Light voice of pure quality suited to cantabile style
Dramatic soprano	c^1 to c^3	Voice with power and brilliance suited to declamatory roles
Mezzo-soprano	b-flat to b-flat^2	A voice both rich and bright combining characteristics of soprano and contralto
Mezzo-contralto	g to g^2	Light contralto quality midway between contralto and mezzo-soprano
Contralto	e to e^2	Rich and full, especially weighty in lower register
Haute contre	c to c^2	Term now largely obsolete denoting high tenor
Tenor	c to c^2	Characterized by brightness of tone and ringing quality
Lyric tenor	d to c^2	Light voice of pure quality suited to cantabile style
Heroic tenor	c to c^2	Powerful, brilliant, and agile, suited to dramatic roles
Tenore robusto	c to c^2	Characterized by fullness, vigor, and power of tone
Tenor-baritone	B-flat to b-flat^1	Combining tenor and baritone characteristics and midway between them
Baritone	A-flat to a-flat^1	Fullness of quality with depth in lower register, brightness above
Bass-baritone	G to f-sharp^1	A voice with depth and power, especially effective in lower register
Basso cantante	G to g^1	A low voice of lyric quality suited to cantabile style
Basso buffo	F to e^1	A low but agile voice suited to roles of comic nature
Basso profondo	C to c^1	Characterized by resonance of its lower register
Contra-bass	F_1 to c^1	Doubly low

variations from singer to singer and each voice changes and develops so that the same voice may exhibit different characteristics at different times.

As an indication of the wide variety of voice ranges and qualities, Table 5 lists some of the terms used to classify voice types. Ranges given are generalizations only, necessarily ignoring the variations among individuals of the same classification in order to reduce the list to reasonable length. Despite the large number of descriptive terms in common use, it is difficult to find a term that describes precisely the range and quality of an individual voice, especially when dealing with adolescents whose voices are not yet fully developed.

The teacher's first step is to reduce the list of voice types to those customarily used in reference to adult singers: soprano, mezzo-soprano, contralto, tenor, baritone, and bass. Where professional singers are concerned, it is normal to expect a voice compass of two octaves or more, but it is advisable to expect a compass of slightly less than two octaves, perhaps a thirteenth, when dealing with untrained singers. As a means of comparison, adult voices might be regarded as having a compass that extends seven tones above and seven tones below the pitches d, f, and a for basses, baritones, and tenors respectively, e^1, g^1, and b^1 for contraltos, mezzo-sopranos, and sopranos. For choral work, these categories may be reduced to four by the elimination of the mezzo-soprano and baritone classifications. The remaining classifications—soprano, alto, tenor, and bass—provide a basis for assigning adult voices to choral parts, sub-divided if necessary for eight-part music. Two other factors are voice quality, having to do with resonance, weight and color of tone, and *tessitura*, the area within the vocal compass in which the voice can be used most comfortably.

In assigning voice parts there are two factors to be considered: the voice and the music it sings. Although in professional groups it is possible to select from a large number of voices those perfectly suited to any one part, eliminating singers whose ranges or qualities are not acceptable, it is necessary when forming school choral groups to use the voices available, selecting music to fit the voices. Although voice quality may determine classification in professional circles, it is range rather than quality that determines the part the immature voice is able to sing. Thus it is necessary to use discretion in applying the old adage that part assignments are based on quality; following that principle inflexibly could cause young singers to develop permanent singing difficulties. In classifying these young singers for choral groups, the teacher must consider range first, placing voices according to quality only when the compass of the voice is wide enough to permit.

JUNIOR-HIGH-SCHOOL VOICES. What practice may the teacher follow, then, to create a degree of order in the confusing array of voice types in the junior high school? A first step is to establish a small number of voice classifications with range requirements such that every singer can be placed in one or another of them, as suggested in Chapter 4. Example 2, page 65, indicates the variety of voice ranges among junior-high-school pupils; Example 3, page 66, indicates the demands made by literature intended for singers of this age. With such information in mind, it is possible to establish classifications arbitrarily, beginning with a pitch centered among those the various voices of any one type might be able to sing and limiting the extremes of the range to a compass all voices should be able to sing with relative ease. These classifications might separate voices as follows: high voices d^1 to f^2; medium voices b-flat to d^2; changing voices g to g^1; changed voices A to c^1. This arrangement suggests a compass of a tenth for all pupils except boys with changing voices, their suggested compass being only one octave. It assumes that all pupils interested in joining a choral group will be able to use the voice with facility and that those unable to sing through the required compass, a narrow one in every case, are not ready for this type of singing activity.

Once these classifications are established, it is the teacher's responsibility to select appropriate materials, rejecting the selections that carry any part beyond the established limits. The teacher is well advised to establish a set of classifications for each choral group, based upon both voice testing and a survey of the appropriate literature; the requirements for the middle voice in a group singing SAB arrangements, for example, would be different from those of the lowest voice in a group singing SSA arrangements. Moreover, the teacher will find it desirable to establish classifications appropriate for the pupils in his own school rather than to accept criteria developed in a different situation; voice ranges and classifications are apt to vary from urban to rural areas and to be affected by other factors in such a way that standards satisfactory in one school are quite unsatisfactory in another.

SENIOR-HIGH-SCHOOL VOICES. Similar procedures are recommended for classifying voices of high-school pupils interested in choral singing. Their voices are somewhat more mature than those of pupils in the junior high school, but still not developed to the point of adult range and quality. It is thus unwise to assume that high-school pupils can be tested and classified according to criteria established for adults; to the contrary, it is essential that the teacher develop a concept of reasonable range through experience in testing voices and through analysis of literature to be sung.

Example 4, page 67, indicates the range demands of choral literature intended for high-school singers. Most of it can be sung by voices with a compass of one and a half octaves, a fact that provides a basis for voice classification. The teacher might establish these ranges arbitrarily, noting each individual's ability to sing beyond the estabilshed compass or his difficulty in singing either its upper or lower extreme: soprano c^1 to g^2; alto a to e^2; tenor c to g^1; bass G to d^1. Parts are then assigned according to these criteria and music is selected to fit the capabilities of the singers. In some instances, the teacher will find that the soprano range can be extended to a^2 or the bass to F. In others, it may be useful to regard the group as being composed of eight parts to permit more accurate classification of voices. In the event it is desirable for some special reason to prepare a choral selection that exceeds the established ranges, one that requires altos to sing down to g, for example, the teacher must decide which voices shall be permitted to sing the part and whether there are enough able voices to make performance feasible.

Voice Testing

Each teacher of music must answer for himself the question of whether a performing group should be open to all who apply, some of whom may possess minimum skill, or whether it should be open only to those who show special talent. One of the basic questions concerning current practices in music education, particularly at the high-school level, is whether music should be for all or only for the talented. If the performing group is closed to those who have comparatively little skill it becomes a specialized organization and does not minister to the needs of all who would benefit from it. It is obvious that the level of performance rises when requirements for entrance are highly selective; the better the performer, the better the performance. It is not proper, however, to deny admission to those of average ability or less, nor is it in accordance with the goals of music education to exclude those who show interest and the will to improve. Thus it is well for the teacher to regard voice tests as a means of discovering vocal characteristics of applicants rather than as a means of refusing participation to those of limited skill.

TEST GOALS. Whether the teacher's intent is to select talented singers or to determine the ability of all who apply, the tryout procedure explores thoroughly the characteristics of each voice and the ability of each singer.

The teacher must have accurate and complete information about the pupil if he is to be assigned to the proper part and to gain from his choral experience. There is a stronger need for careful testing of the weaker singers than of those who are outstanding. To guide the pupil properly, the teacher should know his (1) vocal range, including both the register and compass of the voice, (2) voice quality, including beauty of tone and suitability for a particular part, (3) pitch accuracy, including sensitivity to blend and tonal memory, (4) general musicianship and sensitivity to musical effect, (5) music-reading ability, including understanding of notation and the ability to hold a part in an ensemble, (6) character, including attitude, interest, and dependability. Each of these factors is pertinent to the teacher's problem of understanding, placing, and guiding the pupil and to the degree of success he will enjoy as a member of the choral group. The means of gathering this information are varied and each teacher develops a testing procedure in accordance with his own preferences, the characteristics of the pupils being tested, and the standards established for the choral ensemble.

RANGE. To determine the range of the voice, it is necessary that the pupil sing alone through exercises that probe the limits of his vocal compass. The exercise might be a scale, an arpeggio, or a brief melodic excerpt that can be transposed easily into a number of different keys. The latter is most acceptable to the pupil because it permits him to sing a familiar melody more natural to him than something in the nature of a vocalise. The teacher chooses a familiar song for the purpose, perhaps one most pupils know through the work of the general music class such as "America" or the first four measures of "Swing Low, Sweet Chariot" or "Old Folks at Home." The pupil sings the phrase in the successively higher or lower keys indicated by the teacher through the piano accompaniment and the process is halted by the teacher when it is apparent the pupil has reached the limit of his comfortable range. Although this procedure is one the pupil can follow easily, it is somewhat impractical in that song texts and melodic patterns sometimes introduce difficulties that should not be present in a test exercise. The difficulty with words can be eliminated by asking the pupil to sing with a neutral syllable or open vowel, but the melodic pattern usually can not be revised without sacrifice of familiarity.

A more practical solution is to create a pleasing but brief melodic pattern supported by an interesting harmonization appealing to the taste of the pupils being tested. This is sung with a neutral syllable or sustained vowel and moved sequentially by the teacher into successively higher or lower keys as necessary. The chief requisites are that it offer a smooth vocal line, that it be attractive to pupil tastes, and that it be simple enough to permit the teacher to transpose it instantly into the desired keys.

Scales and arpeggios are popular as exercises for exploring range because they permit quicker testing and may be modified easily to fit the requirements of each test situation. The scale that ascends five degrees and then returns offers a smooth vocal line, is easily transposed in sequential fashion, and can be accompanied by the teacher without concentration upon the keyboard. The arpeggio, such as one that ascends through a major chord to the octave and then returns, is advantageous in that it does not require the singer to dwell on pitches at the upper limit of his compass and in that the only accompaniment required is the chord itself. The disadvantage of both scales and arpeggios is that they tend to be mechanical and to give the pupil the impression he is singing an exercise rather than an attractive melodic line. If pupils are strongly interested in joining the choral group, understand the nature and purpose of the test, and especially if they have been tested on previous occasions, the teacher can turn to scales and arpeggios to complete the testing quickly without sacrificing accuracy or results. If pupils are not entirely at ease or if the teacher wishes to hold pupils not certain of their interest, it is preferable that he use melodic patterns in this portion of the test, presenting them as examples of pleasing music rather than as vocal exercises. In either case, it is desirable that the piano be used to accompany the test. The accompaniment supports the melodic pattern, creates a pleasing effect, and gives confidence to pupils unaccustomed to singing alone. This requires that the teacher develop piano facility, especially a familiarity with the keyboard sufficient to permit easy transposition of test exercises into different keys.

VOICE QUALITY AND MUSICIANSHIP. The teacher may also ask that the pupil sing a short song to listen to voice quality and to estimate the pupil's general musicianship. These factors can be observed as the pupil sings exercises intended to demonstrate his range, but can be determined more accurately through a song suited to the purpose. Here too it is necessary to select a song known to the pupil, perhaps by permitting him to choose from a list prepared for the occasion. In preparing for voice testing, the teacher selects a number of songs suitable for each vocal range that encourage attention to such details as phrasing and dynamics and are of appropriate musical quality. Song books containing these selections are kept at hand along with a list to which either teacher or pupil can refer. The teacher asks that the pupil sing the song to the best of his ability, giving proper attention to both his manner of singing and the interpretation of the song, and helps the pupil by providing an artistic accompaniment. In addition to listening for voice quality and musicianship, the teacher can draw conclusions concerning pitch accuracy through listening to the song and the range-testing exercises. For further evidence of pitch sense and tonal memory, the teacher may ask the pupil to sing a short melodic phrase without accompaniment and to repeat a succession of pitches played by the teacher at the piano. As the pupil sings a short melodic excerpt, such as the first four measures of "America" or "Sweet and Low," the teacher listens to each tone, especially the second, third, and sixth of the scale, to judge the singer's accuracy of pitch. To test tonal memory, the teacher asks the pupil to sing a series of pitches dictated from the piano, beginning with an easily remembered pattern based on the scale or primary chords and progressing to more difficult patterns less closely related to a tonal center.

READING ABILITY. To evaluate reading and part-singing ability, the teacher turns to easy arrangements in three or four parts, using either a song book or octavo music of the type sung by the choral group. The pupil is given the first pitch and a first chord to establish the key and sings his part as the teacher plays the others at the piano. The procedure can be adjusted to any level of difficulty by judicious selection of test materials and the teacher can aid the pupil as necessary by emphasizing his part. In most instances it should include only the easiest music, but the teacher may wish to use more difficult music when choosing members for a highly selective choral group, raising standards to offer a challenge to each applicant and to identify those of outstanding ability. In this phase of the voice test as well as in certain of the others, there are possibilities for placing applicants in quartets. If it is practical to arrange schedules so four pupils of appropriate range can be present at one time, the teacher can evaluate reading ability, voice quality, blend and musicianship realistically as the applicants sing together. The quartet procedure is impractical when large numbers of pupils are being tested for admission to a chorus or glee club, but is essential in the selection of voices for small ensembles.

ATTITUDES AND INTERESTS. In addition to evaluating each pupil's music abilities, the teacher gathers information concerning non-musical traits such as character and attitude. Where performing groups are concerned, these personal characteristics are of consequence, sometimes exerting more influence upon the success of the pupil and his value to the group than his music skills. The disinterested pupil with outstanding talent creates many problems through his influence on other pupils and his lack of concern for the responsibilities of membership. The pupil with less talent but stronger interest often reaches higher levels of competence and makes greater contributions to the success of the group. The teacher examines any available information concerning the pupil's interest, dependability, scholastic standing, industry, leadership potential, and activity in extra-curricular affairs. The pupil's permanent records provide much of this information as well as scores of intelligence and aptitude tests. Other teachers can be consulted if time permits, especially those who know the pupil through his participation in extra-curricular activities, his homeroom teacher, and the teacher who may have guided his work in instrumental music. There are pupils who "find" themselves in choral music despite lack of interest in any other phase of school work, of course, but the teacher may assume that pupils who are successful scholastically and active in extra-curricular affairs will become valuable members of the choral group.

PLANNING THE PROCEDURE. These suggestions for voice testing and evaluating the general desirability of applicants are possibilities the choral teacher considers in establishing a test procedure. Not all of them are needed, however, in every test situation. When testing applicants for a glee club intended to stimulate interest and provide for large numbers of pupils, the teacher might decide to use nothing more than a test for range, drawing conclusions about other factors during the course of this one test. For an advanced and more selective choir, the teacher determines range, quality, pitch sensitivity, and musicianship with considerable accuracy. For small ensembles, all factors are important, including the manner in which the voice blends with others in a quartet. In every case, the test procedure is determined by the nature of the group being formed, the general level of abilities among applicants, and the time available for testing. It is important also that the teacher develop a system for conducting the test once its content has been determined, establishing a pattern that can be followed with every pupil to prevent waste of time. If it is possible to meet all applicants in one group before voice tests are conducted, the teacher can insure that testing proceed smoothly and swiftly by explaining the nature of the test and by asking pupils to sing the test exercises together before singing them individually.

TIME-SAVING DEVICES. Voice testing requires a great deal of the teacher's time if it is to be done properly, but the teacher's load can be markedly reduced through advance planning and systematic procedures. Voice tests can be conducted in the spring of one year for choral groups that are to be active during the next. This prevents the loss of several weeks for testing during the beginning of the year when rehearsal time must be used to greatest advantage. It also permits the teacher to conduct tests without conflict with the activities natural to the beginning of the school year and without competing for the attention of pupils trying to become accustomed to new classes, teachers, and perhaps a new school. In setting dates for the voice-test period, the teacher first checks his own schedule for performances and other responsibilities and the school calendar to avoid conflict with examination periods and other special events. It is advisable to arrange for testing voices of interested pupils in the final year of nearby elementary or junior high schools. For this, the teacher secures the approval of the principal and enlists the coöperation of the music teacher in the lower grade. Tests are given by scheduled appointment, the teacher posting appointment sheets on the bulletin board to permit pupils to sign their names after preferred times. This requires that the teacher estimate the time required for his test procedure, establish a testing schedule, and adhere to it to utilize the available time efficiently.

A mimeographed form is a useful time-saving device. File cards, perhaps 5″ × 7″, are desirable because they are easy to file. The form might provide space for data from cumulative records, coded as necessary to prevent disclosure of confidential information to pupils, questionnaire items to be completed by the pupil, giving complete name, address, telephone, training, experience, and other desired information, and a series of items to be checked by the teacher during the voice test to record voice range, quality, intonation, and so forth. One form might be prepared in advance for each student who signs the appointment sheet and the questionnaire items completed immediately before or after the pupil is given the voice test. The teacher might further reduce the burden of this work by selecting a student assistant, an officer or member of the choral group for which tests are being conducted. The assistant is given the responsibility of ushering pupils in and out of the testing room at their appointed times, answering questions as applicants complete questionnaires, and doing other clerical work to free the teacher for the more important work of testing voices.

Choral Balance

In setting the size of the choral group and determining the number of voices to be assigned to each part, the teacher's aim is to create a body of tone and balance of parts that will produce a pleasing effect. In many instances the teacher has little opportunity to adjust balance to his satisfaction because of the scarcity of voices for certain parts. High-school groups often suffer from a shortage of tenors and altos. Groups in the junior high school have similar difficulties with sopranos and basses. The teacher develops a concept of choral balance nevertheless and in striving to achieve it observes a number of basic principles.

Superior voices sound well alone, in small ensembles in which there is one voice to each part and in small choral groups in which there are only a few voices to each part. The sound has vitality and resonance, can be accurate in pitch, negotiates changes in intensity with ease, and is generally pleasing. Thus the trio, quartet, and quintet must be composed of capable singers and the advanced choir can be limited to a small number of voices for each part.

Immature voices need the support of large numbers. The young singer is unsure; both boys and girls gain confidence when singing with a large group. The uncertainty is in the singer's manner, in his inability to hold his part, and in the tone of the voice itself. The voice is uncertain in pitch, lacking in carrying power, and deficient in quality. When dealing with immature voices the teacher overcomes some of these difficulties by expanding the choral group to the point where the mass of voices masks inaccuracies of pitch, compensates for the lack of resonance, and obscures the quality of individual voices. The teacher works for the improvement of tone quality, of course, but provides the security of numbers until voices can be developed.

Minor inaccuracies of pitch among voices singing the same part are obscured by an "averaging" effect when a large number of voices is involved. Two voices of good tone quality and accurate pitch create a pleasing effect when singing in unison, but two voices inaccurate in pitch produce an effect that borders on the painful. The discomfort of the listener decreases as more voices join in the singing. A reasonable explanation is that two tone-producing instruments, devoid of vibrato or any fluctuation in pitch or intensity, can be adjusted until their pitches coincide at, for example, 440 vibrations per second. At this point they produce a very clear and incisive tone. The same two instruments adjusted to produce 440 and 445 vibrations respectively create the two basic pitches plus a "beat" occurring five times each second whenever the wave of one pitch happens to coincide with that of the other. The listener experiences aural discomfort because the two basic pitches conflict with each other and the beat emphasizes the lack of equilibrium in their relationship. The result is quite different if the number of instruments is increased until the pitches produced include a dozen or more different frequencies between 440 and 445. Beats then occur so frequently that the listener is unable to distinguish one among the others and the tone appears to be constant. Instead, he hears without discomfort a tone of somewhat indeterminate pitch with a spectrum five vibrations in width. The tone is deficient in brilliance and does not have a sharp edge of either pitch or tone quality, but it is not unpleasing to most listeners.

Similarly, a large number of singers unable to sense the precise matching of pitches produces tone with a wide vibration spectrum that does not cause the listener great discomfort. This wide tone is undesirable in music for many parts or that which is based on complex and dissonant harmonies, but can be acceptable in music simple in structure appropriate for singers with uncertain voices. Thus the choral group composed of untrained singers seems to improve in quality as it increases in size.

The teacher chooses between selecting a small group of superior voices or forming a larger group on a less selective basis. The smaller group achieves excellence quickly and is less difficult to direct; the larger group can be successful but requires that the teacher teach. The larger group is to be desired and, within reasonable limits, the teacher strives to increase membership in the choral organization. The growth of the group is halted, however, before it becomes so large as to be musically unwieldly or difficult to control.

Balance of parts is another factor that affects the success of the choral group by helping determine the quality of its performance and the response of its audience. There is little unanimity in opinions concerning ideal balance in terms of the proportionate number of voices assigned to each part. Partially, this is due to the fact that few choral teachers can draw from enough singers to experiment with part distribution. In addition, there are differences of taste among choral teachers, differences in strength and quality among voices available, even differences in the acoustical characteristics of rehearsal rooms and concert halls. Here too, however, there are general factors to be considered when determining the number of singers needed for each part.

Male voices are usually stronger than those of women. The trained soprano may develop resonant, ringing tone that penetrates to the uppermost reaches of the concert hall, but untrained female voices, particularly those of girls who have not attained full maturity, tend to be deficient in power. The male voice, on the other hand, even the newly changed voice of the adolescent, tends to carry to greater distances and to penetrate through other sounds. The penetration is not always desirable, due to the gruffness and rasp of the male voice particularly noticeable during adolescence. Moreover, the rasp sometimes becomes more pronounced when the voice is forced to greater volume.

Parts sung by basses are usually important in that they provide a foundation for the rest of the musical structure. Rarely in choral music is one part important for itself alone, but the bass part merits special attention due to its function of supporting the other parts and because it generates the harmonic patterns of the music. In performance, the balance that awards prominence to the bass part produces an effect of solidity and fullness appealing to audiences, whereas a balance weak in its lower register seems thin and may be less pleasing.

Soprano parts are needed and must be distinguishable. They frequently present the melody necessary to make music intelligible to the listener. If the listener is unable to hear the melody and follow it easily he is left with nothing more than a succession of harmonic colors difficult to comprehend and tiresome to follow. Unless the style of a particular selection relies solely on harmonic color and requires that individual parts be perfectly welded into a single mass of tone, the director is considerate of his audience when he presents the thematic basis of the music with unmistakable clarity.

Untrained voices of adolescent girls tend to be thin, lacking in resonance and color, and breathy in quality. This is especially true of girls who would be classified as second sopranos, unable to sing either the higher pitches required of sopranos or the lower pitches of the alto part. In many instances, the necessity for classifying the singer among the second sopranos arises not because the voice is without potential but because its potential has not been developed. In either case, the treble parts in a choral group of mixed voices may be deficient in tone quality and barely audible unless the number of girls singing the parts is augmented beyond normal proportions.

Newly changed voices of boys need the support of numbers. When the boy's voice drops in register, its power and penetrating quality increase. The voice is not weak in power, but it is weak in that it is difficult to control and in that its owner is lacking in vocal assurance. The support of numbers is needed because it lends assurance to the singer and because the voice negotiates scales and intervals more easily when it does so in the company of others.

These conditions create an interesting but complex problem for the choral teacher. Despite the difficulties created by voices different in quality, power, and assurance, he must adjust the size of the group and the distribution of parts to create the best possible choral balance. He considers the musical effect created by the singing and the necessity for presenting a pleasing performance to each audience, but realizes that in doing so he may not sacrifice the immediate welfare or future development of the singers. He strives to attract large numbers of pupils to membership to compensate for the lack of vocal resonance, to achieve the effect of satisfactory blend, and to build group confidence. He expects to have fewer boys than girls, but enough basses to provide solidity and to eliminate any tendency toward forced singing and harsh tone. Sopranos must be numerous enough to assure that the upper part will be clearly distinguishable and there must be added strength in the second soprano to compensate for the lack of body in the voice of the adolescent girl. If one part is being sung by boys with changing or newly changed voices, their group must be large enough so that each voice is supported by a number of others.

There is no mathematical formula through which choral balance can be achieved. For one choral group, a distribution of parts based on a multiple of three sopranos, four altos, two tenors, and three basses might be satisfactory, whereas best results might be achieved in another through an almost equal distribution of parts. The girls' glee club in the high school might sound best based on a pattern of four sopranos, five second sopranos, and three altos, but a similar group in the junior high school might need four sopranos, an equal number of altos, and six second sopranos. The final arbiter of such questions must be the ear; a balanced chorus is one that *sounds* balanced. There are so many variables in the choral equation that it is impossible to predict what the results will be in any given situation. The choral teacher listens critically to his choral group to judge the effect and make whatever adjustments are desirable. It is probable that most directors of choral groups achieve balance through adjusting dynamics rather than part strength. In the public schools, the teacher accepts all applicants who show interest and reasonable ability and often finds that regardless of the size of the choral group there are fewer altos and tenors than would be desirable. Numerical balance is easier to achieve in selective groups of limited size, but even in these groups there is no substitute for the discerning and critical ear of the director.

Choral Seating

There are many reasons for examining the various ways in which any chorus or glee club can be assigned to seats in the rehearsal room or standing positions on the concert stage. In arranging and re-arranging the seating plan, the teacher seeks to improve the musical effect and to adjust other factors as well. Where musical effect is concerned, the teacher strives to improve balance, intonation, and blend and to achieve ensemble and homogeneity of tone. He tries to provide support for the weaker parts and to place important parts next to each other to improve enesmble in special passages. The reasons other than musical have to do with the visual effect created by the placement of the group on the stage, the control and discipline of a large group of high-spirited pupils, and, not unimportant, the ease and speed of checking attendance at rehearsals.

Balance can be improved by placing weaker voice-groups where they can be heard and stronger ones where their tone is absorbed or covered. The weaker voice-group is normally moved to the front so its tone carries to the audience without having to penetrate the others. On some stages the weaker voice-groups carry better if moved to the side or rear against a reflecting surface or if placed in an area of the stage that is acoustically live. Stronger voices are often placed behind the weaker ones or at either side. If placed at the sides, the singers can be turned to face the center of the stage, their voices being directed toward the conductor and the other singers rather than toward the audience. To reduce further the power of the stronger voices, they can be placed against and under stage draperies that absorb some of the tone.

Intonation can sometimes be improved by moving the offending part closer to the piano or another part that offers harmonic support. Sopranos, for example, may find it easier to sing in tune if they are placed close to basses who sing the foundation of the harmonic structure. Blend, closely related to intonation, can sometimes be improved by experimenting with the seating plan, moving certain parts closer to the piano or placing out-of-tune parts adjacent to those likely to be in tune. One source of difficulty is the common practice of placing boys behind the girls. Voices of adolescent boys tend to be heavy and guttural, especially basses whose natural desire is to sound like mature basses and who force their voices to achieve this effect. Placing these boys at the rear of the stage may cause them to force their voices even further and makes it difficult for them to hear the piano and the other parts. If they do sink below the pitch, they then pull the rest of the parts with them.

The singing group achieves "ensemble" when it develops unanimity of feeling for attacks, releases, rhythms, dynamics, and the contours of phrases. To some extent, this depends upon alert response to the conductor's signals, but it depends also upon each singer's musicianship and his intuitive feeling for the reactions of the other singers. Ensemble can be improved by revising the seating plan, moving certain singers or parts closer to the conductor or the piano, or by placing singers otherwise slow to respond between those who can lead them and provide assurance. Homogeneous tone can be achieved in the same way, voices of distinctive quality being placed among other voices to create a well-mixed choral tone in which no one voice is distinguishable in the mass. Weaker singers chronically uncertain of their parts or likely to deviate from the correct pitch can be surrounded by stronger singers. Finally, parts that often sing together can be placed next to each other so that each part can hear and follow the other in the passages they sing together.

Appearance is one of the non-musical reasons for examining various seating possibilities. Rectangular, semi-circular, and wedge-shaped groupings are desirable on some stages, whereas larger stages may suggest that the director place the chorus informally in several separate groups if the music and the skill of the chorus permit. In any case, the object is to please the eye and to relieve the monotony of static grouping. In rehearsal, an established seating plan aids the director in maintaining control over a large group. The very existence of a seating plan in which each singer is assigned to a permanent seat gives an impression of stability and order and acts as a deterrent when adolescent singers are tempted to indulge their volatile spirits. The teacher can take advantage of the seating plan to separate pupils who disturb the work of the group when seated together. An established seating plan speeds the chore of checking attendance, whether it is done by the teacher or by a student assistant. To this end, the teacher keeps a seating chart always at hand and the student assistant should have access to one when recording absences. A duplicate chart posted in the rehearsal room permits singers to find their seats quickly until they become accustomed to sitting in their assigned places.

The almost universally popular seating plan is the rectangle or semicircle in which all voices singing one part are grouped together. Groups are placed front or rear, right or left depending upon the strength and ability of the singers who make up each part and upon the acoustical characteristics of the rehearsal room or concert hall. No choral director is content to follow an arrangement favored by another director working with a different chorus under different acoustical conditions. The final authority, always, is the ear of the director. It judges the effect created by the voices in his chorus singing the music he has selected in the concert hall in which his chorus must perform.

The relatively standard seating plan consisting of four groups of singers placed to form a rectangle can be varied to produce many different seating plans simply by changing the relative positions of the four groups within the rectangle. The chorus that has developed reading ability and vocal assurance can be grouped in quartets. This makes it almost impossible for the conductor to give cues to single parts, but results in superior blend and balance. The members of each quartet stand beside each other or can be arranged so that sopranos are in the front row of the chorus, altos in the second row, tenors in the third, and basses in the fourth. The teacher might find it interesting to experiment also with a heterogeneous seating plan, provided the singers are thoroughly familiar with their parts and can sing them independently with assurance. To achieve the heterogeneous mixture, the singers simply assemble informally without regard for part groupings in much the same way a congregation assembles in the pews of a church. Although this seems to conflict with all the rules of choral singing, the singers learn something from the experience and the director, if his chorus has been well trained, may be agreeably surprised by the tonal result. Another possibility has to do with increasing the distance between singers. Many choral singers feel it is necessary to stand close to a neighbor so that the chorus becomes a tightly packed mass, assuming that proximity to other singers makes it easier to achieve unity of response. This is often true, but here again the director may experiment by asking the chorus to expand in width and depth until singers are four, six, or even ten feet apart. This forces the singers to be independent and at the same time requires that they listen intently for the other voices, and both of these results are desirable.

A seating plan, therefore, is more than a formula to be followed rigidly. There are almost limitless possibilities for varying the plan and for achieving special effects through re-arranging the singers. There are general principles to be considered, but the principles need not be followed inflexibly. Each choral director grasps the opportunity to discover the seating plan best suited to his chorus. In doing so, the director resists the tendency to accept stereotyped solutions and searches for originality because it may point the way to improved musical effect. A seating plan is another means for achieving satisfying musical results and is judged by the quality of the music it produces.

ADMINISTRATIVE CONSIDERATIONS

Many factors of an administrative nature have been discussed in the preceding pages. Proposals to superintendents and principals concerning the organization of new choral groups are administrative matters, as are the scheduling of rehearsal periods and voice tests, recruiting new members, and the efficient use of cumulative records and mimeographed forms specially designed for the use of the choral teacher. Relationships with parents and the community are administrative responsibilities, including publicity devices, bulletins and letters to parents, and the formation of "booster" organizations. Such duties are not musical in nature, but the successful choral teacher is one who realizes that efficient solution of administrative problems clears more time for purely musical work and paves the way for a successful choral program. The choral teacher can not withdraw from all other responsibilities to devote his time exclusively to conducting rehearsals and performances. As the choral program grows in size and quality, and as it becomes more and more important to the school and the community, the work required to sustain its efficient operation multiplies.

A source of assistance is the choral group itself. The teacher needs willing hands to help with clerical and other routine work. The usual choral group contains many pupils eager to help with behind-the-scenes duties. By permitting pupils to aid him in these tasks, and to shoulder certain responsibilities themselves, the choral teacher not only frees himself for musical work only he can do, he stimulates pupil interest and coöperation as well. Adolescent pupils, especially, want to feel they are accepting adult responsibilities, that they are directing their own efforts with some degree of independence, and that they are respected for their abilities and their opinions. The teacher caters to these normal adolescent desires by delegating some of his duties to pupil assistants and by adopting democratic procedures for the non-musical phases of the choral program. By doing so, he provides opportunity for outstanding pupils to give the enthusiastic participation of which they are capable.

One means of providing this assistance is through the establishment of parliamentary organization in the glee club or chorus. Once each year, or more often if necessary, the chorus nominates and elects officers, determines needed committees, and discusses the duties of each office. Thereafter it holds business meetings as necessary to conduct the business of the organization. A president and secretary are needed and other officers such as treasurer, business manager, and publicity manager may be elected or appointed as necessary. Certain posts must of necessity be filled by appointment, the teacher selecting pupils who have the special abilities required of the several needed accompanists, assistant conductor, librarian, wardrobe supervisor, and stage manager.

Committees, if they are needed, may be elected by the group. A membership committee is helpful in planning and carrying out the annual recruiting drive and the publicity that precedes it. If the chorus is in demand for out-of-school performances, a steering or program committee can evaluate all performance requests, handle related correspondence, and make transportation and other arrangements for concert appearances. A social committee is sometimes desirable to discuss the possibilities of an annual dance, picnic, or other activity, to make plans, secure extra pupil assistance, and arrange for details. The possibilities for this sort of organization are almost limitless. There are pitfalls for the teacher, of course, if the multiplicity of officers and activities converts the chorus from a musical to a social organization, requiring that rehearsal time be given up to business meetings and committee discussions. Further, there is the ever-present possibility that elections determine who is popular rather than who is best qualified for each post. With proper guidance, however, the student organization can become indispensable to the teacher as a means of administering the choral program.

The choral teacher must be a person of many talents. He must be a thorough musician and a skillful administrator. He must be able to win the esteem of administrators, other teachers, pupils, parents, and the public. He must know adolescent voices to utilize them effectively. He must know and be sensitive to the factors essential in the development of outstanding choral performance. Above all, he must be a music educator, sensitive to the goals of music education and to the function of the choral program in developing among large numbers of pupils the ability to participate in and find enjoyment through choral music.

8: *the choral rehearsal*

The choral rehearsal is a segment of the school day of great interest to the choral teacher because it permits him to indulge his desire for making music with pupils carefully selected for ability and interest. More important, the rehearsal is the choral director's opportunity to teach, an opportunity that becomes a responsibility because of the basic purposes of the choral program. The choral rehearsal is his classroom, not for preparing concerts, but for furthering the music interests and abilities of the singers.

Like every other phase of music teaching, the choral rehearsal has goals. They guide the work of every rehearsal and help the teacher use rehearsal time efficiently. They serve as a checklist to which the teacher returns periodically to determine whether choral rehearsals are being properly planned and are achieving proper ends. Such goals include the development of attitudes, interests, and understandings sought for all pupils through the total music program.

Goals pertinent to choral performance are those sought naturally by the choral director. Singers must be taught something of the physical aspects of singing. This includes posture, breathing, and the support of tone through proper use of physical resources. Pupils must achieve something in the area of tone itself, developing vocal resonance, sensitivity to intonation and blend, and the tone-thinking ability to image and recall pitches. The rehearsal includes the study of music in the choral repertoire and increases the singer's ability to read choral music. It teaches stage deportment, provides motivation for the work of rehearsal and the culmination of this work in performance.

Other goals are those that apply to the general music class, the choral program, the instrumental program, and every other activity conducted under the banner of music education. They have to do with the well-rounded musical growth of all pupils and require that the choral director be a music educator in the best sense of the term. Goals of this type are discussed at length in Chapter 3. Their value is less immediate and less apparent to both the choral director and the singers than the performance goals, but they can be achieved through choral activities and deserve an important place in the choral director's thinking.

It is improbable that one teacher will follow the same path as another toward these goals. It is inevitable that there be differences of opinion concerning the relative merits of the various goals, even a lack of agreement that all of them are important. The demands for performance vary from school to school, forcing some teachers to devote virtually all their effort to preparing performance materials but permitting others to divide rehearsal time between concert preparation and the teaching of music. There are differences of opinion concerning the means for achieving the various goals, the materials to be used, the manner of their presentation, and the best methods for teaching music knowledge and skill. There are teachers who believe that the choral group which works toward performance also makes progress toward the general goals; conversely, there are teachers who believe that progress toward the general goals improves the quality of performance. Both may be correct. Progress in both the performance and general areas is possible if the choral group is directed with this double progress as its purpose.

THE PHYSICAL ASPECT

Singing is a physical act. Vocal tone is produced, amplified, modified, and controlled by the physical mechanism of the body. Portions of this act are voluntary, subject to the conscious control of the singer and directed by his will. Other portions are involuntary, occurring without the singer's direct control and in such a way that the singer is not conscious of the physical factors involved. Singing is also a mental process. Certain of the involuntary reactions can be adjusted through the subtle influence of mental concepts. The voluntary processes can be directed by the will or influenced less directly by a state of mind. In any case, the singer must learn to use his physical resources effectively and builds habits through which he becomes the master, either consciously or unconsciously, of his physical powers.

Preparing to Sing

To help the singer use his physical powers properly, the teacher in some instances directs attention to the portion of the body concerned; in others, he directs attention away from the body so that involuntary responses can occur freely without being hampered by the singer's mental concern or fruitless attempts at control. In some instances the teacher's objective is to encourage singers to utilize muscles that affect singing; in others the teacher helps the student relax muscles which if tensed cause vocal fatigue and constrained tone. In either case, there are exercises that can be done by the entire chorus to achieve the desired result and to build the desired habits slowly and surely. Such devices are not equally successful with all choruses. It is useful for each teacher to give consideration to these teaching devices and to experiment with them to draw his own conclusions concerning their effectiveness.

Since their success depends upon each teacher's manner of presentation and the responses of the pupils in each group, one teacher may find the exercises very useful even though another is unable to derive great benefit from them. Some of these devices may be used during rehearsals on a regular or irregular basis; others may be used only on special occasions to solve a problem inherent in one piece of music or to remedy a difficulty created by some other special condition. For example, certain exercises might be used only at the time of a concert, the singers being led through them in a warm-up room prior to going onstage to relieve tension and nervousness.

To relieve physical and general tension, especially in the few minutes before a concert or midway through a long rehearsal, the teacher may ask singers to pommel each other in much the same way a *masseur* loosens the muscles of his patient. Pupils are asked to stand in rows or circles, turned so that each faces the back of another. Midway through the process they face in the opposite direction, so no one goes "unpommeled." Each pupil bends his elbows to bring his hands to chest height in front of his body with fingers pointed upward, straight and together. Each pupil then uses the edge of his hands, from the base of the little finger to the wrist, to pommel the back of the singer standing before him. This is done gently, with hands alternating in short, rapid movements covering an area from the base of the neck to the belt line and across both shoulder blades. There is real physical benefit in this procedure, the pommeling serving to release muscular tension in both pommeled and pommeler. More important, perhaps, is the release of mental and emotional tension through the inevitable laughter that accompanies the pommeling. There is always the possibility that devices such as this cause the teacher to lose control of the group, but kept within reasonable bounds they send singers to the stage relaxed, in good spirit, free of nervousness and tension, and ready to sing their best.

Other exercises can be devised for specific parts of the body for release of general tension or to free muscles used in singing. The head can be turned from side to side, nodded up and down, or rolled so the chin describes a circle. Shoulders can be pulled forward and back, raised and lowered, and these movements combined so the shoulders move in circular fashion. The singers can be asked to "shake loose," letting the arms hang limply at the sides and shaking the head, torso, and arms to free all muscles simultaneously. Any such exercise is done in rhythm when possible, the entire group doing it together, and stops well before there is any possibility of fatigue.

To encourage a feeling of looseness in the jaw and throat, there are devices derived from motions done instinctively by many singers. The lower jaw can be stretched downward and then closed in a chewing motion, moved from side to side without turning the head, and moved through a large circle including the stretch downward and to both sides. It can be thrust forward and then down to simulate the motion of a yawn, or singers can be asked to try to yawn, moving the jaw and inhaling deeply at the same time. The chorus can sing "ma-ma-ma-ma-ma" or some other succession of consonant and vowel sounds that can be done in rhythm, the consonants being produced by dropping the jaw rather than using lip muscles. The object of the device is to give the singer the feeling of a loose, "floppy" jaw that drops from the jaw hinge. The chorus can go through the motions silently, can say the words in a speaking tone, or can sing them in unison or in parts following the tonal patterns prescribed by the teacher, striving to develop tone quality while loosening the jaw.

Inherent in such teaching devices are possibilities for stimulating interest and improving singing. Adolescent singers in particular find physical exercises satisfying because their physical energies demand release and tend to prevent them from either sitting or standing still for long periods of time. Young singers are impressed by the knowledge that professional singers turn to such devices on occasion and enjoy playing the role of the professional. More important, the exercises relieve mental, emotional, and physical tension when properly directed. In some instances, a sufficient reason for using these teaching devices is that they draw attention away from the voice and throat. With inexperienced singers in general, and adolescents in particular, one of the director's larger problems is to prevent singers from thinking about the throat to such an extent that voices tire and become strained. If physical exercises do nothing more, they are worthy of a place in the rehearsal plan.

Singing Posture

Despite the fact that operatic singers are able to perform creditably when seated, lying prone, bound in chains, or caught in the throes of a struggle with death, inexperienced singers achieve better results when their posture places the body in attitudes that permit the vocal mechanism to function freely. The prone position has certain advantages; it permits a general relaxation of muscular tension and causes the head, shoulders, back, and hips to settle into alignment without slumping or restriction of breathing. Similarly, there are advantages in the stance adopted by the baseball player at bat, the golfer preparing to swing, or the stevedore lifting a heavy object. In this semi-crouch, with feet apart, knees slightly bent, and torso straight, the body is in perfect balance. There is equal tension in all muscles and the singer is able to exert physical energy instantaneously when necessary. None of these positions is practical for the choral singer, of course, but suitable posture including the advantages of each is to be desired.

The normal singing posture is one in which the singer is naturally erect and perfectly balanced and which does not require muscular effort or cause fatigue. The torso is straight and vertical with shoulders positioned naturally, neither slumped forward nor pulled back. The head is balanced easily, the chin neither raised nor pulled down toward the chest. When standing, the feet are slightly apart, perhaps placed so one is advanced slightly, the knees straight but not rigid, with the weight over the balls of the feet. When sitting, the feet are placed flat on the floor, perhaps with one foot slightly forward and the other pulled back until it is under the front edge of the seat, and the weight of the torso is over the thighs rather than against the back of the chair.

The secret of seated posture is in the lower back close to the belt line. To assume good posture, the singer rolls the hips forward until the lower back feels straight, this act automatically raising the head and shoulders and balancing the torso over the thighs in such a way that further adjustment of posture is unnecessary. The position to avoid is that in which the lower back feels rounded and slumped toward the back of the chair. The position of the lower back is less noticeable when the singer is standing, but posture is improved when the lower back is straightened. If attention is directed to the lower back, it reduces the tendency of young singers to force the shoulders back unnaturally at every mention of posture, a position that is neither correct nor comfortable.

The young singer often has a faulty notion of good posture, feeling it necessary to raise the chest, force the shoulders back, and pull the chin down and in. This position requires the exertion of inordinate muscular energy to hold the body, especially the chest, in an unnatural position. It quickly produces fatigue and convinces the singer that the slump is more comfortable. The correct position produces little fatigue once the singer acquires the habit of adopting it automatically. One device for demonstrating correct posture is to ask the members of the chorus to stand, raise the arms above the head with elbows straight as though pointing toward the ceiling, and then lower the arms to the sides without changing the position of the shoulders or torso. Raising the arms in the air this way straightens the torso and places the shoulders in a naturally erect setting without forcing the body into a strained position. Once the arms are lowered it is possible to relax the body slightly without materially changing the posture, provided the singers resist temptation to sink back into a slouch. This is the ultimate secret of good posture, whether for singing or for the exertion of physical energy as in sports; the position must be natural and comfortable, yet balanced and alert with every bone and muscle free to act. The teacher's problem is to erase any false notions concerning posture and to help pupils build habits that permit free use of the voice.

There is a need for the description of correct posture to pupils in the choral group and for occasional reminders about it during rehearsal. It is also desirable for the teacher to encourage good posture through subtle means, improving habits indirectly rather than through constant reminders to which pupils ultimately become insensitive. The pupil who assumes correct posture because he is impelled to it by some subtle influence develops better posture and maintains it longer and more easily than the pupil who forces himself to sit straight because he is told to do so. The teacher's best course is to encourage correct posture through adjusting other factors related to posture and singing.

A first step is to secure rehearsal-room chairs that permit and encourage singing posture. Rehearsals held in a classroom or auditorium with immovable desks or writing-arm chairs impede the development of posture habits. Desks are often too large or too small and force pupils to slide awkwardly into their seats from the side. The writing surface is undesirable in that it gives pupils something to lean on and encourages slumped shoulders and a rounded lower back. A much better chair is one of the folding type with a low back but without writing surface or arm rests. This chair permits pupils to rise and sit easily, offers nothing on which to lean, provides support for the lower back when needed, but discourages pupils who tend to slide down to let their shoulder blades rest against the back of the chair. Of further posture benefit is the practice of asking pupils to stand from time to time during rehearsals, for the posture of a choral group is usually better when the group stands. The entire chorus can be asked to stand for the final reading of a selection after it has been rehearsed, or selected part-groups can stand for brief periods to rehearse their own parts. Because long periods of standing are tiresome also, the logical procedure is to alternate between sitting and standing or to bring the chorus to its feet whenever the singers show fatigue or a tendency to slouch in their seats.

Of particular significance to posture is the manner in which the singer holds his music. It should not be in his lap, nor should it be held at chest height with arms or elbows propped against the sides. To hold his music, the choral singer should feel that he is reaching forward and around as though embracing a large beach ball, the hands almost at shoulder height and the music slightly below eye level. The object of this position is to move the arms and elbows away from the sides of the body and to create a feeling of lift and spaciousness in the chest. In addition, this places the music immediately below the line of sight between the singer and the conductor and permits the pupil to see the conductor's signals while watching the music and without taking his eyes from it. Because of this line-of-sight factor, today's practice of using choral risers in the rehearsal room and on the stage sometimes has an unfortunate effect upon posture. When singers are seated on risers and the conductor stands on the floor, many of the singers are above the conductor and must look down to see him. This causes them to lower their music and their arms, destroying the feeling of lift and spaciousness in the chest. For this reason it might be better in the rehearsal room to place singers' chairs on the floor and the conductor's stand on a platform, encouraging the singers to look up and to raise their music to a height conducive to good posture.

One of the most important factors in posture is fatigue. The singer who is tired is prone to slump in his seat, to permit his shoulders to slouch forward, and to forget the importance of the lower back. To prevent fatigue, the teacher avoids lengthy rehearsals and provides frequent rest periods of one sort or another even during shorter ones. These can be short discussion periods in which the singers express opinions, opportunities for the teacher to explain something pertaining to the music, or moments of respite in which the teacher clarifies instructions to the accompanist or works with only one part-group. During such moments, those who are not singing are encouraged to relax completely. Similarly, singers who have lengthy rests in their parts are encouraged to lean back in their chairs to take advantage of the rests both vocally and physically. If the rehearsal must necessarily be either long or intense, there may be a point at which it is wise to stop singing, rise, shake loose, and move the head and shoulders as in the exercises previously described. Other factors contributing to fatigue include room temperature and ventilation, both of which are adjusted to offer reasonable stimulation to the singers. If the teacher is attentive to details of this sort, good posture is encouraged subtly and constantly and the number of needed reminders concerning posture is materially reduced.

Supporting the Tone

Tone support, posture, and breathing are closely related to each other. Correct posture frees the organs of the body for proper and effortless breathing; correct breathing in its turn helps support the singing tone. Habits of posture and breathing can be developed concurrently, but reasonably good posture must be achieved before breathing can become easy and natural. Here too it is often necessary to overcome the erroneous notions many young singers acquire about breathing. This can be done through demonstration of the more desirable breathing process and through exercises that help the singers feel in their own muscles the proper function of the breathing apparatus. In this area also, it is desirable that the teacher encourage the development of good habits of breathing through subtle and indirect means that do not focus the singer's attention upon breathing itself.

To overcome false notions concerning breathing, it is sometimes necessary for the teacher to permit singers to experiment in such a way that they actually feel where breathing occurs. From camp and other experiences they sometimes conclude that breathing is done with the chest and that to inhale deeply it is necessary to raise the chest unnaturally high, resulting in explosive exhalation when the chest is dropped. This quickly produces fatigue because of the necessity of raising and lowering the weight of the chest. It is difficult to maintain a singing tone of uniform intensity when the singer must exert great muscular force to raise the chest and is tempted to let it fall suddenly through complete release of muscular tension.

To feel the sensation of correct breathing, and to identify the muscles that control it, the teacher asks the chorus as a group to inhale slowly but deeply without raising the chest, trying at the same time to note which portions of the torso are effected. In doing so, the pupil should feel that the abdomen tends to move outward, pushing against the belt, the sides of the torso in the area of the floating ribs push outward, the small area of muscle immediately below the sternum pushes forward, and the rib cage tightens, seeming to expand in all directions simultaneously. The singer then purses his lips to form a small aperture and exhale slowly against this resistance to note the torso areas which support the singing tone. As exhalation begins, the singer should feel that pressure is being exerted against the belt around the entire circumference of the torso, including front, sides, and back. As exhalation continues, there is a pull inward felt in the lower abdomen, the upper abdomen immediately below the sternum, and in the area of the floating ribs. At the end of exhalation there is a feeling of tightening or contraction in the entire rib cage. Through this procedure the pupil acquires the feeling that breathing occurs and is controlled below the chest by muscles in the front, sides, and back of the torso, and that it is unnecessary to raise the chest to breathe deeply.

To show the manner in which these muscles affect singing, pupils are instructed to place the fingertips of both hands against one area of the torso and to press repeatedly and rapidly while sustaining a soft, singing tone on one pitch. Fingertips can be placed first immediately below the sternum, then in the area of the belt buckle, next one hand at each side immediately below the ribs, and finally in the areas of the back between the lower ribs and the line of the belt, far enough from the center of the back so they do not press on the "backbone." Pupils recognize immediately that rapidly repeated pressures by the fingertips in any one of these areas create an obvious fluctuation in the volume of the tone. For further evidence of the effect upon singing, pupils may place the hands on any one of these areas, pressing inward with the hands while resisting the pressure with the muscles of the torso. They may also place the hands behind the head with fingers interlaced, pulling forward with the arms while resisting this pull with the muscles of the neck, shoulders, and back. In each instance, they will note that the tone grows in volume, and perhaps improves in quality, as energy is exerted by the muscles of the torso.

Exercises and experiments of this sort are intended only to dispel erroneous impressions singers have acquired and to show the effect of proper breathing and muscular support. They are not intended to be exercises for the development of muscular strength or even for regular use as a reminder concerning the breathing process. Exaggerated muscular tension or too much emphasis upon the physical aspect of singing is as harmful as none. There is the possibility that even one demonstration may cause the pupil to place too much emphasis on the muscular aspect of breathing; it is more likely, however, that the establishment of these concepts during early periods of instruction will help him develop proper breathing habits and tone support as he continues to sing. The singer who is encouraged to focus attention on the torso as a source of voice support is less likely to think of the throat as the source of the vocal tone, a factor that helps prevent the tightness of throat to which adolescents are prone. Once these ideas concerning breathing and voice support have been presented to the young singers of the chorus, further development of either good or bad habits is controlled by the teacher through the influence of the daily work of the rehearsal.

One group of devices for encouraging pupils to utilize the abdominal muscles in breathing is based upon the rapid repetition of a suitable vowel sound, each sound preceded by a strong "H." Pupils begin by panting rapidly to feel the abdominal action that produces the "H." They then say "huh-huh-huh-huh-huh" or laugh vigorously by saying "ho-ho-ho-ho-ho." Next, they sing these sounds on one convenient pitch, perhaps sustaining the last tone. Finally, they sing a portion of the scale in this fashion, ascending to the fifth of the scale and descending again to the pitch with which they began. The intent of such exercises is to stimulate what is usually referred to as "breathing from the diaphragm." The exercises are advantageous because they do not require any reference to the action of the muscles; the teacher can lead his chorus through a series of such exercises simply by instructing the group to say the desired words, laugh, or pant. The attention of the singer is not focused on any set of muscles, but on the sound produced.

Other indirect means of encouraging supported tone include the development of correct posture, the prevention of fatigue, and the attention to details of room temperature and ventilation already mentioned. The teacher influences singers through the judicious selection of music, choosing texts that suggest vitality and intensity of mood or music that requires controlled dynamic intensity. Singers can be influenced through exposure to models of good tone, listening to recordings of competent soloists or choruses and imitating the voice of the director as he demonstrates the manner in which parts are to be sung. Finally, the teacher can focus the attention of the choral group upon its own tone, being alert for the occasions when the chorus achieves the desired quality of supported tone, pointing it out to the singers and asking that they duplicate it in other passages or other selections. Here, again, the success of the chorus depends upon the ear of the director. If he is sensitive to tonal effect, can identify the desired quality when it occurs, and can evaluate the efforts of the chorus as it strives to improve its tone, he is equipped to help the singers reach a tonal goal.

These physical aspects of singing exert a strong influence on the choral effects created by the vocal group. Each singer develops habits through which he uses his body to produce singing tone and to adjust its quality and intensity in the interpretation of choral music. If the group as a whole develops or is permitted to persist in faulty habits, it establishes limits beyond which it can not progress toward choral excellence; if correct habits are established, many of the barriers to choral excellence are removed. The physical potential for singing possessed by each individual is great. Rarely does the singer, even the trained soloist, make full use of his physical resources. If the young singer can be trained to use even a portion of this physical potential, his singing can be markedly improved. The inherent danger is a mental one. It is not desirable for the younger singer to be so imbued with ideas concerning the physical aspects of singing that he concentrates on physical processes to the extent that singing becomes laborious and the tone forced. It is far better that he be led to the proper use of his physical powers through other means—influences, conditions, and ideas that induce correct habits of singing without directing attention to the specific muscles involved. It is this respect in which singing is mental. The teacher strives to implant ideas and develop concepts that influence physical factors indirectly, turning to physical exercises and teaching devices only when necessary to define or clarify such ideas, guiding singers in this way to free but vital singing.

THE TONAL ASPECT

The voice is capable of producing an almost limitless variety of tones, its characteristics determined in part by the physical qualities of the tone-producing mechanism and in part by the manner in which the mechanism is used. It is possible that the operatic singer is gifted with a voice mechanism far superior to that of the person who sings less well, and that most young choral singers can not hope to achieve operatic levels of vocal skill. Young choral singers, however, can be trained to use their voices in such a way that the tone is pleasing and combines with others to produce a satisfying choral effect. For the young choral singer, difficulties imposed by limitations of the vocal mechanism are relatively negligible. The possibilities for improvement through effective use of existing potentials are numerous. The teacher can justifiably be optimistic about the prospects for creating a successful choral group composed initially of untrained singers. It is the function of teaching to create skill where none exists by nourishing and guiding native capacities for improvement.

Where choral music is concerned, one of the goals is beauty of tone. This is one of the unique advantages of the human voice, the characteristic that makes it superior to any other instrument man has been able to devise—it produces tonal beauties, tonal warmth, tonal expressiveness, and tonal flexibility of which no other instrument is capable. The effect of a mass of carefully trained voices of even mediocre native capability can be more moving than the effects created by an outstanding group of instrumental players. To achieve these effects, the choral teacher works with singers to develop vocal resonance, suitable tone quality, sensitivity to intonation and blend, and the ability to distinguish, remember, and produce tones. This is the tonal aspect of choral teaching. It is related to the physical aspect but goes beyond it to vocal habits that may seem divorced from the physical and govern the vocal characteristics in which beauty resides.

Developing Resonance

The term "resonance" is commonly used in reference to the human voice to indicate a characteristic including both carrying power and pleasing quality. The loud voice that carries to great distances is not necessarily resonant, nor is the pleasing voice that can be heard only when close at hand. In common usage, this term refers only to the voice possessing both qualities and implies that they are achieved without great effort on the part of the singer. A more accurate definition, such as one produced from a standard dictionary, implies the re-sounding of tones by surfaces or enclosed spaces separate from the mechanism that produces the tone initially. These surfaces or spaces prolong the tone, or reinforce it, by reflecting its vibrations and returning them to the human ear.

In mountainous terrain or in a large, empty room, resonance is heard as an echo, the tone continuing to ring because it is reflected from distant surfaces. Resonance requires a tone source and one or more resonators. This is one of the principles involved in the function of man-made music instruments. The violin, for example, produces tone through the vibration of a string and the action of the violin body that functions as a resonator. The string alone is virtually worthless as a music instrument; it is the body or resonator that produces the sound we find pleasing. Tone quality, as opposed to intensity or volume, is affected because the resonator or resonators emphasize certain of the tone's components and minimize others. To return to the violin, the scraping of the bow is a component of the tone we hear, fortunately minimized because it is not exaggerated by the resonator. In addition, the tone we hear is made up of a number of different pitches, called overtones, harmonics, or partials, and the relative intensity of these partials in the single pitch identified by the ear affects our judgment of its quality. Thus the violin body affects the carrying power of the string tone by echoing and amplifying the vibrations and affects the quality of its tone by minimizing certain partials and intensifying others.

The human voice functions in a similar manner. Although it is difficult to prove with scientific accuracy any hypothesis concerning the human voice—because of the difficulty of measuring the action of tiny, invisible muscles and cartilages and because of the infinity of minor variations from singer to singer—we are persuaded that the voice depends on a tone source and tone resonators in much the same manner as does the violin or any other instrument. The source of the vibration that produces vocal tone is in the larynx, and if the analogy to the function of the violin is at all accurate, this area of the throat is among the factors of lesser importance to singing. This is an important principle for the teacher to remember: singing can be discussed as though the larynx were of relatively little consequence in the act of singing, needing attention only if its action is impaired by some unnatural physical or mental attitude. The source of vocal power and tone quality is in the resonator. Where the voice is concerned, tone emanates from the larynx but it is the entire column of air set in motion within the body that gives the tone its power and quality. This air motion is not to be regarded as the expulsion of a large quantity of air from the body as in explosive exhalation. To the contrary, comparatively little air is expelled during singing; much of it remains within the body and produces or transmits tone through a species of vibration.

The resonators influencing vocal tone are the hollow spaces of the body in which the air vibrates—cavities that function as echo chambers—found in the head, throat, and chest. It is reasonable to believe that the air in the chest vibrates when tone is produced. As evidence to support this belief, many singers are conscious of vibration in the chest and more notably in the lower back, especially when using all the resources of the voice in singing a *forte* passage. The throat vibrates in a way that can be detected by placing the fingers lightly against the throat while singing. In the head, the mouth cavity itself functions as a resonator as do the cavities and canals referred to as "sinus passages." These are the resonators that function in the manner of the violin body. They provide hollow spaces in which the tone echoes and is amplified, intensifying some partials while minimizing others to give the voice its distinctive quality. Because each individual is unique in his physical make-up, each individual's vocal resonators are different from those of any other singer and each voice has different tonal characteristics. There are possibilities for developing resonance, however, despite limitations imposed by the physical characteristics of the singer.

Although the chest and throat do influence vocal resonance, voice teachers and singers favor procedures that focus attention on the resonating chambers of the head. It is particularly undesirable with young singers to call attention to the throat. Similarly, the chest need not be singled out because young singers, especially boys with newly changed voices, are prone to sing with "chesty" voices. The remaining resonators are those of the head, and it is the development of head resonance that is most rewarding. One reason is that head resonance is needed and highly desirable, lending to the voice a pleasing quality not obtained when the voice is either "chesty" or "throaty." Further reason lies in the fact that the voice seems to function better, to be more flexible and less subject to fatigue, when the singer's concept of tone placement directs his attention to the head. This is one of the ways in which singing is mental, being influenced beneficially by a state of mind even though it is difficult to identify a direct relationship between the mind or will of the singer and the manner in which his voice functions.

It is more difficult to control resonance, unfortunately, than to discuss it. The organs or muscles of the body that affect vocal resonance are for the most part beyond the control of the untrained singer. Attempts to direct the singer's attention to them may lead to actual impairment of singing facility. It is important that the teacher proceed carefully when attempting to improve the singing of a choral group in this respect. Here, as in other aspects of vocal teaching, the best methods are those that influence the singer subtly and indirectly without focusing attention on the portions of the body that interfere with voice production if they become unduly tense or strained. The approach is through ideas and concepts that induce good singing habits.

One device that often produces desired results encourages pupils to adjust their singing until the vibration of the tone can actually be felt in the head. The teacher first presents the idea that sound is vibration, that resonating chambers are important both in music instruments and in the human voice, and that the tone of the voice is improved when it utilizes the various resonating chambers in the head. Pupils then place the thumb and fingertips of one hand lightly against the bridge and along the side of the nose. While touching the nose in this way, they sing a sustained tone on one pitch to see whether they can detect vibration through the fingertips. They are most likely to feel vibration if they sing the word "hung," prolonging the "ng." This prevents the tone from reverberating only in the mouth and forces it to ascend into the head where it fills the sinus cavities and causes vibration in the area of the bridge of the nose. After they have been able to detect vibration in this way while singing "ng," they sing the word "hum," prolonging the "m" while attempting to feel vibration through the fingertips. This may be somewhat more difficult, because the mouth cavity supplies a portion of the resonance, but pupils still should be able to feel vibration without great difficulty. The next step is to sing "hunguh," dropping the tongue after "ng" far enough to create the sound of "uh" and permitting the tone to escape through the mouth without being forced into the head. Feeling the vibration is more difficult here, of course, but pupils who have been led to this point, achieving head resonance while singing "ng" and "m," should be able with practice to develop similar resonance while singing "uh." The teacher can continue from this point by directing the chorus to sing other vowel sounds such as "eh" and "ah," the mouth opening further for each new vowel. As the jaw drops lower and lower there is less and less natural reason for the tone to ascend into the head, but the object of the teaching device is to encourage pupils to place tone in the head or "mask" and to keep it there regardless of jaw position and the vowel being produced.

In this device there is no attempt to direct the singer's conscious attention to any physical mechanism or to encourage him to exert physical effort in singing. There is no mention of muscular action or any contortion of the vocal mechanism, nor are the singers permitted to indulge in any unnatural singing practice that produces vocal strain. To the contrary, the intent of the device is to exert an almost purely psychological effect on the singer. The discussion of head cavities, the gentle pressure of fingertips against the nose, and the effect of a cupped hand before the face create the impression of a focus of tone in the head and mask and establish a mental concept of tone placement.

Although this procedure might be used only once to demonstrate tone placement, or on rare occasions to remind the singers of the importance of head resonance, its principles can be utilized regularly during rehearsals to help pupils improve their singing habits. Selections being rehearsed can be hummed or sung in their entirety with "ng," "uh," or one of the vowel sounds. The vowel sound "oo" is particularly useful for this purpose, helping the tone float upward and resonate in the head and mask. The teacher who favors the use of vocalises or other "warm-up" exercises at the beginning of each rehearsal can use these sounds for the scales, arpeggios, and chord patterns the chorus is accustomed to singing. New exercises can be created using appropriate words such as "mellow moon," "minimum," "nevermore," or "domino." Through all such devices, the singer is encouraged to think of the tone as being placed in the mask, through constant practice developing the ability to move the tone upward away from the chest and throat.

In addition to these more direct approaches to vocal resonance, the teacher takes every opportunity to stimulate pupils to sing with vitality of tone. Correct posture makes its contribution, especially that which produces the feeling of spaciousness and lift in the chest and permits the tone to float upward freely. Breathing is a factor in that it provides a plentiful supply of air to support the tone and expands the chest to form a spacious resonating chamber. The constant attention to phrasing, dynamic shadings, and generally pleasing musical effect helps young singers develop a concept of suitable tone. It is the combination of concept with constant practice on which the choral teacher relies in working with the young singers of the choral group.

Tone Quality and Color

Vocal tone quality is closely related to resonance and is influenced by the size and shape of the various vocal resonators. In working with choral groups, however, it is helpful for the teacher to *think* of tone quality as being separate from resonance in order to devote special attention to the gradual improvement of the group in this respect and to direct the attention of singers to a facet of their voices over which they can develop a degree of control. As has been mentioned, it is probable that the presence or absence of overtones, their relative intensity, and the shape of the sound wave of the audible pitch cause some of the variations we identify as differences in tone quality.

One of the resonating chambers causing these variations, the mouth or oral cavity, can be shaped easily by the singer. This possibility permits the demonstration of various tone qualities in the choral rehearsal. To do so, the teacher directs the chorus to sing a sustained, unison pitch, shaping first the sound "ee," then "oo," then "oh," then "ah." The difference in tone quality is readily apparent and should convince the singers of the possibility of adjusting the quality of their tone easily through tongue, jaw, and lip adjustments they are accustomed to making in speech. It is also possible to adjust tone quality by blocking the flow of tone into the nasal passages and by distending the throat, but for young singers the attempts to produce these changes, or even the suggestion that they are possible, may cause unnatural tension in the voice mechanism. Shaping of the oral cavity, on the other hand, is done so easily and naturally that it is unlikely to impair singing facility and provides a means through which the teacher can demonstrate and improve tone quality.

Because the shape of the oral cavity exerts such a strong influence on tone quality, there are several principles the teacher can follow when working with the chorus. Remembering the different tonal effects created by singing "ee," "oh," and other vowel sounds, the teacher adjusts the tone of the choral group by bringing about the desired change in the shape of the singer's oral cavity. Tone quality is "set" by training the chorus through constant practice with the desired vowel sound. Uniformity of tone quality is approached by decreasing the variety of oral-cavity shapes utilized by the singers and by reducing the tendency to exaggerate jaw, lip, and tongue motions in shaping certain vowel sounds. Word sounds can be projected while singing through attention to consonants without requiring exaggerated differences in vowel sounds, thus helping the chorus achieve uniformity of tone color.

To test the validity of these principles as they apply to his own chorus, and to demonstrate them to the singers, the teacher might experiment by asking the chorus to sing an appropriate familiar passage such as the first eight measures of "Auld Lang Syne" in a number of different ways. First, sing the passage and project the words by exaggerating the lip and jaw movements which produce the vowels, at the same time listening intently to the character of the choral tone at each new vowel sound. The teacher and perhaps the chorus as well will note that the quality or color of the tone changes as the singers shape their mouths to sing "ee," "oo," "aw," and "ah." Next, experiment with different vowel sounds. Sing the same passage, retaining the consonants but using only one vowel sound during the entire eight measures. Sing it first using the sound "uh," then again using the sound "ee," and a third time using "aw." Note that the tone color is different in each instance, "ee" producing a tone that is bright and brilliant, "aw" a tone that is dark and covered, "uh" a tone color midway between the others. Note also that the meaning of the words is projected because of the effect of the consonants despite the sameness of the vowel sounds.

To continue the experiment, the teacher directs the chorus to sing a long, sustained tone in unison, shaping the neutral vowel "uh" with the oral cavity while thinking a series of different vowel sounds. This can be accomplished if the teacher points successively to vowel sounds written on the board, such as "uh-oh-oo-oh-uh-ee-eh-uh-ah-uh," as the chorus sustains its unison pitch. Although the singers are shaping the sound of "uh," thinking the other sounds causes almost imperceptible changes in the shape of the oral cavity sufficient to make each of the other vowels distinguishable. This indicates the possibility of shaping vowel sounds through mental concepts without contorting the oral cavity or facial expression. As a next step, the chorus sings "Auld Lang Syne" again, pronouncing the vowels but remembering to avoid exaggerated lip and jaw movements and retaining a mental concept of "uh" while shaping the normal vowel sounds of the words. The result is that words are understandable, that lip and jaw distortions are reduced, and that the tone color is more nearly uniform than when the singers think and shape each successive vowel sound. Moreover, it indicates that the teacher can adjust the tone color of the chorus by establishing a mental concept of a bright, dark, or neutral vowel to influence the singers as they project the words of a song.[1]

Applying these principles to the daily work of rehearsal, the teacher develops and "sets" the tone color of the choral group by following a pattern of rehearsal techniques to establish both mental concepts and singing habits. First, there is the possibility of using vocalises or other warm-up exercises as an integral part of every rehearsal. The chorus can sing a sustained tone in unison using only one vowel sound with (1) level pitch and intensity, (2) level pitch and changing intensity such as

[1] For a particularly lucid explanation of this concept, see James E. Richards, "The Ubiquitous Phonetic Antithesis!", in *Music Education in Action*, Archie N. Jones, ed. Boston: Allyn and Bacon, Inc., 1960, pp. 161–67.

pp-p-mf-p-pp, (3) level intensity and changing pitch such as a scale ascending from the tone center to the fifth and returning, (4) changing pitch and intensity such as the scale passage that increases in intensity as it ascends and decreases in intensity as it descends.

Similar exercies that tend to develop resonance as well as tone color are those in which the chorus sings a sustained tone in unison but initiates the tone with a consonant sound—"muh," "nuh," or "nguh," dwelling on the consonant long enough to achieve a feeling of resonance before proceeding to the vowel. This exercise can be varied by utilizing (1) only one sustained vowel such as "muh," (2) repeated vowel sounds such as "muh-muh-muh-muh-muh," (3) successive vowel sounds such as "muh-moh-moo-mah-muh." The exercises can be varied further, and to good advantage, by utilizing three- or four-part harmony instead of the single pitch sung in unison, either (1) one sustained chord or (2) a progression of several chords, permitting the chorus to strive for tone color, resonance, and blend simultaneously.

Other possibilities in the use of scales and arpeggios can be explored and exercises devised to meet the needs peculiar to each group. Each such exercise should be sensitive to the singers' range and compass, its *tessitura* lying in an area comfortable for all singers, neither too high nor too low. In general, the exercises should descend rather than ascend, the total pattern of the exercise being repeated on successively lower degrees of the diatonic or chromatic scale. Because young singers, especially, are often sensitive to the difficulties of singing in the upper portions of their voice compasses, the psychological effect of beginning in a comfortable middle register and moving downward from there is more to be desired than the effect created by exercises that force the singer to struggle upward to higher pitches that cause vocal discomfort.

For each of these exercises there are two goals. One is the improvement of tone quality; the other is the creation of musically beautiful sounds. Where the latter is concerned, both teacher and pupils should realize that there is beauty in music even when it takes the form of a vocalise or exercise. One sustained pitch sung in unison by a chorus can be either beautiful or ugly, as can be scales, arpeggios, single chords, chord progressions, and meaningless sounds such as "muh" or "nguh." The difference between beauty and ugliness is a matter of attention, concentration, attitude, and musicianship. It requires that teacher and pupils avoid any tendency to regard these exercises as a matter of routine. Each exercise is given the complete attention of teacher and pupils, reflecting serious attitude and the conviction that there is beauty in the abstractions of choral tone and music interval; it is performed with all the attention to details of accurate rendition and sensitive interpretation devoted to any worthy item of choral literature.

Without this attitude exercises are worthless, perhaps detrimental to good singing; approached with proper attitude, the exercises themselves become satisfying musical experiences. Moreover, the exercises must be approached in this way if they are to serve the other goal, that of tone quality. Tone quality improves of its own accord if the exercises are performed with musicianship. To adjust tone quality, the teacher chooses vowel sounds that tend to brighten or darken the tone, judging the needs of the chorus through listening to its tone. The teacher suggests that the singers listen intently as the exercises proceed, calling attention to the instances in which the tone approaches the desired quality and asking the chorus to duplicate it in other exercises. The object is to improve the tone quality until it meets the teacher's standards and to develop uniformity of tone color regardless of the vowel or word being sung. Although many of these devices are best performed without accompaniment, the teacher emphasizes their musical qualities by devising interesting harmonizations for those that demand use of the piano; the mechanical thumping of tonic and dominant chords is replaced by artistic playing of chords and progressions more appealing to young singers.

The teacher who prefers not to use warm-up exercises or vocalises can turn to other means during the normal course of rehearsal activities. To direct attention to the desired tone quality and practice its production, the chorus devotes some of its rehearsal time to singing softly, striving for vitality of tone and a constant level of volume. This eliminates the necessity for thinking about dynamic changes and tends to focus the attention of the singers on tone quality, resonance, and blend. Humming is sometimes effective, the chorus practicing complete selections with lips together or producing something similar to a humming tone with lips parted only slightly. This tends to focus tone in the oral cavity and mask and directs the singer's attention to the quality of his tone. Complete choral selections or excerpts are practiced with one vowel sound or with a neutral syllable. Different vowels may be selected by the teacher to brighten or darken the tone, as needed. Selections can be practiced with more than normal attention to dynamics, not with the intent of exaggerating contrasts in volume, but with special attention to retaining uniform vitality and color of tone at all dynamic levels.

The use of recordings, visiting soloists, and choral groups offers further opportunity for influencing the singing of the chorus. Recordings are most convenient and can be used regularly during rehearsals to introduce new selections, to assist singers in learning parts, and to show the results expected after the chorus completes its study. Whenever recordings are used, the singers are exposed to models of good tone and influenced to imitate what they hear. Similar results can be anticipated when the chorus is exposed to models of good tone provided by visiting soloists and choruses. Visiting artists can be secured for assembly programs and other special occasions and in some instances can be invited to visit the school during the chorus rehearsal to explain and demonstrate tone production for the singers. It is also useful to have a tape recorder in the rehearsal room so that any portion of the rehearsal may be recorded and played back immediately for the singers themselves to judge the degree of progress achieved.

One means of demonstrating tone is always at the choral director's disposal—his own voice. The choral director maintains and improves his own vocal powers. He is careful to sing to the best of his ability whenever he shows the manner in which a melodic line should be interpreted, helps one group of singers with a part, or in any way displays his voice before the group. The chorus is exposed to the quality of the director's voice many times during every rehearsal and is more likely to imitate his tone than any heard through recordings or assembly programs. This is especially true of younger singers who learn by imitation and who have established few concepts or habits of singing.

Intonation and Blend

Both intonation and blend have to do with accuracy in pitch and are closely related to each other. "Intonation" is sometimes used to refer to the agreement between the pitch of the singer or chorus and that of some absolute reference, such as the piano, whereas "blend" is used to refer to the degree of pitch agreement of singers with each other within the choral group. The singer's pitch accuracy, whether in relation to another singer or to the piano, may be influenced by a number of factors including states of mind, emotion and health, nervous tension and fatigue, temperature and humidity, music experience and training, innate music talent, the physical characteristics of the voice mechanism and the manner in which it is used.

One of the frequent causes of problems of intonation and blend in the choral group is lack of concentration. This is another of the mental aspects of singing and one most singers can learn to control. To sing in tune, the singer needs a mental awareness of the distance and direction traversed by his voice as it negotiates his part. The control of his voice must be based on an understanding of the intervals he is to sing and an assurance that the pitch he chooses is the correct one. In short, he must have the aural ability to hear each pitch *before* he sings it, not in any absolute sense, but in terms of its relation to pitches already sung. More important, he must have the ability to concentrate aural attention on each pitch sung to make the fine adjustment that shifts it into precise agreement with its harmonic context and the pitches sung by other voices in the ensemble.

The teacher's goal is to create an awareness and understanding of pitch among the singers of the chorus. He develops their sensitivity to minute but critical pitch adjustments through any devices that prove effective. To begin, the chorus is asked to sing one pitch in unison, perhaps matching a pitch sounded at the piano, each singer taking small breaths as necessary to sustain the tone indefinitely and listening intently to the sound of the combined voices to bring his own voice into perfect agreement with the group. As the group begins to sing the pitch the tone may be cloudy and dull because each singer is producing a tone of slightly different pitch. As each singer adjusts his voice to achieve perfect unison, the tone improves in quality and resonance until, when all voices are well in tune, it acquires a distinctive resonance and ring. The experience of hearing this perfectly tuned, ringing tone is the first step in the development of the singer's awareness of pitch.

As a next step, the teacher directs the chorus to sustain its unison tone and follow his directions to move up or down a specified interval or to a specified pitch. To accomplish this the teacher may say, "Match this pitch; up a half tone; up a whole tone; down a minor third; up a fourth; down a whole tone; up a fourth." Through this process, the chorus learns and practices intervals, listens to each pitch sung to achieve perfect unison, and becomes increasingly sensitive to pitch accuracy. The teacher may also say, "Match this E; sing F; sing G; sing E; sing A; sing G; sing upper C," or can do the same exercise by pointing to notes on the staff. This procedure tends to increase the reading skill of the chorus as well as its sensitivity to pitch. In either form, the device can be adjusted to the level of ability of each chorus or to permit practice of a specific interval. The logical point of beginning is that which asks the chorus to move by half and whole tones only. From here it can progress to major and minor thirds, perfect fourths and fifths, and other, more difficult intervals.

A variation of this device is one in which the chorus sings chords instead of a unison pitch. The easiest chord for the teacher's purpose, and perhaps the easiest one for pupils to hear and sing, is the triad in open voicing with tenors and basses singing the root, altos the fifth, and sopranos the third. The chorus sings the chord in the same way it sang the unison, sustaining the triad until it feels perfectly in tune. The teacher then directs the singers to move up or down by half and whole tones, creating the same chord on successive degrees of the chromatic or diatonic scale, by saying, "All down a half tone; another; another; up a whole tone; a half tone." The resulting chord shifts surprise the singers and capture their interest. The device impels them to listen to their own pitches and the blend of voices as well as to concentrate on the intervals as they shift from one pitch to another. The exercise can be varied in numerous ways by using major, minor, augmented or diminished triads, triads with added sevenths, ninths and thirteenths, or by experimenting with different voicings of the chords.

A further and interesting variation is to direct the chorus in such a way that only one pitch in the chord is moved at one time, the teacher saying, "Sopranos down a half tone; altos up a half tone," and so forth. This causes the color of each chord to be different [illegible] phasizing further the importance of pitch changes a[illegible] the singer's attention even more sharply on pitch accura[illegible] perform this exercise, the singers must be certain of intervallic distances and concentrate on singing them correctly without the aid of a sense of tonality or a feeling of chord progression. By planning his instructions in advance, the teacher can create chord progressions within a key, can move diatonically or chromatically, and can if he wishes duplicate the harmonic style of the choral literature being rehearsed. This procedure demands intense concentration on the part of the director as well as the singers but can be both enjoyable and profitable for all.

Similar exercises can be devised with chord progressions. The teacher presents one or several chord progressions by notating them on the board, each progression beginning and ending with the same voicing of parts so that one progression may lead easily into another. The chorus begins by reading the progressions from the board and may then memorize them for review during subsequent rehearsals. In singing them, the chorus first sustains the pitches of the initial chord until it is well in tune, then moves to successive chords at the direction of the teacher. Without stopping, it may then proceed through the other progressions, and the teacher may at his discretion instruct all parts to move up or down a half or whole tone while sustaining the final chord of one progression so the next may be in a different key. If the teacher wishes, he may ask the chorus to memorize the progressions and identify them by number so that during subsequent rehearsals he can say, "Sing progression one;

all voices up a half tone; sing progression two," and so forth. The progressions may be either simple or complex and may be related to or derived from the literature being studied. The intent of this exercise, like the others, is to encourage singers to concentrate on intervals and pitches and to help them develop awareness of intonation and blend.

These devices and their variations provide almost limitless opportunities for practice and drill. If the teacher wishes, a number of them can be combined to form a sequence of exercises suitable for use in every rehearsal as a regular pattern of warm-up vocalization. They can be used irregularly as a basis for occasional but extended periods of instruction in which the teacher devotes rehearsals or portions of them to work appropriate to the voice class. Single exercises can be turned to as needed during the study of specific choral selections to help the singers learn difficult melodic or harmonic passages, to combat fatigue or waning interest, or to remedy the pitch difficulty every [illegible]us encounters during [illegible]casional spiritless days. S[illegible] more than educate [illegible] from the last, em- [illegible]p tone support, reso- [illegible]d tending to focus [illegible] other purposes. [illegible]. To perform [illegible]or on exercises that might be regarded by the chorus as tedious drills, their principles can be applied during the study of choral literature. Here, also, the singer is encouraged to concentrate, to be aware of distance and direction, to become sensitive to intervallic distances, to image pitches before singing them, and to listen intently. In appropriate choral passages, the singers can work to achieve the ring of a perfect unison or precisely blended chord. Successive phrases of suitable selections can be sung in different keys by moving all voices up or down as the final chord of each phrase is sustained. Selected passages can be sung without words as chord progressions, the chorus departing from the tempo and rhythm patterns of the music to sing successive harmonies in the manner of block chords. The latter procedure is especially useful in helping the chorus master a particularly unusual chord progression. In doing so, the chorus begins at some convenient starting point before the difficult passage where a comparatively simple chord provides key feeling and permits good blend. It then moves forward through the more complex chords, thinking the intervals required in each voice part, listening intently to the blend and making necessary fine adjustments in pitch, repeating the excerpt until each singer acquires a feeling for the chord colors and the relation of each chord to its successor. Although this does not duplicate the feeling of the passage when sung in proper tempo and rhythm, it is a means of giving the singers experience to serve as a foundation for the more accurate rendition of the music.

In the event that intonation problems are centered in one part, the teacher may direct that the offending part be sung with words or a neutral syllable as the other parts are hummed. The humming provides a harmonic background against which the pitch accuracy of the difficult part may be judged by the singers themselves, a far better way to learn it than by imitating a series of pitches sounded at the piano. The other singers are permitted to hum and practice their parts and are not forced to sit silently for long periods during which the director's attention is occupied by one part only. To reverse the process, the conductor may signal various parts to become silent or to change from words to humming as the selection is being sung. This removes the harmonic support provided by the silent parts, forces the remaining voice to develop independence, and may expose difficulties of which the director and singers were previously unaware.

Other factors affecting intonation are also subject to the teacher's control. The teacher can influence the singers' states of mind and emotion by adjusting his own manner, showing a sense of humor, selecting appropriate materials, and being generally sensitive to pupil attitudes and reactions. He can combat nervousness and fatigue and be attentive to the temperature and humidity of the rehearsal room. He can use rehearsals to increase singers' music experience and training, developing innate music talent and training all pupils in the proper use of the voice. All such factors have some bearing upon intonation and are worthy of the teacher's attention. When a specific problem of intonation or blend arises, the teacher analyzes the difficulty, determines its cause and then plans a specific sequence of teaching procedures to remedy it. Although problems of intonation and blend do not lend themselves easily to analysis, it is likely that many such problems result from lack of understanding and attention and that pointed teaching devices similar to those described above will often prove effective.

Attention and Tone Thinking

One of the basic problems in working with young, untrained singers is that of training them to give concentrated attention to the music at hand. To achieve artistic performance the singer must focus all his mental and physical powers on the act of singing. He must utilize all his knowledge of the structure of music, applying an understanding of scales, intervals, harmonies, rhythms, and so forth. He must exercise aural skill to listen intently to the sounds being produced and to image those yet to come. His physical resources must be utilized effectively, including not only the voice mechanism but the physical powers that support it. Even the capacities for emotional response are of consequence to singing and must be developed. Thus the factor of concentration is important in itself as well as in the ways it applies to problems discussed in foregoing sections. This is another of the teacher's specific goals—to build habits of concentration through rehearsal procedures and teaching devices that encourage pupils to give close attention to choral singing.

Many of the subjects discussed under previous headings bear upon this problem. Alert posture encourages attention both directly and indirectly. The singer who sits and stands properly does so in order that he may be attentive to the music and correct posture itself is a subtle influence toward a generally alert attitude. Holding music properly requires the attention of the singer and permits him to give attention to the conductor. Every measure taken to decrease or prevent fatigue increases the singer's reserve of attentive capacity. Every invitation to relax during moments of respite reminds the singer that an interval of concentrated attention is to follow. The procedures followed by the teacher in training the chorus to sing with supported tone turn the attention of the singer to the full and effective use of his physical resources. Similarly, the devices that prompt the chorus to listen intently help build habits of concentration. Whenever the chorus works to develop vocal resonance, improve tone quality and color, or adjust intonation and blend, intense listening is required and habits of concentration are cultivated. In each of these aspects of choral teaching, the teacher has opportunities to stimulate concentrated attention and gives special thought to gaining maximum benefit from them.

The teacher's own attitude is important also. The seriousness with which the teacher approaches each piece of choral literature is reflected in the attitude of the singers. This is one excellent reason for choosing worthy choral literature for the group and for regarding even the lightest selections as opportunities to create music rather than as outlet for jubilant spirits. Exercises, vocalises, and drills may be approached with serious attitude also; they are musical in nature, can be performed artistically, and must be treated as music if they are to produce the desired results.

A very important factor in developing attentive attitudes among singers is the manner in which the conductor conducts. He can be a true conductor, developing and playing upon the responsiveness of the group, or can become an automaton who starts and stops the music and beats time while it is in progress. The accompanist is a key figure in this process and must be trained to follow the conductor. It is all too easy for the choral director to give a vague signal to the accompanist to begin playing an introduction, to beat time unconcernedly during the introduction, and to turn then to the chorus to begin his conducting. At this point the chorus may have lost interest in the conductor and be ready to rely solely on the sounds of the accompaniment. To prevent the chorus from becoming dependent upon the accompanist, the conductor regards him as an integral part of the forces under his control, thinks of introductions and interludes as important parts of the musical fabric he weaves with his baton, and persists in demanding that the accompanist follow his conducting flexibly until he dominates accompanist and chorus alike. The conductor makes every motion meaningful and eliminates those that are unnecessary. He gives cues, indicates every change in dynamics as well as subtle shadings of nuance, outlines phrases, and reflects the emotional content of the music, in this way proving to the singers that they can look to him for assistance in singing their parts and that they must watch his directions to function as a group.

Although daily attention to the many factors mentioned above is probably most influential in developing intensity of effort, it is possible for the teacher to attack the problem in a more direct way. One device for this purpose requires that the chorus sing a familiar melody in unison, but that the separate groups within the chorus—sopranos, altos, tenors, and basses—take turns singing successive phrases of the melody. The teacher conducts the exercise, beginning with either the entire chorus or one part-group, and at each new phrase gives cues to indicate that one group is to stop singing and another is to begin. This requires that the singers remain alert, but requires further that they learn to hear their pitches before they begin singing. A more challenging version of the exercise is one in which the chorus sings music arranged for four-part singing instead of a melody in unison. Each part-group then responds to the conductor's cue by singing its own part rather than the melody. This prevents the singers from simply following the melody and going on with it when another group stops, requiring that each singer develop the ability to hear and follow his own part when silent despite the fact another group is singing an entirely different part. The exercise is accomplished most easily when the music is arranged in simple hymn style, but can be made more difficult by selecting music in which parts move with some degree of rhythmic and melodic independence. To sing four-part music in this way, singers must develop tone-thinking ability of a high order and the exercise therefore tends to increase reading facility as well as sensitivity to pitch. The singers can be instructed also to sit erect when singing and to rest against the backs of their chairs when silent, further emphasizing the need for alertness in the exercise.

Choral Diction

Because choral music combines the art of music and the art of poetry, the choral director trains his choral group to project words and their meanings as well as choral tone and texture, seeking in this way to make clear to the audience everything that enhances the beauty of the performance. The choral director's task is made especially difficult by the fact that song is by nature less clear than speech. The sounds and rhythms of speech are determined only by the need to transmit meaning, whereas song must modify speech to create singing tone, changing the sounds and rhythms of words and making them less easy to understand. For this reason, song requires more effort than speech, the singer achieving clarity of diction by taking special pains not required of the speaker. Clarity, however, is not the element of supreme importance in song, especially when song takes the form of choral music. It is the tonal beauty of massed voices that gives choral music its unique appeal. To achieve it, vowel sounds must retain a measure of uniformity and consonants may not be exaggerated lest they distort the oral cavity. Thus the choral director faces a dilemma. The burden of clarity rests on consonants, but there are limits to the emphasis that may be placed upon them.

The origin of the diction problem is often in the speech habits of the singers. If they are careless in speech, speaking too rapidly, running words together, slurring consonants, and neglecting the purity of vowels, they sing in the same manner. The effect of this carelessness is magnified by the changed rhythm of choral diction. One means of improving choral diction, therefore, is to be attentive to enunciation, observing the same rules and making the same changes which would be necessary to clarify speech. Vowel sounds are given close attention naturally as the chorus is trained because they are vehicles of choral tone. Consonants tend to be ignored, even consciously eliminated, because they tend to interrupt or distort the singing tone. Hence the first step in improving choral diction is one of being attentive to the articulation of consonants.

This does not imply that consonants must be exaggerated or that the organs of speech must be contorted. Neither does it imply that the singer must dwell on consonants and exaggerate their duration, for the proportion of consonants to vowels, in terms of duration of time, is less in song than in speech. Consonants must be sounded distinctly and their brief appearance timed to give meaning to the sounds of the vowels without disturbing them. The best procedure for this purpose is constant practice. Speech characteristics are matters of habit, developed over long periods of time. Correcting them requires the development of new habits; it does not require the development of new or difficult skills. To train the chorus, the director explains and demonstrates the results he hopes to achieve. Success comes ultimately when the singers are reminded frequently and encouraged to practice constantly, through many repetitions building habits that make clarity of choral diction come easily and naturally.

The director can increase the clarity of choral texts through his interpretation of the music. First, it is necessary that the singers be aware of the text and sensitive to its meaning. In the process of learning a choral selection, they benefit from hearing the text read as a poem, from discussing its meaning, and from reading it aloud, striving to project its meaning through careful diction. Once the singers understand the text, it is the director's responsibility to interpret the music in such a way that he projects its meaning by taking advantage of every appropriate factor in the music itself. Proper phrasing is of benefit because it groups together words that form sentences or shorter units of thought. Improper phrasing often destroys meaning by divorcing objects from verbs and adjectives from nouns. To achieve meaningful phrasing, the conductor must be especially attentive to passages in which music phrases do not agree with the phrases of the text; choral music sometimes suffers because both conductor and singers have grown too accustomed to four-measure phrases and other neatly symmetrical musical units.

Another way to project meaning through interpretation of the score is through adjustment of dynamics and nuance. Here, too, changes in intensity suggested by melodic and harmonic characteristics may be at variance with those suggested by the text. To project the meaning of the text, the conductor has recourse to subtle changes in intensity and to the subtle emphasis of key words, treating the choral selection as though it were poetry being read sensitively and artistically. Actually, this is the key to many aspects of choral interpretation—the state of mind that regards choral literature as poetry clothed in music rather than a succession of choral tones upon which words have been imposed. If the director approaches choral music in this way, being sensitive to and projecting its poetic characteristics through his conducting, it is likely the meaning of the text will be intelligible to his audience.

A device for helping both teacher and pupils achieve this state of mind is choral speaking. It can be practiced during rehearsal and is not out of place in the choral concert. In rehearsal, selected poems can be read aloud by the chorus under the teacher's direction to improve diction, gain sensitivity to the meters of poetry, and to transmit meaning. The poems can be selected from the literary repertoire or taken from choral literature, in the latter case helping the chorus learn new choral selections. For the concert, a particularly effective poem recited sensitively by the chorus might well be a high point of audience enjoyment.

In either case, the practice of choral speaking has much to offer. First, it provides ensemble training, helping the singers develop unanimity of response without the guidance provided by musical rhythm. Second, it emphasizes the need for clarity and beauty of diction, demonstrating to the chorus the need for crisp, well-placed consonants and pure vowels. Because the beauty of singing tone is not at hand to cover imperfections in the spoken words, the singers may see the need for proper diction more clearly through one exercise in choral speaking than through many reminders concerning diction in singing. Third, and perhaps most important, it introduces singers to the expressive possibilities of poetry and makes them sensitive to the rhythms of words and the effects of emphasis. The disadvantage of choral speaking is that it may be somewhat difficult to master. The conductor needs a new repertoire of gestures and the chorus must learn a new manner of choral response. In view of the advantages to be gained, however, it is worthy of the time and effort it requires.

THE TEACHING ASPECT

Despite the inevitable and desirable emphasis on performance in the choral program, the choral director remains a teacher of music and accepts the need for guiding the general musical growth of the pupils in the singing group. The topics discussed in the foregoing sections are directly related to choral performance, yet require teaching of a high order. Pupil progress in the areas of posture, tone support, vocal resonance, tone quality, intonation, tone thinking, and diction are all part of the singing skill which, once acquired, opens new doors to music enjoyment and participation during adult years. In addition to these learnings that bear directly on choral performance, there are other areas that may affect it indirectly and provide solid foundations for future music enjoyment as well. Developing facility in music reading is such a goal even though it too is related to choral performance and strongly desired by the teacher because of the rapid choral progress it makes possible. The exploration of choral literature is advisable both because it expands the performing repertoire and because it introduces pupils to new facets of music literature. The acquisition of knowledge concerning music itself—its structure, rhythmic, melodic, and harmonic characteristics, and its place in man's social and political progress—helps pupils understand and become sensitive to the musical art. Finally, and perhaps most worthwhile, the teacher strives to develop pupils' capacities to enjoy and appreciate music and to raise levels of music taste. This is the area in which the choral director serves as a teacher, preparing pupils to be intelligent consumers of music in later life and opening for them new avenues to deeper and more satisfying pleasure in music.

Teaching Music Reading

It is obvious that the ability to read music is of value to the choral singer and almost equally obvious that in many cases the members of public-school choral groups do not read with facility. Neither is skill in music reading common among adults despite the fact that participation in choral music, from congregational singing in the church to membership in community choral groups, would appeal to more people and be more enjoyable if there were some degree of reading ability. It is also true that participation and enjoyment are possible for those who do not read and that there are objectives more important than reading in the music program. Nevertheless, it is possible to develop a degree of reading skill through choral activities. Moreover, there are good reasons for including the study of music reading in the work of the chorus because of the strong motivation provided by the purpose of the group and pupil interest in its activities.

Suggestions for developing reading facility are offered in Chapter 3 in terms of the abilities and interests of pupils in the general music class. Similar procedures are appropriate for the members of the chorus, increased in intensity and raised to their higher levels of ability and interest. Choral singers should be encouraged to use the score as a guide, focusing their attention on the notation and using whatever knowledge they possess to obtain singing directions from it. Some singers may be able to derive precise information, such as the difference between perfect and augmented intervals, whereas others may see no more than the difference between ascending and descending passages. Each will in his own way be reading music and practicing the skill. Choral singers, like pupils in the general music class, can look for repeated phrases and other characteristics of music form, using this knowledge to aid reading. They can learn scales, intervals, chords, and other tone and rhythm patterns as they appear in the literature, subsequently applying this knowledge in reading. Through directing attention to the score, the teacher helps the singers develop a repertoire of these patterns, building a vocabulary of sounds they know and can image aurally. As this fund of directed experience and knowledge increases, the singers find more and more opportunity to apply it in the music they study, advancing steadily along the road to reading facility. The difference between the general music class and the choral group is that the stronger interest and many opportunities for application of knowledge in the latter permit the teacher to devote more time to drill.

Although the term "drill" is used with caution today because of certain past excesses in the use of drill procedures in the classroom, drill itself is essential in the study of music, especially where the skill of music reading is concerned. One learns a skill through practice, by repeating actions until the habit of correct response is well established. There are different ways to conduct drill, of course, including some that make it a routine and tedious exercise from which little is learned but discipline. But drill need not be tedious. It can be challenging, interesting, and enjoyable.

Drill becomes interesting when the teacher exercises imagination and originality. Drills are varied so they do not become routine. The teacher searches for new exercises or devices and for ways to revise the old ones. They are used only as needed and at different times during the rehearsal, never with such regularity that pupils know the first ten minutes of every rehearsal, for example, will be devoted to drill exercises. Most important, drill grows out of literature being studied. Practice of drill-like exercises occurs when a problem in the literature shows its need. The exercise is an excerpt from the literature itself or closely related to it, the skill developed through drill is applied immediately in the literature being studied, and the drill is put aside as soon as it has served its purpose. Every repetition of a difficult passage is drill, as is the practice of rhythm or interval patterns written on the board, and each has its place in the process of learning to read.

Devices can be created by the teacher as needed to learn difficult patterns that occur in choral selections. There are three things the singer must do to read music—read rhythm patterns, read pitch or interval patterns, read patterns in which pitches and rhythms are combined. Singers usually learn rhythms most easily, pitch and interval more slowly, and have most difficulty with passages that require reading of pitches and rhythms simultaneously. For this reason, the teacher begins with rhythms, an area in which pupils can progress quickly and feel the satisfaction of success before attempting the more difficult problem of learning to read pitches.

In choral literature, it is natural that the rhythms of the music should reflect the rhythmic patterns of the words and that the words themselves should be used as a point of departure in studying rhythms. One of the first steps in learning note values and rhythm patterns is to read the words of the choral compositions as they are introduced. To focus attention on the notes themselves and to achieve greater rhythmic accuracy, the next step is to recite the rhythm using a neutral syllable and a speaking tone. To vary the procedure, the rhythm may be tapped or clapped rather than spoken. Muscular response such as conducting or foot beating should accompany the exercise to mark the beat. As a final step, the group may be asked to read rhythm patterns from the board by clapping, tapping, or speaking a neutral syllable, the patterns being made up of difficult rhythms selected from the literature being studied or relatively simple and regular patterns chosen to show the relationships among notes of different duration.

To practice thinking and reading pitches, it is often necessary to divorce them from the rhythms in which they occur in the choral selection, permitting the singers to move slowly and to think each pitch before singing it. In addition, it is helpful to use either syllables, numbers, or letter names as a means of measuring intervallic distances. This eliminates the words of the text which may actually hinder the singers as they try to image the successive pitches. As the work of learning to read is begun, it may be necessary to give the pupil an initial understanding of scales and intervals to build a vocabulary of known pitch patterns. Although the singer is likely to have a beginning vocabulary acquired through previous singing experience, it is probable that his vocabulary will be small and his understanding of the sounds he has sung, indistinct. When this becomes apparent to the teacher, he turns to teaching devices that help pupils learn the scales or intervals concerned, including their sound, their appearance on the staff, and the names with which they can be labeled.

The exercises described under previous headings can be helpful here. Whenever the teacher uses exercises or vocalises to improve intonation, tone quality and so forth, he uses proper terminology in giving directions; he names the interval, chord, or scale in order that pupils become familiar with the terms and associate them with specific tonal patterns. A more direct approach to learning pitch relationships utilizes various forms of dictation. The teacher might sound middle "C" at the piano, telling the chorus its letter name, then strike a succession of white keys asking the chorus to sing the letter name, syllable, or number of each pitch immediately after it is played. The teacher may dictate by saying letter names, the chorus responding by singing either letters or a neutral syllable, or the teacher may notate a complete scale on the board and dictate by pointing to the desired note. The exercise is done in rhythm, the teacher dictating pitches in a distinctly rhythmic pattern and the chorus duplicating the rhythm in its response. To vary the exercise or make it more challenging, the teacher dictates three, four, or more pitches at one time. The chorus may be asked to respond to the dictated pitch by singing its upper or lower diatonic neighbor, the pitch a third, fourth, or fifth above it, or by singing a triad in the manner of an arpeggio using the dictated pitch as the root. Exercises such as these can be made either difficult or easy, are adjusted to the ability of the group, and are used sparingly. Their purpose is to provide a challenging means of defining specific intervals and each exercise is terminated as soon as this has been accomplished.

The form of drill needed most is that in which pupils practice reading from the score. In doing so, they must read rhythms and pitches simultaneously, but are aided by the rhythmic and harmonic flow of the music, the recurrence of phrases and other elements of music form. One distinct difficulty for the beginning reader is learning to think of the relativity of pitches in a key. The beginner is often confused by the fact that middle "C" is the first tone of the scale in one key and the fifth in another; he has difficulty learning to read note patterns in relation to a key center regardless of their position on the staff. This is one of the ways the vocalist's sight-singing differs from the instrumentalist's music reading. The remedy for the singer's difficulty lies in reading a great deal of music in a variety of keys.

For this, one possibility is to secure books of graded exercises and to devote portions of the choral rehearsal to reading from them. The disadvantages of this procedure are that suitable collections are not plentiful and that pupils have little interest in this kind of reading practice. A more practical alternative is for the teacher to build a library of graded reading materials by selecting octavo music or collections of choral music for the purpose. In actuality, much of the music sung by the chorus should be appropriate for reading practice, provided the teacher makes it a rule to select music within the limits of the pupils' ability. Although there may be occasions when the teacher must prepare music too difficult for the chorus to read, because of a special program or holiday season, every effort should be made to avoid selections that require protracted drill on parts and cause pupils to lose interest.

Teaching the Repertoire

The procedures for teaching reading ability suggest a method for teaching choral selections. The first step in teaching the new selection is to examine the total score with the chorus, asking the singers to note repeated phrases, melodic sequences, changes in tempo, key, and meter. Next, examine the text by reading it aloud for meaning and in the style of choral speaking to feel its rhythm and to focus attention in diction. Now read the rhythm of the notes, speaking either a neutral syllable or the words of the text while conducting to mark the meter and tempo. If necessary, clap or tap the rhythm as well. If there are patterns new to the chorus, place them on the board for practice by speaking or clapping, returning to the music as soon as the chorus has gained a feeling for the pattern. Once the rhythm has been learned, examine the melodic characteristics of the parts. Note the key signature, the position of "do," passages built from the scale or chords, accidentals, and passages that are especially difficult as well as the sequences and repeated phrases that make reading easier.

At this point, the chorus attempts to read through the music. If the teacher feels the chorus can read it successfully, all voice-groups sing their own parts simultaneously, observing the rhythm and singing the words. Rather than risk failure at the first attempt, the teacher may ask the group to move slowly from chord to chord, or may ask that only one or two voice-groups read their parts as the others follow theirs silently in the score. The reading is done with piano accompaniment if possible, for the harmonic and rhythmic support it provides, but the voice-parts may be played if it seems desirable to give singers this additional aid. The goal is to read through the entire selection despite errors and uncertainties before going back to study troublesome passages.

In the event the chorus does not possess reading ability, it is necessary to turn to a procedure utilizing the devices for rote teaching. The rote procedure is similar to the reading procedure in some respects, using the score to the fullest possible extent, encouraging the singers to look to the notes for hints concerning melodic direction and note duration, and to recall portions already learned. Here, too, the first step is to examine the score to search out any help it can give. Words need not be taught, but may be used to help learn the rhythm of the selection, the pupils first reading them aloud for meaning and rhythmic flow. To learn the rhythm more accurately, the chorus follows the text and notation in the score as the voice parts are played at the piano.

After only one hearing, the sopranos may be able to sing the melody softly as all voice parts are played at the piano, the other voices following the score and humming as much of their parts as possible. Once the sopranos have become acquainted with their part, the teacher chooses the part to be attempted next, probably the bass because the boys should be able to sing portions of it by ear, but possibly any other part that moves in thirds with the sopranos or forms an easily followed duet. The pupils in this voice-group then sing their part, following the score and listening as the piano plays all voice parts. At the same time, the sopranos review their part by singing softly and the remaining voices try to hum their parts, relying on both the score and the piano for assistance. The teacher then directs attention to the other parts in turn, in each instance playing all parts at the piano, asking the remaining voice-groups to hum or sing softly, and singing with any group that needs special assistance.

In this process, no voice-group is asked to remain silent for a long period while one group is drilled. Each part is learned through a combination of listening and reading. The piano plays voice parts if necessary or the accompaniment if several voices have already become secure in their parts and can hum them to aid those learning the new part. A phonograph recording can be used for one or more hearings to help singers learn their parts and to provide an example of finished performance. Each part helps the others, humming or singing softly to establish the harmonic framework in which each new part finds its place. If necessary, any one part can be singled out to practice a particularly difficult passage, but this is necessary infrequently if the music is appropriate to the abilities of the singers. Not all of the process need be completed during one rehearsal, a much wiser course being to persist with the new selection only until the chorus can feel the satisfaction of attempting it once with all parts or singing one portion successfully, further study being deferred until a subsequent rehearsal.

In both these procedures there is the implication that the chorus will sing many different selections during each rehearsal. Some are sung purely for pleasure, having been learned and polished in earlier periods. Others are sung for review and further study, and one or more new selections may be introduced. This permits the teacher to build repertoire and develop reading ability simultaneously, but most important provides variety and interest in each rehearsal. It requires also that materials be selected carefully, with due regard for pupils' ability to learn. The result is that the chorus explores a large quantity of choral literature, sings within the range of its capabilities, and is encouraged to continue its efforts and to improve its skills.

Teaching for Musical Growth

General musical growth is that which carries over into adult years and offers benefits in addition to those of choral performance. Teaching for musical growth requires that choral rehearsals be planned to advance the pupil's interest in and knowledge of music and that the teacher's goals reach beyond the preparation of concert programs.

The teacher's first step is to accept the belief that membership in a choral group should give each singer a broad acquaintance with choral literature. Rather than polishing a few selections needed for concert programs, the teacher introduces the chorus to many selections of varied type. Some of these are rehearsed carefully for concert use; others are read through or studied briefly so they can become part of the pupils' background. This may prevent the chorus from singing certain especially difficult works in concert, due to the necessity for limiting the time devoted to any one selection, but may also result in better concerts as well as freeing rehearsal time for the survey of other worthy literature. The selections not destined for concert use may be sung with double purpose, for practice in reading and for acquaintance with literature, for example, or simply for the pleasure of becoming familiar with new and interesting music. Instead of spending the several months prior to a concert working intensely with the same repertoire, the singers meet one or two new selections at each rehearsal, review several that were introduced during earlier meetings, and look forward to enjoyable singing that includes but is not exclusively devoted to achieving perfection of the concert repertoire.

Learning about the history of music is a natural counterpart to the survey of music literature. Pupils who sing choral music from the various eras of music history can develop a much clearer understanding of the progress of musical development than pupils who learn about it through study in the music history class. The experience of participating in the music and responding to its intellectual and emotional content leaves an impression no amount of reading can duplicate. The choral director who takes rehearsal opportunities for exploring choral literature is simultaneously taking an important step toward the teaching of music history. What remains is the task of giving direction to the experience by identifying and emphasizing the ideas to be learned.

Directed exploration results when the teacher plans concert and rehearsal programs to include works from the various periods of music history. In the course of a school year, some thirty-five weeks of from two to five rehearsal hours each week, there is opportunity for the choral director to present music from every significant period by every significant composer. This should be his aim. To define this learning more clearly, the teacher need give up only small portions of rehearsal time to discussion of the literature and its historical importance. A few words about the composer, his life, and his historical position suffice as a beginning. His musical style may be shown by singing and discussing a few selected measures from the music being studied. Finally, notebooks, reviews, and quizzes are useful if the teacher accepts the desirability of teaching music through choral activities and plans toward this end.

To supplement the survey of literature and history and make it more meaningful, the teacher draws on normal rehearsal activities to teach other aspects of music. The skill of music reading is developed as a necessary part of the training of a performing group. Aural sensitivity is developed through attention to intonation, blend, tone quality, and color. A knowledge of music form develops from attention to repeated or recurring phrases and through extension of this knowledge to a general understanding of the larger forms. Pupils learn meters, note values, and rhythm patterns as part of the reading process. They become acquainted with scales and intervals through learning to read, through vocalises, and through the various devices used to call attention to intonation and blend. Chords and chord progressions are introduced during rehearsal to help the singers feel more clearly the character of the selections they sing and to improve the singing. To relate this knowledge to the exploration of literature and the survey of music history requires only a small extension of the teacher's planning, creating a well-rounded program of music study based on both performing and understanding.

PLANNING THE REHEARSAL

The choral rehearsal must be planned with care if it is to be productive of pupil progress and efficient in use of rehearsal time. The teacher's goal is to make every rehearsal a balanced program of music of various styles and moods attractive to the singers, combined with activities that advance the pupil's knowledge of music. The plan provides for variety within each rehearsal and from one rehearsal to the next. The rehearsal, therefore, has some of the characteristics of both the concert program and the music class and merits similarly careful planning.

A first step is to determine what needs to be done. One area is that of general choral development, including the improvement of such things as tone quality, intonation, diction, and so forth. A second area is the preparation of music needed for impending concert programs. If a concert calendar is maintained and programs planned well in advance, the teacher can begin study of concert selections early. This permits each rehearsal to be devoted partly to concert preparation and partly to other work, eliminating much of the tension created when the week prior to a public appearance finds the program only partly prepared. Third, the teacher establishes goals in the area of general music knowledge and skill. This is a continuing project worthy of attention during every rehearsal. Fourth, the teacher selects the choral music and other materials to be included in the rehearsal program. Some of these are concert selections, some are chosen because they lend themselves to the development of choral techniques or the teaching of general music knowledge, and some are included simply because the group enjoys singing them. By considering these needs as well as those peculiar to each chorus, the teacher charts a course for rehearsals to follow through a period of weeks, months, or the entire year and defines the specific goals to be achieved in each rehearsal.

Score study is one means of determining rehearsal goals and the essential in rehearsal planning for the director. It brings to light both the difficulties that must be overcome before successful performance is possible and the factors in the music that provide opportunities for teaching general music knowledge. If the conductor studies the score, he can identify the problems likely to arise during rehearsal—difficult rhythms, melodic intervals, harmonic progressions, and so forth—before the chorus makes its first attempt to sing the music. This is one of the skills demanded of the conductor and one he develops rapidly if he is alert to the manner in which his chorus responds, applying his knowledge of pupil limitations as he studies the music to be presented. Once he has identified the problems in each selection, he searches for a means of overcoming them. This may require only that he point out a change of key or tempo before the chorus begins to sing, or that he turn to a special teaching device if the problem is a difficult passage containing new rhythms or intervals. In either event, it is in finding solutions to problems before they occur that the director saves rehearsal time through score study.

Planning also includes the search for approaches to new music being introduced for the first time. Motivation is often thought of as important to class lessons, but less frequently considered when the choral group is to begin its work with a new selection. Yet motivation is one of the forces that impels the chorus to be attentive to the work at hand, interested in the music, and concerned about singing it artistically.

Once the director has completed this preliminary work of deciding upon goals to be achieved, selecting materials, identifying problems, and finding possibilities for their solution, he is ready to plan the rehearsal schedule. Here, too, the rehearsal is like the class in that the sequence of events is calculated to preserve the interest of the group. It must not dwell too long on any one activity, must provide for variety, yet must permit concentrated work when needed. Among the types of activity it can include are "warm-ups," singing familiar selections for pleasure, reviewing those that need additional rehearsal, intense study of especially difficult passages, introduction of new music, and the artistic performance of music that has been mastered to provide a satisfying conclusion to the rehearsal period.

It is common practice to begin the rehearsal with materials that permit the pupils to sing freely without strain in order to approach the more strenuous work of the rehearsal gradually. For this, some directors prefer familiar materials that can be sung easily and well, whereas others prefer vocalises or other warm-up exercises. For the latter, the devices suggested in earlier portions of this chapter permit the teacher to control the vocal demands made upon singers and to teach some aspect of choral technique or music knowledge simultaneously. It is desirable to plan the conclusion of the rehearsal also, selecting music that can be sung well and with pleasure so the singers leave the rehearsal with a feeling of accomplishment and satisfaction. For the balance of the time, new music is interspersed among that which is familiar and difficult music among that which can be sung more easily, the director planning for variety to prevent fatigue and sustain interest.

A complete plan is made for the rehearsal, the director planning the sequence of events and estimating the time required for each to insure that necessary work is completed and the rehearsal ends on time. As he conducts the rehearsal, he makes every effort to follow his plan, to maintain the tempo of his teaching, and to accomplish the goals he has set for the period. With experience, he learns to estimate accurately the capabilities of his chorus and the amount of time required for each activity, finding that careful planning enables him to use rehearsal time to best advantage and achieve noteworthy progress even in the short span of one rehearsal period.

Although the chorus is often thought of as a performing group first and a means of music education second, there are good reasons for regarding it as a type of class and for considering the use of teaching devices not usually associated with the chorus rehearsal. There are many possibilities for outside study, pertinent "homework" that contributes to performing success or music learning. Singers may be asked to study their parts at home to reduce the time devoted to drill in rehearsal. They may be asked to do exercises in writing melodies, scales, and intervals or chord progressions to develop familiarity with music notation and increase reading facility. The study of music literature and history may be pursued outside of class. Notebooks are a further possibility. Small portions of rehearsal time can be devoted to presenting information to be included in the notebooks, the pupils using additional time outside of rehearsal to organizing the notebook, gathering additional information, or review. This leads naturally to quizzes that encourage the pupils to study. Written quizzes are in order when the director gives continuing attention to teaching music literature, history, and theory. Oral reviews may be conducted to ascertain whether the pupil's information is complete and whether he is making satisfactory progress. Quartet auditions may be used to test pupils' progress in learning their parts or in developing reading ability, providing a means of judging whether outside assignments are being completed faithfully.

In these and other ways the chorus is conducted in the manner of a general music class. If the music program offers a sufficient number of general music classes, and if these classes reach a sufficiently large segment of the school population, the teacher may decide against including general music study in the choral program. There are, however, worthy reasons for teaching choral groups in this way regardless of other school offerings. Performances improve as the singers' fund of general music knowledge and skill increases. Pupils have greater respect for the performing group that establishes definite requirements, work harder, and are more interested in the music they sing. There are benefits to the teacher in that the teaching program encourages careful planning and compels the teacher to use rehearsal time efficiently and effectively. As a result, rehearsals proceed more smoothly, are more successful, and offer greater satisfaction to the director. Finally, there are indirect benefits to the total music program, the choral group demonstrating the effectiveness of competent music teaching, justifying the allotment of rehearsal time and the award of school credit, and creating a favorable climate of opinion for further program developments.

9: choral performance

The choral performance is a natural outcome of the choral program and its sequence of rehearsals. It has values of a general, educational nature as well as others important to the music program. Performance is essential to the maintenance of interest among members of the choral group and highly desirable as a means of demonstrating progress to the public, school administrators, and parents. Many kinds of choral performance are possible and performance opportunities are plentiful. Planning the concert calendar is sometimes one of the director's more difficult problems and additional planning is devoted to the programs themselves. Although there is little need to justify or stimulate choral performance, there is good reason to give careful thought to its various aspects and problems.

THE GOALS OF CHORAL PERFORMANCE

Because there are many reasons for presenting a choral group in performance, and the possibility of many desirable outcomes, it is well for the choral teacher to establish goals he hopes to achieve through every concert. These may have to do with pupil development, with community relations, or with the advancement of the total choral program.

Learning through Singing

Performance can be a learning experience for the singers, helping them advance beyond the limits of progress possible through participation in rehearsals only. Performance provides motivation for rehearsal, offering incentive which spurs the group to concentrated effort. Performance provides for the application of skill, requiring that singers be alert and that they exercise their skills to sing well despite the pressures and tensions created by the presence of an audience; the difference between the atmosphere of rehearsal and that of performance impels pupils to concentrate all their powers and raise their singing to a peak of perfection not common to the rehearsal.

There are further advantages in choral performance in that it tends to promote pupil development in areas not directly related to the performing skill. It is one means of raising the pupils' level of music taste. In the classroom or in the choral rehearsal, pupils respond best to music they enjoy and the teacher is prone to seek this response by selecting materials to maintain interest rather than widen acquaintance with superior music. When preparing for a concert, however, pupils accept the necessity for studying music that has less immediate appeal for them. They are quick to see the desirability of offering music that appeals to the many different tastes among audiences and are willing to work hard to prepare music of high caliber, knowing that by doing so they win the approbation of those who listen. When the director applies this knowledge to the selection of materials for concert programs, he takes advantage of pupils' higher levels of interest to introduce them to superior music, persevering in its study until the chorus reaches a level of performing excellence that displays the beauties of the music.

One of the important performance goals is to develop the singers' poise and self-confidence, qualities which can be developed rapidly through the experience of appearing before an audience. Of further benefit to pupils is the fact that choral performance is enjoyable and stimulating in a general way. Pupils of all ages enjoy the experience of appearing in public, especially if they appear as members of a large choral group and are spared the stronger pressure of solo or small ensemble performance. This enjoyment is a physical and emotional outlet, worthy for itself as well as for the stimulation it provides for music study in rehearsal.

Improving Community Relations

Performing music groups are among the most effective means of arousing community interest and support. The choral concert is of especial interest because it is enjoyable; audiences gather to be entertained and parents are gratified to see their children perform. When the concert offers a lesson to the audience through its implications concerning the general value of the educational program, the lesson being combined with entertainment and enjoyment, it makes a deeper impression than similar information presented through other public relations devices.

There is a more practical financial aspect to the choral concert. In some instances admission can be charged to raise funds for special purposes. Money can be gathered to augment the choir-robe fund, to expand the choral library, or to purchase special equipment necessary to the choral program. The choral group can lend its assistance to other school departments, helping the dramatics group gather funds for scenery and costumes, helping clubs buy special materials or equipment, or participating in fund drives of benefit to the entire school.

Many educators feel it is improper for the choral group to charge admission to its concerts. The school chorus is a tax-supported educational activity and its concerts should be open to the public and free. The choral director is a teacher of music whose function it is to guide the music development of pupils in his charge; it is not his responsibility to participate directly in the gathering of funds to support either the school or the music program. If he does so, especially if the funds obtained are used solely for the advancement of the choral program, he may be trespassing in an area beyond the proper limits of professional endeavor. There is something unfair, too, about a practice that permits the chorus to exploit its entertainment value to serve its own ends when other and more basic subjects in the school program are unable to resort to similar measures.

Nevertheless, there are many school music organizations that raise funds through concerts. The practice may be justifiable when the performing group is new and growing, when it is obviously below the standard of similar groups in neighboring schools, and when the school budget is such that the allocation of regular funds must be postponed until later years. In these circumstances school administrators may agree to the necessity for raising funds through extraordinary means and other teachers may endorse the project and even coöperate in carrying it out.

Because the choral concert can be used effectively to secure extra-musical benefits, the music teacher must be especially alert to the dangers of exploiting pupil abilities to achieve ends neither musical nor educational. There are similar dangers arising from the entertainment value of the choral concert. Because audiences respond favorably to entertaining concerts, and pupils are especially responsive to concert music they enjoy singing, the choral director is often tempted to build concert programs with these ends in view. Entertainment, however, is not the principal goal of choral activity. Neither is it proper to use pupils to further the cause of choral music or to achieve objectives desired by the choral director if this use exploits the group at the expense of educational progress. Proper goals are those that have to do with education in general and with the teaching of music in particular.

THE VARIETY OF CONCERT OPPORTUNITIES

Because the performing experience is of educational value, it is appropriate that the choral director seek opportunities for his pupils to appear in public. These opportunities are legion. There are school concerts of many different kinds and for many different groups as well as public concerts under the auspices of various community organizations. By scheduling concerts for different audiences, the teacher provides repeated performing experience without requiring the preparation of an extensive concert repertoire. This is advantageous in that the young singers are not forced beyond the limits of their interest because of the pressures of a heavy performance schedule. Each concert selection can be prepared carefully and without sacrifice of the rehearsal time that should be devoted to other learning experiences. Once worthy selections have been thoroughly prepared, they can be performed on repeated occasions; it is neither reasonable nor efficient to spend months in the rehearsal of concert music used only once before the group must begin the study of an entirely new program.

School Concerts

In the school itself the chorus can participate in regular assemblies, utilizing an entire assembly period for its concert or occupying only a short portion of a number of programs. The latter procedure is desirable because the chorus can present its performance after mastering only a few selections, permitting the teacher to offer this kind of motivation without waiting for the several months required to prepare music for a lengthy program. School songs, patriotic songs, and other appropriate music can be sung by the chorus alone as a regular part of every assembly or the chorus can be used to lead and accompany the singing of the entire student body. During holiday seasons or on other special occasions the chorus can prepare a complete program in the form of a choral concert. This may be solely for the enjoyment of the student body, may prompt the invitation of parents to visit the school assembly, or may serve as a dress rehearsal for a public concert. On still other occasions, the chorus can coöperate with a dramatics group or some other school club in presenting an assembly program of a special nature in which choral music plays a subordinate role.

Similar programs can be arranged for presentation in other schools of the community, the high-school chorus offering programs in junior high and elementary schools. In addition to providing performance opportunities for the high-school singers, this practice stimulates interest in the high-school chorus itself, encouraging pupils in the junior high school to plan in advance for membership and reducing the problem of recruiting in the high school. The appearance of the high-school chorus in a junior high school assembly may have a desirable influence on the junior high school as well, encouraging membership and providing a model of good singing and choral practice for the junior high school choral group to imitate. A further possibility is that of exchange concerts with schools in neighboring communities to broaden pupils' experience and acquaint them with the work done by other schools. This coöperative arrangement is much to be desired and creates a far better atmosphere than the competitive spirit fostered by music contests, school sports, and other such activities.

An area worthy of exploration, especially for the small ensembles and soloists who may be a part of the larger choral organization, is the music recital. In some schools, extended lunch periods leave pupils with unoccupied time during the middle of the day. In others, there are club, homeroom, and other activity periods that can be utilized for music. The hour immediately after school and in some cases a period of perhaps fifteen minutes before school might be made available for special musical purposes. These periods are ideally suited for the music recital, a brief, informal concert presented by soloists or small groups. Concerts of this nature may be open to anyone who wishes to attend, there being no necessity for requiring the attendance of the entire school or an entire class. In some instances, individual pupils may be excused from homeroom or club periods to attend the recital. Carefully planned programs of special materials might be pertinent to the work of English, social studies, or language classes or to the projects of extra-curricular clubs, these groups substituting recital attendance for all or part of a regular class meeting.

The experience of appearing in recital is a valuable one for the chorus members. An audience of almost any size, from a few pupils to an entire class or the entire school, is suitable and provides the desired performing experience. Recitals encourage the performing pupils to gain independence, arranging their own rehearsals, planning recital dates and programs, and conducting the recital itself. It also permits the performers to explore types of music of special interest to them and to various segments of the student body. Music of a popular nature is almost certain to be successful and music representing a particular country or historical period may be of interest to special classes. Once interest is developed and the recital performers have gained skill and assurance, the recital program may be extended to include evening concerts in the school building or to presentations for various community groups.

The school public address system may be of service, especially during the portions of the school day when classes are not in session. Music performed by the glee club, small ensembles, or soloists can be broadcast to the school as a whole or to selected locations or classes. Music can be broadcast in the cafeteria during the lunch period, to the auditorium when it is used during bad weather as a place where pupils wait for the beginning of classes, or to homerooms and classes on special occasions. If a tape recorder is available, appropriate music can be recorded during rehearsal if the entire chorus participates, or during free periods, before or after school if the recording is to present a smaller group. To serve the interests of other school departments, the chorus might even present singing commercials advertising dramatic productions, sports events, or school social functions.

Public Concerts

Opportunities for public concerts are equally numerous. Formal public concerts can be presented on a regular basis throughout the school year, appropriate programs being arranged during holiday seasons or for annual concerts in the spring or fall. The chorus can appear before PTA meetings or for other school functions to which the public is invited. Other concerts for interested community groups offer a means of supplementing the regular school concert programs. Churches of the community may welcome the high school glee club, especially if it is possible to arrange a combined program shared by the glee club and the church choir. Service clubs and other community organizations present special programs in which the high-school singers can participate. The chorus can be of real service by presenting concerts in hospitals and other community institutions. In some communities, radio and television stations are willing to provide time for broadcast concerts, especially during holiday seasons. The broadcasting experience is an exciting one for the singers, creating strong interest and stimulating the improvement of singing. The teacher must exercise good judgment, however, in scheduling radio and television appearances, for imperfections of intonation and ensemble are magnified by the microphone.

Public concerts, including those on radio and television, are of value because they permit the chorus to appear before audiences composed of adults, creating a concert climate quite different from that of the school concert in which the chorus sings for other pupils of their own age. The opportunities for public concerts, combined with those for concerts in the school or at school functions, are so numerous that the choral teacher may find it necessary to select performance opportunities carefully to prevent the too-frequent performance that overtaxes his chorus. If good judgment is exercised in scheduling concerts, however, the experience is of great educational value to the singers.

ARRANGING THE CONCERT CALENDAR

The necessity for planning the concert calendar carefully is evident when one considers the limitations of the young singers in the high-school or junior-high-school choral group. They are neither physically nor vocally capable of an extended series of concerts. Because they are not trained musicians with highly developed vocal skills, reading abilities, and music sensitivity, they must be given adequate time to master the concert repertoire. Reheasal time is limited. The singers' interests and energies are divided among music activities, school studies, and many extra-curricular projects. If the chorus is to be a source of general music learning, rehearsal time must provide for surveying the literature and history of music, learning numerous music skills, and developing interest and appreciation. The choral teacher can not justifiably regard the singing group as an organization having performance as its sole objective. Moreover, the choral group should not be permitted to develop to the point where it claims the major share of the pupils' attention or occupies too many of their hours either in or out of school. Other school subjects must take precedence in the curriculum and in the demands placed upon pupils' time. Thus it is important that the teacher restrict the performance schedule and plan it carefully so it can be carried out effectively without making unreasonable demands on the pupils.

Aspects of Scheduling

In planning the concert calendar, the teacher begins by considering the concerts of a regular nature that occur on an annual basis, perhaps placing these on the calendar a year in advance. In doing so, he considers the demands placed on pupils, the probability of extraordinary situations which might require that pupils be called out of classes for special rehearsals, the quantity and type of music needed to fill these concert programs, and the necessity for securing administrative approval for every concert and rehearsal not held during regularly scheduled hours.

It is especially important that the choral teacher concern himself with the manner in which choral activities interfere with or detract from other portions of the school program. The choral teacher who constantly requests that pupils be excused from other classes for special rehearsals quickly generates antipathy among administrators and other teachers for the choral program. Similarly, it is important that the school principal or superintendent be consulted about the advisability of scheduling public concerts that may conflict with other school or community activities. The choral program needs the support of administrators and other teachers and the fact that it is of natural interest to the public and receives much public attention may create resentment among teachers whose important work must be confined to the classroom.

Andrews and Cockerille [1] suggest a faculty steering committee for this purpose. Such a committee might be composed of the music teacher, teachers from several other departments, including those with interests in athletics and dramatics as well as the core subjects, and the principal as an *ex officio* member. By discussing the concert calendar and other problems with this committee, the choral teacher in effect seeks the advice and assistance of the entire faculty. He informs them of the problems involved in managing the choral program, of providing the best educational experi-

[1] Frances M. Andrews, and Clara E. Cockerille, *Your School Music Program: A Guide to Effective Curriculum Development*. Englewood Cliffs, N.J.: Prentice-Hall, Inc., 1958, p. 150. Reprinted by permission.

ence for chorus members, and insures that planned concert activities have the full approval of the entire school. As a further safeguard, the recommendations of this steering committee can be presented to the faculty during regular faculty meetings so plans can be discussed and approved by the entire group when necessary.

A first step in planning concert appearances is to consult the school calendar. In many school systems, a master calendar is maintained in the office of the principal or superintendent. This calendar shows dates when school begins and ends for the year, vacation periods, and special holidays. It should also show the dates set aside for special events, including the administration of achievement and placement tests for the entire student body, the ends of marking periods, dates for completion of records and forms, periods for health examinations, inoculations, and so forth. Each of these might offer sufficient reason for postponing a choral concert. In addition, this calendar should show dates selected for various extra-curricular activities such as sports, dramatic productions, special school assemblies, and PTA meetings. The choral teacher consults this calendar before selecting concert dates to avoid conflict with other school functions and to make certain all concert dates are entered on the master calendar for the information of groups planning other extra-curricular activities.

Teacher-Pupil Planning

To free himself from some of the details of concert planning, and to encourage pupil participation, the choral teacher designates a student group as a planning or program committee. It is the teacher's responsibility to plan aspects of the choral program that require his experienced music judgment and to approve or revise the decisions of the committee, but much of the clerical and routine work can be carried out by competent pupils. This is a desirable application of principles of student government to the choral program. The existence of a student committee increases interest in the performing activities of the chorus, stimulates pupil cooperation, and prevents some of the problems that arise when concert dates conflict with the singers' other activities. The latter problem is of consequence, especially when the chorus becomes capable of artistic performance and receives many concert invitations from community groups. If the concert calendar is planned by the students themselves, it is less likely that soloists and leaders of the various sections will have conflicting social engagements on the evenings of important concerts. The student committee reviews invitations from community groups and other sources, recommending their acceptance or rejection. The existence of the committee is valuable from the teacher's point of view because it relieves him of some of the necessity for explaining to community groups the reasons for refusing certain concert invitations; because the concert calendar is arranged by a committee according to an organized and equitable system, it is possible to avoid the implication that some community groups are given preferred treatment.

Whether these decisions are made by the student committee or by the director, it is often advisable to prepare form letters to accept or reject invitations and to furnish the information needed by the sponsoring group in planning for the guest appearance of the chorus. These letters describe the standard policy governing appearance of school groups during hours other than those of the regular school day and in places other than the school auditorium. The letters permit the director to note the limitation placed on frequency of performances, the necessity for securing administrative approval, the person to whom invitations should be addressed, and the desirability of submitting them well in advance of the concert date. Information is given concerning any regulations that affect the appearance of the group or any special accommodations required for the performance. These include such things as transportation to and from a central meeting place, a room in which the chorus may assemble, deposit hats and coats, don choir robes or other attire, and sing any warm-up exercises the teacher may wish. Further, such letters describe the function of the student planning committee and any other pertinent information concerning the manner in which the chorus establishes its concert calendar. With such form letters available, a great deal of time is saved for the choral director and the student committee, and each community group can be assured that its invitation has been courteously considered.

Keeping Useful Records

Planning is made easier if records are maintained, permitting the director to refer to them for information concerning the events of previous years. By preserving concert calendars, the choral director can at any time determine which concerts arise annually, which community groups submit concert invitations, the frequency with which invitations from any one group are accepted, and the general pattern of concert activities as it develops over a period of years. By establishing a file of printed programs from past concerts, he can determine which choral works have been performed, which have been presented to various community groups, and which have been studied in previous years by singers who are still members of the choral group. By adding a few brief notes after every concert, he can record information concerning audience reaction, quality of performance, and the degree of pupil interest in each concert selection.

These notes are of inestimable value to the choral director as he plans subsequent programs. They permit him to select from the choral repertoire music appealing to audiences and students. The file of printed programs provides information on which to base a rotating schedule of music to be studied in rehearsal so that pupils who remain in the group for more than one year do not study the same music over and over again. By examining the choral files, the director projects the concert schedule for the coming year, including both the concerts that arise regularly and those likely to be needed for special occasions or in response to invitations from community groups. In addition, the files permit him to project rehearsal schedules for an entire year, indicating the number and kind of concert selections needed, the amount of rehearsal time to be devoted to them, and the amount of rehearsal time that may be reserved for other music study.

With this planning completed, the choral director is able to post a concert schedule in the rehearsal room for the information of the pupils in the group, advising them of concert dates well in advance so their other activities may be planned accordingly. If he wishes, he can post rehearsal schedules several weeks in advance for the information of members and to guide the librarians who distribute music before it is to be rehearsed and remove it from the choral folders after it has been presented in concert. The files and other records then serve a useful purpose, guiding the work of the chorus, saving time for both director and singers, and helping rehearsals and concerts proceed smoothly.

BUILDING THE CONCERT PROGRAM

The choral concert is both an educational experience and a public relations device. In planning the program, the choral teacher considers its effect upon the music development of the singers and the impression it will make on members of the community in the audience.

The choral program has an influence on music taste, the succession of rehearsals devoted to intensive study of choral literature providing the extensive experience, the repeated contact, and the increased knowledge that strengthen pupil interest in and understanding of worthy music. Similarly, the concert is a means of acquainting audiences with better music, taking advantage of parents' natural interest in the achievements of their children to direct their attention toward great works of choral music that might otherwise be of little interest to them. Because the concert presented by a public-school singing group offers unique opportunities to capture audience interest, it is an effective means for stimulating appreciation of the best examples of choral literature and providing experience that contributes to the improvement of music taste.

Unity, Variety, and Contrast

In building each concert program, the director strives to include both unity and variety in a presentation of reasonable length. It is necessary that audience interest be sustained and that the concert be brought to a conclusion before the listener becomes fatigued. A unified program provides a thread of continuity to lead the listener from one selection to the next, whereas variety and contrast combat the natural waning of interest as the program continues. Unity can be provided through the selection of a theme for each concert, or several themes that permit the grouping of selections into related units. Themes may be suggested by the season of the year, important holidays, or periods in music history. Holiday programs are usually successful because of the atmosphere generated by the holiday itself and because the appropriate music is often well known to and enjoyed by the audience. Programs devoted to a historical period or a particular type of choral literature may arouse interest because of the presentation of unusual types of music. In addition, they give the choral director an opportunity to extend his teaching to include the listeners as well as the singers. In doing so, he builds audience acceptance of worthy choral literature unfamiliar to his audiences and paves the way to subsequent choral concerts of high caliber.

Variety and contrast may be achieved in a number of ways. Because the public-school chorus usually presents concerts consisting of a number of short choral selections rather than a lengthy cantata or oratorio, it is possible to choose contrasting selections and to arrange the order of their presentation to provide changes in mood, tempo, and style.

The program may be varied further by the inclusion of soloists and small ensembles such as trios and quartets. This is desirable in that it provides a challenging outlet for the more talented members of the group and avoids the vocal fatigue young singers may experience when presenting a lengthy concert composed entirely of choral music.

As for the length of the concert program, from sixty to ninety minutes is a reasonable maximum. This may vary, being influenced by the type of music presented, the abilities of the singers, and the interest of the audience, and being further adjusted by the inclusion of an intermission. Moreover, the director may find that a concert well received by one audience subsequently proves too long or too short for another. In any event, the choral director may well follow the show-business adage that it is better to sing one song too few than one too many.

The usual audience of pupils or of parents who gather to see their children perform shows a limited capacity for listening and may become restless during an extended program. Thus it is advisable to plan the concert in such a way that audience fatigue is avoided and that even the last selection can be presented to interested and attentive listeners. Principal offenders in this respect are the departmental concerts in which an attempt is made to display to the public all the choral groups in the school music program. Concerts of this kind are sometimes planned for the end of the school year, music festivals which show the progress of the many pupils in the various groups. Although there may be a festival atmosphere about such a program and an air of excitement caused by the massing of large numbers of pupils, the audience sometimes sees little beyond the parade of one group after another before the footlights, an interminable process of little interest to parents whose children appear for only a few brief selections before being replaced by other pupils in other groups. Rather than permit a concert of this sort to grow beyond reasonable time limits, the teacher is well advised to plan several concerts, each featuring only one or two singing groups.

In planning the program itself, many conductors prefer to select first some outstanding work to serve as a high point and to build the rest of the program around it. This provides a climax for the concert, one memorable experience to make a deep impression on both singers and listeners, more likely to be remembered vividly and with pleasure than a program that either has no climax or is held to high levels of intensity throughout. By selecting one especially stimulating work and others that are relatively subordinate, the director considers the capacities for emotional response of the performers and the audience and the vocal capabilities of young singers.

The concert may have subordinate climaxes and is in this respect similar to a dramatic performance. The principal climax may be preceded by others to set the mood and whet the appetite and may be followed by a lesser climax or one of a different type to avoid ending the concert too abruptly. If the concert includes one or more intermissions, it is appropriate that each segment have its own high point but that the different segments be unequal in intensity. The climactic work may be placed in the early portion of the concert, near its end, or close to the middle. If it makes heavy demands on the singers it may be necessary to place it near the beginning of the program so the chorus sings it before other selections have taxed vocal endurance. If the climactic work is of a lighter type and likely to prompt enthusiastic applause, it may be used as a final selection. If it is of a very serious nature, noteworthy for musical beauty but quiet in mood, it may best be placed near the middle of the program so that other music may be used to prepare the mood of the singers and the audience and so it can be followed by selections that stimulate applause.

Planning in terms of climax, pupil capabilities and audience response suggests a general pattern for the choral concert. The first selection is often for "warm-up" purposes. The members of the choral group must be given time to become accustomed to the stage, the unfamiliar lighting, and the knowledge that an audience is watching. More important, they must be given opportunity to flex their vocal muscles and become accustomed to singing in these unusual conditions before undertaking the performance of demanding choral music. A warm-up selection may be appropriate for the audience also, giving the listener time to settle in his seat and preparing him for the music to follow. For this purpose, the director chooses music that is easy to sing, does not require extraordinary efforts of concentration by conductor, singers, or audience, and that functions as a curtain-raiser to arouse the enthusiasm of all concerned. He avoids subtleties of mood or style and turns instead to music that makes an immediate appeal, is colorful in harmony and has rhythmic vitality, but avoids exaggerated effects and extremes of vocal range, dynamics, and ensemble precision.

As a next step in program building, the director places the selection that is most demanding of the singers and is the high-point of the program. The logical place for music of this kind is in the early portion of the program, shortly before intermission. If the climactic work is not especially difficult to perform or for the audience to understand, it may better be placed later in the program, shortly after intermission, so the audience retains a clear impression of it when the concert is over.

Immediately before intermission it is often desirable to present a short selection with strong audience appeal. Although those who attend public-school choral concerts are in effect captive audiences and not likely to leave before the concert ends, it is well to stimulate their desire to hear more music and to provide strong incentive for them to return to their seats after intermission. This is especially desirable if more than one performing group participates in the program and parents may feel content to leave after they have heard their children perform.

One reason for ending the first portion of the program with a flourish is that the segment before intermission is often longer than that which follows. If two halves of a program are of equal length, the second may seem unduly long and tiresome. Singers and audience are fresh and interested when the program begins, but tend to become less able to concentrate on the music once intermission has passed. Thus the director plans a comparatively lengthy first half to take full advantage of the natural alertness of singers and listeners, but ends this portion of the program with a selection calculated to re-awaken enthusiasm. A selection for this purpose should be short, vigorous, and exciting, productive of applause that leaves the singers in high spirits and the audience eager to hear more.

For the first selection after intermission, the director may again choose music for warm-up purposes. The release of tension that follows successful performance and the fatigue felt by singers after they have concentrated their vocal powers during the first half of a concert may find them even less ready to sing freely after intermission than they were at the beginning of the program. A successful first half raises the spirits of the singers, especially those of high-school age, to such an extent that the second half of the program may suffer. The elation of having sung well before an audience coupled with the volatile spirits of adolescents may cause the chorus to forget much of what it has learned about the music to be sung after intermission, to remove their attention from the conductor, and to sing too jubilantly with raucous voices. Similarly, the audience may benefit from hearing music chosen to recapture the mood of the concert. These considerations suggest a selection that is short, rhythmic, and bold in its appeal, but compels the attention of the singers and requires controlled singing. This is followed by music lighter and more entertaining than that of the first half, chosen to hold the attention of singers and audience and considerate of the young singers' lack of vocal endurance.

To end the concert effectively, the director chooses music especially impressive but not necessarily difficult. Depending on the nature of the audience and the skill of the chorus, it might be either vigorous, rhythmic, and exciting or slow, hushed, and of serene beauty. In most instances, a rousing chorus may be the best choice to stimulate enthusiasm and applause. In special circumstances or to vary the pattern of the concert program, the director may find it effective to close with a quiet selection or a respectful presentation of the *alma mater*. In either case, the object is to bring the concert to a memorable close, giving the chorus and the audience an impressive music experience to carry away from the concert.

In determining the order in which the various choral selections are to be presented, the director continues to think in terms of variety and contrast. This may be a matter of keys, moods, tempos, music styles, or even the lengths of the various selections. The director can build the program in terms of a cycle of keys, following the lead of symphonic composers who begin and end their works in the same key and use contrasting but related keys for inner movements. A definite key scheme is seldom practical for the choral concert, but the director examines the key relations of successive selections nevertheless. In general, he avoids the juxtaposition of several selections in the same key unless they are sufficiently different in mood to offer contrast to each other. He also avoids the other extreme of juxtaposing two selections of sharply different key. Two reasons for this are that the singers' sense of tonality may be destroyed by a new and unrelated key, sufficient to influence intonation or even to cause them to sing incorrect pitches, and that the listeners' aural sense suffers a shock when the final cord of one selection is shattered by the opening tones of the next. Major and minor modes must be considered also, it being better in many instances to place a selection in minor mode between two in major rather than to place two minor modes together. Mood, tempo, and length are treated similarly, exciting music being followed by that which is quiet, fast by slow, short by long. The question of music styles may be treated somewhat differently. Here it is usually preferable to group selections of similar style together. Music of contemporary flavor or popular in nature does not mix well with that of the seventeenth and eighteenth centuries. With some exceptions, each type of music is most effective when presented with other selections of compatible style. Groups of different styles can be separated by intermissions, by a change in the seating arrangements of the chorus, or by interludes created in some other way.

There are many different patterns for the concert program, of course, the sequence of selections varying from concert to concert. In general, however, the principles described above merit consideration when any program is being planned and the director's goals might be summarized as follows:

1. To achieve unity through selection of a theme.
2. To provide variety and contrast through the succession of keys, moods, tempos, and lengths and the inclusion of music of different styles or historical periods.
3. To build around a high-point or series of climaxes.
4. To provide warm-up opportunities at the beginning of each segment of the program.
5. To provide a memorable conclusion for each portion of the concert.

6. To place difficult music in the early portion of the concert and be considerate of the singers' capabilities throughout.
7. To make the later portion of the concert shorter, lighter, easier to enjoy and less demanding for singers and audience.
8. To limit the program to reasonable length and provide an intermission or other interlude when possible.

By following these precepts and adjusting them as necessary to fit each concert situation, the choral teacher takes the first step in assuring that the program will be successful. If it is planned with care, the concert presented by even a newly formed group of inexperienced choristers can offer satisfactions to both singers and listeners, providing incentive for further choral development and the raising of choral standards in subsequent concerts.

Sustaining Audience and Pupil Interest

The variety show is successful because it presents a varied program with something to appeal to each taste and interest. The choral teacher may well heed the lesson it contains. The audiences for which his groups perform are as complex in their make-up as any that applaud the variety show. There is good reason to include selections appealing to each level of taste. In addition to choosing varied music, he considers the performing medium itself. Although the human voice is regarded as the perfect instrument and massed voices produce choral tone of unique beauty and expressive power, the chorus is far more limited in its abilities to produce contrasting tone colors and intensities than is, for example, the orchestra or band. It is reasonable to expect that an audience might find an hour or more of choral singing a tiresome listening chore and experience indicates that audiences become restless more quickly at choral concerts than at those that feature instrumental music.

Here is something the choral teacher can do—provide a variety of sounds for the audience to hear. By using sections of the chorus both together and separately, he can perform music for mixed chorus, boys' voices alone, and girls' voices alone. The program can include music arranged in four parts, three parts, two parts, or for voices in unison. The latter is a neglected type, naturally overlooked when the choral program is being planned, but offers interesting opportunities to vary the choral program with exciting and appealing music. The choral group can be the source of soloists and small ensembles, providing welcome variety in the concert program and stimulating audience interest.

Most choral concerts require accompanying instruments. Here too is opportunity for varying the sounds heard by the audience. Accompaniment is most frequently provided by the piano, but other instruments of the keyboard family may be substituted with good effect. Organ, celesta, harpsichord if one can be obtained, or even instruments of the marimba family are suitable and markedly different. To this accompaniment can be added the effects produced by percussion instruments, including snare and bongo drums, tom-toms, maracas, claves, castanets, guiro, and tambourine. For music of a popular nature, the piano can be replaced by a "combo" consisting of guitar, bass, drums, and wind instruments including the saxophone. Other instrumental groups are suitable for more serious music, including string quartet or small ensemble, brass quartet or choir, woodwind ensembles and other groups of mixed instruments. These groups not only provide interestingly different accompaniments, they permit the choral director to include in the choral concert a selection or two featuring the instrumental ensemble alone. This, too, is a neglected practice. The use of instrumental groups requires that the choral teacher seek the assistance of the instrumental teacher and perhaps that special parts be provided for the instrumentalists, but the rewards of increased pupil and audience interest more than compensate for the extra effort entailed.

Creating Visual Appeal

Perhaps the most neglected aspect of the choral concert is that of movement. We are accustomed to seeing choral groups file on-stage in a disciplined manner, take seats in neatly arranged chairs or stand in orderly rows on choral risers. Beyond this there is little movement except when the choristers rise from their chairs to sing or file off the stage at the end of the program. This leaves the audience with very little to watch and provides little to hold visual attention. The chorus need not be visually static. Movement that holds the listener's visual attention helps hold his aural attention as well. A first step is to change the position of the chorus from one selection to the next. Form a compact group in the center of the stage, then change to a widespread arrangement that fills the space from wing to wing. Let one group of singers step forward for the selection that includes solos for their part. Place the various part-groups about the stage in a visually attractive arrangement. For one selection an echo choir in the rear of the auditorium or in the balcony might be suitable, whereas for another a group might sit cross-legged on the floor, on barrels and boxes, or dangle their legs from an improvised rail fence. There is the possibility of using carefully rehearsed gestures, of planning stage movements in the nature of choreography, or of inviting a dance group to pariticipate in the concert by interpreting music sung by the chorus.

Choral concerts can be made visually interesting by varying the costume. The traditional uniform is the chorister's robe, a long, flowing garment of solid color and solemn effect. This is appropriate for the cathedral choir and for concerts presented on solemn occasions by the public-school chorus, but it need not be the only costume in the choral wardrobe. It is inappropriate for some of the lighter music presented and provides little of visual interest to hold audience attention. A similarly formal but more interesting costume is dark suits for the boys and pastel dresses for the girls. Bright blazers or vests can be used to add color. Open-throated sport shirts and blouses combined with slacks or skirts may be suitable for some selections. Brightly colored rectangles of cloth can be used imaginatively as head coverings, scarves or shawls, sashes or apron-like skirts. Special hats or gloves might be used to good effect. Even the traditional choral robe, purchased in one color for boys, a different color for girls, and with reversible stoles in contrasting colors can be used to provide visual variety. This is particularly effective if the boys stand in a compact group for one selection and mix with the girls to form quartets for the other. Original and often excellent ideas can be suggested by the pupils themselves for other costumes that can be devised at little or no expense, and the possibilities for using costume effectively to reflect the mood or text of the music and for varying it from one portion of the program to another give the choral director a means of holding audience interest.

Natural additions to stage movement and costumes are lighting, scenery, and props. Dramatic lighting can be used to intensify musical effect simply by changing colors from one portion of the program or one selection to the next. Spotlights focus attention on soloists, ensembles, or even on a tableau or decorative picture or object hung against a backdrop or over the heads of the chorus. Backdrops and scenery are more difficult to devise, but pieces once used for dramatic productions or made with the help of another department can sometimes be secured for special concerts. Props can be of any variety, from furniture moved from the teachers' room to articles brought from home by the singers. Lighting, of course, is the most convenient means of heightening the concert's visual appeal, but each of the other means should be explored and experimented with by the teacher who wishes the choral concert to be an outstanding success.

Variety through Speech

Further variety is added to the choral concert through the use of speech. Choral speaking has been suggested as a useful device in rehearsal, but can be included in the choral concert to provide relief from the singing tone. If the poetry is carefully selected and well performed, it is an enjoyable change for the audience and an interesting experience for the chorus, although one or two spoken selections in each choral concert are probably sufficient. In addition to selections in choral speech, the group might offer a dramatic presentation in the form of a recited poem with choral background. In one selection, a vocal soloist might be replaced with a speaker who declaims the words in the rhythm of the music. In another, the chorus might chant a portion of the selection in the tones of speech. For one portion of the concert, a student narrator could be used to provide spoken continuity for a series of choral selections.

The director himself can make good use of his speaking voice by talking to the audience. Although it may seem strange for a conductor to speak informally at a formal concert, there is no tradition that forbids it and there are precedents in the talks of various kinds given by conductors of major symphony orchestras for breaking the barrier of silence between the choral director and the audience. This practice is particularly desirable for concerts offered by public-school groups because of the close relationship between performers and listeners and because it is one of the goals of the public-school concert to transmit certain non-musical information and impressions to the listener, especially when the audience is composed of parents and other adults. The choral director in this instance is a teacher as well—informed, articulate, and charged with the responsibility of furthering music education with every means at his disposal. At the choral concert, he has the opportunity to educate his audience, to make the program more interesting and understandable for the listener, and to improve public relations.

The director can function as a program commentator, in effect teaching music history, literature, and appreciation to his audience while increasing the listener's pleasure in the music performed. He can give oral program notes, offering appropriate information concerning the composer, the history of the music, and the circumstances of its composition. He can discuss the text of the choral composition and the manner in which its spirit is captured in the music. He can explain music forms, describe the significance of themes, and discuss characteristics of harmonic style. In addition, he can use the chorus to illustrate his remarks, asking pupils to sing selected themes, harmonic progressions, and interesting rhythms. This is especially desirable because it interests the listener and helps him follow the music when the selection is performed in its entirety. The listener should have the benefit of program notes at every concert, printed in the program but supplemented when practicable by the conductor's spoken remarks. In the same vein, the conductor might introduce soloists, describe voice qualities, and explain something of the utilization of voices in choral singing.

Of particular interest to parents are teachers' remarks about teaching procedures and techniques. Parents are often deeply impressed by the quality of the music produced by their children through the instruction offered in the public schools and enjoy hearing performances in the school setting. They enjoy even more knowing how these performance levels are achieved. They want to know what procedures are used, what philosophy the teacher follows, and what their children must do to progress in their music work. During concert programs, or at PTA meetings or wherever parents are assembled, the choral director may find it useful to talk frankly and informally about the work of the music program. He can demonstrate rehearsal procedures, voice-training devices, procedures for studying new literature, even the manner of developing sight-singing ability; he can discuss problems of recruiting, scheduling, membership requirements, plans for future expansion, and special concerts or trips.

USING CONCERT SHOWMANSHIP

Showmanship is usually associated with the vaudeville stage, the circus performance, television productions, or other diversions from the entertainment world. It calls up visions of the impresario, wigs and make-up, or performers in spangled tights. Our first reaction is that all of these are incompatible with the formal concert, the goals of education, and the workings of the music education program. We think of concerts as being devoted to the music of Bach, Beethoven, and Brahms. Our mental image of the performers includes men and women in strictly formal dress seated on a severely decorated stage in well-disciplined rows or semicircles. We see the audience file sedately to their seats, sit in hushed reverence during the presentation of great works of musical art and greet the conclusion of each with appreciative but controlled applause. This point of view is natural to music educators and others who are conditioned early in life to the formal concert, to the necessity for sitting quietly still, and to the accepted response.

Is it necessarily true, however, that even the greatest music must be dressed in black and denuded of all the trimmings that increase audience appeal? "Showmanship" is not a term that need be excluded from polite music conversation; it implies nothing more harmful than displaying one's wares in the best possible light. The term "wares" is used advisedly because music education has an important selling function—it must sell worthy music to as many people as possible. The fact that music is an art does not imply that it must be either esoteric or admired only from a distance. To the contrary, it is of value because it has meaning for all and because it is unique among the arts for its personal significance to the performer and the listener. It is proper that music education make every effort to promote the enjoyment of music and present it in the most favorable light. Doing so is helpful to the audience and provides benefits for those who teach or perform.

Showmanship is not out of place in concerts presented by public-school choruses. The concert can be made appealing to the eye as well as the ear and entertaining as well as enjoyable in the aesthetic sense. To do so, the teacher examines the techniques of television and Broadway, noting the devices used to capture audience interest and arouse enthusiasm, borrowing those appropriate to the concert.

The successful Broadway or television show is a model of effective showmanship. It utilizes all the resources commensurate with good taste to sell its wares to the public, knowing that its life-span depends on the size of the audience it attracts. Television has given millions of people repeated opportunities to see outstandingly entertaining programs compared with others that fail to win public approval, and it is not wise to offer a choral concert that appears dull, lifeless, and uninteresting when compared with standard television fare. This is not to imply that the serene beauty of masterpieces of musical art should be hidden under cheap costumes and gaudy make-up. Showmanship is offensive when it exceeds the limits of good taste or trespasses in areas reserved for the quiet contemplation of great beauty. Utilized properly and with good judgment it is a potent weapon with which music education can combat the influence of cheaper music and its effect on music taste.

Many of the topics discussed in this chapter are factors in good showmanship: the unity, variety, contrast, and climax provided by the sequence of choral selections; the presentation of a variety of vocal ensembles and accompanying instruments; the use of stage movement, costume, lighting, scenery, and props; the inclusion of choral speaking and program commentaries.

Two additional items are worthy of mention: audience participation and humor. Most people enjoy singing. The community sing, even though it is a rapidly disappearing phenomenon, is an enjoyable and social form of singing activity. The concert is an opportunity to capitalize on any desire the audience may have to join forces with the singers. The choral singers function as leaders to help those in the audience follow their parts, the accompanying instrument provides additional support, and the conductor helps keep everyone together. The song can be a familiar excerpt from musical comedy, a hymn or patriotic song, a camp or fun song, or any other selection familiar to and enjoyed by the audience. As for humor, choral concerts not devoted exclusively to religious or other serious music can be brightened considerably by that which induces a smile. Humorous songs are appropriate on many occasions, humorous antics by the singers may be well received if conceived in good taste, and the director is well advised to display reasonable humor in the remarks he makes to the audience.

A final element of showmanship is the printed program. As a matter of course, it should show the date, time, and place of the concert and the name of the school and other sponsoring organizations if any. The list of selections to be performed, composers, arrangers, soloists, accompanist, and suitable program notes are essential. Equally essential but sometimes overlooked are the names of chorus members and all others who contribute to the success of the concert. Both pupils and parents are interested in seeing the roster of personnel and may save the program as a souvenir, and the teacher may find the list of members useful for reference in later years. Others who assist as "dressing-room" supervisors, stage managers, ticket-sellers, and ushers deserve mention. Their names should appear in the printed program as a matter of courtesy and to encourage their assistance at subsequent concerts.

All of this is showmanship as it may be applied to the choral concert offered by a public-school group. The only caution is that it must be used with good taste, the teacher being careful not to overstep the bounds of propriety in presenting music of a serious nature and being wary of any device of showmanship that might transform the concert into a species of vaudeville. Used with discretion, showmanship makes the concert interesting and enjoyable, stimulating pupil enthusiasm and heightening audience interest. In an indirect way, it contributes to the success of the total choral program and helps the choral teacher achieve educational goals.

part four: The Instrumental Program

10: *establishing the program*

Instrumental music, like choral music, is included in the public-school music program because it is an effective means of achieving the goals of music education and those of the total educational program. A point worthy of emphasis is that instrumental music strives to achieve the same basic goals as the general music class and the various choral activities. Its aim is to develop immediate interest in and enjoyment of music and to lay foundations for continuing interest through later years. It strives to reach large numbers of pupils. It regards them as potential consumers of music, those who ultimately make up adult audiences and become amateur participants. It explores the instrumental-music literature searching for appeals to a variety of interests and abilities. It develops music taste by acquainting pupils with superior music and by giving them repeated and extensive contact with it. It offers planned instruction to help pupils move upward to higher levels of discrimination and appreciation. It teaches music skills of value to the informed listener and necessary for the participating amateur. It identifies pupils of exceptional talent, offering them special instruction and experience and encouraging them to continue music study through private channels beyond the public-school years.

Instrumental music is different from the general music class and the activities of choral music because of the specialized skills needed by members of bands, orchestras, and ensembles. The ability to play an instrument is an obvious necessity; pupils must achieve a relatively high degree of proficiency before they can be accepted as members of a performing group and before they can derive satisfaction from playing an instrument. For this reason, the instrumental teacher accepts the desirability of developing technical skills of an advanced nature, often requiring that his pupils progress well beyond the point considered adequate by teachers of general music classes and choral groups. The instrumental teacher requires that his pupils learn to read music with accuracy, developing the ability to interpret correctly the symbols of rhythm, pitch, and dynamics. He pays close attention to ensemble skills, training pupils to respond to conductors' signals and to the ensemble spirit of the group. Although these are technical skills, they are taught because they help the pupil progress toward the more general objectives already mentioned.

In addition to the goals common to the total program of music education and those accepted because they are peculiar to instrumental music, there are other goals imposed by circumstances not necessarily related to the teacher's philosophy of music education. The instrumental teacher works toward the development of a marching band capable of participating in parades and of presenting entertaining shows at football games and other school athletic events. He may teach such non-musical skills as baton twirling or develop an outstanding corps of majorettes. He searches for ways to provide uniforms for both the music and non-music personnel of the band organization. He concerns himself with floats, animal mascots, props, and other special effects. During one portion of the school year he may be occupied with the presentation of a variety or vaudeville show. During another, he may have time for little else but contests and festivals, raising money, arranging trips, and enlisting the support of various school officers and community groups.

Not all instrumental teachers agree upon the desirability of these "imposed" objectives. There are those who object strenuously to the non-musical work of preparing the football show and still more to its effect upon the music progress of their pupils. They say that show planning and practice drastically reduce the time available for music instruction and that the results of football-game playing are faulty tone and careless musicianship. Some deplore the football show because they are unwilling to accept their annual conversion from music educator to impresario.

Although there are reasons undoubtedly valid for criticizing certain of the instrumental activities in the current school-music scene, it is possible to cite benefits derived from them. Pupils who participate in the marching band, shows, contests, and festivals learn the importance of coöperation and discipline. The marching band can teach democratic procedures and social skills. Each of these activities helps pupils develop poise and self-confidence and provides worthy leisure-time activity. They may contribute to pupils' music development, arousing interest and enthusiasm and providing motivation for study and practice. The football band and variety show may serve a recruiting function, attracting large numbers of otherwise uninterested pupils who respond to colorful uniforms and the glamour and excitement of public appearance.

Not least among the benefits derived from such activities are their effects upon parents and the community. Instrumental activities have public relations value. They persuade parents to encourage their children to become active in instrumental affairs, to take lessons and purchase instruments. The football band, for example, reaches audiences far larger than could be expected at band concerts and generates community enthusiasm for the music program and the work of the schools in general. Football and variety shows, contests and festivals may have a desirable influence on school finances and on the budget for music instruction, especially during the years in which a new instrumental program is struggling for status, funds, and equipment.

One difficulty arising from public interest in marching and football bands is that it tends to shift attention away from orchestra, chorus, and other music activities. It also tends to shift emphasis away from the concert band and the type of music instruction it requires. The marching band is displayed to the public more frequently than either the orchestra or the chorus. Its colorful uniforms leave lasting impressions on the audience. The band is easier to develop than the orchestra, can be organized and presented in performance more quickly, and permits early demonstration of progress. This is advantageous if the marching band is used as a stepping-stone to other music organizations and instruction. It is unfortunate if the teacher develops a successful marching band and is content to do little more.

In this situation are problems that demand the serious attention of music educators. The cost of maintaining the band, particularly the successful football band, is higher than the cost of maintaining either a chorus or an orchestra. It must be determined whether the importance of the band is sufficient to warrant this unbalanced expenditure. It must be determined whether it is wise to feed pupils a diet of marching-band music, often of poor quality, in simplified arrangements, and poorly played because of football-game excitement and outdoor acoustics. It is time to examine the policy that devotes a large portion of band time—rehearsals, marching practice, and show planning—to a type of instrumental playing that is sometimes actually unmusical and may be detrimental to music progress. If the attitude that glorifies the marching band persists and causes an emphasis on marching and shows at the expense of music instruction—a situation that already exists in some communities—it is possible the band as a worthy music organization may disappear from the school scene. If the band becomes a source of entertainment rather than a means of music education, it may again sink to the extra-curricular status it occupied when first introduced, causing music education to lose much of the ground gained in recent years.

Another objective of the instrumental program has to do with the development of soloists and ensembles. The instrumental teacher who discovers pupils of extraordinary talent through an efficient program develops these talents to the limit of their potential. It is his duty as a teacher and a musician to help each pupil achieve this potential however great or small it may be.

The intent of the program, however, is to reach many pupils and to build for all of them a basis for future music enjoyment. For some few pupils the instrumental program serves as vocational preparation. It gives them skills with which to earn a livelihood in post-school years. These pupils are in the minority, however, and instrumental training is not designed for their needs alone. If the teacher's practice is to train outstanding performers rather than to develop music interest and appreciation among an entire student body, the program ignores the needs of many who may profit from music education. This situation invites criticism. It raises justifiable questions of whether such highly specialized training should be within the province of the public, tax-supported school and whether instrumental activities of this type are worthy of curricular time.

The instrumental program offers instrumental training and attempts to teach pupils to play with skill and artistry. It encourages the talented pupil to develop to the limit of his ability. It encourages participation in contests and festivals as motivation for further achievement. It also seeks the interest of those with less talent. It utilizes brilliant uniforms, pageantry, showmanship, and popular music to capture pupil and public interest. While doing all this, however, instrumental music remains true to its basic purpose. It regards itself as part of a program tuned to the needs of large numbers of pupils as they prepare for membership in society. It teaches music, its importance as a cultural heritage, its value as a repository of man's visions and ideals, and its function as a means of expression and a source of aesthetic satisfaction. It may be that instrumental music is still in its infancy where the public-school program is concerned. It has achieved much, but the possibilities for further achievement are numerous and offer great educational rewards.

RECRUITING NEW MEMBERS

The instrumental-music program encourages a constant flow of new pupils into classes through which they become qualified for membership in the performing groups. The recruiting program is a determining factor in the success of the advanced groups and the continuing growth of the instrumental program as a whole. It speeds the development of instrumental activities and makes later phases of instrumental teaching much easier by providing a constant supply of competent players.

As part of the recruiting program, the teacher strives to arouse interest in instrumental music, to discover talented pupils, to help pupils select the instruments they wish to study, to provide instruments for beginners and certain of the more advanced players, and to insure balanced instrumentation in the performing groups. It is important that pupils be chosen wisely and that each be guided to an instrument he can learn to play. A high mortality rate is inevitable if pupils are selected carelessly. The unfit drop out of the program and those with ability become discouraged if they are frustrated by an instrument that offers either too much or too little challenge. A large number of drop-outs is costly. Improperly selected pupils make demands on the teacher's time and energy to no purpose and reduce the number of instruments available for deserving pupils. This waste can be avoided if the recruiting program functions properly and if the instrumental teacher provides for the careful consideration of each pupil.

The recruiting program embraces more than the selection of new pupils to receive instrumental lessons. Interest must be aroused among adults as well as pupils, including parents, other members of the community, school administrators, and teachers. The instrumental teacher becomes a familiar figure at PTA and community meetings, offering lectures, concerts, and demonstrations to enlist the aid of parents and the general support of all.

The recruiting program requires a continuing series of activities through which pupils progress once they have begun instrumental study. This is of obvious importance but sometimes overlooked because of the teacher's preoccupation with performing groups. The pupil who has completed a few lessons is not ready to participate in an advanced group. He must be able to join an elementary group and then an intermediate group before he acquires the skill and experience needed to join the advanced players.

The experienced teacher is well aware of this. The new teacher in a new position, enthusiastic about creating an effective instrumental program, may overlook it. He is well advised to complete his planning for the entire program before recruiting large numbers of pupils. This is especially true if the recruiting program planned by a high-school teacher reaches down to the elementary grades. It can not be completely successful unless there are training groups of one kind or another in both the elementary school and the junior high school. Unless other instrumental teachers are available for these levels, the high-school teacher may find it necessary to extend his teaching into the elementary school.

The extension of the instrumental program into the elementary school is a virtual necessity, even though the instrumental teacher in a small community must do the work alone and may feel that his strongest interest is in high-school teaching. Although other music activities may achieve a degree of success by dealing only with high-school pupils, instrumental skill can not be developed in a few months or even in the course of one or two school years. The band can reach much higher performing levels if its members have had instruction beginning in the elementary school, and orchestral playing is virtually impossible unless there is a nucleus of string players developed through a program in the elementary school. To a considerable degree, the quality of high-school performing groups is determined by the level at which instrumental instruction is first offered.

Arousing Interest

One of the teacher's first objectives is to arouse interest in instrumental activities. An interested student body is necessary to insure a flow of new members to replace those lost through graduation. Interest is aroused to encourage beginners and sustained to insure the continued participation of those in the intermediate and advanced groups. The teacher thinks in terms of interest as he goes about his daily work throughout the school year. He plans special interest-arousing procedures as part of the recruiting program. He directs his attention to the high school and junior high school, but concentrates his attention on the lower grades from which instrumental players are first chosen.

DEMONSTRATIONS. Perhaps the most successful device for arousing interest is the demonstration. The instrumental teacher first secures the approval of the principal of the school concerned for a program in which instruments of the band and orchestra are to be displayed and demonstrated.

It may be an assembly program for the entire school, a similar program for selected pupils, such as those in the fifth grade, or an informal demonstration in one or more classrooms. For the display, the teacher selects one of each type of instrument, being especially careful to choose instruments that are in good condition, well shined, and can be displayed to good advantage.

The program itself consists of the display, playing demonstrations of the instruments, remarks concerning their use in bands and orchestras, and interesting sidelights concerning their history. When practical, selections by an instrumental ensemble lend further interest to the program. In most instances it is advantageous to ask competent members of the band or orchestra to demonstrate the instruments. The audience is more interested in the playing of a pupil and most teachers are not capable of demonstrating all the instruments adequately. The remarks concerning each instrument may be made by the student instrumentalists and supplemented as necessary by the teacher. At some point in the program, the teacher explains that instrumental instruction and perhaps the instruments themselves are provided by the school, describes the instrumental program briefly, and invites interested pupils to apply for lessons.

The success of the demonstration stems from the children's natural curiosity and the irresistible attractions of shiny instruments. Children, especially those of elementary-school age, find it hard to resist the lure of the instruments on display. They want to see them at close range, are curious about the sounds they produce, ask to hold the instruments, press valves and keys, and even to produce tones. Interest is heightened by the appearance of older pupils as performers and by the presentation of music played by the instruments in various combinations.

An assembly program of this type is usually an unqualified success. If the assembly program is impractical, the teacher can obtain equally satisfactory results by appearing in a classroom with only a few instruments, perhaps trumpet, clarinet, violin, and flute, and with only one or two student instrumentalists to assist him. Although the program is best presented in the elementary school, it is equally worthwhile in the junior high school if limitations of time or equipment do not permit the establishment of an elementary-school instrumental program.

CONCERTS. The concert is a similarly useful interest-arousing device. The teacher who wishes to stimulate interest makes it a practice to give regular concerts for the junior high and elementary schools from which new players are recruited. The concert can be presented in the junior high or elementary school or pupils from these schools can be invited to a special concert in the high-school auditorium. If the audience is small, the concert can be given in the instrumental rehearsal room. This desirable arrangement permits the visitors to see instruments at close range and to become acquainted with "behind-the-scene" rehearsal procedures in an informal atmosphere. Concerts should be short, considerate of the limited attention span of the young audience, and as varied and entertaining as possible. Concert selections are adjusted to the age and interests of the audience, are light and gay in mood, and include special arrangements of familiar and popular songs. Novelties lend interest to the program as does the inclusion of soloists and ensembles.

Because this type of concert is given as part of the recruiting program, the teacher takes full advantage of the opportunity to display and demonstrate the various instruments to the pupils in the audience. He may talk briefly about each instrument, ask a member of the performing group to show his instrument and play a characteristic passage, and point out portions of the concert selections that feature one instrument or a family of instruments. When practical, the audience may be invited to walk through the band or orchestra at the end of the concert to look more closely at the instruments and ask questions. Included in the program is the teacher's invitation to begin instrumental lessons.

On a smaller scale, concerts can be provided for elementary-school and junior-high-school pupils by soloists and ensembles that appear in assemblies or individual classrooms. These concerts offer excellent performance outlet for advanced players from the high-school orchestra and band. The practice serves three purposes: it is useful in the recruiting program, gives valuable performing experience to advanced instrumentalists, and helps improve the music programs of the lower schools. The value to the recruiting program is that it gives pupils in the lower grades close contact with the instruments. The experience of seeing and hearing them at close range in the classroom is far more meaningful than seeing them in the relatively formal atmosphere of the auditorium concert and generates stronger interest. When presenting programs of this sort, the student players tell the younger children something about the instruments, demonstrate them, and answer questions asked by the audience. Such programs are supervised by the high-school teacher and planned in advance with the coöperation of the teacher responsible for the music work of the lower grade.

Another type of concert is that offered by bands, orchestras, and ensembles from schools of neighboring communities. These are especially useful if it is desired to stimulate the interest of school administrators, parents, or the community. To begin an entirely new instrumental program, the appearance of an outstanding group from another school may be all that is required to provide the needed impetus. A concert presented during a school assembly serves to arouse the interest of the student body. An evening concert may be used to stimulate community enthusiasm. Similar concerts can be arranged if it is desired to improve an existing program or to expand it through the addition of new offerings or organizations.

PRE-BAND INSTRUMENTS. To make full use of the interest-arousing possibilities in the regular elementary-school program, the high-school teacher of instrumental music encourages the use of pre-band or "exploratory" instruments. An organized teaching program including both class lessons and ensemble experience is established for the grade immediately before the one in which the teacher first invites pupils to study band and orchestra instruments. If band instruments are offered in the fifth grade, for example, pre-band instruments are presented to pupils in the fourth grade. Due to the limited progress possible with the simple instruments, one year or less of systematic instruction is sufficient in most instances, the span of instruction being reduced for pupils in the upper elementary grades because they master the instruments quickly and tend to lose interest if the instruction is continued beyond a one-year period.

The chief advantages of the pre-band instruments are that their cost is small, they are easy to play, and they can be taught through class rather than private lessons. Because they are inexpensive, pre-band instruments can be provided for an entire class or for an entire grade including one hundred or more children. In some instances the school bears the entire cost; in others parents make this relatively small expenditure. Because they are simple instruments, children learn to play them quickly without the difficulties of embouchure or fingering encountered in wind instruments of the band. Finally, because instruction can be given to large groups it is not necessary for the teacher to devote a large number of hours from his schedule to this teaching. Thus the pre-band instruments can be taught effectively and economically and contribute to the success of both the elementary-school vocal program and the high-school instrumental program.

For the instrumental teacher, pre-band instruments serve as a fairly reliable indicator of instrumental aptitude and interest. The teacher is usually able to separate easily those who have natural ability from those who have difficulty; the child who is unable to play a pre-band instrument because he is deficient in coördination or rhythmic sense is not a good candidate for further instrumental instruction. In addition, the extended period of instruction separates the pupils who have only transient interest, because of the novelty of the pre-band instrument, from those who want to learn to play and are capable of sustained interest and effort.

It is possible to teach through these instruments skills of value in both instrumental and vocal music. Children gain music-reading skill much more quickly through the instruments than through the vocal program. They learn to finger the instrument, to use the tongue, to provide breath support for the tone and to play with others in an ensemble. Although children learn less in these areas than is needed to play a band or orchestra instrument, and although it is necessary to learn new fingering patterns and embouchure sensations when transferring to other wind instruments, the experience with pre-band instruments gives them an acquaintance with instrumental techniques and makes the initial stage of learning to play another instrument much less difficult.

OTHER DEVICES. To stimulate interest still further, the instrumental teacher can make use of the devices suggested in Chapter 7 for the choral program, adapting them as necessary to fit the needs of instrumental recruiting. School bulletin boards and display cases are used to feature notices, articles, photographs, and the instruments themselves. School and community newspapers carry feature articles or regular columns devoted to instrumental activities. Posters and homeroom bulletins are utilized during the portion of the year in which the active recruiting campaign is conducted. Members of the performing groups are encouraged to conduct a student-directed recruiting campaign. Questionnaires are distributed to all pupils in the grades for which beginning instrumental instruction is planned, the questionnaires supplemented by bulletins to parents describing the opportunities for their children. The excellent films dealing with instruments and instrumental music can be shown to pupils in the appropriate grade immediately prior to a demonstration or concert, planned in cooperation with the vocal-music or classroom teacher as part of the regular music work of that grade. Visiting instrumental soloists or ensembles can be scheduled as part of the regular assembly program.

By using these devices at the appropriate grade level and planning their sequence in relation to other activities of the recruiting program, the instrumental teacher arouses the interest of large numbers of elementary-school pupils and assures a large number of applications for instrumental instruction. In planning this phase of recruiting, the teacher attempts to establish a fixed pattern that can become an established part of the school calendar, recurring almost automatically year after year. This lends continuity to the program and, while placing minimum demands on the teacher's time and school facilities, helps insure a constant flow of competent players into high-school performing groups.

Talent Testing and Discovery

Once pupil interest is aroused, the next step is the selection of those who are likely to be apt students. This is an important step in the recruiting program. In many instances, the instrumental teacher finds there are more interested applicants than can be accepted into beginning classes restricted in size by the number of instruments available, the possibilities of scheduling classes, and the amount of time the teacher can devote to this portion of his instrumental teaching. Ultimately, the instrumental teacher tries to expand the facilities for instruction, purchasing additional instruments, devising improved scheduling arrangements, and recommending the employment of additional teachers. In many instances, however, these improvements are postponed until the need can be made apparent—until the existing program is functioning smoothly and its desirable results can be demonstrated. In other instances there are restrictions of a permanent nature, imposed by the school budget, to which the instrumental teacher must adapt his program. In any case, it is unwise to accept more pupils than can be properly instructed.

Among the applicants for instrumental instruction there are pupils who have interest but little or no talent. These often are excluded from the instrumental program during the years in which it is attempting to produce acceptable performing groups with minimum resources. The inept pupil who is encouraged to begin instrumental study and perseveres through an extended period of lessons without achieving reasonable progress undergoes a frustrating experience. He becomes discouraged to such an extent that he may turn away from other forms of music activity in which he could find worthwhile satisfaction. Because of inevitable errors of judgment, inadequate testing, or circumstances beyond the control of the teacher, there are cases also in which the pupil withdraws from the instrumental program soon after he begins his study. The teacher does everything possible to prevent such cases by being careful in his selection procedure. The pupil suffers least disappointment if he is excluded from the program before he has acquired an instrument and before any instruction has been given. Permitting him to begin instrumental study wastes the teacher's time and prevents another pupil who may have more talent from making good use of the instrument. Parents deserve consideration too. It is important that children lacking in capability be identified before instruments have been purchased or rented. Finally, scheduling arrangements and the efficient use of the teacher's time demand that instrumental classes remain constant in size once they are established. The teacher's time is not used to best advantage if a class established at the beginning of a year is reduced to a fraction of its size by pupil withdrawals as the year progresses.

Even among the acceptable applicants for instrumental instruction there will be different degrees of talent that must be evaluated carefully. From this evaluation the teacher selects the instrument with which the pupil should begin and, at some later date, the instrument to which he might be transferred. He may search for pupils with an especially keen sense of pitch to encourage them to begin study of a stringed instrument. He might identify those with relatively weak pitch sense but strong rhythm and coördination, encouraging them to study percussion instruments. He selects those with adequate pitch and rhythmic sensitivity as well as good coördination for the various wind instruments. If complete and accurate information is gathered through tests administered at this early stage, the teacher may return to the test data at a later date to select pupils for transfer, for example, from clarinet to oboe or from trumpet to French horn.

Talent testing is one of the keys to a successful instrumental program. It is a species of diagnosis that establishes conditions favorable to the pupils' future progress. It helps assure that performing groups will be composed of competent players, each with the ability to understand and respond to music and the ability to master the instrument. It helps the teacher use his time and school facilities with maximum efficiency, assuring that instruction will be given to pupils who can profit from it.

Talent discovery is another important aspect of the recruiting program, a process distinct from the testing of pupils who express interest in instrumental lessons. Some pupils with marked talent do not respond to the interest-arousing devices. It is unfortunate if these talented pupils are not encouraged to enter the program. As a case in point, the author discovered a student in a college class who had been given no special training and who had not participated in music activities in earlier school years, but who had the unique sensitivity called absolute pitch! To one engaged in teaching music, this seems a tragic waste of talent. It is this sort of pupil the music teacher tries to identify as early as possible in the elementary school. It is imperative that they be discovered and proper that they be encouraged to develop their talent. Talent discovery may be regarded, therefore, as both an extension of the recruiting program and a normal function of music education. It reaches beyond the interested pupil to every member of the student body, seeking to identify those with extraordinary talent as well as those with lesser degrees of aptitude, encouraging them to begin participation of some sort in the instrumental program.

There are many ways to search out music talent and to test the aptitude of those who express interest. There are standardized tests devised for the purpose and in common use by instrumental teachers. There is the possibility of devising informal tests to measure the abilities of special interest to the instrumental teacher. The instrumental teacher confers with teachers of vocal music or with classroom and homeroom teachers, gathering further information about the music potentials of the pupils they know well through daily contact. Permanent school records are examined for data concerning aptitude, intelligence, curricular and extracurricular music activities and interests.

INFORMAL TESTS. The informal test devised by the teacher is desirable for a number of reasons. It can be adjusted to local conditions—to the size of the group taking the test, the age of the pupils to be tested, and the extent of their backgrounds and experience. It is often easier and quicker to administer than the standardized test. Answer sheets can be eliminated so that pupils of elementary-school age are not hampered by the necessity of reading and writing terms they may not understand or following instructions that require abilities other than music talent.

There are two important factors to be discovered concerning a pupil's music potential. (1) Does he have rhythmic sense and sufficient muscular coördination to respond accurately to rhythm patterns? (2) Does he have sufficient pitch sense to judge and adjust intonation? Other factors such as tonal memory, aesthetic judgment, and sensitivity to degrees of loudness may be indicative of music talent also. It is believed, however, that pitch and rhythm are the factors of greatest interest to the instrumental teacher and that a test which measures these aspects of music talent provides an adequate basis for selecting pupils for beginning classes.

To test rhythmic sense, the teacher turns to a testing procedure that utilizes rhythmic physical movement. One such test[1] is shown in Table 6. In this test the pupil is required to coördinate hand and foot movements in much the same way the beginning instrumental student learns to use his body in playing an instrument. He taps his foot to establish and maintain a rhythmic pulse and claps his hands to produce rhythm patterns indicated by easily read symbols. The letters "D" and "U" in Table 6 indicate motions of the toe as it moves "down" and "up," tapping the floor rhythmically to mark the pulse of the rhythm. The letter "x" written

[1] This procedure was suggested by Damon D. Holton, Director of Music, Norristown, Pennsylvania.

above the letters "D" and "U" indicates that the pupil is to clap his hands at this point in the rhythm. The "x" occurs sometimes as the foot goes down, sometimes as it comes up, and there are lines in which there are two claps for each "D" or "U." Using this simple notation, the teacher

TABLE 6. TEST FOR RHYTHMIC COÖRDINATION

```
     x               : x               : x               : x
 1)  D   U   D   U   : D   U   D   U   : D   U   D   U   : D   U   D   U

     x       x       : x       x       : x       x       : x       x
 2)  D   U   D   U   : D   U   D   U   : D   U   D   U   : D   U   D   U

     x   x   x   x   : x   x   x   x   : x   x   x   x   : x   x   x   x
 3)  D   U   D   U   : D   U   D   U   : D   U   D   U   : D   U   D   U

         x       x   :     x       x   :     x       x   :     x       x
 4)  D   U   D   U   : D   U   D   U   : D   U   D   U   : D   U   D   U

     x   x   x       : x   x   x       : x   x   x       : x   x   x
 5)  D   U   D   U   : D   U   D   U   : D   U   D   U   : D   U   D   U

     x   x       x   : x   x       x   : x   x       x   : x   x       x
 6)  D   U   D   U   : D   U   D   U   : D   U   D   U   : D   U   D   U

     x       x       : x   x   x       : x   x       x   :     x   x
 7)  D   U   D   U   : D   U   D   U   : D   U   D   U   : D   U   D   U

     xx xx x         : xx xx x         : xx xx xx xx     : xx xx x
 8)  D   U   D   U   : D   U   D   U   : D   U   D   U   : D   U   D   U

     x  xxx          : x  xxx          : x  xxx          : x  xxx
 9)  D   U   D   U   : D   U   D   U   : D   U   D   U   : D   U   D   U

     xxx x           : xxx x           : xxx x           : xxx x
10)  D   U   D   U   : D   U   D   U   : D   U   D   U   : D   U   D   U

     x  xxx      x   : xxxxx           : x  xxxxx        : x   x   x
11)  D   U   D   U   : D   U   D   U   : D   U   D   U   : D   U   D   U
```

can indicate a variety of rhythm patterns, including the simplest succession of quarter and half notes as well as complex patterns including sixteenth notes and syncopation.

As a first step in administering the test, the teacher prepares the pupils by giving them an opportunity to practice the hand and foot movements. A large group of pupils can be led through this practice at one time. The symbols may be written on the board so that all may practice reading the test or, if the teacher anticipates reading difficulties, he may begin by asking the group to practice motions he demonstrates and describes verbally. In the latter case he might proceed as follows.

1. Tap your foot on the floor as I do. Be sure you can feel both the "down" motion and the "up" motion.

2. Tap your foot as you did before and clap your hands every time your foot goes down.
3. Tap your foot again. Clap your hands every time your foot goes down and every time it comes up.
4. Now clap every time your foot comes up, but do not clap when your foot goes down.
5. This time clap once when your foot goes down and twice when it comes up. Watch me as I show you how to clap this way.
6. Now clap twice when your foot goes down and only once when it comes up.

When the teacher feels the group has practiced enough to understand the tapping and clapping procedure, he places a number of exercises on the board. Both the rote practice and the written exercises can be adjusted to any level of difficulty the teacher thinks appropriate. Once the symbols are on the board, the teacher leads the entire group through the series of exercises, explaining and repeating lines as necessary to make certain the group understands the symbols and the desired motions. Although this procedure helps the pupil become familiar with the test procedure, it does not improve his response enough to overcome his deficiencies in rhythmic sense or coördination.

The next step in the procedure is to test the pupils. They may be tested individually or in groups of six or more, preferably in a room away from the rest of those to be tested. In the test, the pupils are asked simply to read the exercises on the board, tapping and clapping as they follow the symbols. The exercises may be the same as those used in the familiarization period or new exercises of greater difficulty may be added. The teacher may again demonstrate certain exercises as necessary to help individual pupils who seem unable to coördinate their movements.

Although a test of this kind may not measure rhythmic sense as precisely or objectively as a standardized test, it does permit the teacher to judge the pupil's rhythmic aptitude for instrumental instruction. It uses symbols and movements similar to those the pupil must learn as he begins to play an instrument. The pupil is less likely to be confused by a test of this sort than by the answer sheets and formality of a standardized test. An entire class may be introduced to the test in from ten to twenty minutes and small groups may be tested quickly without unduly disturbing the work of the balance of the class. With a minimum of experience, the teacher learns to recognize the symptoms of lack of rhythmic sense and muscular coördination and can quickly identify the pupil who claps slightly before or after the beat or who can not coördinate his movements. The pupil who can not feel these rhythms or coördinate his movements is not a good prospect for instrumental lessons.

Equally simple and informal procedures are used to measure the pupil's pitch sense. Tests of different degrees of difficulty can be devised for pupils with different backgrounds and experience. Pupils who have been taught to use syllables or numbers in reading vocal music can be tested accordingly. For those with no such vocal instruction the test can be based on familiar songs. In either case, the test requires that the pupil sing a series of pitches as directed by the teacher. The teacher listens to each child individually and judges whether he sings the pitches accurately and in tune. Here again the test relies on subjective judgment rather than accurate measurement. The teacher quickly discovers, however, that he can immediately identify pupils who sing in tune and those who seem to have little feeling for pitch. As he listens to pupils sing the test exercises, he can identify those who have begun to develop pitch sense also and can judge the desirability of exposing each pupil to special instrumental instruction.

The test itself can consist of one or several parts. First, the pupil may be asked to sing a phrase of one or more familiar songs. Suitable songs are those that are moderate in tempo, contain only simple and regular rhythm patterns, and offer both interval and scale passages to test the pupil's feeling for pitch. The teacher selects songs that have been taught in the music classes or that the child has learned outside of school. "America," "America the Beautiful," "Lovely Evening," "Brother John," and "Now Thank We All Our God" are examples of suitable songs. As the child sings the songs or phrases selected for the test, the teacher listens to determine whether he sings intervals accurately and moves with certainty from one scale-tone to the next. The child who does not have pitch sense is apt to sing the second, third, and sixth tones of the scale out of tune and to be uncertain when he sings intervals of a third, fourth, or fifth.

A simple tonal memory test is the next step in the procedure. The teacher dictates a series of four or more pitches or a short phrase, using the piano or some other instrument to produce tones in the child's vocal range. The child then sings the phrase as the teacher listens to determine whether he has remembered the series accurately and whether he sings each pitch and interval in tune. If the child is capable of responding by singing either syllables or numbers, he does so. If the child does not have this background he responds by singing neutral syllables.

The final step in the procedure is to test the child's feeling for scale relationships. This portion of the test requires that the child be familiar with some method of naming the tones of the scale—syllables, numbers, or letters. If these scale names have not been taught in other music work, the instrumental teacher may find that in some classes he can teach a portion of the scale ladder in a few minutes and that this brief introduction of scale names is sufficient to permit him to use this portion of the test. If these few minutes of teaching are not successful he simply eliminates this step of the testing procedure. For the test, he writes a portion of the scale ladder on the board as shown below, using whichever system of names is familiar to the pupils—syllables, numbers, or letters. He then dictates tonal

Fa	4	F
Mi	3	E
Re	2	D
Do	1	C
$\overline{\text{Ti}}$	$\overline{7}$	$\overline{\text{B}}$

groups to each pupil, sounding "do" at the piano and then pointing to the pitches he wants the pupil to sing. He begins with an easy succession of pitches, such as "Do-Re-Do," and progresses to more difficult series such as "Do-Mi-Ti-Do." As the pupil sings the syllables in response, the teacher listens to determine whether he sings the tones in correct succession and whether each pitch is in tune. In this way he tests the pupil's aural imagery, tonal memory, pitch sense, and his feeling for scale relationships.

A pitch test of this sort can be adjusted easily to the abilities of the groups to be tested. The teacher can add or delete exercises as necessary to challenge the talented pupil or to give the untalented pupil a feeling of accomplishment and success. The entire sequence of test exercises can be practiced in class prior to the test so that each child will understand the procedure when it is his turn to be tested. Small groups of from four to six pupils can be taken to a separate room for the test so that the balance of the class may continue its regular work.

To administer an informal rhythm and pitch test the teacher might proceed as follows:

1. Arrange to meet with either an entire class or a selected group of pupils who have expressed interest in instrumental music.
2. Briefly explain to the large group that each pupil is to be given a short, informal test to determine whether he is ready to begin instrumental lessons.
3. Lead the entire group through the rhythm test. Teach the movements first by rote and then read the test exercises from the board.
4. Lead the group through the pitch test. Sing the familiar songs or phrases selected for the test. Practice the tonal memory test by dictating from the piano for group response. Practice the scale relationships test by placing the scale ladder on the board and pointing to the tones sung by the group.
5. Arrange to have smaller groups of from four to six pupils sent to a separate room according to a schedule arranged with the classroom teacher.

6. In the testing room ask each pupil to read the rhythm exercises from the board. Then ask each pupil to sing the test song or phrase, to sing pitches dictated from the piano, and to sing pitch groups from the scale ladder.
7. Before pupils leave the testing room, interview each as necessary to determine family interest, instruments available, instrument desired, and so forth.

Through an informal test the teacher obtains information from which he can judge the pupil's aptitude for instrumental instruction. In some instances he can also form a tentative conclusion concerning the type of instrument with which the pupil might be successful. The test permits the teacher to have personal contact with each pupil. He can be alert for signs of nervousness or fatigue, giving individual help as necessary, and can ask for needed information as in an interview. The test is short and not conducive to fatigue or nervous tension. It does not require that the pupil read or write beyond his level of comprehension and it does not tax his attention span in long periods of listening. Disadvantages are that it requires the personal attention of the instrumental teacher and permits the testing of only a few pupils at one time.

STANDARDIZED TESTS. The standardized test does not offer the disadvantages of the informal test. Some can be administered by any music teacher, others by any teacher. Large groups of pupils can be tested at one time so that the test can be scheduled once for an entire school or grade without subsequent interruption of class work. Test construction is intended to eliminate subjective judgment through mechanical grading which can be done with a key by a person having no knowledge of music or of the test. There are established norms with which results can be compared and which permit easily understandable scores to be entered in the pupil's permanent record.

Standardized tests also offer certain disadvantages. Instructions and test procedures may be difficult for some pupils to understand. Answer sheets that require literary reading and writing may test the pupil's reading ability and powers of comprehension rather than his music talent. The test is sometimes long enough to exceed the pupil's attention span and cause fatigue even if given only a portion at a time. The test that relies on equipment such as the phonograph introduces mechanical difficulties having to do with the equipment itself, its operation, room acoustics, and so forth. Finally, some standardized tests are more difficult than necessary, exploring aspects and degrees of talent with which the instrumental teacher need not be concerned when selecting pupils for instrumental instruction.

In view of these disadvantages, the instrumental teacher selects standardized tests with care. He writes to the publisher of each test to ask that a copy be sent for examination or for literature describing the test in detail. He may be able to secure one or more tests from local libraries or discuss the tests with teachers who have used them in neighboring communities. He studies each test carefully, perhaps even administering it to a small group of pupils. In the process, he judges the test against local conditions to determine whether it meets his needs and is suitable for the pupils to be tested.

In evaluating the test, the teacher first considers its validity. Does it measure what it is intended to test, or are results affected by other, nonmusical factors? Has its validity been measured by the authors or publishers? Is it reliable, i.e., is it likely to be consistent in its results, giving the same evaluation for each pupil even if given more than once and despite unavoidable variations in test conditions? Must it be administered all at one time, or could it be given a portion at a time to reduce fatigue? Are answer sheets easy to understand and complete, or do they require well-developed abilities to read, write and understand? Is special equipment required by the test and is suitable equipment available in schools in which the test is to be used? Can the test be administered and marked by any teacher, or must the instrumental teacher give it his personal attention? Even though many such questions have been investigated by the test authors, each instrumental teacher asks them again in the light of his own complete knowledge of his needs and the conditions peculiar to his own school system.

After investigating all the tests to which he has access, the instrumental teacher is ready to select those appropriate for his testing program. He may choose one for all pupils or several to be used at different grade levels or for different groups. He may select single portions of several different tests, combining them to form one test meeting his special requirements. He may devise his own answer sheets, adjusting them to the abilities of the pupils to be tested, and may adjust the length and difficulty of the tests themselves. In doing so he may create a new test to which established norms do not apply, a sacrifice compensated for by the increased usefulness of the test in his music program.

The following is a list of tests available to the instrumental teacher, designed to measure music talent and the pupil's potential as an instrumental player.

Drake Musical Aptitude Tests. Raleigh M. Drake.
Distributed by Science Research Associates, 57 West Grand Avenue, Chicago 10, Illinois.

Tests for (1) rhythm; (2) musical memory. Age 8 to adult. Includes examiner manual, self-scoring answer pads, one microgroove 33⅓ recording.

Elementary Rhythm and Pitch Test. C. L. McCreery.
Distributed by Lyons Band Instrument Co., 223 W. Lake St., Chicago 6, Illinois.
Tests for (1) rhythm; (2) pitch. Grades 4–8. Includes instruction pamphlet, pupil's blanks. (No recording. Teacher taps rhythms and plays pitches using piano and/or other instruments.)

Kwalwasser Music Talent Test. Jacob Kwalwasser.
Distributed by Mills Music, Inc., 1619 Broadway, New York 19, N.Y.
Two tests: Form A, junior high school through college; Form B, children through grade 6. Includes instruction manual, test blanks, scoring key, one 78 rpm plastic record (tones produced by electronic instruments).

Measures of Musical Talent. C. E. Seashore.
Distributed by Psychological Corporation, 522 Fifth Avenue, New York 17, New York.
Tests for (1) pitch; (2) intensity; (3) time; (4) consonance; (5) tonal memory; (6) rhythm. Recommended for grades 5 and 8. Includes manual of instructions, test blanks, six 78 rpm recordings.

Music Aptitude Test.
Distributed by Conn Corporation, Elkhart, Indiana.
Tests for (1) rhythm; (2) tempo; (3) pitch; (4) melody; (5) chords; (6) vision; (7) mathematics. Grades 4–8. Includes instruction manual, test cards, grading masks. (No record. Rhythms and pitches played by examiner or advanced pupils using drum, piano, and/or other instruments.)

Musical Aptitude Test (Series A). Harvey S. Whistler and Louis P. Thorpe.
Distributed by California Test Bureau, 5916 Hollywood Boulevard, Hollywood 28, California.
Tests for (1) rhythm recognition; (2) pitch discrimination; (3) advanced rhythm recognition. Grades 4–10. Includes instruction manual, answer sheets. (No record. Examiner plays examples at piano.)

Test of Musicality (Fourth Edition). E. Thayer Gaston.
Distributed by Odells Instrumental Service, 925 Massachusetts Street, Lawrence, Kansas.
Grades 4–12. Includes manual of directions, scoring key, test form, one 33⅓ rpm recording.

Tilson-Gretsch Musical Aptitude Test. Lowell Mason Tilson.
Distributed by Educational Department, Fred Gretsch Manufacturing Co., 218 South Wabash Avenue, Chicago 4, Illinois.
Tests for (1) pitch; (2) time; (3) intensity; (4) tonal memory. Grades 4–12. Includes test blanks, key corrector, letter to parents, test certificate, press releases, two recordings.

OTHER INFORMATION SOURCES. Additional information about each pupil can be obtained from other sources. Vocal teachers are familiar with the pupil's general music ability, singing ability, and interest in music, all of which is directly pertinent to the selection of instrumental beginners. Classroom and homeroom teachers know whether the pupil is quick to learn, interested in school work, dependable in his work habits, and generally successful in his school work. They often know whether he comes from a musical home and whether his parents might look favorably on extra music instruction. Permanent record cards maintained by each school show test scores dealing with such factors as intelligence, aptitudes, and interests. They offer a complete scholarship record showing degrees of success in various subject areas as well as a record of participation in extra-curricular and out-of-school activities and comments concerning the pupil's conduct. They give information about the pupil's parents, their occupations, socio-economic status, and other conditions in the home.

All this information is of use to the instrumental teacher. He collects as much as he can before reaching a decision about each pupil. He considers the pupil's talent as indicated by rhythm, pitch, and standardized tests. He consults other teachers to ask their opinions about the pupil's music potential and general character. He searches for pertinent data in permanent school records. Ultimately, he talks with the parents of the pupils he has identified as likely prospects. With the information derived from all these sources he is equipped to make informed judgments and to select pupils who will profit from instrumental instruction.

This data-collecting process involves many steps and is important to the success of the pupil and of the instrumental program. The teacher therefore establishes a carefully conceived testing program as a regular part of the annual school calendar. It includes a sequence of steps that recurs automatically year after year and requires only minimum effort on the part of music and other teachers.

A talent test is administered each year to all pupils in a particular grade. The intent is to test every pupil who passes through the school system and to identify talented pupils before instrumental classes are formed. Every pupil is then re-tested one or two years later to make certain no talented pupil was overlooked during the first testing. This step is highly desirable. Teachers often find that a significant number of pupils who ranked low in the first test—due to nervousness, minor illness, or some unidentifiable cause—achieve markedly higher scores when re-tested. Either the same or a different test may be used. When scheduling arrangements permit, both tests are given in the spring so that organized classes may begin promptly at the beginning of the next school year.

Scores or anecdotal comments are entered in the pupil's permanent record and further information is gathered at the same time from the permanent records, other music teachers, and classroom teachers. This gives the instrumental teacher complete information about each pupil who ranked high in the tests and permits other teachers to suggest the names of pupils who might benefit from special instruction despite low test scores. With this information available, the instrumental teacher is able to identify likely prospects for instrumental classes. He can write appropriate letters to parents of children who scored high in the tests, talk with the pupils, and make plans for the necessary beginners' classes.

Matching Pupils and Instruments

Many pupils who express interest in instrumental lessons do so because they want to play a particular instrument. Others simply want to play in the band or orchestra and have no particular instrument in mind. Still others are identified through the testing program before they have developed either music interests or preferences. Each of these pupils, regardless of his preference, must be guided to the instrument he can learn to play. Many instruments require specialized music talent or unique physical capabilities. Persons who study these instruments without the requisite music talent or physical capability may achieve a degree of success, but make progress slowly and only through great perseverance. The pupil is more likely to succeed if he chooses an instrument that matches his capabilities.

Physical characteristics of the player have an important bearing on the speed with which he masters his instrument and the extent of his progress. Each of the various wind instruments uses a mouthpiece of unique type or size. The player finds the instrument easier to master if his lips and teeth are suited to the mouthpiece. The string instruments differ in size. They must be matched to the size of the player and to his capabilities for highly refined arm and finger movements. Percussion instruments require manual dexterity as well as general fluidity and grace of movement. It is possible to cite examples of players who achieved virtuoso skill despite their physical characteristics, but such cases are the exception rather than the rule.

All instruments require music talent of the player, but not all require the same degree of talent or the same mixture of the several related talents. Pitch sense is essential for the beginning string player, but is less important for the beginning wind player, and is of least importance for the beginning percussion player. Rhythmic sense is important to all, but the need for coördinated movement is strongest for the percussion player.

PHYSICAL CRITERIA. The instrumental teacher considers the requirements of each instrument as he guides the interest of pupils entering the instrumental program. He helps each pupil select an instrument, basing his recommendations on scores achieved in music talent tests and on observable physical characteristics. A list of such characteristics similar to the one below serves as a guide to the teacher.

Trumpet: Keen sense of pitch, rhythm sense, physical coördination, lips of normal thickness, even teeth, rounded rather than pointed jaws.

Trombone-baritone: Keen sense of pitch, rhythm sense, physical coördination, lips of full or medium thickness, relatively even teeth, rounded jaws, normally developed arms and shoulders, long arms and/or fingers (to reach seventh position).

Tuba: Normal pitch sense, strong rhythm sense, physical coördination, full lips, rounded jaws, relatively even teeth, appropriate body size and strength.

French horn: Keen pitch sense, rhythm sense, physical coöordination, normal lips, even teeth, rounded or pointed jaws, strong interest in music and the French horn.

Clarinet-saxophone: Normal pitch sense, rhythm sense, physical coördination, even lower teeth, rounded or pointed jaws, fingers long enough to reach all keys without distortion of hand position.

Flute-piccolo: Normal pitch sense, rhythm sense, physical coördination, lips of normal thickness, even lower teeth, rounded or pointed jaws, long fingers.

Oboe: Keen pitch sense, rhythm sense, physical coördination, medium or thin lips, normally even teeth, fingers long enough to reach all keys, interest and perseverance.

Bassoon: Normal pitch sense, rhythm sense, physical coördination, medium or full lips, normally even teeth, rounded or pointed jaws, large hands and long fingers, interest and perseverance.

String instruments: Keen pitch sense, physical coördination, rhythm sense, finger dexterity, long fingers for viola, strong fingers for double bass, arms long and free, appropriate body size and/or stature, interest and perseverance.

Percussion: Strong rhythm sense, physical coördination, flexible fingers and wrists, general music ability (avoid assigning percussion instruments to those who lack music talent!).

The difficulty with a list such as this is that it makes no allowance for pupil interest or exceptions to the rule. The pupil's strong interest in music or in a particular instrument may more than compensate for his physical ineptitude or lack of music talent. Although pupils with long, agile fingers may be equipped by nature to achieve success in playing instruments requiring finger dexterity, there will be pupils with stubby fingers who surpass them. For this and other reasons there are wide differences of opinion concerning the physical capabilities required by each instrument. It is possible that interest, perseverance, and other qualities have a more important bearing on the pupil's success than the shape of his lips or the length of his fingers. The teacher therefore relies heavily on his own judgment and applies the requirements of any such list with discretion.

As an alternative to rigid standards of music talent and physical capability, some instrumental teachers use actual playing tests to indicate the instrument for which the pupil is best suited. Even though the playing test does nothing more than permit the pupil to experiment with an instrument for as little as ten minutes, it may be a better indicator of potential success than any list of criteria. A more reliable procedure, however, is one the teacher devises to include test scores, physical characteristics, and a playing test, relying on all three to determine which instrument the pupil should study.

EXPLORATORY DAYS. A relatively simple procedure for the playing test is one that permits the pupil to experiment with one or several instruments under the teacher's supervision. The teacher announces "exploratory days" on which interested pupils can come to him singly or in small groups to experiment with the instruments available. The teacher provides a trumpet, clarinet, flute, violin, and snare drum or practice pad, avoiding for these beginners the less usual instruments such as oboe and bassoon or the larger ones such as trombone and tuba to which pupils may transfer at a later date. To simplify matters even further, he may provide only mouthpieces for the wind instruments. This eliminates any difficulty the pupil might encounter in holding the instrument or manipulating the keys, but requires the teacher to base his conclusion solely on the ease with which the pupil produces a tone from the mouthpiece. Actually, the playing test is equivalent to a private lesson. The teacher works with the pupil, experimenting with one or more instruments as necessary, searching for the instrument the pupil can hold and manipulate satisfactorily and from which he can produce acceptable tone most easily.

TRIAL PERIODS. A more elaborate procedure is the "trial period." The teacher assigns instruments on a trial basis, using his best judgment in selecting the instrument for each pupil. Pupils are then given lessons for one week, two weeks, or a month, either privately or in classes. During this period the teacher watches the pupil's progress closely, noting his music aptitude, skill in manipulating the instrument, tone quality, interest, and perseverance. During or at the end of the trial period the teacher confers with each pupil, advising him to continue, to transfer to a different instrument, or to postpone his entrance into the instrumental program.

"Exploratory days" and "trial periods," like the talent tests, are scheduled to fit conveniently into the sequence of the instrumental program. If the teacher wishes to begin instrumental classes early in the school year, the playing tests are offered as early as possible in September. Where summer music programs are possible, a week or more may be set aside in late summer for a "Summer Band School." In still other situations, the teacher may conduct playing tests immediately prior to the end of one school year so that instrumental classes can begin as soon as school opens in the fall. This is particularly advantageous if facilities can be provided for lessons through the summer, but undesirable if the absence of summer lessons permits the pupil's initial interest to wane. If the normal pattern of the school year permits re-scheduling of classes at the middle of the year, in January or February for example, talent and playing tests can be scheduled in the fall.

Providing Instruments for Pupils

In the well-organized instrumental program, the teacher accepts responsibility for providing instruments for pupils who want to learn to play them. Pupils must have instruments to participate in classes, of course, but few have instruments at their disposal. Some pupils may be able to use an instrument previously played by an older brother or sister or may be able to acquire a used instrument from some other source. In other instances, parents may be willing to purchase a new instrument. In general, however, most pupils will have no instrument and those who have access to used instruments may progress more rapidly if they begin with instruments selected to match their capabilities rather than those that happen to be available. Even in the case of the pupil who is able to buy a new instrument, there is good reason to postpone the purchase for six months or a year until both teacher and parents are certain that interest and ability have been evaluated correctly.

For beginning classes, the needed instruments are those that might be called "basic"—clarinet, trumpet, flute, violin, and snare drum. These are provided for every beginning pupil if possible. As the class progresses, and after the teacher has been able to re-evaluate each pupil's interest and ability, many pupils are encouraged to obtain instruments of their own. Even at this stage, the teacher may want to provide the basic instruments for pupils who show promise but are unable for financial reasons to buy them. As the group progresses still further and selected pupils are ready to transfer to instruments other than the basic ones, the teacher will find it necessary to supply tubas, euphoniums, French horns, and the larger instruments in every family. Even advanced players of the high-school band rarely own the larger and more costly instruments. For these reasons the teacher develops a plan through which large numbers of basic instruments can be provided for classes of beginners, smaller numbers of basic instruments can be provided for advanced pupils, and certain expensive instruments can be supplied for both beginning and advanced players.

One plan is the *school loan*. Under this plan, the schools buys the necessary instruments, lends them to qualified pupils, keeps them in repair, and eventually re-distributes them to new generations of beginning players. An advantage of this arrangement is that there is no cost to the parents of beginning pupils. It is easier for the teacher to get parental consent for the participation of all pupils and therefore easier to establish beginners' classes. Parents whose children withdraw from instrumental classes suffer no loss and the teacher can recommend withdrawal freely in the event his original estimate of the pupil's interest and ability was in error. Once pupils have proved their ability and interest by making progress, parents can see the need for an instrument and more readily provide for its purchase. The plan is evidence of the good judgment and good intent of the instrumental program.

The chief disadvantage of the school-loan plan is that it requires a large investment of school funds and careful management of expensive school property. The initial investment required for the purchase of even a small number of music instruments is large. This initial investment must be supported by regular appropriation of additional funds for normal repairs and the replacement of instruments no longer serviceable. Because of the large investment, it is especially important that this school property be well taken care of. The instrumental teacher must accept the responsibility for making certain the instruments are kept in playing condition and not misplaced or stolen. This is a heavy responsibility requiring that detailed and accurate records be kept and that the entire plan have the constant supervision of the teacher.

The details of the school-loan plan can be arranged to minimize certain of its disadvantages. The teacher establishes an annual budget for repair, replacement, and regular addition of new instruments. He keeps records for each instrument showing make, type, inventory number, purchase date, cost, repairs, borrowers and so forth. Parents and pupils are asked to sign a loan agreement under which they assume responsibility for the borrowed instrument. The agreement may stipulate the conditions under which the borrower is required to repair or replace the instrument in the event it is damaged through neglect or accident. It may require a deposit to be forfeited if the instrument suffers excessive damage. It may state a maximum loan period, implying that pupils who wish to continue study beyond that point will be asked to purchase their own instruments. Finally, the agreement may include practice and participation requirements, permitting the teacher to withdraw the loan privilege if the pupil neglects to practice or does not meet other requirements of the instrumental program. These stipulations are desirable in that they emphasize the value of the instrument, place responsibility for its care with pupils and parents, and encourage the pupil to practice.

The *school-rental* plan is similar to the school-loan plan except for the addition of a small rental fee. Charges may be payable on a monthly or semi-annual basis, or the rental fee for an entire year may be paid at the beginning of that year. The rental fee is a return on the original investment. It can be small, providing funds for repairs only, or can be large enough to provide for both repairs and eventual replacement of the instrument. The latter arrangement makes this instrumental program self-sustaining, requiring no additional school funds once the original instruments are purchased. School administrators are quick to see the advantages of the rental system and may approve it more readily than a school-loan plan. Parents tend to accept the rental system also, understanding the necessity for the rental charge and agreeing to pay the relatively small fees to provide instruction for their children.

The disadvantages of the rental system are that it requires careful bookkeeping and that it is difficult for the teacher to avoid entering into business relationships with parents. Both disadvantages can be overcome by establishing a system in which the school office collects all fees and maintains all financial records. This protects the teacher from criticism and permits him to devote his time to teaching rather than to record-keeping. A contract is essential under this plan, similar to the loan contract except for the addition of information concerning the amount of the rental fee and the manner of its payment. Some schools apply rental fees toward purchase of the rented instrument. In doing so the school can become the target for criticism for conducting a business in the sale of music instruments in competition with local merchants. For this reason many schools set low fees to cover only repair, or repair and replacement. The income reduces the burden on the school budget but can not be criticized for being business income. The fees are small enough to be paid by families of low income and the mere existence of the fee emphasizes the value of the instrument and encourages careful use and practice.

The *dealer-rental* plan is a third possibility. It permits the teacher to provide instruments for beginning pupils at low cost without incurring responsibility for keeping records or managing funds and without requesting school appropriations for instrument purchases. Local dealers offer the instruments to pupils under a plan similar to school rental. The pupil or his parents sign a loan contract, pay a small fee, and can usually apply the fee toward purchase of the instrument. The dealer supplies the instruments, keeps them in repair, and collects all fees. The instrumental teacher does not participate in the arrangement except by informing his pupils that instruments can be secured in this way.

The school has an implied responsibility under the dealer-rental plan even though it is not directly involved in the transaction. The school must assure that the rented instruments are of reasonably good quality, are kept in repair, and that the rental fee is equitable. The school is also responsible for recommending dealers impartially, thus avoiding criticism for interfering in the business affairs of the community. Through arrangement with participating dealers, the school can help establish policies concerning maximum rental periods and, in some instances, practice and participation requirements.

A fourth possibility, the *manufacturer-rental* plan, has become popular in recent years. Nationally known instrument manufacturers offer this plan because it is desired by many school districts. The plan is similar to the dealer-rental plan except that it is operated or supervised by the instrument manufacturer, often with the coöperation of local dealers. The school benefits from the manufacturer's interest in furthering the development of instrumental music and is less subject to criticism for its dealings with local merchants. The manufacturer supplies instruments of appropriate quality and offers the benefits of extensive rental experience. Fees are equitable and rental contracts and policies are firmly established. The disadvantage, overcome when a local dealer coöperates in the plan, is that the manufacturer's facilities are not near the school. Repair and replacement of instruments as well as adjustment of other complaints are hampered if the manufacturer's representative is not readily available or if these matters must be taken care of through correspondence. An advantage is that the manufacturer may be able to offer better facilities for instrument repair.

Regardless of the plan adopted, most schools find it necessary to own and lend many instruments. Tympani and other percussion instruments are of necessity owned by the school, as are the large and expensive winds. Once these instruments are acquired, it is easier to take the succeeding steps of acquiring other low brasses and woodwinds and ultimately a small inventory of basic instruments. Many instrumental teachers succeed in acquiring a large supply of instruments in this way, beginning with those that are essential and progressing to the purchase of large numbers of basic instruments for beginners.

The choice of plan for each school depends on local conditions. Where funds are available in the school budget and the teacher has time for the necessary administrative work, the school loan or rental plans are often preferred. Many teachers find that one of these plans evolves naturally as the instrumental program develops, the purchase of essential instruments setting the precedent for regular additions to the inventory. Rental from local dealers or the manufacturer is warranted when the school is unable to purchase instruments or during the beginning phases of the instrumental program when large numbers of instruments must be provided before funds can be allocated from the school budget. These latter programs are especially convenient in that the teacher is not hampered by a limited supply of school-owned instruments and can expand the instrumental program to meet pupil needs as necessary.

Planning for Balanced Instrumentation

Every instrumental director strives toward the goal of balanced instrumentation in his performing groups. To achieve it he formulates a plan to guide him as he establishes beginning instrument classes and encourages pupils to transfer from basic to other instruments. The plan helps him achieve or maintain the desired instrumentation, raise the level of musicianship in performing groups, and serve all potential players in the school population. In schools with a poorly developed instrumental program or none at all, the plan provides a means for (1) establishing performing groups with a minimum number of players, and (2) the addition of new players each year until the desired instrumentation goal is reached. In schools with an established instrumental program, the plan helps maintain existing standards of instrumentation and musicianship.

The well-conceived plan considers these factors.

1. The need for beginning classes at the earliest possible grade in the elementary school.
2. The desirability of offering instruction in basic instruments in beginning classes—trumpet, clarinet, flute, violin, snare drum.
3. The necessity for transfer of selected pupils from basic instruments to others such as low brasses, woodwinds, strings, and double reeds when the pupil's music progress and physical development permit.
4. The goal of balanced instrumentation in bands and orchestras in the junior high school and senior high school.

5. The effect of drop-outs, transfer to other instruments, high-school graduation, or any other factor which may influence the number of players who continue to participate.

Among the most important elements of the plan are the beginning classes. The establishment of new classes for beginners year after year is the best assurance of a steady flow of advanced players into the performing groups. Although it is desirable to organize these classes at the earliest possible grade in the elementary school, the grade may vary for several reasons. First, the physical maturity and music experience of children in any one grade varies from school to school. In one school, pupils in the fourth grade may be mature enough to begin instrumental study. In another school, the teacher may find that fourth-grade pupils are not sufficiently mature and postpone the beginning classes until the fifth grade. Second, difficulties of scheduling or the press of other work may force the instrumental teacher to postpone formation of beginning classes. Some teachers find time to direct elementary-school classes as well as the ensembles of the junior and senior high school. Others find it necessary to sacrifice elementary-school classes to permit other work, postponing beginning classes until the junior high school.

Another influence is the scheduling of pupil transfers from basic to other instruments. The pupil must meet certain requirements of physical and musical development before he transfers from trumpet to trombone, or from any basic instrument to one of the larger instruments, the double reeds or French horn. This fact, plus the need for finding time and schedule hours to instruct pupils who transfer to new instruments, requires that the director's plan be thought out carefully in terms of the local situation.

Although the grades in which the various classes are offered may vary for a number of reasons, one possible scheduling is shown below. This plan includes the use of exploratory instruments prior to the beginning class, transfer to larger but related instruments after one year of instruction, and transfer to the less usual instruments such as double reeds after two years of instruction.

Grade 4: Pre-band, exploratory instruments.
Grade 5: Beginning classes in basic instruments—trumpet, clarinet, flute, violin, snare drum.
Grade 6: Intermediate classes and/or beginning ensembles for basic instruments plus beginning classes for related instruments—alto and bass clarinet, saxophone, trombone, baritone, viola, cello.
Grade 7: Beginning ensembles for basic and related instruments plus beginning classes for oboe, bassoon, French horn, tuba, and string bass.

The transfer student is a perennial problem. When he transfers from clarinet to saxophone after one year of instruction, or from clarinet to oboe after two years of instruction, he needs for a short period to be regarded as a beginner and to be given careful instruction in his new instrument. Because of his previous training in the basic instrument, however, he often makes progress quickly, especially because the instrumental teacher selects apt pupils for transfer. For this reason, many teachers arrange informal instruction periods for these pupils instead of establishing a beginning class. The pupils are taught either privately or in small groups for as little as a few weeks and then take their places in ensembles for which they are qualified.

There are two instrumentation factors to be considered in the director's plan: (1) the desired number of basic instruments in the performing groups and (2) the necessity for at least a minimum number of the less usual instruments. The band needs relatively large numbers of clarinets and trumpets, the orchestra large numbers of violins, and both need double reeds as well as lower instruments of the brass, woodwind, and string families. As a graphic record of the development of the desired number of each type of instrument, and a guide to the establishment of beginning classes and the recommendation of transfers, the director can construct a chart showing the number of each type of instrument in each grade. The chart can show simply the desired number of instruments or can include figures for both the desired number and those currently available. Table 7 is a "director's chart" showing desired numbers only, dealing with the development of players for junior-high-school and senior-high-school bands.

The chart in Table 7 includes an estimated mortality rate to allow for pupils who withdraw from the instrumental program because of lack of interest or conflict with other classes and school activities. The drop-out rate will be an estimate only as the director begins his program, but after a few years can be revised according to the director's experience with local conditions. The chart provides for transfers from basic to other instruments and establishes goals in terms of a desired instrumentation for the high-school band, another variable determined by the director's standards, numbers of instruments available, the size of the school population, and other factors.

Planning of this sort is vital to the growth and sustained success of the instrumental program. Without it, the high-school director runs the perennial risk of having no double reeds, no French horns, and unbalanced sections of basic instruments. With proper planning he can assure balanced instrumentation, noting gaps and weaknesses as they develop and remedying them years before they affect the performance standards of the advanced groups.

TABLE 7. DIRECTOR'S CHART SHOWING DESIRED NUMBER OF PLAYERS OF EACH TYPE OF INSTRUMENT IN EACH SCHOOL GRADE IN THE INSTRUMENTAL PROGRAM.

Grade	*4*	*5*	*6*	*7*	*8*	*9*	*Jr H S Band*	*10*	*11*	*12*	*H S Band*
Pre-band	60										
Flute		5	4	3		3	6	3		2	5
E-flat clar				1	1	1	3	1		1	2
B-flat clar		24	16	9	9	8	26	8	8	8	24
Alto clar			2	1	1	1	3	1		1	2
Bass clar			1	1	1	1	3		1	1	2
Oboe				2	1	1	4	1		1	2
Bassoon				2	1	1	4		1	1	2
Saxophone			4	3	2	2	7	2	2	1	5
Trumpet		18	10	5	5	4	14	4	3	3	10
Fr. Horn				2	2	2	6	1	1	2	4
Trombone			4	3	3	2	8	2	2	2	6
Baritone			3	2	1	1	4	1		1	2
Tuba				2	2	1	5	2	1	1	4
Percussion		4	3	2	2	3	7	2	2	3	7
Totals	60	51	47	38	31	31	100	28	21	28	77

INSTRUCTING THE BEGINNERS

Beginning instrumentalists can be taught in either of two ways, in classes or through private instruction. Class instruction is desirable because it uses the teacher's time economically, permitting him to teach forty or more pupils in one group. It is often the only solution to difficult scheduling problems, a means of teaching all pupils during one activity or other "free" period in the school day. Pupils gain security through playing in a group. Each learns through the mistakes of others. Each begins to learn the skills and disciplines of ensemble playing in the first lesson. Perhaps most important, pupils find more enjoyment in the ensemble experience than in private lessons.

There are distinct advantages in private instruction also. Each pupil can be given individual attention and may make more rapid progress than the pupil who receives only class instruction. Whereas in the class the teacher may have to deal with several different types of instruments simultaneously, he can deal with the problems of only one instrument in the private lesson. As a result, lesson materials and teaching techniques can be adjusted to the needs of each pupil.

Because of limitations imposed by the school budget, scheduling possibilities, and requirements concerning teacher load, many schools choose class instruction. Classes may be homogeneous, heterogeneous, or may take the form of the junior band or orchestra. Each type of class has its own advantages and disadvantages but each may be used effectively to advance pupil skills.

Homogeneous Classes

The homogeneous class is one made up of like instruments, as compared to the heterogeneous class of unlike instruments. Although these terms imply a clear distinction, the dividing line between the two categories of classes is not clear. This is illustrated by the list of class groupings below. Although certain classes made up of mixed but related instruments are not truly homogeneous, the relationship is close enough to permit the teacher to treat the group as a homogeneous class. These groups include instruments from the brass and woodwind families only, excluding double reeds. Many other groupings are possible when strings, percussion, and double reeds are included.

1. B-flat clarinets only.
2. B-flat and bass clarinets.
3. Mixed clarinets, including B-flat, alto, and bass.
4. Mixed single reeds, including clarinets and saxophones in B-flat and E-flat.
5. Mixed woodwinds, including clarinets and saxophones in B-flat and E-flat and flutes in C.
6. Trumpets only.
7. B-flat brasses with valves, including trumpets, baritones, and tubas.
8. Mixed B-flat brasses, including trumpets, baritones, tubas, and trombones.
9. Mixed brasses, including trumpets, baritones, trombones and tubas in B-flat, French horns in F, and tubas in E-flat.

In each of these classes, teaching is simplified because the instruments are either alike or similar. Because the instruments in each group share one or more characteristics, a portion of each lesson can be devoted to "class" teaching in which the same playing problem can be discussed and practiced with all pupils simultaneously. The degree of homogeneity in the group, however, determines the proportion of class and individual teaching in the lesson. In the brass groups listed above, for example, the degrees of homogeneity are as follows:

Group 6. Trumpets only—all instruments offer the same problems of embouchure, fingering, range, register, and transposition. The entire lesson can be devoted to "class" teaching.

Group 7. B-flat brasses with valves—all instruments offer similar problems of embouchure, fingering, range, and transposition. The principal difference is one of register, the trumpets, baritones, and tubas sounding octaves apart. This difference is not sufficient to prohibit "class" teaching.

Group 8. Mixed B-flat brasses—all instruments are similar in embouchure, range, and key. There are differences in register and in that some pupils must learn fingerings while others learn slide positions. Much "class" teaching is possible, but some lesson time must be devoted to teaching slide positions to a relatively small number of trombone students.

Group 9. Mixed brasses—instruments are related in embouchure, range, and general playing characteristics. "Class" teaching, however, is difficult. Pupils studying French horn face embouchure problems quite different from those of the other brasses. The teacher must explain several different fingerings as well as a slide position for any one pitch. Because the French horn is pitched in F, and one or more tubas possibly in E-flat, there are only limited possibilities for playing passages in unison. In a class of this type much time is devoted to individual problems until each pupil has developed enough skill to permit the group to play as a brass ensemble or junior band.

Similar variations in homogeneity exist in other groups made up of either woodwinds or strings. Although the true homogeneous class is one consisting of identical instruments only, the label attached to the class is relatively unimportant. In practice, it is the teacher's point of view that establishes the dividing line between homogeneous and heterogeneous classes. This point of view is often determined by the teacher's success in teaching classes of similar but not identical instruments.

The intent of the homogeneous class is to create a group in which the teaching procedure of the private lesson can be combined with opportunities for ensemble playing. As in the private lesson, serious attention is given to the development of technique. Each problem is explained to and practiced with the class as a whole. Drills and exercises are part of the lesson and are practiced in unison. Regular assignments are noted for outside study and practice by all. The lesson combines this instruction with ensemble playing. It strives to develop the ensemble skills that are an important goal in the instrumental program of the public school. Ensemble playing is an effective means of teaching rhythmic precision, intonation, tone quality, and dynamic balance. It acquaints the pupil with conductors' signals. It permits the pupil to experience the satisfactions of ensemble playing, introduces him to music he could not meet in the private lesson, and transforms the work of learning to play his instrument into an enjoyable and musical experience.

Homogeneous classes vary in size from three or four identical instruments to thirty or more mixed instruments of the same family. From the school administrator's point of view, the group of only three or four pupils does not utilize the teacher's time economically and should not be regarded as a class. The teacher's load is often computed in terms of the number of hours spent with classes of thirty or more pupils, or in terms of the total number of pupil-contact hours per week. A teacher who meets 25 classes of three pupils each per week, for a total of 75 contact hours, is said to have a lighter load than one who meets the same number of classes of thirty pupils each, a total of 750 contact hours. This difference in contact hours has important consequences for the school budget and it is for this reason some schools disapprove of small homogeneous classes. Other schools justify the small classes by arranging the teacher's schedule to include perhaps ten rehearsal periods each week with performing groups of from 50 to 100 players each. When this is possible, the teacher can justifiably teach a number of small homogeneous classes and give pupils the benefits of individual instruction.

The advantages of the homogeneous class are many. It uses the teacher's time and schedule hours efficiently, especially when classes consist of twenty, thirty, or more pupils. It deals with learning problems common to every pupil in the class. It is enjoyable for pupils and sustains their interest because ensemble playing is not deferred until a year or more of lessons has been completed. Instructional materials are plentiful. The usual instruction books can be used to develop technique and easy band or orchestra arrangements can be used for ensemble playing. In addition, there are method books designed for this type of class offering both technique instruction and ensemble experience.

One of the principal disadvantages of the homogeneous class is the problem of scheduling. It is difficult to find a period during the school day in which all clarinet students, for example, can be excused from other classes. The result is that the teacher must choose between the small class of three or four identical instruments and the larger class of twenty or more mixed instruments. Whether they are large or small, a relatively large number of classes is needed to teach all instruments in homogeneous groupings. Ensemble playing is sometimes unsatisfactory because of poor balance or because all instruments of an important register, such as those in the bass clef, are missing. Finally, the homogeneous class gives too little opportunity for the individual attention especially important to beginning players. Problems of embouchure, tone quality, posture, and so forth have their roots in the pupil's first lessons. Unless the teacher sees and corrects these faults as they begin to develop, they become established playing habits and retard the pupil's later progress. In the class, the teacher is often unaware of these problems until they seriously affect the pupil's progress.

Many of these problems are eliminated by the circumstances surrounding the formation of the beginning class. The "director's chart," Table 7, shows the possibility of beginning with two large classes and two smaller ones. One large class might consist of clarinets only, the other of trumpets only. Flutes and percussion might be combined with the clarinets and trumpets respectively, taught separately as small classes, or postponed until the following year. After the first year of instruction, when selected pupils have transferred from basic to related instruments, the mixture of related instruments in two large classes creates few problems because of the knowledge and experience gained by the pupils during their first year. It is for this reason that class instruction is practical for beginning players in a well-organized instrumental program.

Heterogeneous Classes

The heterogeneous class is one made up of instruments of different families or of different instruments within the same family. It may include all instruments of the band or orchestra and is then in effect a junior band or orchestra. As in the homogeneous class, there may be different degrees of homogeneity. The number of different types of instrument can be reduced to eliminate certain teaching problems, bringing the class closer to the homogeneous type.

A common type of heterogeneous class is that composed of band instruments, including woodwinds, brasses, and percussion. Also common is the class made up of string instruments, including violin, viola, cello, and double bass. The "orchestra" class, made up of strings, woodwinds, brasses, and percussion, is not popular due to the many problems that arise when all families are taught in one group. Other types of class are possible, such as those made up of brasses or woodwinds only.

The heterogeneous class uses the "band" or "orchestra" method of teaching rather than the "private" method. The classes can be larger than the homogeneous class, numbering sixty or more pupils. There is of necessity less emphasis upon technique and less use of drills and exercises. There may be fewer assignments for outside study because the lesson offers less opportunity to check this outside work. The elements of the private lesson are replaced with ensemble playing. Instruction books are based on song materials and easy band or orchestra arrangements. The development of technique is often more gradual than in the homogeneous class but there may be more rapid development of ensemble skills.

The important advantage of the heterogeneous class is one of scheduling. The class can meet during an activity period and all pupils free to join the class can participate in the lesson regardless of the instruments they play. Fewer separate classes are needed. One band class and one for strings will suffice. One teacher can then serve many pupils. Whether the class is for band instruments or for strings alone, it can be better balanced than the homogeneous class. The complete instrumentation produces a more satisfying ensemble tone and ensemble skills can be emphasized and developed quickly. Because it gives pupils the "band" or "orchestra" feeling, it can be called "first band," "junior band," or "beginning orchestra" to stimulate the interest of pupils whose strongest desire is to belong to a performing group.

The chief disadvantages of the heterogeneous class stem from the mixture of instruments and the large number of pupils in the group. The mixture of instruments creates many teaching problems. Much class time is occupied with describing fingerings, embouchure positions, playing posture, and similar matters to each smaller group within the class. Possibilities for unison practice are limited. The variety of keys and transpositions makes it difficult for the teacher to discuss pitches with the group. The variety of tone qualities, particularly when the class is made up of beginning players, makes it difficult to establish concepts of good tone.

Because of the size of the group, all pupils must be held to the same rate of progress. The class must play as an ensemble, the teacher limiting his selection of music to that which every pupil can play. The pupil who progresses rapidly loses interest in the easy ensemble pieces. The pupil attempting to master French horn or one of the double reeds, and progressing more slowly than pupils playing other instruments, gives up in despair when the group plays passages or exercises requiring fluent technique. In the large heterogeneous class individual attention is all but impossible and playing problems multiply unnoticed. Instructional materials are not plentiful, partly because the writers of "band" and "orchestra" methods must solve awkward problems. It is difficult, for example, to choose a "starting tone" for the first lesson, one which beginning players of trumpets, clarinets, flutes, and French horns can produce with equal ease.

Many teachers feel that the heterogeneous class is impractical for beginning pupils. It is less impractical for the second or third year of instruction after pupils have gained basic familiarity with their instruments and some have transferred from basic to related instruments. In the "director's chart," Table 7, the 38 players in the seventh grade might form a heterogeneous class. All players in the sixth grade might be included in one heterogeneous class instead of two relatively homogeneous classes. By utilizing its advantages and minimizing its disadvantages through careful lesson planning, the teacher can use the heterogeneous class effectively at this level, teaching many different instruments in one group at a substantial saying of time and effort.

Junior Band and Orchestra

Junior band and junior orchestra are especially important because they are group activities. The adolescent is attracted to them because it is his nature to want to belong to a social group and to pursue both his work and his recreation in the company of others. The pupil of elementary-school age, though less impelled to group activity than the adolescent, has similar desires for the company and esteem of others of his own age.

The junior instrumental group is therefore a desirable social organization as well as an instructional device. Its schedule includes rehearsal periods during which pupils learn about music and their instruments as well as concerts and festivals that provide both musical and social motivation. It is uniformed when possible to add to the distinction of membership and may adopt club organization with officers and committees to emphasize its social nature.

The junior group is a type of heterogeneous class open to intermediate players rather than beginners. Pupils in beginning classes look forward to joining the junior group after a year or more of instruction and accept membership as a reward for progress. It is a stepping-stone to "first" or "senior" band or orchestra, a means of participation for those who have learned the lessons of the beginning class but are not yet ready to join the advanced players.

Although performance is desirable and necessary, and may be a goal, the purpose of the junior group is to increase the skills of its members. It offers instruction in musicianship and technique and develops ensemble disciplines, all through ensemble experience. Lesson periods are conducted like rehearsals and many of the instructional materials are selections from easy band or orchestra literature. Musicianship and technique are advanced through the study of this ensemble literature, but supplementary materials —such as chorale books, ensemble technique books, collections of rhythm patterns, scales and arpeggios—are used as necessary to develop technical facility, tone quality, intonation, and reading ability. This makes the junior band or junior orchestra a productive teaching device combining the advantages of the instrumental lesson and the performing ensemble.

The junior group may be of almost any size. Composed of only ten or fifteen pupils playing instruments of the same family, it is a brass, woodwind, or string ensemble. Composed of fifty or sixty pupils playing instruments of several families, it becomes a junior band or orchestra. Each of these types is desirable, both as a performing group and as an instructional class. Because the junior group is a stepping-stone to a more advanced ensemble, and because the players of the junior group ultimately become the advanced group, the teacher strives for balanced instrumentation and the good ensemble tone it makes possible. Selected pupils are encouraged to transfer from basic to related instruments before they enter the junior group, and the teacher's recommendations are based on instrumentation needs as well as the pupil's music ability and progress.

Despite the variety of instruments, "class" instruction in the fundamentals of playing is not an insurmountable problem. Pupils accepted into the junior group have already acquired certain basic abilities. They have become familiar with their instruments, have developed embouchure habits, and have learned proper playing position. They have learned to produce tone of acceptable quality and enough facility to play scales, arpeggios, and "technique" passages in a number of keys. They are able to read music of reasonable difficulty and have been trained to respond to conductors' signals. Although the intermediate players need additional training in each of these areas, the knowledge gained in beginning classes is sufficient to permit the teacher to discuss new learnings in general terms without taking class time to apply it to each different type of instrument.

If the group is treated as a junior band or orchestra, selected pupils can be drawn from it for smaller ensembles such as brass quartet, woodwind quintet, or string ensemble. The smaller ensembles are instructional groups although they are useful also as performing groups to provide variety at concerts and to reduce the number of selections that must be prepared by the larger group. Because there is not time during regular class periods to coach the ensembles, much of their work is done at other times. The director assigns music to be prepared, meets with the group when possible to direct attention to new problems in the music and to offer constructive criticism.

As the small ensemble rehearses, its members gain invaluable experience, become acquainted with new music, and acquire new skill in playing. In forming some ensembles, the director chooses only outstanding pupils to give them experience they can not get by playing with the larger group. The teacher's aim, however, is to give every pupil this kind of ensemble experience, the weaker pupils learning from it and strengthening their interest in instrumental music.

Junior bands and orchestras are common to many schools, partly because they are effective teaching devices and partly because they create comparatively few scheduling or other administrative problems. The group can meet during activity periods or as a class during the heart of the school day. All pupils free to attend can participate in the rehearsal-lesson. In doing so, they improve their music skills, gain ensemble experience, and earn continuing membership in a desirable social group.

Private Instruction

Private instruction, as has been indicated, is superior in many ways to class instruction. Teaching materials can be selected in accordance with the needs of each pupil and each pupil can progress at his own rate. The teacher can help each pupil with his problems as they arise. The teacher's task is simplified in that he deals with only one pupil and one instrument at a time. Materials are plentiful and varied, permitting the teacher to choose materials appropriate for concentrated study of any aspect of technique or musicianship.

Despite its advantages, private instruction is rarely practical in the public schools. The high cost in school funds and teacher time is prohibitive. There is the question of whether private instruction is proper within the system of public education; an educational system philosophically directed toward the training of large numbers of pupils through group experience at public expense must look searchingly at any arrangement that permits the teacher to work with only one pupil at a time. The advantages and results of private instruction are much to be desired, nevertheless, and many instrumental teachers search for means of providing private lessons for some or all of the pupils in the instrumental program.

For the pupil who participates in the classes and ensembles of the organized instrumental program, the private lesson is a desirable supplement. Regardless of the amount of time devoted in the class lesson to musicianship and technique, the pupil does not receive the intensive instruction of the private lesson. The ideal arrangement might be a combination of private lessons and ensemble experience, all pupils studying with private teachers and participating in one or more performing groups. In this arrangement, the pupil would develop skills under the direction of his private teacher and apply them during ensemble rehearsal. The homogeneous and heterogeneous classes are attempts to combine the benefits of private instruction and ensemble experience in the group lesson. They succeed to a degree, but they do not replace the private teacher.

One solution to this problem is based upon full use of private teachers in the community. The private teacher may be supplied by a local music store as part of the instrument-rental program, giving lessons in the store with fees established and collected by the instrument dealer. Teachers may be found among the adults of the community, giving lessons in studios or their homes for established fees. The instrumental teacher encourages pupils to study privately and accepts responsibility for guiding each pupil's choice of teacher. He also has a responsibility for being impartial in these recommendations. Carefully guided, this solution (1) enables pupils to make rapid progress, (2) reduces the burden on school personnel and facilities, and (3) improves the quality of the school instrumental program. It also relieves the tension sometimes created when the school gives free instruction in competition with private "fee" teachers.

Another solution is the in-school "fee" teacher. These teachers are drawn from the adult musicians of the community, but give lessons in school buildings during the school day. The school establishes or approves lesson rates which may be paid through the school office or to the teacher. Teachers travel from school to school as necessary, following the schedules established by the school office. Under this arrangement the school has control over the selection of teachers and the cost of lessons. It offers facilities and administrative assistance to compensate teachers for fees lower than those charged for studio lessons.

A third solution is one adopted by instrumental teachers who can adjust their schedules and are willing to give the needed time. The teacher himself gives private lessons during the regular school day. He may fill all his periods and part of his lunch hour with private teaching. He may remain in school until five or six o'clock each day, teaching as many pupils as possible during after-school hours. This is a burdensome schedule, but many teachers accept it. It is natural for the teacher to want to improve his program and equally natural to want to help the talented pupil. The temptation to offer private instruction is therefore hard for him to resist. Pupils pay no fee and the teacher receives no additional salary. The teacher feels impelled to teach, nevertheless, and accepts pupil progress as his reward.

In many schools, one of these systems for private instruction develops out of necessity or because of its obvious benefit to the school instrumental program. The danger is one of over-emphasis. The program based on a philosophy of "music for all" is wary of practices that tend to develop into vocational education for the minority of pupils who may some day become professional instrumentalists if these practices detract from other phases of the music program. The public-school instrumental director is fortunate, however, if he can draw on the skills of community teachers and arrange a system of private instruction for either advanced or all instrumental players. The quality of the school program increases markedly as does the benefit to all pupils who participate in the program.

The Class Lesson

The instruction of beginners is an especially important phase of the public-school instrumental program. It is during this early instruction that pupils build foundations for playing habits and lasting concepts of rhythmic accuracy, intonation, tone quality, and general musicianship. The beginning class should not be entrusted to an unprepared teacher or one with less than vital interest in this teaching. Requirements for the teacher include musicianship, knowledge of music and instruments, sympathy for pupils and their problems, great patience and superior teaching ability. The instrumental director therefore secures well-qualified teachers for beginners and teaches one or more classes himself to keep in touch with their problems.

In any instrumental class—beginning, intermediate, or advanced—there are pupils of different levels of ability. There may be those with less previous training than others in the class. There may be intermediate players who have advanced beyond the work of the beginning class but who are not yet ready to join the advanced groups. There may be capable players who are unable to participate in the rehearsals of advanced groups—because of schedule problems or for some other reason—who must either meet with a less advanced class or remain inactive. Even in classes of pupils with no previous training, differences in natural ability and interest result in different rates of progress and quickly create differences in playing ability. Although the teacher groups pupils according to ability, he accepts the fact that individual differences exist within each class and plans lesson procedures accordingly.

To plan effectively, the teacher needs a wide knowledge of appropriate literature and an available supply of materials of different kinds. This includes materials of different levels of difficulty, appropriate to pupils' levels of skill, as well as materials to develop specific areas of instrumental playing and musicianship—"method" books, technique books, chorale collections, and easy pieces selected from band, orchestra, or ensemble literature. The teacher evaluates and selects these materials carefully, studying each to become familiar with its content and suggested use. Among the most difficult to select are the method books designed for heterogeneous classes, the "band" and "orchestra" methods intended for the instruction of large classes of mixed instruments. He examines each book to note whether it contains these features:

1. Pictures showing correct assembly of instrument, playing posture, hand positions, and embouchure.
2. Easily playable starting tones for each instrument.
3. Correct and thorough training in fundamentals—embouchure, tonguing or bowing, rhythms, phrasing, dynamics.
4. Presentation of fundamental learnings in logical sequence.
5. Musical exercises of melodic and rhythmic interest.
6. Progressive development of technique.
7. Variety of music material, including unison exercises, ensemble exercises, and program pieces.
8. Special materials for problems peculiar to each instrument.
9. Teacher's book containing full scores of exercises and pieces.
10. Text matter in pupils' books describing proper care of each instrument.

To make full use of available lesson time, the teacher establishes a system for dealing with routine administrative matters. These include arranging music stands and chairs, adjusting light and ventilation, distributing and collecting ensemble books and parts, checking attendance, and taking care of minor instrument repairs and adjustments. Much of this work can be done by student assistants or monitors. Each monitor is given a designated task and instructed to accomplish it quickly at the beginning of each lesson period without further instruction from the teacher. If this is done, the teacher is free to deal with special problems during the first few minutes of the period. The lesson can begin promptly and the time can be used efficiently for teaching.

When monitors are used it is appropriate that they be given recognition. If the class is a junior band or orchestra, it can be organized with elected and appointed officers and committees. This student-government organization places responsibilities upon the pupils themselves and tends to improve group spirit and rehearsal discipline. Monitors can be given recognition in other ways as well, whether they are elected officers or appointed student assistants. Among the possibilities are points, badges, arm bands, and insignia. Appointments can be made as rewards for attendance, punctuality, outside practice, or on the basis of a cumulative total of points awarded for these and other acccomplishments. In this way the monitor system gives tangible rewards for conduct and progress, relieves the teacher of routine work, and permits more effective teaching of the class.

In planning class lessons the teacher strives for progress in playing facility and general musicianship. Progress in certain areas can be made in each lesson. In other areas progress may be measurable only after a semester or entire year of study. These separate areas are worthy of attention:

1. The study of progressively more difficult music to develop skill and knowledge, beginning with music within pupils' ability.
2. Steady improvement of instrumental skills—tone quality, technique, and articulation.
3. Steady improvement in musicianship—reading ability, knowledge of rhythms, attention to dynamics, correct intonation, artistic phrasing.
4. Development of rehearsal skills—knowledge of conductors' signals and ensemble disciplines.
5. Learning proper care and use of instrument.

The development of ability to read rhythms accurately is worthy of special note. Pupils taught only through class lessons quickly develop the ability to "play by ear." They follow the rest of the group and neglect to read the rhythms of their own parts. If this tendency is not checked, their lack of attention to rhythms becomes a serious handicap when they join the advanced performing groups. It retards each pupil's own progress and interferes with the rehearsal efficiency of the group. For this reason the teacher gives special attention to reading rhythms. He utilizes exercises in method books, collections of rhythmic exercises, rote drills, and sight-reading pieces.

In addition to guiding class progress in the development of instrumental skills, the teacher sets goals for each pupil's general music development. The class provides more than an opportunity to learn to play an instrument. As part of the program of music education, it rightly gives attention to the pupil's interest in music of many kinds, his ability to find enjoyment in music, and his capacity to appreciate music as an art form.

When studying an instrument the pupil should learn something about the instrument itself, including its acoustical principles, history, use in band and orchestral music, and virtuoso players of the past and present. Instrument classes should acquaint him also with the history of music, the harmonic and formal elements of music structure, and the principal characteristics of music styles. These goals merit the teacher's attention as he plans class lessons, for it may be that the most effective work in general music education can be done through instrumental instruction.

As he plans and directs each lesson, the teacher observes certain basic principles of class management.

1. Maintain strict control so that all class activities are under the direction of the teacher.
2. Prohibit individual "tooting" between exercises and pieces or at any other time during the class session.
3. Talk little and play much, eliminating pupils' temptation to play while the teacher is talking.
4. Keep individual and sectional playing to a minimum, interspersing necessary sectional practice with ensemble playing and making each sectional exercise as brief as possible.
5. Plan the lesson to move swiftly and teach at a rapid tempo, avoiding lengthy discussions and needless repetition of instructions, page numbers, and so forth.

The lesson itself is a sequence of different activities. The activities serve different purposes and are arranged in a logical sequence, often as follows:

1. *Warm-up.* The class prepares for the work of the lesson by playing long tones, chords, chorales, or scales and arpeggios.
2. *Tuning.* Pupils are encouraged to tune their instruments before class begins by using a tuning bar or other reference, and to make other needed tuning adjustments during the warm-up period. Once this habit is established, the teacher suggests further tuning adjustments during or following warm-up after listening to the blend of the entire ensemble or separate sections.
3. *Review.* In this portion of the lesson, the class plays exercises and pieces learned during earlier lessons, refining them by being increasingly attentive to such factors as dynamics and phrasing.
4. *Fundamental exercises.* The class concentrates on elements of technique, playing passages from technique books or by rote, many in unison but some in ensemble arrangements.
5. *Testing of groups and sections.* The teacher evaluates progress and checks completion of outside study assignments by asking sections, groups, or individuals to play alone. The teacher rotates these recitations, asking only two or three sections to play alone each day, devoting most of the lesson time to ensemble playing.
6. *New materials.* Exercises and pieces for study are introduced in each lesson as appropriate. The presentation normally includes a first playing, brief drill on difficult passages, explanation of new terms, and assignment for outside practice.
7. *Sight reading.* Music for sight reading is normally less difficult than "new materials" but more difficult than warm-up pieces. The intent of sight reading is to give pupils regular experience reading music of reasonable challenge but within the range of their abilities.

8. *Culmination.* Class interest and enthusiasm are sustained by ending the lesson with a satisfying playing experience. The teacher selects one or more favorite pieces pupils can play well, providing not only satisfaction but a sense of accomplishment as well at the close of the lesson.

In planning the sequence of lesson activities, the establishment of a routine procedure permits pupils to anticipate each portion of the lesson and prepare for it. This helps the lesson move swiftly, eliminates much waste of time reduces individual tooting, and improves discipline. Interest may be heightened, however, by planning minor variations in the routine from lesson to lesson. If it is possible to vary the sequence of the activities, or the procedure in any one activity, there is less opportunity for pupil attention to wander. The routine of the lesson can be varied also through use of dictation drills, singing, piano accompaniments, playing-by-ear, or by changing the interpretation of familiar pieces. Dictation is a useful device to engage pupil attention and develop aural accuracy. Rhythm and pitch patterns can be dictated for playback by the ensemble in unison, the teacher dictating from the piano, with an instrument, verbally, or by tapping. Pupils can be asked to sing their parts when ranges permit or to recite the rhythms of their parts by saying "ta" for each note. Singing the exercises is especially valuable in string classes, and in wind classes as well, to develop pupils' ability to hear the pitches they play and to adjust intonation. Pupil attention can be encouraged by varying the tempo and dynamics of exercises in successive readings, the teacher signaling these changes through his conducting. If the class is small, piano accompaniments added to portions of the lesson provide variety and enhance the ensemble effect.

The "progress chart" is a helpful motivating device for pupils who receive either class or private instruction. The chart may be a large sheet showing the names of all pupils in one class, suitable for posting on the classroom bulletin board, or may consist of separate sheets for each pupil. If separate sheets are used, they are more convenient if placed in a loose-leaf binder in an easily accessible location in the classroom. Pupil names can be listed by instrument in score order on the large progress chart, but the separate sheets in a loose-leaf binder are best arranged by pupil name in alphabetical order for easy reference. Some information is posted by the teacher who enters dates or his initials to show the completion of assignments and requirements. Other information, such as the number of minutes of practice each week, may be entered by the pupil.

Each teacher constructs his own chart, including items appropriate for the system of teaching he adopts for each class. Once the content of the chart is decided, blank forms can be mimeographed or printed in quantity and new charts posted every week, month, or other report period. Possible items in the progress chart include:

1. Completion of specific lesson assignments or pages in method books.
2. Satisfactory execution of technical exercises, including scales and arpeggios in specified keys.
3. Sight-reading facility as indicated by completion of graded sight-reading material.
4. Mastery of various articulations and bowings.
5. Correctness of initial tuning; intonation while playing.
6. Familiarity with music vocabulary, including terms for tempo and dynamics, articulation, keys and key signatures, historical information.
7. Development of good playing posture.
8. Participation in rehearsals of small ensembles.
9. Participation in public performance.
10. Attendance.
11. Punctuality.
12. Care and cleanliness of instrument.
13. Number of minutes of practice—daily or weekly.

The chart is useful as a basis for awards and promotions, including appointment of monitors, accumulation of points for award pins or badges, order of seating, and promotion to advanced classes or performing groups. It is useful also as a basis for regular reports to parents describing the progress of each pupil. These reports are evidence of the school's concern for each pupil and are gratefully received by most parents, stimulating their interest and encouraging them to supervise practice and support participation. Most important, the chart permits each pupil to see the record of his own progress. It stimulates practice and encourages effort toward the completion of graded requirements.

The foundation program, as its name implies, is the basis for all success in the total instrumental program. It includes (1) arousing interest, (2) talent testing and discovery, (3) matching pupils and instruments, (4) providing instruments for pupils, (5) planning for balanced instrumentation, (6) homogeneous and heterogeneous classes, (7) junior bands and orchestras, (8) private instruction, and (9) lesson planning. Every phase is guided by clear and purposeful goals established in accordance with the director's philosophy of music education. The foundation program may consist of many activities and classes or may be reduced to only a few, its extent determined by the size of the total instrumental program, the number of teachers available, and other factors. In any case, the instrumental director plans the foundation program with great care to assure the success of the more advanced instrumental activities and performing groups.

11: *teaching advanced players*

The teaching program in instrumental music does not terminate with the pupil's completion of beginning and intermediate classes. It continues throughout his school years, from the time he enters the program in the elementary school until his graduation from high school. For those who have achieved levels of skill and musicianship close to their potentials, group instruction and performing experience are adequate as means of continued instruction. For those of outstanding talent, private instruction is desirable in addition to these group experiences. The chief responsibility of the school, however, is to provide group instruction and experience.

PERFORMING GROUPS

Instrumental performing groups form the foundation of the instructional program for advanced players. They permit the teacher to instruct large numbers of pupils, are efficient in use of teacher time and school facilities, and provide the performing experience without which advanced players quickly lose interest. The band, orchestra, ensembles of woodwinds, brasses and strings, and the dance band or stage band are included in this portion of the instrumental program. Each organization has its own purpose and offers unique music experience to the participating pupils.

Band

The band has two principal functions. (1) As a concert ensemble it is a magnificent wind instrument. It is expressive, sensitive, has an almost limitless spectrum of tonal colors and dynamics, and is capable of performing many types of music with artistic effect. (2) As a parade organization it is a colorful and impressive spectacle. It is capable of playing stirring music and is usually viewed by the public with enthusiasm because of the musical and visual impressions it creates.

INSTRUMENTATION. Band instrumentation is flexible and has been the subject of many experiments. The experiments have been attempts to improve balance, tone quality, and intonation. They will continue as long as there are band directors interested in developing the band as a medium of artistic music performance. Flexibility exists because there is as yet no firmly established instrumentation pattern. This flexibility is desirable because it permits the director to adjust instrumentation to meet special playing requirements and because the composition of the band is not always a matter of the director's choice. In the public school, instrumentation is often determined by the number of instruments or players available, and these are determined by the school budget and the amount of time the director can devote to instrumental teaching.

The "director's chart," Table 7, shows the band instrumentation that might develop in the junior and senior high schools as the result of an organized program of instrumental instruction. These patterns are neither ideal nor inevitable. Each director establishes his own instrumentation standards in accordance with requirements set by band arrangements, discriminating music taste, and the peculiarities of his own teaching situation. Table 8 is a table showing suggested instrumentations for bands of three different sizes through which any one band might develop. These instrumentation patterns may be regarded as guides for the director as he builds his band and progresses toward his instrumentation goal. They are not ideal or inflexible and should be revised as necessary by the director. The best balance and tonal effect are produced when each director adjusts instrumentation to compensate for such factors in his own situation as the tone qualities of the sections of his band and the acoustics of his rehearsal room and concert hall.

INSTRUMENTATION VARIATIONS. The instrumentation of the band can be revised to compensate for missing instruments, to adjust band tone to different playing conditions, and to create major changes or improvements in the tone quality and intonation of the concert band. Some of these revisions are made from necessity. Others may be made at the discretion of the

TABLE 8. INSTRUMENTATION PATTERNS FOR BANDS OF 30, 60, AND 90 PLAYERS.

Instrument	*30 Players*	*60 Players*	*90 Players*
Flute-piccolo	2	4	6
Oboe & English horn	1	2	3
E-flat clarinet			2
B-flat clarinet	8	18	24
Alto clarinet		1	3
Bass clarinet		1	3
Bassoon		2	2
Soprano saxophone			1
Alto saxophone	1	2	2
Tenor saxophone	1	1	2
Baritone saxophone	1	1	2
Bass saxophone			1
Cornet & trumpet	5	8	10
French horn	3	4	6
Trombone	3	5	6
Baritone	1	2	3
Tuba	2	4	6
String bass		1	2
Percussion	2	4	5
Harp			1

director in accordance with his own taste and judgment. The director may experiment with a variety of tone qualities to create an interesting and unique performing group.

1. Minor changes involving addition of special instruments to improve balance and tone quality or substitutions for missing instruments and those not played well by inexperienced pupils.
    a. Deletion of E-flat clarinets if played with poor intonation by inexperienced pupils.
    b. Addition of contra-bass clarinet to improve balance of clarinet choir.
    c. Deletion of soprano saxophone if played with poor intonation or tone quality by inexperienced pupils.
    d. Addition of lower saxophones (baritone and bass) for increased richness of woodwind choir and to compensate for absence of low brasses.

   e. Addition of fluegelhorn to increase richness of upper brasses.
   f. Substitution of E-flat alto horns if capable French horn players are not available.
2. Changes to improve the effect of music played outdoors and on the march.
   a. Deletion of flutes and substitution of a reasonable number of piccolos.
   b. Deletion of oboes and bassoons.
   c. Deletion of alto and bass clarinets and addition of alto, tenor, and baritone saxophones for increased richness of tone.
   d. Substitution of E-flat alto horns for French horns.
   e. Addition of trombones, baritones, and tubas to increase richness of tone and carrying power.
   f. Deletion of string basses.
   g. Addition of percussion instruments, especially snare and scotch drums.
3. Major changes influencing concert-band tone.
   a. Addition of large numbers of flutes of various keys to create a balanced flute choir, compensated for by reduction in numbers of clarinets.
   b. Addition of large numbers of alto, bass, and contra-bass clarinets to create a balanced clarinet choir, compensated for by reduction or elimination of saxophones.
   c. Addition of brass instruments, especially those of lower register, and reduction in number of woodwinds to approach the tone quality of the brass ensemble.
   d. Reduction of all instruments to approximately one instrument for each part, approaching the tone quality of the wind ensemble.

BAND SEATING. Seating arrangements for the band are as flexible as its instrumentation. Here, again, there is much experimenting to improve balance and tone quality and the director is free to seek the solution most appropriate for the characteristics of his situation. These characteristics include the total number of players, the number of each type of instrument, the relative size of sections, and the size, shape, and acoustics of the rehearsal room and concert hall. Figures 1 and 2 are two possible seating plans. The basic difference between them is in the placement of clarinets, normally the largest single section of the band. Many directors feel the clarinets are best placed in one large section as in Figure 1. Other directors have experimented by dividing the clarinets and placing all woodwinds close to the audience as in Figure 2.

In any arrangement there are almost limitless possibilities for variation. One rarely used plan seats all players in straight rows facing the audience, the conductor moving away from the band to be seen from each stand. The more common seating plans are based on semi-circular rows with the conductor close to or at the center of the first semi-circle. Many variations are possible even in this semi-circular arrangement, but the principles to be considered when determining any seating plan are as follows:

1. Instruments with subdued tone are usually placed toward the front to permit their parts to carry to the audience.
2. Instruments with piercing tone are usually placed toward the rear, behind the screen of tone produced by other instruments.
3. Inner parts are sectioned together to improve their blend and facilitate ensemble playing.
4. Each section is grouped together, including the brass and woodwind sections in total and the sub-sections within each.
5. Flutes and oboes are usually placed well forward so they can be heard and because of the frequency of solo passages in their parts.
6. Basses and percussion are usually placed in the last row, often in the center of the row, to be clearly audible to the rest of the band.
7. Horns are often placed directly in front of tubas, a practice desirable if programmed marches depend on the rhythmic interaction of their parts.
8. Trombones are often placed in the last row because it permits wide spacing and adequate slide room.
9. Baritones are placed where their frequent solo parts can be heard clearly by the audience.
10. Trumpets are placed in the last row because of their piercing tone, often toward the side of the stage so bells point across stage instead of toward the audience.

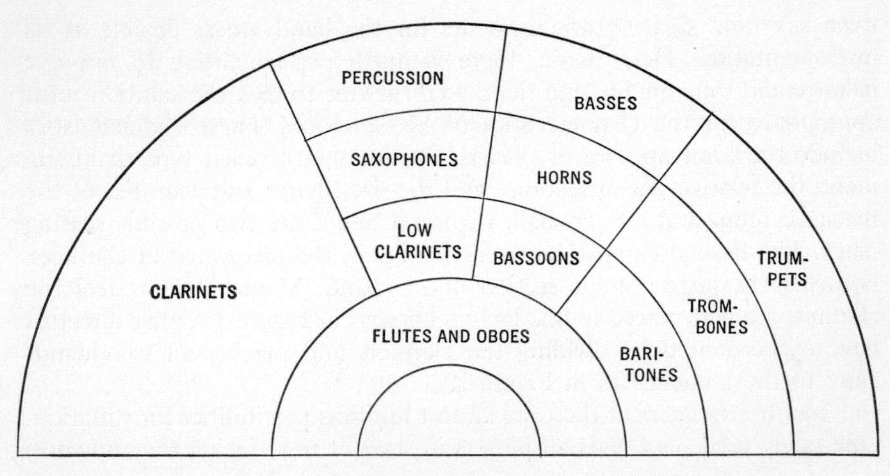

FIGURE 1. BAND SEATING ARRANGEMENT WITH CLARINETS TOGETHER.

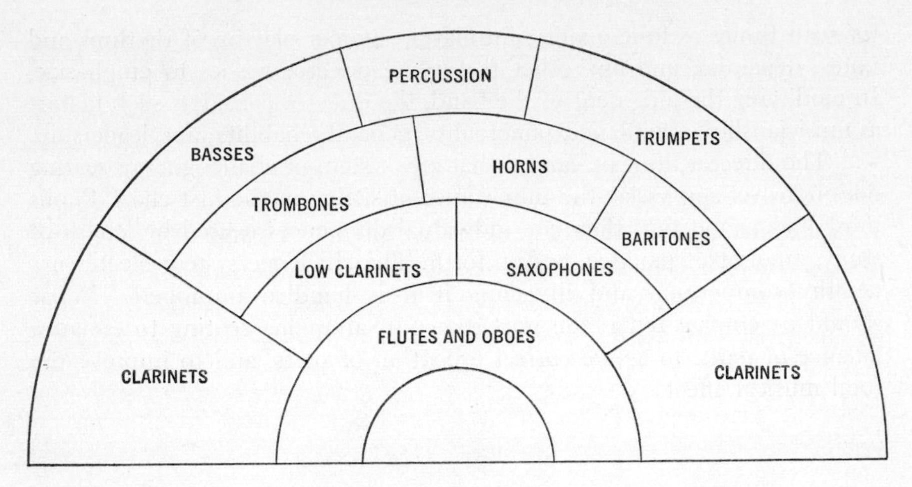

FIGURE 2. BAND SEATING ARRANGEMENT WITH CLARINETS DIVIDED.

SEATING ORDER. Band players are accustomed to being assigned to seats for regular use during rehearsals and performance. There is merit in this practice in that it tends to eliminate confusion and helps pupils ready themselves for playing at the beginning of the rehearsal period. A standard procedure is to place players in order of ability—the best player in the first chair, the next best player in the second chair, and so on. Another possibility is to seat the best players where they can be of most help to pupils of less ability. One such plan is to place advanced players in outside positions on each stand, pairing each with a player of less skill. Another practical plan is to place best players in first chairs in each section—the best player on first stand, first part, the next best player on first stand, second part, the third best player on first stand, third part. This assures that each part will be played equally well and that balance will be even.

Many directors feel it is wise to establish a system of challenging to determine the order of seating. Under this system any player who believes he is qualified for a more advanced chair challenges the player occupying that chair. The two players then compete with each other to determine which merits the higher chair. The players may compete before the rest of the band and with the band itself rendering judgment, the teacher reserving the right to modify the judgment of the band members. This prevents the director from neglecting seating changes and encourages pupils to develop healthy rivalry in improving their playing. It gives the band members experience in evaluating performance and may be regarded as citizenship training. Band members who listen to the play-off are instructed to listen for such things as tone quality, intonation, proper playing of rhythms and notes, dynamics, and any other factor the director wishes to emphasize. In modifying the judgment of the band, the director considers such factors as musicianship, attendance, punctuality, general reliability, and leadership.

The director must be careful that any system of challenging or seating does not over-emphasize the importance of sitting in the first chair. Pupils must understand that there are individual differences caused by length of study, amount of practice, and so forth. The challenge system creates unhealthy competition and ill-feeling if it is handled improperly. What should be emphasized is the importance of arranging seating to enhance balance of parts, to assure correct execution of parts, and to improve the total musical effect.

Orchestra

The orchestra's sole performance function in the public school is that of the concert group. It provides music for school plays, assemblies, and other special events as well as presenting orchestral concerts. It does not match the band in showmanship or public relations value, but excels it in the artistic presentation of standard concert music.

One of the tragedies of today's school-music scene is that the orchestra does not occupy a more prominent place among the performing groups. The orchestra is in many communities a neglected organization, partly because of the difficulty of training string players in the limited time available to the teacher. Another factor is the unfortunate impression made by some school orchestras in the early and more recent years of music education. In many schools the "orchestra" consisted of a few strings, piano, "trap" drums, and large numbers of winds. This mixture of instruments was necessary to make performance possible but created the effect of a "pit band" rather than an orchestra. In other schools, large orchestras with almost a full complement of strings played with such poor intonation that their concerts were painful experiences for even the untrained ear. This situation is almost unavoidable if string players are placed in the orchestra before they have had sufficient training. Yet the orchestra can be a superb performance medium and can be developed through the public-school instrumental program.

The solution to this problem is chiefly a matter of teacher time and budgeted funds. What seems to be a lack of interest in string playing can be overcome. It has been said that teachers, pupils, and parents have little interest in string teaching or playing. This is not surprising in view of the absence of organized string programs in many schools. There can be no string program if there is no interest, and there can be little interest in what does not exist. For pupils, interest can be aroused if there are opportunities to see and hear string performances and opportunities to play a string instrument. For parents, interest can be created if the results of string teaching can be demonstrated. For many teachers, interest is futile because there is no time in the schedule for string teaching and because instruments are not available. If these conditions are remedied, the teacher's interest is revived. The organized string program can begin early in the elementary school and can be nourished until it produces the outstanding performing groups possible at the high-school level.

INSTRUMENTATION. The instrumentation of the orchestra is less flexible than that of the band. Its general pattern has been established by existing professional orchestras and the requirements of standard orchestral literature. There are fewer simplified arrangements and transcriptions for school orchestras than for bands and much of orchestral literature is most effective when performed by the prescribed instrumentation.

Table 9 is a chart showing suggested instrumentations for orchestras of three different sizes. Like the instrumentations suggested for bands, they are not inflexible. They can be adjusted by the director to meet the needs

TABLE 9. INSTRUMENTATION PATTERNS FOR ORCHESTRAS OF 30, 60, AND 90 PLAYERS.

Instrument	*30 Players*	*60 Players*	*90 Players*
Flute-piccolo	2	2	3
Oboe		2	2
Clarinet	2	2	2
Bassoon		2	2
French horn	2	4	4
Trumpet	2	3	3
Trombone	2	3	3
Tuba		1	1
Percussion	2	3	4
Harp			1
Violin I	6	12	20
Violin II	4	10	18
Viola	3	6	10
Cello	3	6	10
Bass	2	4	7

of his pupils and should be experimented with to determine the best proportions for tone quality and balance under local conditions.

INSTRUMENTATION VARIATIONS. Variations in the instrumentation pattern are due principally to the differences among requirements established by composers of the baroque, classic, romantic, and other periods. These differences provide flexibility to meet the needs of many teaching situations. The director with a small orchestra or an ensemble of strings only can turn to music of the baroque and early classic periods. There is a distinct advantage in doing so in that music of this era is often in easily playable keys, contains few accidentals, uses plateau dynamics, is rhythmically regular, and does not rely on difficult bowings. The director of a larger orchestra with a small complement of winds can select from music of the late classic and early romantic periods. Here too there is music suited to the abilities of young players. Selections from contemporary music can be played by the normal orchestra, sometimes with the addition of a small number of winds and percussion. For the beginning orchestra, there are published collections of graded pieces and easy arrangements of standard favorites.

Other variations in the instrumentation pattern are possible when it is necessary to compensate for missing instruments or to give orchestral experience to larger numbers of pupils. String sections can be expanded or reduced within reasonable limits. Flutes, B-flat clarinets, and alto and bass clarinets can be substituted for missing oboes and bassoons. Certain woodwind parts can be doubled and alternate players can be provided for brass parts. The practice to be avoided is that of compensating for missing strings by substituting instruments of the brass and woodwind families. The characteristic string tone is a requisite for the orchestra. If strings are too few to permit the formation of an orchestra, the director is better advised to organize them as one or more small ensembles.

SEATING ARRANGEMENT. The seating arrangement of the orchestra has been generally established during the years of its growth. There is less variation than in the seating arrangements for the band because of the relative newness of the concert band and the continuing experiments to improve its concert effect. The chief differences in orchestral seating are those resulting from differences in size and instrumentation. The small orchestra playing baroque and early classic music may use a seating plan different from that of the large orchestra playing late romantic and contemporary music. The addition of large numbers of winds and percussion, and the distribution of solo passages among relatively unusual instruments, sometimes requires a revision of the seating plan.

Figures 3 and 4 are diagrams of two possible seating arrangements. The principal difference between them is in the placement of violins, the heart of orchestral tone. Figure 3 shows what is perhaps the most popular arrangement with all violins to the conductor's left. Figure 4 shows an arrangement which places first violins to the conductor's left and second violins to his right. Possibilities for variation of these seating arrangements are many and it is to the conductor's advantage to experiment with different arrangements to discover which is best for his orchestra.

The factors to be considered in planning the seating arrangement are as follows:

1. Violin sections are seated together and placed where they can be heard by the audience. Because the instrument rests on the violinist's left shoulder with f-holes pointed toward his right, violins are most frequently seated to the conductor's left so that f-holes, rather than the backs of the instruments, face the audience.
2. Violas are sometimes given seating preference because they are usually few in number but must be heard. They might best be placed to the conductor's left if that position were not occupied by first violins. As an alternative, violas are often placed next to the first violins to the conductor's left, as in Figure 4, or next to the cellos and almost in front of the conductor, as in Figure 3.
3. Cellos are less of a problem than the other strings because their playing position tends to direct the tone forward. They are usually seated to the conductor's right, chiefly because other locations to his left are occupied by other strings.
4. Basses, like violins and violas, are somewhat "directional" in tone. They are normally played in a position that directs the tone to the player's right. For this reason they too might be best placed to the conductor's left so that f-holes face the audience. Because they frequently play passages in octaves with cellos, however, basses are usually placed in the last row near the cello section.
5. Flutes, oboes, clarinets, and bassoons are seated well forward near the middle of the orchestral semi-circle. This permits their tone to carry to the audience and places them together to facilitate playing of ensemble passages.
6. Horns are seated near both woodwinds and brasses but as far forward as the seating plan permits. Their tone then carries to the audience and they can join either woodwinds or brasses in ensemble passages.
7. Trumpets, trombones, and tuba are placed toward the rear and grouped together as a section with the tuba close to both percussion and basses.

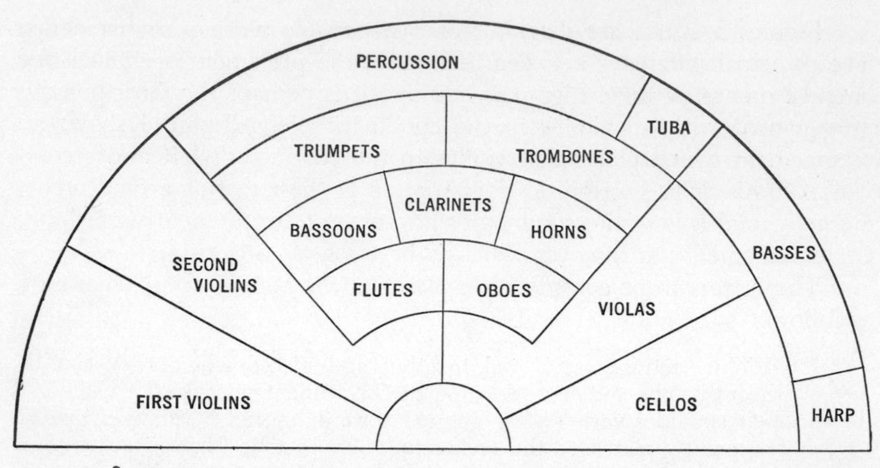

FIGURE 3. SEATING ARRANGEMENT FOR ORCHESTRA WITH VIOLINS TOGETHER.

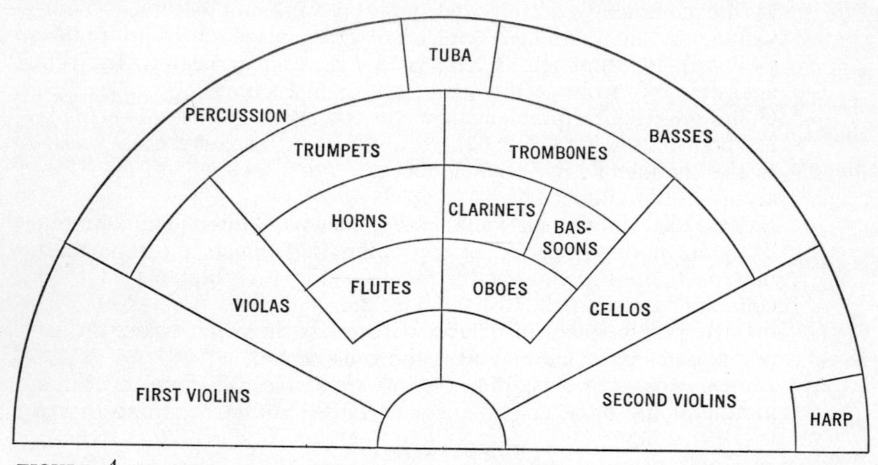

FIGURE 4. SEATING ARRANGEMENT FOR ORCHESTRA WITH VIOLINS DIVIDED.

SEATING ORDER. Considerations affecting seating order in the orchestra are similar to those mentioned in relationship to the band. Better players are seated where they are most useful to the orchestra and where they can be of most help to players of less ability. The challenge system is helpful in determining the placement of large numbers of strings and is an incentive to pupil progress.

It is especially important in the orchestra that better players be distributed throughout the sections instead of being concentrated at the first several stands. There are often wide differences of ability among the string players and many of the less advanced players need help with bowings, fingerings, and positions. For this reason it is desirable to place violinists in this order:

Player 1: Violin I, first stand, first chair
Player 2: Violin II, first stand, first chair
Player 3: Violin I, second stand, first chair
Player 4: Violin II, second stand, first chair

In this arrangement, better players occupy first-chair positions at each stand and less able players occupy second-chair positions at each stand. A good player is paired with a weaker player at each stand. First and second violins are well matched in both tone and technical facility. Bowings will be more nearly uniform. When pages are turned, usually by the second-chair player at each stand, the strings retain much of their tone. If better players are concentrated at the first several stands, string tone may drop as much as 75% at each page turn because half of the better players must stop playing to turn the page and many of the less able players at rear stands become confused or lose their places. In addition to following these general principles, the conductor who knows his players can pair pupils at stands for instructional, psychological, social, or other reasons and may find that minor changes in seating order result in major improvements in the playing of the orchestra.

Small Ensembles

Pupils can be drawn from both the band and the orchestra, as well as from junior groups, as indicated in Chapter 10, to form small instrumental ensembles. Because small ensembles are of great interest to pupils and are an especially effective medium of instruction if properly supervised by the teacher, they are a virtual necessity in the instrumental program. Many different sizes and instrumentations are common, making it possible for the teacher to provide ensemble experience for almost any combination of instruments and any number of interested pupils.

VALUES. As mentioned in Chapter 7 in the discussion of vocal music, small ensembles are an outlet for the advanced skills of talented pupils and offer invaluable training in musicianship. Ensemble players quickly learn the necessity for developing ensemble disciplines. They gain concepts of tone quality, intonation, and rhythmic precision they would develop much more slowly, if at all, in the band or orchestra. Ensembles lighten the performance load of the larger groups by providing music for PTA, service clubs, churches, and other community organizations that otherwise would call on the band or orchestra. They lighten the rehearsal schedules of the larger groups also by presenting ensemble selections at band and orchestra concerts and reducing the quantity of music that must be prepared by the larger group.

Small ensembles are an excellent means of influencing community attitudes toward music and the school music program. The ensembles can be of markedly higher caliber than the larger organizations and make better impressions on the public. They can be readily available, permitting the teacher to accept requests from community organizations immediately without concerning himself with the problems of transporting a large band or orchestra of from sixty to one hundred players. The ensembles are unique, rarely heard by many of those who make up concert audiences, and can be relied on to arouse interest.

Ensembles are especially worthwhile, particularly those made up of strings, because they are helpful in achieving one of the principal goals of music education. The intent of music education is to give pupils something they can carry into their later lives and into their homes. Bands and orchestras accomplish this when they develop appreciative attitudes among their members, but the instrumental skills they teach are useful only to the relatively few pupils who continue to play in professional or amateur groups. Pupils who discover the pleasures of playing with small ensembles, however, can continue this kind of music participation much more easily than membership in bands and orchestras. String players, and woodwind and brass players to a lesser degree, can discover these pleasures and develop permanent interest in chamber-music playing through the school-music program. For this reason, the teacher is justified in stressing ensemble participation and in devoting large blocks of school time to ensemble training.

ENSEMBLE TYPES. Although ensembles can be formed with many different combinations of instruments, not all are practical due to the difficulty of finding published arrangements suitable for young players. The more popular ensembles, consisting of three or more players and for which materials are readily available, are as follows:

Woodwind Ensembles

Flute trio
B-flat clarinet trio
B-flat clarinet quartet
Saxophone quartet
Mixed clarinet quartet
(2 B-flat, 1 bass, 1 alto or 3 B-flat, 1 bass)
Woodwind quintet

Brass Ensembles

Trumpet trio
Trombone trio
Horn quartet
Trombone quartet
Brass quartet
(2 trumpets and 2 trombones or 2 trumpets, horn, and trombone)
Brass sextet

String Ensembles

String trio
String quartet
String quintet
Many ensembles of various strings with and without piano

Percussion Ensembles
Drum trio—3 snare drums
Drum quartet—4 snare drums
Percussion quartet—2 snare drums, cymbals, bass drum
Percussion quintet—3 snare drums, cymbals, bass drum
Other ensembles of from five to eleven players

The saxophone quartet and brass sextet are worthy of special mention. Saxophones have sometimes been regarded as undesirable instruments by instrumental directors, chiefly because they are too frequently played with poor tone and intonation by young players. The saxophone quartet is a means of remedying these playing difficulties by giving young players experience with the kind of music that requires good musicianship. A large amount of material is available for saxophone quartet, much of it of outstanding quality, and the teacher who investigates it for the first time is likely to be agreeably surprised by the musical potential of the ensemble. The brass sextet is an equally worthy ensemble, although not as neglected as the saxophone quartet. It may consist of two trumpets, two trombones, baritone, and tuba, or the instrumentation may be varied by the inclusion of French horns. For this group there is also a wealth of published material of good quality. The balance of brass sonorities and the expressive potential of the group make the brass sextet an effective performance medium and a rewarding experience for pupils.

PUPIL SELECTION. Small ensembles are not for talented pupils only. They are a means of instruction which should be open to all. This includes members of junior bands and orchestras, as mentioned in Chapter 10, and all members of advanced performing groups. In forming ensembles, however, the director groups players according to ability. This is necessary if each ensemble is to develop satisfactorily, studying music suited to the players' ability. Some ensembles will be composed of advanced pupils, others of those who play less well. All ensembles are given opportunities to perform, but those composed of advanced players and capable of artistic performance appear in public more frequently, especially in response to requests from community organizations.

Because of the popularity and utility of the well-rehearsed small ensemble and the frequency with which it may appear at other than school functions, the teacher strives to develop qualities of independence and responsibility in the players. To this end, he selects players on the basis of character as well as musicianship and appoints student directors, especially in the better ensembles. The student director is able to take charge of ensemble rehearsals, selecting music and special passages to be rehearsed, checking tuning, setting tempos, and being generally responsible for the conduct of the group. When the ensemble appears in public, especially at community functions, the student director may be assigned the responsibility of supervising not only the performance, but the conduct of the group when away from school as well. This practice is desirable. It permits the teacher to send ensembles to community functions without sacrificing his own teaching time and, more important, develops leadership qualities in ensemble players.

Dance Band

The dance or stage band is a small ensemble and is affected by many of the factors discussed in the preceding section. It is an outlet for talented pupils and offers musicianship training. It has many values and is flexible enough to be useful in almost any school situation.

GENERAL VALUES. The dance band can be relied on to arouse strong interest among all pupils and is especially effective in sustaining the interest of advanced pupils not strongly attracted to other music activities. It has entertainment value for non-participating pupils, is a useful adjunct to school shows and can provide music for school dances. It is like other ensembles in that it develops qualities of independence and responsibility. The dance band can be a means of elevating taste through development of appreciation of the jazz idiom and various jazz styles. It is desirable as vocational training for those who plan to play professionally in later years and is better conducted under teacher supervision than at the initiative of pupils and without competent guidance.

MUSIC VALUES. The dance band is an instructional device through which pupils learn a unique type of musicianship. It requires intense concentration on the disciplines of ensemble playing. It develops perfection of intonation and blend essential because of the complex chords common to popular music. It promotes rapid development of reading facility and a feeling for rhythmic precision. For advanced players it goes beyond the experiences of band and orchestra playing by creating sensitivity to certain niceties of playing such as evenness of vibrato and the matching of tone qualities.

The elements of music theory can be taught more effectively through the dance band than through larger performing groups. It provides incentive for formation of classes in music theory and arouses pupil interest in arranging. It can teach transposition and ranges of instruments, including the tone qualities and characteristics of their various registers. The experience with popular music develops a feeling for chord progression and a knowledge of chord structure. The teacher will find that many pupils who become interested in dance-band playing and arranging progress to broader interests and increased knowledge of many areas of music learning.

INSTRUMENTATION. The instrumentation of the dance or stage band is flexible. It may vary from the small group of five or six players to the large orchestra of five saxophones, four trumpets, three trombones, rhythm instruments, and strings. The large ensemble is effective because of the variety of effects it can produce. The small group may be of more interest and result in more rapid music progress for advanced players, but it is impractical in some instances because it requires especially capable instrumentalists, is best suited to improvisation, and exposes the skill or lack of it possessed by each player. The standard instrumentation is most practical because it can use published arrangements, but other combinations are useful in that they stimulate interest in arranging.

SELECTION OF PUPILS. The teacher exercises considerable care in his selection of dance-band members. They must be capable instrumentalists with feeling for the jazz idiom, strong rhythmic sense, good tone, and sensitivity to intonation. Leadership qualities are needed because the dance band functions with the same independence as other ensembles. Scholarship and general character are worthy of consideration because dance-band players are looked up to by other pupils in the instrumental program and occupy prominent positions at many school affairs.

SPECIAL CLASSES

Although performing groups are the foundation of the school instrumental program, supplementary instruction is needed for the improvement of both the performing groups and the participating pupils. The group instruction provided by band, orchestra, and ensembles is not sufficient for advanced players who have strong interests in instrumental music. They need either private lessons or a type of group instruction that offers intensive training similar to that gained through study with a private teacher. Among the possibilities for this intensive training, for both advanced and other pupils, are sectional rehearsals, technique classes, and special lessons.

Sectional Rehearsals

Sectional rehearsals are desirable for both band and orchestra. Devoted to careful rehearsal of concert literature, they save time in the rehearsals of the larger group and greatly improve its performance. As the group rehearses concert selections it can omit long rests during which other sections of the band or orchestra play alone. Phrasings, attacks, dynamics, balance, and blend can be worked out carefully in terms of the instruments of that section. The sectional rehearsal permits the teacher to devote class time to technique studies and improves the playing of individuals as well as that of the total group. Because instruments are normally of the same family, teaching is simplified and the teacher can give attention to individual problems. The problems of any one player are encountered by all pupils in the group and the same exercises can be studied profitably by all.

SECTIONAL GROUPINGS. The band can be separated into two sections, woodwinds alone and brass and percussion together. Further subdivision is useful if rehearsal time can be arranged, often on a less frequent basis or as needed. All B-flat clarinets can meet together to study particularly difficult passages. All lower brasses of the band, or cellos and basses of the orchestra, can meet for special rehearsals as needed. The orchestra, of course, is normally subdivided into one group of strings alone, another of winds and percussion together.

SCHEDULING. When schedule arrangements permit, the director may find it desirable to schedule rehearsals of major sections on a regular basis. If there is a possibility of five band rehearsals each week, for example, the band may progress more rapidly by meeting only three times each week if the remaining two periods are used for one woodwind rehearsal and one brass and percussion rehearsal. Time is often wasted, however, if the smaller sub-sections are scheduled for regular meetings. A weekly meeting of cellos and basses, for example, is often unprofitable. Although these players would derive benefits from regular sectional instruction, the teacher accomplishes more by reserving regularly scheduled meetings for larger groups and working with the smaller sub-sections in unscheduled time before or after school when the need arises.

The regularly scheduled sectional rehearsal is desirable in the school instrumental program. It leads the teacher to plan teaching procedures in terms of the instrumentation of that section and to search for materials of many kinds for use with the instruments of each family. It encourages pupils to prepare for rehearsals, practicing difficult passages, readying themselves for recitation, and prompting them to ask the teacher about individual problems. If available schedule hours are few, sectional rehearsals can be scheduled on a rotating basis, brasses meeting one week, woodwinds the next. If no schedule hours are available, sectional rehearsals can be held before or after school or during homeroom and activity periods.

TEACHING PROCEDURE. As indicated above, the sectional rehearsal can be devoted to practice of literature being prepared for concert performance, to technique instruction, or to both. If concert pieces are used, the director selects passages for study by the section, usually practicing these passages only instead of taking time to read through the entire composition. He chooses passages by studying the score of the selection before it is read through by the concert group, or marks passages during the rehearsal of the concert group for intensive practice in subsequent sectional rehearsals. If technique is to be studied, he provides collections of exercises, method books, and other suitable materials. Some of these may be used during rehearsals of the concert group, but others are purchased for the use of the sectional group only. Because the sectional group is small, it is practical as a means of instruction in matters other than concert literature and technique—posture, breathing, tone quality, intonation, and reading. If instruments are of the same family, there is the further possibility of using special materials written for small woodwind, brass, or string ensembles, doubling parts if necessary to permit all pupils to participate. In many respects, the sectional rehearsal is a class lesson and utilizes the procedures described under that heading in Chapter 10.

Technique Classes

The technique class differs from the sectional rehearsal in composition, scheduling, and teaching procedure. Its objective, as the name implies, is to develop technique and general playing ability. It is not intended for the practice of concert literature, although band and orchestra parts can be used for instructional purposes. The intent of the class is to improve technique, breathing, articulation, tone quality, and ability to play the literature characteristic of each instrument. The class is of value because it is part of the continuing program of instrumental teaching and raises the level of ability of individual pupils.

COMPOSITION OF THE CLASS. The technique class, like others in the school instrumental program, is an attempt to achieve the benefits of private study through group instruction. It is usually a homogeneous grouping of like instruments or of instruments of the same family, although it is possible in rare instances to conduct the class successfully if the instruments form a heterogeneous group. The class is composed of advanced players and the material it studies is devoted to the technical peculiarities of each instrument. For this reason, the class is most successful when it is small in size, is made up of identical instruments, and includes players of similar ability. The larger class of unlike instruments creates teaching problems because exercises necessary for technique development for one instrument can not be played by the others of the group.

The ideal technique class consists of from two to six identical instruments—four to six B-flat clarinets, trumpets or violins, two oboes or bassoons, four trombones or French horns. It is impractical if it consists of more than six or eight pupils because the possibilities for effective teaching decrease as the number of pupils increases, and it is impractical for scheduling and budget reasons if too few pupils are included.

SCHEDULING. Technique classes are best scheduled on a regular basis, meeting at the same time week after week. Because of the small numbers of pupils involved, this can sometimes be accomplished by forming classes from pupils in study halls, homeroom, or other activity periods. To plan the program more effectively, the instrumental director announces a tentative schedule of available class times. He talks with pupils and suggests arrangements of their academic programs that will permit participation in a technique class. By planning in this way, and with the coöperation of administrators and other teachers, it is possible to form technique classes of carefully selected pupils by drawing them only from what would otherwise be free periods.

When it is possible to rely wholly on free-period scheduling, the schedules are easy to arrange. When free-period scheduling is impossible, the rotating schedule can be used. This requires the director to make up a roster of technique classes and the pupils in each, and a calendar showing the date and time of every meeting of every class. Each class meeting is scheduled at a different time or on a different day. The French horn class, for example, might follow this schedule: first week, Monday at 9:00; second week, Monday at 10:00; third week, Monday at 11:00; and so on. Meeting only once each week, pupils in the French horn class would be absent from any one academic or other class not more often than once in six weeks. Although it is not desirable to rely on any system that requires consistent absence from academic courses, the relative infrequency of absence under the rotating schedule makes it acceptable in many schools. Once the practice is approved by administrators and other teachers, copies of the roster and calendar are given to all concerned to serve as excuses and records of absence.

TEACHING THE CLASS. The subject matter of the technique class is that of the private lesson and homogeneous class. It places emphasis on the development of general musicianship and specific instrumental techniques, including alternate fingerings, mastery of extremes of range, and advanced problems of fingering, embouchure, and articulation. The materials used are chiefly method books and collections of technique exercises, but attention is given to the preparation of solos and ensemble pieces if time permits. Although the class is not intended for study of band and orchestra parts, these are used if they contribute to the lesson or if particularly difficult passages merit class time. Assignments for outside practice are made regularly and checked during subsequent lessons.

Each lesson follows a basic teaching pattern. The sequence may be added to or shortened as necessary, or the order of the lesson may be changed, but the plan of the lesson provides for each of these activities:

1. *Warm-up and review.* The class plays exercises or pieces learned previously, warming up, adjusting tuning, and reviewing simultaneously.
2. *Technique practice.* The class plays previously assigned exercises for additional practice and further development of technique or musicianship.
3. *Recitation.* Pupils play individually or in groups of two or three to permit the teacher to judge whether assignments have been satisfactorily completed.
4. *Solo playing.* Individual pupils play portions of assigned solos for criticism by the teacher and other class members.
5. *Assignment.* New materials are presented, read through to identify passages needing explanation or special practice, and assignments are made for the next lesson.
6. *Culmination.* The class plays material learned during earlier lessons, including ensemble pieces which offer satisfaction and a sense of achievement.

The lesson procedure described above is suited to the class made up of identical instruments. It is not practical if the pupils available during any one period form a heterogeneous mixture of instruments. The heterogeneous mixture sometimes occurs when the teacher is unable to plan a schedule of technique classes and must teach as best he can with pupils drawn from study halls. One solution is a system of supervised practice. Each pupil is assigned a practice room for the lesson hour and works by himself for a portion of the hour. The teacher visits each practice room in turn, spending as much time as possible with each pupil, checking assignments, criticising the pupil's performance, and assigning new work. This arrangement is less desirable than the class lesson, but does permit technique instruction where class lessons are impossible.

Special Lessons

The several methods mentioned in Chapter 10 for securing private instruction are appropriate for advanced pupils as well as beginning players. Private lessons can be offered by members of the school instrumental-music staff, private teachers of the community, or school-approved fee teachers. One problem in the use of fee teachers is that many states prohibit in-school instruction by persons who do not possess state certificates. Some laws apply to all teachers who use school facilities or are sanctioned by the schools in any way, whether salaries are paid by the school board or fees are paid by the pupil to the teacher. Each instrumental director is responsible for discussing any proposed program of private instruction with his principal or superintendent and making certain it does not conflict with established laws or school policy.

THE SCHOOL STAFF. The instrumental director and other members of the instrumental staff are free to offer special lessons during whatever time they can make available. The lessons can be given without fee during free periods or before or after school. In some communities, members of the school staff can give private lessons for a fee without incurring criticism as long as the lessons are not given during school time. In general, however, it is not desirable for school personnel to give private lessons in school unless a large staff is hired for the purpose and lessons are scheduled in school time. This is a desirable arrangement, but one few school budgets can support.

In most schools, the instrumental director and other teachers can ill afford to devote hours during the school day to private instruction. To do so, they must take time away from class work and burden themselves with more teaching duties than can be performed effectively. At best, the teachers of the school staff can free enough time to teach only a few private lessons to advanced pupils. Other members of the performing groups are then denied lessons and the disparity becomes even more pronounced between advanced pupils and those who receive no instruction. Finally, it is not common for the instrumental teacher to know all instruments of the band and orchestra well enough to give competent instruction to advanced pupils. In doing so, he may either retard their progress or teach them incorrectly.

COMMUNITY TEACHERS. For advanced players, it is necessary to find private teachers who are both skilled instrumentalists and competent teachers. These are available in many communities. Once a system of private instruction is formulated, they can be made available to all pupils in the instrumental program. The easiest, but not necessarily best, way to encourage private study is to describe its benefits to band and orchestra members and to urge them to seek private teachers. This saves time for the instrumental director, who is spared the necessity of planning an effective instructional program, but permits pupils to choose teachers without guidance. As a result, their work with a community teacher may lead to slow progress or faulty playing habits.

A better way, and one that requires time and tact of the instrumental director, is to compile a list of approved private teachers. The list is distributed to pupils and parents with the strong recommendation that pupils study with one of the teachers listed. Before compiling the list, the instrumental director must find a satisfactory means of evaluating the private teachers of the community. This can be done by (1) announcing that a system of private study is to be established, (2) that private teachers are invited to submit their credentials for school approval, and (3) that credentials will be evaluated according to specified criteria. Criteria can include such factors as diplomas and certificates, conservatory or other study, and experience with professional bands and orchestras. This is the point at which the instrumental director must exercise tact and good judgment. Ill will is created easily if standards are not carefully formulated and applied and if they are not endorsed by school authorities.

Fee Teachers

Competent musicians of the community can be utilized as fee teachers giving lessons in school and, if possible, in school time during pupils' free periods. Because it is difficult to find time in the school day for private instruction, some teachers begin by establishing instruction periods after school or on Saturdays. Fee teachers are brought to the school at these times for full schedules of private lessons and fees are paid by pupils either weekly to the fee teacher or on a monthly or semester basis to the school office. The Saturday-morning session is popular, especially where transportation is available to and from the school and where other activities do not occupy Saturday mornings for the pupils. The instrumental director selects private teachers for each instrument and assigns a practice room or classroom to each teacher. Pupils come to the school for their lessons and often stay for the entire morning, participating in ensembles, sectional rehearsals, or even a full band or orchestra rehearsal if time permits. If the Saturday-morning program grows, and more pupils apply for lessons than can be scheduled in one morning, the program can be extended to include one or more weekday afternoons.

SUMMER PROGRAMS. A useful extension of the fee-teacher program is the summer band or orchestra school. The summer program is especially successful because many pupils have little to occupy them during the summer months and welcome the opportunity to participate in school-centered music activities. From the director's point of view, the summer program is desirable because it is a means of giving continuity to the program. It sustains interest through the long summer vacation and prevents the loss of skill gained during the regular school year.

The summer band or orchestra can be extended through a long period of four or six weeks, or even through the entire summer. If so, it meets infrequently, perhaps on Saturday mornings only. As part of the program, pupils take lessons from fee teachers and participate in ensembles, sectional and full rehearsals as in the Saturday sessions held during the school year. This long term is impractical for a number of reasons. It interferes with family vacation plans, attendance at summer camps, and pupils' summer employment. It requires the teacher's presence for many weeks without providing full-time teaching opportunities. It requires that the school building be opened only one day each week through a period of many weeks, an inconvenient and costly schedule. For these reasons, the long summer program is not in general favor.

The two-week summer program is more practical. It is most conveniently scheduled in August, shortly before the beginning of school in September. It then permits pupils to "warm up" for the coming year, recovering from the effects of an idle summer by strengthening embouchures and regaining technique and general playing facility. The two-week session can be filled with intensive work. The group meets as many as five mornings each week, taking lessons and practicing with ensembles, sections, and the entire group. Fee teachers take part in the program by giving lessons, coaching ensembles, and assisting with sectional or full rehearsals. Pupils regain much of their instrumental facility and at the end of the summer program look forward to the beginning of school with revived interest.

GROUP INSTRUCTION AND PERFORMANCE

School bands and orchestras, as indicated earlier in this chapter, are instructional groups. They are part of the school program because they are teaching devices. Their entertainment and public relations functions, though of value to the school, are not their reasons for existence. For the same reason, band and orchestra rehearsals are in many respects more important than the concerts to which they lead. The director gains more contact hours with the pupils and has more opportunity to teach during rehearsals than at concerts. Concerts and other public appearances are instructional devices also. They provide motivation for practice, raise pupil performance to a peak of excellence seldom achieved during rehearsal, and are unforgettable experiences pupils carry with them into later life.

Instruction through Rehearsal

The general goals of the band and orchestra rehearsal are similar to those discussed in Chapter 8 in reference to choral performing groups. The rehearsal is a means of teaching musicianship and instrumental technique, building familiarity with band and orchestra literature, developing appreciation and taste, and preparing concert programs. From the point of view of music education, music appreciation is possibly the most important of these objectives.

REHEARSAL GOALS AND CONTENT. The instructional program for members of advanced performing groups is a continuation of the program for beginning and intermediate groups. The goals and content listed here and discussed in detail under *The Class Lesson* in Chapter 10 apply to all instruction given to advanced players, whether in special classes or in rehearsals.

1. The study of progressively more difficult music.
2. Steady improvement in instrumental skills.
3. Steady improvement in musicianship.
4. Development of rehearsal disciplines.
5. Learning proper care and use of instrument.
6. Becoming acquainted with the history of instruments.
7. Understanding the acoustical principles of instruments.
8. Surveying music history and literature.
9. Learning about harmony and music form.
10. Gaining awareness of music styles.

For advanced performing groups, these goals are adjusted to the skills and knowledge of the members. Instead of progressively more difficult music, the band or orchestra might study music of different types or of progressively better quality. Less attention need be given to the development of rehearsal disciplines and to training in proper care and use of instruments. Study in the areas of music history and literature, harmony, form, and music style is devoted to more advanced learnings once foundations have been laid in earlier classes.

The director achieves these goals through rehearsal planning and the selection of appropriate music. Some music is selected because it can be played well in performance, because it suits the tastes of audiences and band or orchestra players, or because it displays the capabilities of the performing group effectively. Other music is selected for instructional purposes. Ensemble exercises and pieces contribute to the development of technique and musicianship. Concert selections, as well as pieces studied only in rehearsal, add to the knowledge of music history, harmony, or style. The director chooses music for study with these thoughts in mind, giving attention to the general music development of each pupil as well as to the requirements of a concert schedule.

REHEARSAL PLANNING. Because the rehearsal is in actuality a music lesson, it is planned with the same care as a lesson for the general music or other class. The procedures in planning discussed in detail in Chapter 6 are applicable to the band or orchestra rehearsal, especially the items discussed under *Principles of Planning.*

1. Choose music appropriate to pupil background and ability, attitudes, and interests.
2. Select music to aid in achieving the specific learning goal or goals of each rehearsal.
3. Devise rehearsal procedures to emphasize learning goals.
4. Search for a means of arousing interest in the skills or knowledges to be learned.
5. Visualize the sequence of rehearsal activities, revising it as necessary

in accordance with principles of (a) approach, (b) participation, (c) activity, (d) variety, (e) tempo.

6. Write a lesson plan, including an estimated allotment of time for each activity.

Intensive score study is required for proper rehearsal planning. The director who begins rehearsal without having studied the score, with the feeling that he reads with more facility than the players and can sight-read his way through rehearsal, is unfair to himself and to the performing group. He sacrifices rehearsal efficiency and music progress. He also creates confusion, disorder, and discipline problems, especially when dealing with performing groups in the public schools. Band and orchestra players are quick to detect the conductor's lack of preparation, lose respect for his ability and interest, and soon reflect his careless attitude in their playing.

Score study shows the need for many rehearsal activities. It permits the conductor to identify passages meriting special study because of technical difficulties or problems of balance, dynamics, phrasing, and intonation. It discloses opportunities for music teaching in the peculiarities of form, harmonic structure, melodic character, and rhythmic pattern of each selection. Finally, it permits the conductor to become familiar with the score and improves the precision, authority, and expressiveness of his conducting.

Once the conductor decides upon his rehearsal program, he prepares a written lesson plan like that of the classroom teacher. The conductor's plan includes the sequence of rehearsal activities, special devices or procedures for emphasis of the knowledge to be learned, notes concerning passages needing special practice, and is written in the form of a timed schedule of events. The estimation of time is essential. It permits the conductor to fill the rehearsal hour with productive work, prevents him from scheduling more work than can be done in one rehearsal, and improves the tempo of his teaching. After rehearsal, the conductor notes on his plan any comments of use to him as he plans subsequent rehearsals and files each plan for future reference. Depending on the skill and experience of the conductor, the plan may be either a full sheet of detailed notations or a card bearing little more than titles of selections and the measure numbers identifying sections for intensive practice. In either case, the plan itself is a necessity and few conductors are successful in rehearsal without it.

REHEARSAL PROCEDURE. The procedure for band and orchestra rehearsals is similar to that for the beginning class described in Chapter 10 and the advanced technique class discussed earlier in this chapter. It may place less emphasis on technique and more on the preparation of music for performance, but follows the same basic procedure. As in other class lessons, routine saves time, variety increases interest, and the cardinal rule is to talk little and play much. These activities are desirable in every rehearsal:

1. Warm-up and tuning.
2. Review of material introduced in previous rehearsals.
3. Technique study through use of ensemble drills.
4. Presentation of new music.
5. Working out of problems in either new or familiar materials.
6. Sight-reading practice.
7. Culmination.

Technique study in the rehearsal of the performing group includes articulation exercises, scales and arpeggios, rhythm drill, and exercises using long tones and gradations in dynamics for development of tone in wind instruments. Rhythm drills can be played from exercise books, read from the board, or played back after dictation by the teacher. They can be played by all instruments in unison, clapped or tapped by the pupils, or pronounced using a neutral syllable such as "ta."

The presentation of new music includes the use of motivating devices unless the judgment of the conductor indicates that no special motivation is needed. As motivation, it is useful to play a recording in which the new selection is performed artistically by a professional band or orchestra. The intent is not only to arouse interest, but to give players concepts of execution, interpretation, and the total effect of the music in finished performance. Interest can sometimes be aroused by brief comments about the composition of the music, its place in history, anecdotes about earlier performances, or the presentation of other information.

The "working out" portion of the rehearsal is distributed among the other activities as needed. It is appropriate for review materials, for technique exercises, and for new music. Where new music is concerned, the conductor isolates passages as necessary and rehearses the group long enough to point the way to solution of technical or other difficulties. Once players understand the passages and know the correct fingerings or the effect desired, they are assigned further practice outside of rehearsal so these passages can be played correctly and with facility at the next rehearsal. Because the rehearsal is a class lesson, the conductor keeps private instruction and sectional practice to a minimum. His goal is group instruction and stimulation of outside practice by the players. In working out difficult passages, and for the general improvement of the band or orchestra, it is useful to have a tape recorder in the rehearsal room. This permits portions of the rehearsal to be recorded for playback so each player may judge for himself the need for improvement.

THE WARM-UP PERIOD. Instrumentalists need a warm-up period to prepare themselves for the work of rehearsal. Wind players need warm-up exercises for embouchure flexibility. All players need an opportunity to flex their fingers, hands, and arms in preparation for manipulating their instruments. The warm-up period is of psychological value also. It focuses attention on the necessity for correct playing and is conducive to the attitudes needed for serious rehearsal.

Although a warm-up period is desirable for string players, it is essential for brasses and woodwinds which are particularly difficult to play if either the instrument or the player is "cold." String players can warm up individually and their unsupervised playing does not disrupt the rehearsal or make it impossible for the conductor to deal with administrative matters in the first few minutes of a rehearsal period. For the band rehearsal, however, the organized warm-up period is essential, partly because wind players need the teacher's guidance during warm-up and partly because their unsupervised blowing quickly becomes deafening.

Young wind players are addicted to a certain amount of raucous blowing, before and after rehearsal or whenever the opportunity arises. They like to explore the extremes of their instruments, playing high tones, low tones, or exceptionally loud tones. They enjoy displaying technical dexterity by racing up and down scales or arpeggios. A certain amount of this is inevitable and the conductor may show good judgment by permitting individual blowing for a brief interval at the beginning of the rehearsal. The kind of blowing indulged in by young players, however, is not always what is needed for warm-up purposes. If it continues for too long, it destroys both the physical and psychological advantages of the warm-up period. The conductor therefore makes it a point to establish order in the rehearsal quickly, calling a halt to individual blowing after permitting it to continue for only a few minutes, and proceeds to ensemble warm-up pieces or exercises.

There are many possibilities for warm-up exercises. Some band conductors prefer a lively march that does not require extremes of range or dynamics. Others choose chorales and other pieces that stress long tones, controlled dynamics and intonation. Still other conductors prefer exercises written for the purpose. These exercises can be taught by rote, read from the board or exercise books. They can consist of long tones played in unison, chords, scales, arpeggios, rhythm drills, or exercises in dynamics. Each of these is satisfactory if the materials are properly selected by the conductor and if the drill is conducted so that players warm up gradually. The best solution for many bands and orchestras is a combination of the materials mentioned, including a march, a chorale, and ensemble exercises.

REHEARSAL TUNING. Tuning and warm-up exercises are often combined. Players tune before the rehearsal begins, checking their instruments against a tuning bar or other reference device. They are asked to listen to intonation as they play warm-up exercises, adjusting their own instruments without being asked to do so by the conductor. The conductor listens intently to the blend and general effect of the group during the warm-up period. If he is unable to tell which instrument of a section is out of tune, he calls for that section to play alone, searching for the source of poor blend and suggesting tuning adjustments to players or sections. The aim is to develop each player's sensitivity to intonation, encouraging him to listen constantly as he plays and to adjust his instrument whenever necessary. With advanced players, it should not be necessary for the conductor to check tuning except in special cases. The conductor works toward this goal by developing the players' ability to tune their own instruments.

The band learns to tune itself by playing both unison and harmonized exercises. The first step is to play long tones in unison, beginning with the tuning note but progressing to others, especially those of the B-flat (concert) major triad and scale. The next step is to play scales, ascending and descending slowly through one octave, beginning with the B-flat scale and progressing to other closely related keys as needed. A third possible step is to play arpeggios slowly, in the same keys as the scales. A final step is to play sustained chords and chord progressions, each player listening to the manner in which his own instrument blends into the total ensemble. Chord progressions can be read from books, from the board, or they can be taught by rote and memorized by the band. The conductor develops pupils' general musicianship by calling for these chords by letter name, asking for changes from major to minor, using chord numbers or tonic-dominant terminology to dictate progressions, or by asking players to transpose parts from one key to another.

TEACHING WITH THE BATON. The director of a band or orchestra increases the effectiveness of his teaching by regarding conducting as more than a means of beating time and giving cues. Conducting is a means of teaching and the baton is a valuable teaching tool, especially in dealing with groups of players in the public schools. It helps maintain control, guides the players, and teaches them musicianship.

Conducting is a means of gaining and maintaining control. The baton controls the musical response of the performing group in a direct way, regulating tempos, dynamics, attacks and releases, phrasing, and every other aspect of music in performance. The baton also controls the attitudes of the players in an indirect but equally important way. Through baton technique, the conductor shows whether he is in command of the performance and expects attention and coöperation, or whether he is a slipshod director with whom "anything goes." If he is slipshod in his conducting, pupils become less alert, less respectful, and discipline problems grow. If he shows that he is in command of the performance, respect and alertness increase and discipline problems decrease.

Conducting is a source of guidance for the players. Some high-school players are competent musicians, capable of playing their parts accurately and artistically. They need the guidance of the conductor, nevertheless, in the same way that members of professional orchestras and bands need guidance. It is the conductor who creates ensemble feeling and causes the group to play with precision and unanimity.

Conducting is a means of teaching musicianship. It shows not only how to play rhythms and dynamics, but describes mood and interpretation as well, teaching the sensitivity required for artistic performance. One simple conducting motion, properly used, takes the place of many minutes of verbal instruction. The baton is a means of communication, transmitting the wishes of the conductor to the members of the performing group. Communication is effective and teaching takes place when the baton is used with skill. The artistic conductor must have good music judgment and the ability to communicate it through the baton. Rarely does a performing group achieve excellence unless the conductor has both.

Although conducting is more than a means of beating time and giving cues, these basic elements of the conductor's art are especially important to the director of public-school performing groups. Young players rely on the rhythmic authority of the conductor's baton. To feel the rhythmic swing of the music, to play each note in its proper place, and to be unanimous in attacks and releases, young players should be able to refer to the conductor's motions to see each element of the rhythm precisely placed. The conductor must do two things: (1) show the occurrence of each beat in such a way that players recognize it every time it occurs; (2) show the rhythmic flow which connects each beat with its neighbors. To show the occurrence of each beat, many conductors adopt a beat "floor" as shown in Figure 5, an imaginary horizontal line, perhaps at the level of the conductor's waist. Each beat occurs when the baton descends to this level and is further emphasized by an abrupt stop or bounce at that point of the beat motion. To show the continuity of the rhythm, many conductors adopt the divided-beat pattern which in effect provides a preparatory motion for each beat by showing the "ands" as well as the beats. By following patterns like those in Figure 5, the conductor shows clearly every beat and every division of the beat, can emphasize any or every beat, and provides the players with a visual reference that can be followed easily.

Cues are especially important for high-school groups in which players often lack the assurance of more experienced players. The high-school player needs cues to tell him to begin playing after a long period of rest or to stop playing after sustaining one pitch for a number of beats or measures. He often needs a cue to tell him to change from one pitch to another during a sustained passage. The conductor gives as many cues as possible, using every means at his disposal. The cue may be a motion of the baton, of the other hand, a nod of the head, or simply a glance at the player to be cued. The cue need not be a big motion or unduly emphasized, but it must be given.

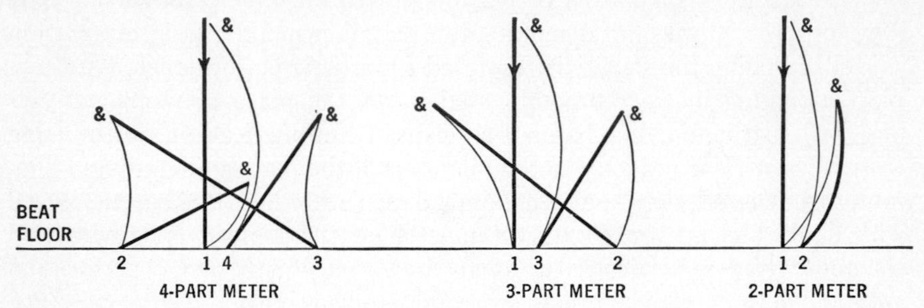

FIGURE 5. CONDUCTING PATTERNS FOR 2, 3, AND 4-PART METERS.

SCHEDULING REHEARSALS. Although it is possible for instrumental groups to rehearse at almost any time of the day, early periods in the morning or afternoon are most desirable. It is well to avoid the period immediately before lunch and the period at the end of the school day because pupils are tired and restless and less attentive to the problems of rehearsal at these times. It is also desirable to avoid the period immediately after lunch so pupils do not have to play wind instruments immediately after eating. One good reason for scheduling rehearsals during the first period in the morning, or the last period in the afternoon, is that extra rehearsal time can be arranged easily if needed. The first period in the morning can be extended by beginning early, before school begins, and the last period of the day can be extended into after-school hours.

Rehearsals ought to be at least a full period long, 45 to 60 minutes depending on the schedule of the school, and double periods are to be desired if they are possible. Much time is occupied in instrumental rehearsals with assembly and disassembly of instruments, warm-up, and tuning. To be productive, instrumental rehearsals must be long enough to give ample playing time in addition to that occupied by these routine matters. Daily meetings are to be desired for instrumentalists who need daily practice. Days that do not include rehearsal permit players to lose skills, forget lessons learned, and are particularly damaging to wind players' embouchures. Rehearsals are scheduled in curricular time when possible, but may be held before or after school or during activity periods when curricular time can not be made available.

USING STUDENT ASSISTANTS. The band or orchestra director profits from appointing student assistants or monitors as discussed in Chapter 10 under the heading *The Class Lesson.* He saves time by selecting pupils to arrange music stands and chairs, distribute folders and parts, check attendance, and adjust light and ventilation. Additional student assistants, appropriate more for the advanced band or orchestra than for the beginning instrumental class, are listed below. These and other student assistants can be elected as part of the parliamentary organization of the group or awarded posts in recognition of service or progress.

1. *Section Leaders.* Supervise tuning of sections, answer questions of other players concerning parts, check attendance, and handle minor problems in their sections.
2. *Librarian.* Supervises the library, distributes and collects parts or folders, is responsible for filing, numbering parts, and so on.
3. *Student Conductor.* Assists with full and sectional rehearsals, takes charge of the group if the teacher is unavoidably absent from the rehearsal room.
4. *Clerical Assistant.* Helps with routine clerical work and performs miscellaneous duties during rehearsal—accepting messages, receiving visitors, dispensing reeds, and dealing with any minor problem that might otherwise force the conductor to interrupt rehearsal.

Performance and Its Values

Performance is essential for any concert organization and is particularly important for pupils in the public-school instrumental program. Performance is necessary to provide a sense of achievement, as motivation for practice and rehearsal, and because it displays the work and achievements of the program. The experience of appearing in concert is enjoyable and educational for the participating pupils and similarly enjoyable and educational for those in the audience.

CONCERT OPPORTUNITIES. Most high-school bands have many opportunities to appear in public. High-school orchestras have similar opportunities but make fewer appearances chiefly because it is not customary for orchestras to play at athletic events. The difficulty is not one of finding enough opportunities, but of using good judgment in selecting from many opportunities to prevent the exploitation of performing groups. This is particularly true in schools where the program of instrumental instruction is effective and develops bands and orchestras of outstanding quality. Community organizations quickly become aware of the excellence of these groups and ask them to perform at community functions, requiring the director to plan the concert schedule carefully and to keep the number of outside appearances within reasonable limits.

The following list includes the events in the school and community at which a high-school band or orchestra might be asked to appear.

1. Regular evening concerts sponsored by the school.
2. Music festivals sponsored by the city, district, or state music education associations.
3. Special school events such as graduation ceremonies and productions by the dramatics department.
4. Music contests sponsored by music education associations.
5. Regular school assemblies at which the performing group provides "entrance" music, accompanies songs, presents single concert selections or a complete concert program.
6. Athletic events, especially football and basketball games.
7. Regular and special meetings of the Parent-Teacher Association.
8. Special exchange programs involving other schools of the same community or the schools of a different community.
9. Special community meetings or parades, including events sponsored by churches, service clubs, and fraternal organizations.
10. Special radio and television programs.

Every high-school band and orchestra should plan for one or more evening concerts each year, making them regular features of the school calendar. The spring concert is perhaps most popular and many schools offer only this one concert each year, but additional concerts are desirable if the performing level of the group permits them. It is equally desirable for the performing groups to undertake other public appearances at events sponsored by the school, including contests, festivals, special programs and assemblies. The band and orchestra can be of service to the school in this way in addition to making use of these events as experiences of educational value to its members. The performing groups render service to the community also by accepting performance requests from the various community groups and taking part in community events. These community appearances are useful as public relations devices and are of educational value to the adults of the community.

PERFORMANCE CONSIDERATIONS. Matters related to performance are discussed in Chapter 9 under the title *Choral Performance.* Much of that discussion pertains to band and orchestra performances as well as to those of choral groups. Goals having to do with music learning, motivation for study, development of poise, and the improvement of community relations apply to both vocal and instrumental areas. The performance schedule is prepared as much as a year in advance, is geared to the calendar of other school events, and is planned coöperatively by the director and members of the group. In building concert programs, the director strives for unity, variety, climax, and contrast, is attentive to the sequence of pieces in the concert program and the physical demands they make on the performers. He observes principles of showmanship to sustain audience interest, creating visual appeal through costume, lighting, and stage movement.

Special attention is given to some of these considerations by the instrumental director, especially those pertaining to the educational objectives of the band. Because of the necessity of providing band music at athletic events and the danger of exaggerating the importance of this band function, the director re-examines the band program constantly to make certain it is directed toward educational goals and the music instruction of band members. Similar attention is given to the band calendar. The many possibilities for appearances at athletic events make it possible to fill the band's performance calendar with "pep" playing, leaving little or no room for concert appearances. The director remains alert to both dangers, striving for a reasonable balance of pep and concert playing and planning the band program so that advancement of skills, musicianship, and general music knowledge is its principal objective.

The instrumental concert is sufficiently different from the choral concert to require special attention to some of the considerations of program building. Because bands and orchestras are made up of instruments of different families, there are many possibilities for featuring differences in tonal color and of increasing the variety and contrast offered by the sequence of pieces in the instrumental concert. The director is particularly careful about presenting concert selections that make heavy demands on the physical endurance of the players. Young players of wind instruments, especially the brasses, do not have the stamina of experienced players. Their embouchures tire quickly, resulting in loss of control and other embouchure problems. The director therefore chooses concert selections that distribute the playing load evenly among the sections of the band or orchestra. He avoids such passages as those that require brasses to dwell in the upper extremes of their ranges or to maintain high volume levels. Where showmanship is concerned, the variety of instruments in the band and orchestra permits unique concert effects. Antiphonal groups can be placed in the balcony or wings, stage movement can be utilized to feature soloists or sections, and special instruments such as herald trumpets can be used to capture audience interest.

CONCERT ACOUSTICS. Special mention of the acoustical problems in concerts of bands and orchestras is merited because of the wide range of dynamic levels and tone colors offered by these instrumental groups. To cite obvious examples, a band fortissimo can be overpowering and an orchestra pianissimo inaudible if the acoustics of the concert hall are not taken into consideration. Conversely, an orchestra fortissimo can be deafening and a band pianissimo inaudible. This is especially undesirable if the director is seriously interested in presenting the band as a worthy concert instrument. Too many of those who make up concert audiences are prone to regard the band as a grouping of raucous instruments best suited to the performance of marches in street parades. The director who knows the capability of the band for producing whispering pianissimos and infinite dynamic gradations up to the impenetrable solidity of its fortissimo requires that it perform under favorable acoustical conditions. The orchestra deserves similar consideration, partly because it is a worthy performing group and partly because the experience of those in the audience leads them to compare it with professional orchestras and to expect good performance.

First, there is the stage on which the group performs. On some stages, sound disappears upward into the emptiness above the heads of the players, while on others it is channeled into the wings. In either case it does not reach the audience. Some stages place the performing group in front of a hard-surfaced wall which reflects sound directly toward the audience, while others surround it with heavy draperies which absorb sound and deaden the stage. There may be live spots from which every whisper is audible in the last row of seats, or dead spots from which a flute player will be unheard regardless of how loudly he plays. Each of these possibilities is explored by the director before he uses any stage for the first time. Stage draperies can be raised or lowered to improve the acoustical effect. The performing group can be moved closer to the audience or closer to the rear wall. Sections and individual players can be shifted and the seating plan revised as necessary to improve balance. For many stages, the best solution is the "box" set, a room-like stage setting open on only one side with walls and ceiling made of painted canvas, plywood, or other materials. The box set functions as a shell, projecting all sound toward the audience, and is constructed so it can be set up and dismantled easily.

Another factor is the concert hall itself. Its acoustical properties are affected by its size and shape, the composition of walls, floor and ceiling, the area covered by window draperies and carpeting, and the number of people in the audience. The director judges hall acoustics by listening to the group from various places in the hall. Because he can usually do little to change the hall itself, he adjusts stage acoustics and the seating plan until he is content with the tonal effect. Because the effect may be quite different when the seats of the hall are filled with listeners, he regards his first adjustments as tentative. He listens again each time his group performs for an audience, continuing to adjust stage acoustics and seating until optimum balance, blend, and sonority are achieved.

There are both advantages and disadvantages in the conditions faced by the conductor of high-school bands and orchestras. Most concerts are given in the auditorium provided in the school building. Acoustical conditions are always the same and problems once solved need not arise again until the composition of the performing group or some other factor changes. The box set or other special equipment can be made at minimum cost by pupils in the industrial arts shops. The disadvantage is that the school conductor may find it difficult to change the physical equipment of the stage, or of the gymnasium or cafeteria if that is where his concerts must be presented. The limited budget is a perennial problem and often does not provide funds for the purchase or construction of special equipment. Auditorium stages and multi-purpose rooms are designed for general use rather than as concert shells and their construction may prevent changes for concert purposes. The benefits of acoustical adjustment are numerous, nevertheless, and the director is amply rewarded for the time and effort he devotes to the improvement of these concert conditions.

12: *administering the program*

The music director has many administrative responsibilities in addition to his teaching duties. His administrative work falls chiefly into two categories, one involving management of school property, the other involving relationships with school personnel and adults of the community. Each of these categories requires his constant attention and best effort. Unless he develops competence as an administrator his work as a teacher is seriously handicapped and his music program can not develop to the limit of its potential.

PROPERTY MANAGEMENT

The instrumental music department must acquire large quantities of expensive equipment to achieve its educational goals. Instruments and uniforms make up two of the largest categories, but music, music stands, electronic tuning devices, and many other necessities increase the required music department investment to a sum larger than that required by most other school departments. All this equipment must be purchased, cared for, and properly recorded for inventory and accounting purposes. The burden of work is large enough to occupy all the teacher's time if he does not manage it systematically, but with careful planning this work can be accomplished quickly and systematically and with great benefit to the development of the music program.

Preparing the Music Budget

The music budget is a systematic approach to the financial problems of the music department. It can deal with instrumental music alone, with all performing groups in one school, both vocal and instrumental, or with the entire music program from grade one through grade twelve. The ideal budget is one that functions effectively year after year, retaining the same basic framework but permitting revision of minor details to compensate for the growth of the music program or other special circumstances. Advance planning is essential. Music department needs must be known in advance so a place for them can be reserved in the total school budget. Advance planning is further required because school funds must be obtained and set aside long before they are spent. Finally, the music director plans in terms of the school population, estimating years in advance the effect increases in enrollment will have on instrument classes and advanced performing groups. Budgeted amounts depend therefore on the size of classes and performing groups, the importance of music in the school program, and, of course, the amount of money available through normal channels of school revenue.

BUDGET CATEGORIES. In formulating a budget it is helpful to establish broad categories of expenditure. Each category is considered separately in terms of its relative importance in the total budget, the amount of funds it requires, and the frequency of its occurrence. Certain new equipment such as instruments and uniforms requires extraordinary expenditure, either a large special appropriation once every several years or regular small appropriations annually. The occasional large appropriation is advantageous in that it sometimes permits the economies of quantity purchase and permits the school to acquire simultaneously a large number of instruments of the same make, model, and quality. The smaller annual appropriation is usually preferred, however, because it spreads the expenditure evenly over many years instead of burdening the budget in any one year. Funds for maintenance and repair are needed every year, are spent as needed, and may be among the largest items in the budget. Other items may be seasonal, such as band uniforms, special Christmas music, and scenery for annual shows. Budget needs for these items are determined far in advance and orders placed with suppliers before their seasonal rush.

A list of possible categories is shown here as an indication of needs that might be common to all music departments. The items in each category are examples only and do not show the wide range of needed materials and equipment.

1. *Instructional materials:* textbooks, band and orchestra arrangements, ensemble pieces, method books, rehearsal folders, librarian's supplies.
2. *Expendable supplies:* bond, carbon, and onionskin paper, music manuscript paper, mimeograph stencils, chalk, answer sheets for standardized tests, recording tapes.
3. *Instructional equipment:* phonograph, tape recorder, electronic tuning devices, music stands, special rehearsal chairs.
4. *Instructional expenses:* film rental, performance cost including program printing, concert-hall rental, janitorial fees.
5. *School equipment:* storage cabinets for instruments, music and uniforms, rehearsal-room risers, phonograph records, duplicating machines.
6. *Maintenance and repair:* instrument repair and replacement, uniform cleaning, repair and replacement, piano tuning, purchase of tools for instrument repairs.
7. *Capital outlay:* purchase of instruments and uniforms.
8. *Insurance:* protection against damage, loss, and fire for instruments, uniforms, and other equipment; liability insurance covering injury to pupils during trips or any out-of-school function.
9. *Miscellaneous and contingency:* festival expenses, including registration fees, transportation, housing and meals; purchase of extra reeds, mouthpieces, and other small supplies.

The size of the budget is determined in two ways: (1) in terms of the total need in each category and (2) in terms of the relative importance of the various categories. The director surveys his situation and determines exactly what is needed in each separate category. The expenditure for each category is increased as necessary to provide for the purchase of all items in the quantity needed without special consideration of the total amount of money required. Because the school budget may not permit the expenditure of this much money, the director also compares the categories with each other. He notes the importance of each and sets percentage weights to show how the budget might be divided among the several categories in the event available funds do not equal the budget request. His budget request can then show total need, recommended apportionment if the total must be reduced, and possible carry-over of balances into the following year.

INSTRUMENT PURCHASES. In a new or growing instrumental program, instrument purchase is often one of the largest items in the music-department budget. Because large sums of money are involved, it is necessary in many schools to formulate a long-range plan under which the instrument inventory can be built gradually to the desired level. Even in an established program, the need for replacing old instruments is such that it is desirable to formulate a similar long-range plan for the purchase of a small number of replacement instruments each year.

To begin, the director requests the purchase of a minimum number of instruments, basing his request on the needs of a small band or orchestra. He assumes that violins, clarinets, and trumpets will be privately owned and that the school need provide only the larger instruments for the band and orchestra. For reasons of economy, he requests only the essential large or expensive instruments, deferring purchase of bassoons, oboes, or any other instruments whose parts can be cued until the growth of the performing group makes them essential. Thereafter, he adds a small number of instruments each year. He may purchase additional tubas, string basses, cellos, and baritones, adding to the number purchased originally to provide for larger numbers of players. He may work toward complete instrumentation by purchasing oboes, bassoons, tympani, and other less common instruments. If he wishes to develop a complete instrumental program, he may request the purchase of basic instruments for beginning classes. In so doing, he considers the desired instrumentation of each performing group, the number of players, and the need for expanding beginning classes.

Table 10 is a possible purchase schedule. It assumes the director will establish a 30-piece band, expanding it to 60 players after two years and to 90 players after four years. There are many possibilities for revising such a plan, depending upon the size of the school, the size of the budget, and the instrumentation needs of the band. The intent of the plan, however, is to provide instruments for a growing band while spreading the cost over a number of years.

The long-range plan is particularly necessary because of the high cost of band and orchestra instruments and the large numbers of instruments required. Expensive instruments such as bassoons, tubas, and harps must be planned for in advance so provision can be made for them in the total school budget. Requests for these instruments are less likely to be refused if one is bought each year, or one every two or three years, than if all are requested at once. Violins, clarinets, and trumpets for beginning classes are purchased in a similar manner, a few each year. The budget is adjusted from year to year to meet the needs of the expanding program. Single instruments are purchased as needed to complete the instrumentation of the band and orchestra, small numbers of basic instruments are purchased each year to permit expansion of beginning classes as pupil interest grows, and related instruments are purchased to permit transfers from basic instruments after one or two years of instruction.

TABLE 10. SCHEDULE FOR PURCHASE OF BAND INSTRUMENTS

Purchases	*1st Year*	*2nd Year*	*3rd Year*	*4th Year*	*5th Year*
Piccolo	1	0	1	0	0
Oboe	1	1	0	1	0
E-flat clarinet	0	0	0	1	1
Alto clarinet	0	0	1	1	1
Bass clarinet	0	1	0	1	1
Bassoon	0	1	1	0	0
Soprano saxophone	0	0	0	0	1
Baritone saxophone	1	0	0	1	0
Bass saxophone	0	0	0	0	1
French horn	3	1	0	1	1
Baritone horn	1	0	1	0	1
Tuba	2	1	1	1	1
Snare drum	1	0	1	0	1
Bass drum	1	0	0	0	0
Cymbals	1	0	0	0	0
Tympani	0	1	0	0	0
Harp	0	0	0	1	0

When optimum size is reached, either by performing groups or beginning classes, further purchases are made to replace instruments no longer serviceable. This requires that the director establish a "depreciation" system. He determines the probable useful life of each type of instrument, determines the cost of each instrument, divides the cost by the number of years of useful life, and includes this sum in the annual budget. This permits the director to build a replacement fund by accumulating small sums each year and eliminates the necessity for requesting large sums every several years. Economies are effected by selecting second- or third-line instruments when their quality is acceptable. Although it is unwise to buy inferior instruments, many manufacturers of first-line instruments offer subsidiary lines of good quality at low cost. Budget problems are reduced if these second- or third-line instruments are provided for beginning classes, reserving first-line instruments for advanced players only.

BUILDING THE MUSIC LIBRARY. Large libraries including concert music and instructional materials of many kinds are needed for school orchestras and bands. The library is developed over a period of years, partly to avoid the need for large expenditure in any one year and partly to permit purchase of new music as it is published. The director establishes a library budget made up of separate categories to show the types of music to be purchased.

If the director feels it is necessary to emphasize the relative importance of the various categories, each can be given a percentage weight. The categorized budget then becomes a guide for requesting funds and purchasing music. It is made part of the total budget and is submitted year after year to build a comprehensive library complete in all categories and balanced to meet the needs of the performing group. These categories might be as follows, adjusted as needed to build a new or maintain an established library or to supply the needs of larger or smaller performing groups.

1.	New music for band or orchestra	
	Heavy concert music	30%
	Light concert music	20%
	Marches	5%
	Novelties	3%
	Chorales	3%
	Solos with full accompaniment	3%
	Ensemble drills and tuning exercises	3%
2.	New music for small ensembles	
	Brass	3%
	Woodwind	3%
	String	3%
	Percussion	3%
3.	Solos with piano accompaniment (loan copies)	3%
4.	Instrument method books (reference copies)	3%
5.	Phonograph records and tapes	5%
6.	Miscellaneous	10%
	File cards, mending tape, and other librarian's supplies.	
	Extra and replacement parts.	
	Band and ensemble folders.	

RAISING FUNDS. The American philosophy of education is that public schools should be open to all and supported by all through taxation. This implies that any school program or activity worthy of a place in the education pattern should be worthy of tax support. This is true of each separate aspect of the music program—it is worthy of tax support if it is of sufficient educational value to merit school sponsorship.

Music teachers in the public schools are responsible for the teaching of music. They misuse their talents and training if they become fund raisers and sacrifice teaching time to promote bake sales, raffles, and other money-raising schemes. Although his public-relations function is undeniable, the music teacher serves the community best in a teaching capacity. He is untrained and inefficient as a public-relations agent, even when money-raising activities are necessary, and his teaching suffers when he is required to raise funds for materials and activities that should be provided for in the school budget.

Many instrumental directors face the problem of insufficient funds, nevertheless, and must choose between promoting fund-raising activities and eliminating needed portions of the instrumental program. When this situation occurs, the music director may be justified in accepting fund-raising activities, regarding them as necessary to the achievement of worthy educational ends. One real value of fund-raising activity is that it stimulates interest in the music program. Pupils, parents, and the community at large become aware of the music program and interested in its improvement by taking part in fund drives. Partly for this reason and partly because adults of the community can offer great assistance and expert guidance, the music teacher solicits community coöperation when fund-raising is necessary. The "Band-Parents Association" is excellent for this purpose. The music director encourages its organization and helps sustain it year after year for its help in fund-raising and for the many other services it renders to pupils, the music program, and the school.

Funds for the music program can be secured from many sources other than the school budget. Some of these sources are found in the school program and do not require promotion of money-making schemes. Other sources are the special activities that can be organized and carried out by pupils and the Band-Parents Association with only minimum participation by the music director. Both types are included in this list.

1. Instrument rental fees.
2. Tuition fees for private lessons.
3. Profits from concerts featuring visiting artists.
4. Sale of advertising space in concert programs.
5. Sale of tickets to special band and orchestra concerts or variety shows.
6. Receipts from sale of athletic tickets.
7. Funds from student activity organizations.
8. Band parties.
9. Benefit sales and parties.

Several of these items are worthy of special note. Although fees for instrument rental and private lessons are usually adjusted to cover the costs of these programs, any surplus is returned to the music budget for music use. Regular band and orchestra concerts, because they are produced through tax-supported school programs, are free to the public. Special benefit concerts, however, are usually permissible and may draw larger audiences than free concerts if their goals are worthy and well publicized. Funds created by the sale of tickets for athletic events are used chiefly to support the athletic program, but the band is entitled to a percentage of athletic receipts if it provides music and entertainment at football and basketball games. Similarly, student activity associations contribute to the music budget if music organizations participate in and enhance student-organized activities for which admission is charged. Band parties such as dances, hay rides, and dinners can contribute to the music budget as can the candy and bake sales, dinners, and other fund-raising activities sponsored by band members or the Band-Parents Association.

SUBMITTING REQUESTS FOR FUNDS. There are a number of principles to be observed when preparing budget requests for the approval of administrative officers. Requests must be business-like in every detail. They are prepared in written form, brief, but with all necessary information included. They are organized logically, showing the need for funds, being considerate of necessary limitations placed upon expenditure, giving accurate figures for current requests, and showing how major improvements can be achieved through long-range planning. Finally, they include any information needed to justify expenditures or to help the administrator form conclusions concerning the relative importance of separate items.

The allocation of school funds is a major responsibility of administrative officers and a time-consuming portion of their work. Because the administrator's time is limited, budget requests are submitted in a form that permits quick initial scanning, detailed later study, convenient filing, and subsequent reference. The administrator respects and is sympathetic toward the music director whose budget requests show careful organization. They save time for the administrator and are evidence of good judgment in the preparation of the budget and the expenditure of school funds. For this reason, the music director who follows business-like principles in preparing his budget can be confident of its approval whenever the school budget permits.

The written budget request might consist of the following:

1. *General statement.* Identifies the department submitting the budget and the period covered, requests special consideration of specific items as necessary, and may state briefly selected facts about goals or needs.
2. *Budget synopsis.* A brief summary of budget requests by major categories suitable for quick scanning and easy reference.
3. *Specific requests.* This is the body of the budget request. It lists all categories of expenditure, states amounts desired, gives costs, discounts, purchase specifications, sources, and any other necessary information.
4. *Supplementary information.* Contains any information useful to the administrative officer, including (a) description of current needs, (b) enrollment figures and trends, (c) plans for additional classes or performing groups, (d) long-range plans, (e) comparative bids, (f) alternate sources.

Selecting Music Instruments

When buying instruments the music director is careful not to become a victim of the common notion that cheap instruments are good enough for beginning players. Too many beginners have been discouraged in their first lessons by trying without success to produce musical sounds from poor instruments. No player can do well with an imperfect instrument. For beginning players it is especially important that instruments function easily and well and produce pleasing tones. Beginners do not have the experienced player's ability to perform well despite the faults of an inferior instrument and their interest and progress depend upon the success of their first attempts.

GENERAL SUGGESTIONS. The instrumental director is rare who is capable of judging the quality of all instruments of the band and orchestra. Although he may be a competent judge of the instruments he plays, and may gain in experience in judging others during his teaching years, the music director who is purchasing large numbers of instruments for the school program is well advised to ask the assistance of others in choosing among the many brands available. Competent players from the community can be of assistance in rating the playing qualities of the various brands. Other instrumental teachers may be able to give valuable advice concerning the durability and performance of these brands in school conditions.

Each instrument is given a playing test. In the test, a capable player first determines whether the instrument is pitched close to the standard adopted by the director for his band and orchestra, probably A-440. All instruments are purchased to meet this standard, with the realization that tuning slides of brasses can be pulled slightly without serious effect on intonation, but that woodwinds, especially clarinets, create serious intonation problems if mouthpieces or barrels are pulled. The player further tests the instrument to make certain all pitches in the lower, middle, and upper registers are in tune and that tone quality is uniform throughout the full compass of the instrument. The instrument should "speak" easily in all registers and its mechanical parts should function freely and smoothly.

In addition to checking the instruments themselves, the director specifies that they include all accessories, such as lyres and mouthpiece caps, and that a case be provided for each instrument. The chief requisite for cases is that they be sturdy and durable, capable of giving long wear despite the careless treatment beginners might give them. Extra zipper covers made of heavy material are an excellent investment also. They protect the hard cases of trumpets, clarinets, and other relatively small instruments and ultimately save money by extending the useful life of the inner case. For the larger instruments such as Sousaphones and string basses, a soft case of heavy canvas or padded plastic is acceptable if pupils are trained to handle their instruments with care. In most instances, however, the added cost of durable hard cases is an indirect economy.

Although no instrument should be exempt from rigid scrutiny and careful testing, the music director can usually rely on instruments supplied by well-known manufacturers. He invests school funds unwisely when he attempts to save money by buying cheap instruments from relatively unknown sources. The instruments themselves are often inferior and replacements and factory repairs may be impossible to obtain. Although professional instrumentalists and advanced players in the high school sometimes develop strong prejudices against the instruments of even the most reputable manufacturer, the director's safest course is to select from well-known brands of instruments with the advice of competent players and other instrumental teachers.

BRASSES. Requirements for instruments of the brass family are determined by the needs of pupils and the needs of performing groups, especially the band. Cornets are to be preferred over trumpets because of their richness of tone, although trumpets are purchased if the school provides instruments for pupils who play trumpet parts in the band or orchestra. For young French-horn players, the school provides single horns in F, purchasing one or two double horns for advanced players. It is usually necessary for the school to provide French horns for all players, but cornets are purchased principally for beginning classes because most players in the advanced groups will want to buy instruments of their own.

Of the lower brasses, school-owned baritone horns and basses are supplied for all pupils, trombones for beginners only. Although tenor trombones are practical for school use, one or two bass trombones are useful for advanced players in the band and orchestra, especially since high-school pupils do not usually buy bass trombones for their own use. Baritones even from the most reputable manufacturers are sometimes badly out of tune, chiefly because of the nature of the instrument. They are therefore selected with special care and are tested by a skilled player to determine the extent of the intonation problems of each instrument. Bell-front baritones with three valves are satisfactory, one or two four-valve instruments being purchased for members of the high-school band. When purchasing basses, most directors first buy a complete set of Sousaphones for the marching band, deferring the purchase of upright tubas until funds can be found for them in later budgets. As a result, the fortunate director finds himself with two sets of basses, Sousaphones for marching band, and tubas for concert band. Although Sousaphones are a necessity for the marching band, tubas are usually preferred for concert work. Their purchase, in the ratio of one E-flat to three BB-flat tubas, should be one of the band director's goals. To protect these expensive and bulky basses, it is wise to buy a rehearsal stand for every instrument.

WOODWINDS. Flutes and piccolos should be metal, pitched in C, and built in the Boehm system. Grenadilla wood is preferred for oboes and English horns, as is the conservatory system of fingering. Bassoons should be Heckel system and made of rosewood. For all double reeds, it is essential that each new intrument be tested by a skilled player and that hand-made reeds be made available to all pupils.

Composition and plastic clarinets are available, some of them of excellent quality, but the music director who is not a clarinetist selects from the available brands only with the help of a skilled clarinetist or other music teachers who have had experience with the instruments in school conditions. These "synthetic" clarinets are desirable for several reasons. They are virtually immune to damage caused by temperature changes or careless handling and are attractive to the beginning pupil because they look and feel like wood clarinets. The school need purchase few if any wood clarinets, for advanced pupils who want them are encouraged to buy their own. Because of the intonation problems created by "tuning down," all clarinets and saxophones should be tested to make certain they are close to the pitch standard adopted for the performing groups.

STRINGS. Stringed instruments are available in a number of sizes, often classified as standard, intermediate, and junior. They can be purchased by the school in an assortment of sizes appropriate for the pupils of different ages in the instrumental classes and performing groups. When buying any stringed instrument, the music director looks for good basic workmanship and evidence that the manufacturer has used proper materials. Backs and sides are best made of maple, tops of spruce. Ebony is used in the better instruments for most "black" pieces—fingerboard, pegs, tailpiece, nut, and saddle. The instruments are not bought separately, but in "outfits," each outfit consisting of the instrument, bow, case, and accessories. In the outfit, the bow is matched to the instrument, the bridge is properly fitted and the fingerboard aligned, strings are matched in sets, and all adjustments are made so the beginning pupil is not handicapped during his first lessons.

The most important accessory is the bow. It is of sufficient importance to the progress of the pupil that it is sometimes wiser to buy an inexpensive instrument than an inexpensive bow. Better bows are made of Pernambuco wood, although Brazil wood and aluminium are acceptable. They must be straight and properly balanced, with a bow screw that turns easily and bow hairs held in place by wedges, not glued. Other needed accessories are chin and shoulder rests for violins and violas, adjustable endpins for cellos and bases, and endpin rests to prevent cellos and basses from slipping on hard floors.

PERCUSSION. Music directors who are not percussion specialists rely on the advice of qualified percussion players to avoid buying instruments not suited for band and orchestra use. Percussion instruments are music instruments. They are purchased with the same care as other instruments, with the same requirements for quality materials, good workmanship, and musical tones. Percussion instruments of good quality enhance band and orchestral effects and encourage young players to develop musicianship. The music director who hopes to develop his percussion section into something more than a collection of noise-makers purchases the best instruments for all players.

Snare drums for orchestral use should be not less than 6½ x 14 inches, parade drums 12 x 16 inches. The tension of each head should be adjustable separately and snares should be made of coiled wire. Skin heads are preferred by many players, but plastic heads have won favor for school use, especially in the marching band. Bass drums may be from 14 x 30 to 16 x 36 inches or larger, the smaller drum for orchestral use. Heavy heads are practical, with the batter head tuned tighter than the opposite head. Paired tympani may be 25 and 28 or 26 and 29 inches in diameter, sets of three consisting of drums 25, 28, and 30 inches in diameter. Orchestral cymbals may be from 14 to 16 inches in diameter, of medium weight, equipped with leather thongs instead of handles, and purchased in matched pairs. Other percussion equipment is purchased as needed and with equal care, the director choosing standard orchestral instruments of the best quality.

CHOOSING THE SOURCE. Music instruments can be purchased through the local music store, from the manufacturer's representative, or from the factory itself. In any case, the director is wise to choose a source in which he has complete confidence and which offers immediate adjustment of complaints and factory repair facilities. Large school systems often require that competitive bids be secured before instruments are purchased. Before seeking bids, the music director establishes precise specifications for each instrument, often without naming brands. This entails a great deal of careful research, but assures that satisfactory instruments will be purchased at reasonable prices. In smaller school systems, however, the music director often relies on one or several reputable dealers and the advice of competent players and other teachers.

Caring for Equipment and Materials

Caring for equipment and materials is one of the major responsibilities of the music director. He is custodian of large quantities of expensive equipment including instruments, uniforms, and music. The protection of this large investment of school funds requires the exercise of administrative skill. This skill is in some respects more important to the music director than music talent or training, for the music program cannot continue to function unless it is well organized and its equipment and materials are protected and preserved through proper care.

A large portion of the music director's administrative work has to do with maintaining record systems for inventory, filing, and control over issue and return of equipment and materials. Much of this work is simplified if correct forms are properly used and systematic procedures are developed. The music director determines what forms are needed, buys them from available sources or requests that they be printed according to his specifications. Each form is designed to meet the needs of his program, providing space and headings for all information to make record-keeping easier and less time-consuming. If forms are properly designed they can be maintained by student assistants with little previous training and little or no supervision by the music director. Although most of the needed forms can be purchased from publishers or other supply sources, the music director may find it preferable to use forms printed to his order. Loan contracts and other agreements of a legal nature are written or approved by school legal authorities. Where record-keeping forms are concerned, the experience of a few years will show the music director what data should be included and what eliminated to meet his needs and simplify record-keeping for student assistants.

Much of this administrative work must be completed well in advance of the time equipment, materials, and forms are actually used. Items needed during one school year must be ordered early enough to be received before the school year begins. Budget requests must be submitted before materials are ordered from suppliers and planning must be completed before budget requests are submitted. This means that planning must be done as much as a year in advance and, if the school budget permits, materials for use in one school year ordered during the preceding year. Inventories of instruments, uniforms, and other equipment are checked during the summer vacation or earlier if possible, when all equipment has been returned to the school for storage. Instruments can be checked for needed repairs during a period set aside during the school year for the purpose and repairs made during a vacation interval when instruments are not in use. The music library is checked during a vacation period, after parts have been returned and filed, to make certain all parts have been returned, are in readable condition, and have been filed in correct order. The music director also checks room equipment—rehearsal chairs, music stands, and so forth—for needed repairs and to determine whether additional equipment should be purchased.

INSTRUMENTS. At least three forms are needed for the records dealing with music instruments.

1. *Instrument inventory card.* One card is completed for each instrument showing (a) type of instrument, (b) manufacturer, (c) manufacturer's serial number, (d) school number, (e) list of accessories, (f) purchase date, (g) price, (h) repair dates, (i) description of repairs, (j) cost of repairs, (k) remarks.
2. *Instrument loan contract.* One contract, in duplicate, is completed for each pupil who borrows or rents an instrument. It shows (a) type of instrument, (b) manufacturer, (c) manufacturer's serial number, (d) school number, (e) list of accessories, (f) value, (g) statement describing responsibilities of pupil and parents and terms of the loan agreement, (h) signatures of pupil, parent, and music director, (i) dates of issue and return, (j) remarks.
3. *Instrument loan record.* Ledger-type sheets are used to list all instruments and the names of pupils who rent, borrow, or use them. Headings include (a) school number, (b) instrument, (c) student borrower, (d) date of issue, (e) date of return, (f) rental payments, (g) condition of instrument.

Each new instrument is given a school number. The number is engraved on the instrument and painted on the case immediately after the instrument is received from the manufacturer. This number is recorded on the inventory card along with the manufacturer's serial number for the instrument and all its component parts. Serial numbers for all parts are recorded to make certain that separate pieces, such as Sousaphone bells, are kept always with the same instrument. The inventory card may include "depreciation" information also—spaces for recording estimated values in successive years.

Forms are filed for easy cross-reference and to permit the music director to find needed information quickly. Loan contracts are filed alphabetically according to the names of borrowers and the loan record lists instruments by school number in consecutive order. Inventory cards may be filed by school number or by type of instrument with the instruments in each group arranged in school-number order.

UNIFORMS. Forms similar to those needed for instruments are used to keep records concerning band uniforms.

1. *Uniform inventory sheets.* Ledger-type sheets listing each item of apparel separately, but grouping all similar items together—blouses, capes, caps, skirts, trousers, overcoats, and so forth. Notations for each piece of apparel include (a) item, (b) school number, (c) size, (d) date of purchase, (e) source, (f) cost, (g) remarks.
2. *Uniform issue record.* Ledger-type sheets listing (a) items by school number, (b) name of pupil to whom issued, (c) date of issue, (d) date of return, (e) remarks.
3. *Pupil uniform card.* File cards showing (a) name of pupil, size and number of (b) blouse, (c) cape, (d) cap, (e) skirt or trousers, (f) overcoat, (g) uniform accessories, (h) date of issue, (i) date of return, (j) remarks.

New uniforms are numbered as soon as they are received from the supplier. The director numbers each item separately, rather than assigning one number to each complete uniform, so items can be issued individually in correct sizes for each player. If storage and dressing-room facilities are adequate, uniforms can be stored in the school building and issued prior to each band appearance. If facilities are not adequate, uniforms are issued in September and retained by pupils for the entire year.

One additional form is sometimes useful to either supplement or replace the pupil uniform card and instrument loan record—the *personnel card.* One card is completed for each pupil. It shows his name, address, telephone number, instrument, parent or guardian. It may also contain some of the information shown on the instrument loan record and pupil uniform card so those forms can be simpler and easier to maintain. If the personnel card is confidential, available only to the music director or other teachers, it may include aptitude scores, comments concerning progress, and pertinent information about the pupil's parents and home conditions. For practical purposes, however, it is desirable to use these forms only for information that need not be confidential so all record-keeping can be placed in the hands of student assistants.

THE MUSIC LIBRARY. Efficient management of the music library requires a large number of records and the constant attention of an industrious librarian. There are many possible systems for filing band and orchestra music, but the following items are required in almost any system:

1. *Library file cards.* Cards are purchased in sets of four so each band or orchestra selection can be indexed under (a) composer, (b) title, (c) character, (d) file number. Each card of the set is a different color and is arranged so the important indexing item appears on the top line. One card contains detailed information about the selection —composer, title, arranger, file number, character, publisher, publisher's catalog number, cost, performance dates. The other three cards of each set contain only the information needed for cross-reference. Cards of the same color are filed together, each color in its own file drawer.
2. *File envelopes.* Envelopes, folders, or boxes are needed to protect the music stored in drawers or cabinets. Envelopes, preferred by many directors, can be purchased in march, octavo, and concert sizes. The face of each envelope provides spaces to show (a) file number, (b) composer, (c) title, (d) arranger, (e) character, (f) publisher, (g) cost, (h) parts list, (i) performance dates, (j) remarks. The parts list is especially important. It permits the librarian to check the instrumentation and number of copies of each part without opening the envelope.
3. *Concert folders.* Folders are necessary to protect music, prevent loss of individual parts, and simplify issue and return of music at rehearsal. They are made of heavy stock or hardboard with inner pockets to hold parts and may have envelope flaps. The chief requisites are that they be made of sturdy material and constructed so that music can not fall out when the folder is closed.
4. *March folders.* Special folders of march size are provided for each member of the marching band. The folder consists of plastic pockets hinged together for easy turning. Music placed inside the pockets is protected from rain and other damage but visible through the plastic face. Folders can be placed in music lyres and pages turned easily, the hinge preventing loss of parts on the march.
5. *Sign-out sheets.* One sheet is provided for each concert folder so players can leave the sheet with the librarian whenever a folder is taken from the rehearsal room for individual practice. Each sheet shows (a) concert folder number, (b) instrument, (c) stand number, (d) date issued, (e) student signature, (f) date returned, (g) librarian's signature.
6. *Music order blank.* These blanks are for the convenience of the director in ordering band and orchestra selections. The director types three copies—for the supplier, the school office, and his own file—or more if the school purchasing system requires. The form provides headings for (a) supplier's name and address, (b) school

name and address, (c) school order number, (d) title of selection, (e) composer, (f) arranger, (g) publisher, (h) publisher's catalog number, (i) list price, (j) discount, (k) parts list, (l) music director's signature and title. The parts list is particularly useful because it permits the director to order standard, symphonic, or other sets of parts plus as many extra parts as needed for his performing group.

The following equipment other than printed forms and folders is of use to the librarian:

1. *Sorting rack.* This is an arrangement of shelves providing space for the display of each concert folder separately. Shelves are tipped forward so all folders are visible and parts can be distributed by placing each part on its proper folder.
2. *Folder file.* A cabinet containing shelves or slots, each labeled to receive one concert folder. Players select their own folders before rehearsal and replace them in the proper slots at the end of each rehearsal.
3. *Work table.* A large table providing ample working surface and drawer space for storage is useful to the librarian for sorting, mending music, cataloging, and so forth.

The most convenient receptacle for file cards is a multi-drawer cabinet. Single wood or steel drawers can be used as the library is being developed and when the number of file cards is small, but the expanding library quickly requires additional drawers. Band and orchestra arrangements can be stored in several ways. (1) Sliding-drawer file cabinets are practical and require that each selection be placed in its own envelope. (2) Selections can be placed in file boxes of heavy cardboard, each selection in its own box and the boxes placed like books on library shelves. (3) Another possibility, suitable for temporary use until filing equipment can be purchased, is the "lay-away" system. Each selection is placed in its own file folder, the spine of the folder is labeled, and the folders are piled on shelves in file order. Of all the possibilities, sliding-drawer cabinets are preferred by many directors because they protect the music fully, occupy relatively little space, and permit easy access.

Although the use of four file cards for each selection helps determine categories for filing, it is sometimes useful to establish additional categories to govern placement of selections in file drawers. Categories might include chorales, marches, novelties, overtures, popular selections, sacred music, solos with full accompaniment, suites, symphonic excerpts, and so forth. All marches are filed together in special drawers of march size. Other selections can be grouped in standard drawers so all selections of each type are filed together. If this is done, each category is identified by a file-number prefix and each selection by the prefix plus the file number. Chorales, for example, would be numbered C-1, C-2, and so on.

Of more importance is the numbering of parts to prevent loss and as an aid in filing. When new music is received, parts are arranged in score order, numbers are entered in the parts list on the face of the envelope, and the parts are placed in the envelope in score order. In addition, each part is numbered, the numbers indicating score order, the number of copies of each part, and the concert folder in which each part is to be placed. The simplest way is to place parts in score order and number them consecutively, but this prevents the addition of extra parts at a later date. A more elaborate but practical method is to assign a block of numbers to each part as in Table 11, reserving unused numbers for later addition of extra parts.

TABLE 11. SUGGESTED NUMBERING SYSTEM FOR PARTS IN BAND ARRANGEMENTS.

Numbers	*Parts*	*Number*	*Parts*
1–9	Flutes and piccolos	90–94	Bass saxophones
10–14	Oboes and English horns	100–109	Cornets
15–19	E-flat clarinets	110–114	Trumpets
20–49	B-flat clarinets	115–119	Fluegelhorns
50–54	Alto clarinets	120–129	French horns
55–59	Bass clarinets	130–139	Trombones
60–64	Contra-bass clarinets	140–149	Baritones
65–69	Bassoons	150–159	Tubas
70–74	Soprano saxophones	160–164	String basses
75–79	Alto saxophones	200–209	Percussion
80–84	Tenor saxophones	210–214	Harps
85–89	Baritone saxophones		

If this system is followed, the first flute part will always be number 1, first cornet number 100, first baritone number 140. Concert folders are then given the same numbers so that part number 1 is always placed in folder number 1. To distribute music, the librarian places concert folders on the sorting rack in numerical order and places a part of the correct number on each folder. Parts are removed from the folders in a similar manner and a missing part can be identified by its number, showing which folder is incomplete and which player is responsible. Collected parts are then piled in numerical order, the quantities of each part checked against the parts list on the file envelope, and the complete selection filed in correct order ready for re-distribution when needed.

HUMAN RELATIONS

As in many other types of administrative work, skill in human relations is among the most important factors in the success of the music superviser. He deals with music teachers, classroom teachers, administrative officers, and the public. He exercises control over the work of other teachers, directs the music program, and pleads the case for music before school authorities and the public. To do this successfully, he must get along well with people and be tactful and diplomatic in all his relations. Although he must be a trained musician, a capable teacher, and an assured administrator, these talents may be useless to him unless his skill in human relations permits him to use them to best advantage.

Music Supervision

The goal toward which the music supervisor strives is the improvement of teaching in every phase of the music program. The music superviser is not an inspector or a critic. Neither does he substitute for other teachers, doing their work in areas in which they are weak or lacking in confidence. A supervisor is one who observes and assists, guiding policies and practices to help the entire program function smoothly. His function is to help other teachers improve their work rather than to compel them to follow prescribed rules.

The supervisor's duties include recruiting new teachers, determining the school to which each will be assigned, arranging schedules, preparing budgets, securing equipment and materials. He is responsible for evaluating the capabilities of applicants for teaching positions as well as the strengths and weaknesses of teachers in service. He is accountable to school administrators and the public for the quality of teaching. In a broader sense, he is responsible for establishing and maintaining an effective music education program in all the schools of the community and for the public relations that affect it.

HELPING OTHER MUSIC TEACHERS. There are several devices the supervisor can use in helping the music teachers of his staff. Demonstration lessons can be presented by the supervisor or by other teachers who achieve outstanding success in their special fields. The demonstration may take the form of a lesson taught in a particular classroom for the benefit of the teacher of that class, or a lesson taught at a special time in a larger room for a group of teachers from the community. Closely related to the demonstration is the clinic. Specialists from other communities or competent teachers of the local staff may be invited to address groups of teachers on special subjects, demonstrating techniques of teaching or conducting workshops devoted to special areas. In a large community, a series of clinics might be devoted to instrumental teaching, one dealing with double reeds, one with strings, one with percussion, and so on. In smaller communities, the supervisor might find it beneficial to arrange clinics dealing with music in the elementary school including rhythmic activities, the use of rhythm and melody instruments, or the use of song texts and other materials.

Other devices are those included in the supervisor's normal schedule. He arranges conferences with individual teachers on a regular basis, often preceded by an observation of each teacher's work in the classroom. During the conference, he and the teacher discuss the teacher's strengths and weaknesses, needs of the pupils, materials, and teaching devices for improving the effectiveness of learning in each class. He arranges periodic meetings of the entire music staff, departmental faculty meetings during which mutual problems are discussed and capable teachers give the benefits of their experience to others. He may arrange visitation days on which teachers can observe each other, learning new techniques by watching the work of another teacher in a different school.

Through these and any other devices possible in his situation, the supervisor maintains a constant schedule of meetings and activities directed toward improving the professional skills of the music teachers of his staff. His most useful device is effective communication. He becomes personally acquainted with the teachers and helps them become acquainted with each other so there can be free interchange of ideas and a constant flow of mutual assistance. He stands as an example of the cooperative spirit and encourages all teachers to develop similar attitudes.

HELPING CLASSROOM TEACHERS. One of the supervisor's important responsibilities is that of providing needed in-service training for classroom teachers. In many communities, some or all of the music program of the elementary school is taught by classroom teachers who receive little or no assistance from music specialists. These classroom teachers are often not completely at ease in their roles as teachers of music. Some feel they have too little music talent, others too little training, to teach music. Those with both ability and training sometimes feel they are lacking in experience or for some other reason do not have the assurance to use their abilities freely. Even though classroom teachers are not part of the music staff, their music teaching and the portions of the music program under their direction are within the responsibilities of the music supervisor. It is his function to provide assistance and advice for them as well as for the specially trained music teachers.

To help the classroom teacher, the music supervisor turns to the same devices useful in helping the music teacher. Observations, conferences, demonstration lessons, clinics, workshops, and visitation days are of value. Through them, the supervisor helps the classroom teacher solve the problems of daily class routine, suggests new or better teaching techniques, and helps the teacher find materials suitable for particular units of work. In addition, he sometimes finds it necessary to provide basic instruction in music, helping classroom teachers use their singing voices, teaching the rudiments of the language of music, and giving instruction in the use of simple rhythm, melody, and chord instruments.

For basic music instruction, and for giving instruction having to do with the teaching of music, some supervisors favor a formal program of in-service training. The supervisor establishes a regular schedule of classes meeting monthly or more often. Classroom teachers from all schools of the community are invited to attend. If feasible, each sequence of classes may be devoted to a specific area or grade level, one group of classes dealing with kindergarten and primary grades, another with the upper grades of the elementary school. Classes are held during afternoons, after children have been dismissed, and meet in a central building to which all teachers can travel without inconvenience. The classes may be taught by the music supervisor or by members of the music staff who are especially well qualified for the work.

Winning Public Support

The music supervisor has an important responsibility in the maintenance of good public relations. Although every teacher on the music staff and every other teacher of the school system shares responsibility for winning public support, the music supervisor in his administrative position is best able to view the entire program and best qualified to direct the public relations effort. This effort is partly a matter of human relations and partly a matter of efficient organization.

The music supervisor makes it a point to speak regularly at meetings of the Parent-Teacher Association, the school board, community service clubs, and to the press. He establishes systematic means of collecting newsworthy information from the teachers of his staff and disseminating it to the public. He is equally diligent in keeping teachers informed of the desirability and results of the public-relations effort. In addition, the music supervisor is the coördinator or originator of the many music department activities worthy of public attention.

IDENTIFYING NEWSWORTHY ITEMS. Many music department activities are of interest to the public, even those that may seem routine to the music supervisor and his staff. Every music department activity affects the pupils who take part, and everything that affects the child is of interest to the parent. For this reason, the problem is not one of identifying the news; it is one of finding time to collect it and developing ingenuity in its presentation. Here, for example, are only a few of the items on which news stories might be based:

1. Regular concerts by school performing groups.
2. Special concerts presented for community organizations or for other schools in other communities.
3. Participation in contests and festivals.
4. Awards received by performing groups and soloists.
5. Pupil achievements and honors.
6. Teacher achievements and honors.
7. Alumni achievements and honors.
8. New classes and activities.
9. Increase in enrollment.
10. Acquisition of new equipment and facilities.

PUBLICIZING THE NEWS. Once news items are identified, they are presented for the attention of the public through every available medium. Some of these media are readily available; others may be established by the music department for the purpose.

1. Community and school newspapers.
2. Radio and television news services.
3. Annual or more frequent reports published by the school board.
4. Special reports published by the music department and directed to the school board or the public.
5. Regular music department publications addressed to parents such as monthly newsletters devoted to matters of general interest.
6. Special letters or bulletins to parents concerning the progress of their children.
7. "Open-house" days or weeks during which parents and other members of the community are invited to visit the school, observe rehearsals, and attend demonstrations.
8. Special demonstrations of teaching techniques, rehearsal procedures,

and new instruments and equipment for service clubs and other community organizations.
9. "Speakers Bureau" through which arrangements can be made for talks to community groups by music personnel, including the superviser, other music teachers, and pupils.
10. "Concert Bureau" to which community groups are invited to submit requests for appearances of soloists and ensembles.

PUPIL AWARDS. In addition to providing motivation for pupil effort, systems of awards are desirable public-relations devices of interest to parents. Awards may consist of letters, pins, certificates, trophies, sweaters, and band chevrons. Their distribution may be determined by the music teachers concerned, by the votes of the performing groups, or by a point system more objective than teacher or pupil opinion. These are some of the factors that might be recognized under a point system:

1. Attendance at rehearsals.
2. Punctuality.
3. Participation in concerts.
4. Participation in solo and ensemble recitals.
5. Participation in contests and festivals, including large performing groups, small ensembles, and solos.
6. Regularity of private lessons.
7. Record of faithful practice.
8. Special service as student conductor, section leader, librarian, stage manager, attendance officer, clerical assistant, or rehearsal monitor.
9. Evidence of music progress.
10. Scholastic achievement.
11. Participation in non-musical extra-curricular activities.

LETTERS TO PARENTS. It is proper that parents in particular, and the community in general, be informed about the policies and activities of the schools. It is proper also that parents receive accurate information through official channels rather than erratic reports relayed by their children. This is the basis for all letters to parents—that they be given accurate information through official channels—and one which applies to almost every activity of the music department. This is indicated in the following list of subjects that might be discussed in letters or bulletins to parents.

1. The music-aptitude testing program, including a general description of the tests and the dates on which tests are to be administered.
2. An estimate of each pupil's probable success in music study based on test results, including the suggestion that parents encourage their children to begin special music study.
3. A summary of information gained from questionnaires completed by pupils.

4. The availability of school instruments and class lessons.
5. A description of available instrument loan or rental plans.
6. Parental permission for class or school-sponsored private lessons.
7. Loan or rental agreements in the form of a contract or bond.
8. Regular reports of pupil progress in music study.
9. Information concerning performing groups or classes.
   a. Benefits of participation.
   b. Requirements for membership.
   c. Standing rules and policies.
   d. Point system and awards.
   e. Time, place, and frequency of rehearsal.
   f. Concert responsibilities and schedule.
10. Description of contests, festivals, or trips.
11. Parental permission for pupils to travel with a performing group or to participate in any special activity.

PARENTS ORGANIZATIONS. The Band-Parents Organization is common, but similar groups related to the orchestra and chorus are possible if these groups are well developed and active. As the name implies, the organization is made up of parents of pupils in the performing group. It is formed through the efforts of the music supervisor or the director of the performing group concerned. It holds regular meetings, sometimes monthly or bi-monthly, and is organized in parliamentary fashion with elected officers and committees for special purposes.

The parents organization is a means of communication and a source of assistance. Through it, the director keeps parents informed about the progress of their children, the activities of the performing group, its needs, goals, and problems. Conversely, it is a means through which parents can communicate with the director, keeping him informed of their opinions and wishes concerning the performing group and its effect on their children. The parents group assists the director in many ways. It is a forum for the discussion and authorization of special pupil activities. It assists in arranging and supervising trips and concert appearances. It helps arouse interest in the purchase of new equipment, instruments, and uniforms. Its annual dinners can be occasions for announcing pupil awards and the presentation of trophies. It plans social activities for parents and pupils, assists with publicity and public relations, and gives valuable aid during fund-raising drives.

Although the parents organization can be of great assistance when it is necessary to raise money for trips, uniforms or new instruments, it is questionable whether a group such as this should be regarded as a fund-raising organization. The performing groups, as worthy educational activities in the school program, are best supported by school funds allocated through normal school channels. Moreover, it is proper that funds be divided equitably among all the school departments; there is cause for criticism if a parents organization contributes to the support of one department at the expense of others. Finally, groups of parents rightfully lose interest when it becomes apparent that the chief function of their organization is to solicit funds. For these reasons the music supervisor or director turns to the parents organization for fund-raising assistance only when there is no alternative. If he uses good judgment in this respect, the parents organization is an invaluable and uniquely effective source of financial aid.

Credit

When performing groups meet regularly during normal school hours they can in some schools be a source of regular credit, helping the pupil meet graduation requirements. High-school credits computed in terms of Carnegie units are based on a minimum number of class hours during the school year, each class hour being balanced by an equal amount of time devoted to outside preparation. Laboratory classes for which half-credit is given are assumed to require little or no outside preparation. If one credit is considered equal to 120 hours of class time during the school year, a year of thirty-six weeks would require that a class meet five days each week for not less than forty minutes each day. This is the standard which can be met by high-school performing groups, rehearsals being considered as class time and individual practice as outside preparation.

High-school graduation standards, often determined or influenced by college entrance requirements, are stated in terms of a minimum number of earned units including stated minimums in certain required areas. The high school, for example, might require a minimum of sixteen units, including at least four units of English, two of mathematics or foreign language, one of social studies, and one of science. In any case, there is often the possibility that one or more units in music, including band, orchestra, and chorus can be accepted toward graduation.

These requirements vary somewhat from community to community and from state to state. It is therefore the responsibility of each music supervisor or director to become familiar with the requirements and policies of his school system and to guide the scheduling of his classes and performing groups toward meeting them. Although in the past, there was much resistance to awarding credit for participation in performing groups, increasing numbers of schools are now finding it feasible and desirable to do so. Music has won a firm footing in the school program and properly is being recognized as a subject worthy of credit.

part five: A Philosophy of Music Education

13: looking to the future

Sooner or later, most music teachers consider the question, "Shall I teach music for the sake of music, or for the sake of my pupils?" As a musician, the teacher is prone to rank music values first, striving for perfection in performing groups and being impatient with unmusical results as well as unmusical people. As a teacher, he is prone to think first of the musical growth of pupils, being tolerant of results that are less than perfect and excusing them as inevitable stages in the music development of young people. It is possible, however, that the person who is both musician and teacher can achieve both ends, working effectively with pupils to achieve satisfying musical results. It is music of high quality that attracts pupils and stimulates their music development; conversely, it is the musically alert pupil who makes it possible to create music of high quality. Actually, the problem is not a simple one. It is related to a number of other questions, some of them having remained without definitive answers through the years, others having been answered in theory but not in practice. Basically, all such questions hinge on a point of philosophy, the personal decisions made by every teacher in formulating a set of ideas about what music teaching ought to accomplish.

QUESTIONS IN MUSIC EDUCATION

Is music for all pupils, or only those with special talent and interest? To answer this question, it is necessary to examine the benefits derived from music study and their relationships to the broader goals of general education.

In all times and all ages it has been one of the aims of education to pass on to younger generations the heritage of the past. This heritage sometimes includes the knowledge and skill that lead to craftsmanship and prepare the younger generation to gather the material necessities of life. At other times, the heritage will be thought to include basic knowledge concerning the natural world, mankind, and the relationships between them, facts studied in the attempt to understand something of man's place in his environment and to explain the mysteries of his existence. In still other times, the heritage is thought to include the arts and the expression of man's thoughts about beauty; this heritage, when passed on to younger generations, is believed to help them find deeper satisfactions in life and to provide nourishment for the soul. Further, it is thought that man's nobler ideas and ideals have been captured in the works of art he has labored to create, and that younger generations will be infected by these ideals and see the nobility of mankind through contact with the arts.

It is commonly said that human beings possess an innate craving for beauty. It is true, of course, that standards of taste have varied widely through the centuries and that man's concept of the beautiful may change as time passes. Nevertheless, we know that from the beginning of time man has tended to adorn himself and to cover the walls of his dwellings with pictures, drawings, or other decorations. He persists in creating things which are of no immediate, practical purpose, but which are pleasant to look upon or to hear. Since this creative urge seems to have been common to all ages and to all cultures, it is reasonable to believe that the hunger for beauty and the need to express it are common to all of mankind and are in each of us to some degree. Without beauty, man's life would be lacking in an important ingredient; he would be reduced to an animal-like existence in which his only concern would be the sustenance of life.

There is, of course, the question of taste. Man's concept of beauty through the ages has not always been the same and in any one society there are likely to be different opinions of what constitutes the beautiful in art. Today, we are engulfed by music. Television, automobile and home radios, the sound systems of restaurants, shopping centers, professional offices and factories bombard us at every turn with sounds more or less musical. We become accustomed to the sounds, but develop immunity and the knack of closing our ears to often unwelcome interferences with thought. Moreover, much of the music we hear in this way is of dubious quality; even though we refuse to listen we inevitably succumb to a lowering of taste. To counteract the insidious influence of this public music, there is a need for forces working to raise the levels of taste of all the members of our society, achieving the same broad coverage enjoyed by the media of mass communication.

Thus, through almost any line of reasoning, we quickly reach the conclusion that music should be offered to every pupil. The system of democratic education is committed to the principle of universal education, that the public schools should minister to all the youth of the nation, preparing each for his role in society. Music teachers, too, must realize that public schools and their programs are established and maintained for the benefit of all pupils, arranging music offerings to provide benefits for every pupil in the school. Our chief aim should be to develop music interests and appreciation in as many pupils as possible, rather than to develop a few outstanding soloists or a few superlative performing groups whose work is polished to perfection. These latter objectives are important and worthy, of course, but only in proper relation to the larger objective of universality. There is a practical and selfish aspect to this point of view, also, in that music needs audiences as well as performers. There would be little point in presenting music of the highest quality to empty auditoriums or to a society uninterested in its support. To sustain the levels of music culture, and to raise them, it is necessary to create music interests and develop discriminating taste in the total population.

In a sense, music education must be prepared to accept a portion of the responsibility for the state of music in our society. Moreover, music teachers might well realize that it is unfair to accept all the credit for that which is musically laudable, even in the performing groups of the public schools. Schools in which performing groups are outstanding due to the skills of pupils studying with private teachers must share the credit with those teachers. Wholehearted coöperation between private music teachers and those of the public schools is to be desired and can lead to striking achievements. In view of the large numbers of pupils under the guidance of the teacher in the public school, this coöperative system may be the only route to thorough instruction and flawless performance. Although the task of reaching an entire school population may be a difficult one, the music educator may regard it as a duty and an opportunity to perpetuate the musical art to which he is dedicated.

Should music education offer a standard and basic course required of all pupils, or a varied program of elective courses? Generally speaking, it is the core subjects which are required of all pupils and which consist of basic sequences supplemented, when possible, by electives. Although such activities as band, orchestra, glee club, and chorus may in some instances meet five times each week, as do the core subjects, music classes at the level of the secondary school, especially the high school, usually meet less frequently, often only once each week, as do the special subjects. Regardless of scheduling, whether once or five times each week, there is no denying that music is thought of as a special subject along with art, physical education, and others. As a special subject, music must give way to English, social studies, and the sciences where there is a conflict in scheduling; it can be offered only to those pupils whose schedules are not filled with required subjects, as an elective.

In this situation are the roots of a number of problems important to the teacher of music. Because they are elective and scheduling is difficult, music classes often accept pupils with little regard for age, grade, or previous music experience, creating the impression that these classes require no skill and little effort. Administrators and advisors inevitably come to regard them as catch-alls, suggesting them to pupils who need extra credits and who happen to have time available in their schedules. Pupils are likely to be less concerned about elective subjects than those they regard as required, giving a larger measure of effort to what they know is necessary to their school progress and slighting subjects they regard as unimportant. This places an especially heavy burden on the teacher of music who must find a way to make music interesting, enjoyable, and productive in terms of pupil achievement.

Despite the difficulties created by music's status as a special and elective subject, music teachers must realize that it is not as important to the total school program or to education in general as the core subjects. Although the school music program receives much public attention and provides many public relations services that benefit the school as a whole, music, with all its activities, rehearsals, and performances, should not infringe on the time required by basic subjects of the curriculum. Moreover, music teachers should understand that school administrators must of necessity provide first for these basic subjects, sacrificing music activities when necessary.

Thus it would seem that music, at the level of the high school, is destined to retain the elective status that makes it impractical to establish a standard course required of all pupils. In a school program consisting of separate subjects each taught by specialized teachers, music must achieve its objectives within the existing framework and without interfering with the patterns of the core subjects. In order to reach as many pupils as possible, music can offer a variety of subjects and activities suited to the variety of pupil interests and the many levels of pupil ability. To maintain standards, music courses can be offered in sequence, rather than haphazardly, with elementary courses serving as prerequisites to those requiring higher levels of skill or interest. In the final analysis, this situation is a challenge to music education and the music teacher rather than an indictment of the educational system.

Should music activities be extra-curricular, or part of the regular curricular program? To answer this question it is necessary to determine which music activities contribute to the aims of music education and are in accord with the general objectives of the total educational program. It is not necessary to build a case for the subject of music as one of the humanities, or as an important part of general education. Music is virtually a cultural necessity, its value accepted unquestioningly by educators and laymen alike. It is vital, however, to examine the various activities pursued as music to judge which of them are musical and of educational significance, and which may be non-musical and out of place in the educational scheme.

Music lends itself readily to the achievement of a number of ends not especially educational in nature. As has been stated, music has great public relations value. Because of the favorable impressions it creates, music is indirectly useful in the area of school finance. On occasion, music groups actually gather school funds in the form of admissions to concerts and shows; at other times they create a favorable climate of opinion concerning the beneficial use to which additional school funds might be put, influencing the approval of new school revenue. The entertainment value of music can be exploited through performances for the student body, parent-teacher associations, and the public at large. Although there are definite educational benefits to be derived from public performance, there is also the possibility that some performances have no purpose other than entertainment, and that there may be a sensible limit to the number of performances needed for educational purposes. For pupils who participate, music groups offer social training and enjoyable social activity. Here, too, there is educational value related to education's larger objectives for which the activities may be judged worthy and proper, depending on the relative proportion of music and social values, the purpose of the organization, and its intended function in the educational program.

In forming an opinion about the relative merits of curricular and extra-curricular status for music activities, the purpose of the activities, the training they offer, and their service to educational aims all merit consideration. In addition, each of the alternatives holds certain advantages and disadvantages for the music teacher and the activities themselves.

Curricular subjects normally offer academic credit, can justifiably be scheduled in the heart of the school day, and tend to be regarded with respect by pupils, teachers, and administrators. Extra-curricular activities, on the other hand, are less bound to certain curricular rules and requirements, are free to meet in whatever time is available, including the hours before and after the regular school day, and often arouse more pupil interest and develop more group spirit than curricular subjects. Generally speaking, curricular status is desirable for the advantages it offers. It has been the goal of music education for decades to win a place in the regular school schedule for performing groups, to secure sufficient scheduled rehearsal time, and to gain approval for the award of credit. The burden on music education, however, is one of constant re-examination of current practices to make certain they are philosophically sound and educationally justifiable. If music teachers contribute to or accede to the exploitation of music groups for the achievement of other than musical or educational ends, they interrupt the forward progress of music education and raise justifiable questions among administrators and the public concerning music's right to school time and credit.

Should music in the public schools have as its objective the development of knowledge and skill, or interest and appreciation? This question is among the most critical of those having to do with music education and contains the roots of many other questions, some of which have been debated for decades. Should classroom vocal music stress music reading or enjoyable singing? Should music be regarded as a subject made up of facts and skills to be learned, or as a mysterious influence on attitudes and emotions? Should the approach to music be through the intellect or the emotions? These and similar questions are legion. Their answers lie in the objectives of music education, the teaching procedures through which these objectives can best be achieved, and in the nature and purpose of the musical art itself.

Music is an aural art. It consists of highly refined sounds arranged in carefully considered combinations, presented to the ear of the listener in meaningful sequence. All of this must be heard, and heard completely and accurately, if the listener is to apprehend the full meaning of music. Unless one possesses certain listening skills, music is only little more meaningful than is literature to the illiterate or painting to the blind. In our rapidly moving and mechanical society, we develop the ability to exercise negative control over hearing, blocking out sounds that are unpleasant, distracting, or impertinent to the task at hand. For music, we must reverse this trend, striving to make progressive gains in attention to sounds and discrimination among them. In this sense, the aural faculty is indispensable in music, a skill which must be developed and which is properly within the province of music education.

Appreciation, understanding, and enjoyment are common terms in the world of the arts. They are also appropriate terms in which to express the objectives of music education. The art of music is meant to be enjoyed. The enjoyment it offers is heightened by understanding and appreciation. Music education might be said to have no other objective than that of building or laying a foundation for the enjoyment of music. There are prerequisites, however, to the unique sort of enjoyment music provides. The deeper satisfactions of music are intensified, perhaps made possible, by knowledge and skill. The term "appreciation" could be defined as "the perception of merit or worth," a perception based on knowledge. As for skill, music performed by others is felt less intensely than music in which one participates, whether in choral singing or orchestral playing. Even those who listen, whether it be to a concert-hall program or recorded music played in the home, find that active listening, in which the listener participates in the performance by understanding and following the music and by being sensitive to its nuances and values, offers greater rewards than passive listening in which music passes almost unheeded. Active listening is that which produces empathy, the power to understand fully and react in sympathy to a work of art, and both active listening and empathy are aided by knowledge and skill.

In music, as in the other arts, there are many levels of enjoyment and appreciation. The level attained by each individual, whether he is a performer or a listener, is a function and an indication of his taste. An important objective of every educational process is the development in the student of the ability to evaluate that with which he comes in contact, distinguishing the good and the bad, the valuable and the worthless.

This dimension of the educational process is particularly significant in the area of the arts. It is what we know as appreciation and might well rank high in any list of objectives in music education. Important to the development of taste is the acquisition of knowledge, for value judgments are based on factual knowledge of the technical aspects of music and its relationship to historical factors as well as sensitivity to its artistic effect. The development of taste is hampered by the lack of knowledge and sensitivity, and neither enjoyment nor appreciation can reach their highest levels without them. If enjoyment becomes the sole objective of music education, then entertainment rather than instruction becomes the result. Although music may serve useful purposes in the school program as sheer entertainment, it is doubtful whether a school subject should be offered for that purpose alone. Moreover, if interest and enjoyment are the teacher's sole concern, it is unlikely that advances will be made in knowledge and skill, there being little reason for persevering in the relatively tedious work needed to achieve them. There would then be no foundation for the development of discrimination and levels of taste would tend to remain static, perhaps even to deteriorate. It is not a question of teaching *either* enjoyment and appreciation *or* knowledge and skill; the art of music and the objectives of education are served best if *both* are taught simultaneously.

Is it to the best interests of music education for the teacher to strive for constant improvement in performing ability or constant growth in the understanding and leadership of young people? It is fortunate, indeed, that those who enter the profession of music teaching usually do so because of a strong interest in music, often stimulated by early success in performance. It is also natural that the music teacher should be the victim of a division of interest, on one hand seeking greater personal satisfaction through development of performing proficiency, on the other seeking a different kind of satisfaction through development of interests and abilities in pupils.

Music is a demanding art, always challenging the performer to overcome frustrating limitations of skill; teaching is equally demanding as a profession, presenting a limitless variety of individuals to be understood and problems to be solved. In some instances, the teacher may be able to follow both interests, but more frequently he will find it necessary to choose between them, chiefly because of the difficulty of finding time for both.

In the hands of a teacher, musicianship becomes an invaluable educational tool. With it, the teacher can communicate musical beauty more effectively than with words. He can compensate for some of the musical inadequacies of his pupils, displaying convincing and infectious enthusiasm for the musical art. Nevertheless, effective teaching is not guaranteed by performing ability. There are outstanding performers whose musicianship inspires, but whose attitudes and temperament conditioned by years of study and practice, are not suited to the instruction of the young.

The effectiveness of teaching is governed by other factors: knowledge of subject matter and pupils, understanding of and sympathy toward pupils' opinions and reactions, appropriate presentation of subject matter, effective communication of ideas, and many others. These can be achieved by teachers who do not perform. It is true, of course, that performing ability added to the other skills of the teacher results in a wider and more effective array of teaching resources, and it is obvious that a teacher is not equipped for effective teaching until he has reached certain minimum levels in musicianship and performance. Nevertheless, the teacher's focus of interest, the weight of his preparation and the concentration of his powers, must be on the musical growth of the pupils under his guidance.

How can lasting music interests be developed among larger numbers of adolescent pupils? The adolescent is addicted to strong opinions and fixed ideas, some shaped by his family and background, others by the friends of his social group. He is emotional by nature, gifted with an active imagination and great intellectual curiosity. He is intensely conscious of social status, motivated by social considerations, and governed by gang standards through pressures of a social nature. Adolescence has been the subject of intensive study and much is understood about adolescent behavior and its causes. Yet, the adolescent is one of music education's most persistent problems, given to erratic behavior, prone to resist the advice and leadership of adults, and reluctant to show interest in subjects not approved by the peers of his own group.

In music, many adolescents lean toward the popular, especially that which accompanies dancing or some other social activity; they tend to reject music of a more serious nature and of better quality, for no apparent reasons except perhaps the desire to conform to adolescent standards. It is possible, however, to enlist adolescent coöperation in music activities and arouse interest and enthusiasm for the acquisition of music knowledge and skill.

Experience proves that adolescents, once their interests are aroused, give themselves to wholehearted effort that results in rapid music progress. In view of the fact that the music instruction of the secondary school may be the last the adolescent receives, it is important that the music teacher make every effort to reach as many pupils as possible, especially in the general music class or the junior high school, laying foundations for the interest, knowledge, and skill that are conducive to a lifetime of enjoyment and appreciation. For the adolescent, music must be made to live. It must be presented in a manner appropriate to adolescent interest, utilizing activities suited to adolescent nature and development. It must impress the adolescent as a vital part of life—exciting, imaginative, and rewardingly expressive of adolescent ideas and emotions.

There is no universal formula which can be followed by the teacher to achieve these ends. Each pupil is unique and each class is different, offering a different set of factors in every teaching situation. To develop lasting music interests in larger numbers of adolescent pupils, the teacher must regard each class as a new and different combination of attitudes, adjusting teaching procedures and materials to the collective personality of the class. Flexibility, originality, and imagination, directed by understanding of and sympathy for adolescent points of view, are the teacher's resources. Employed wisely, they lead to the music interest and growth that are the aims of music education and the goals of every teacher of music.

DEVELOPING A POINT OF VIEW

In any endeavor, man's progress is swifter and more certain if he has clearly defined goals reinforced by a set of beliefs concerning the value of his goals and the manner in which they can be attained. Such beliefs constitute a philosophy or a point of view and are important to every phase of every endeavor. Because the teaching process is influenced by many variables, a well-developed point of view is particularly important to the teacher. Without a philosophy to define the teacher's purposes, education could easily become aimless, leaping from one hastily conceived task to the next in response to criticisms and pressures from every source, confounded by the appearance of each new variable in pupil reaction, environmental characteristics, and the attitude of the public, and turning to make-shift expedients to serve short-sighted ends. It is the well-defined and well-grounded point of view that gives direction to education and to the daily work of the teacher, making possible steady progress toward the large and worthy educational goals that are in keeping with man's social, cultural, and intellectual development.

The goals of general education and of music education are long range. Although they are sensitive to man's changing way of life and minister to new needs as they arise, the larger goals of education are tuned to society rather than to individuals. They are in keeping with its nature and purpose, designed for its advancement, preparing pupils for society and society for other generations of pupils. Similarly, the larger goals of music education are far-sighted, looking ahead to the future of society and the role of music in a better way of life. The function of music as an art and an expression and reflection of man's spiritual nature, the true purpose of education as an influence on man's physical and intellectual well-being—these are the cornerstones of any worthy philosophy of music education. To serve the daily needs of the teacher and define the goals of teaching more clearly, a philosophy of music education must also consider the needs of each pupil as an individual and as a future citizen with adult problems and responsibilities, the characteristics of each pupil as they affect the manner in which he responds to music and education, and the place of music in his later life.

Although a comprehensive philosophy considers many factors and requires the examination of large and far-reaching concepts, it is important that every teacher formulate his own point of view for his personal guidance in both daily teaching and long-range objectives. A personal philosophy is dynamic rather than static. It changes constantly as it is affected by new considerations. It is based on knowledge and modified or emphasized by experience, both of which grow continuously as the teacher observes and works with class after class of young pupils. This is as it should be, for a philosophy that ignores changing conditions and new evidence can not long serve as a useful guide for the teacher. There are many questions in music education, most of which merit the consideration of every teacher and have an important bearing on the planning of every music class and activity. Defensible and useful answers are the product of a carefully considered point of view, and the search for answers leads to the development of a philosophy. Every teacher should be able to say, "I believe," and to describe his own convictions concerning his function as a teacher. With a well-conceived philosophy he is equipped for teaching service, to guide youth toward significant goals and rewarding achievements, and to experience the deep satisfactions of effective teaching.

BIBLIOGRAPHY

Part I. Reference materials pertinent to general music and other music classes and the broad aspects of music education in secondary schools.

ANDREWS, FRANCES M., and COCKERILLE, CLARA E., *Your School Music Program: A Guide to Effective Curriculum Development.* Englewood Cliffs, New Jersey: Prentice-Hall, Inc., 1958.

ANDREWS, FRANCES M., and LEEDER, JOSEPH A., *Guiding Junior High School Pupils in Music Experiences.* Englewood Cliffs, New Jersey: Prentice-Hall, Inc., 1953.

COLE, LUELLA, *Psychology of Adolescence,* 5th ed. New York: Holt, Rinehart and Winston, Inc., 1959.

DYKEMA, PETER, and CUNDIFF, HANNAH, *School Music Handbook.* Evanston, Illinois: Summy-Birchard Company, 1955.

DYKEMA, PETER, and GEHRKENS, KARL W., *High School Music.* Evanston, Illinois: Summy-Birchard Company, 1941.

FISHBURN, HUMMEL, *Fundamentals of Music Appreciation.* New York: Longmans, Green & Co., Inc., 1955.

GARRISON, KARL C., *Psychology of Adolescence,* 5th ed. Englewood Cliffs, New Jersey: Prentice-Hall, Inc., 1956.

HARTSHORN, WILLIAM C., *Music for the Academically Talented Student in the Secondary School.* Washington, D.C.: Music Educators National Conference, 1960.

HENRY, NELSON B. (ed.), *Basic Concepts in Music Education.* Fifty-seventh Yearbook of the National Society for the Study of Education, prepared by a joint MENC-NSSE committee, Thurber Madison, chairman. Chicago, Illinois: University of Chicago Press, 1958.

JERSILD, ARTHUR T., *The Psychology of Adolescence.* New York: The Macmillan Company, 1957.

JONES, ARCHIE N. (ed.), *Music Education in Action.* Boston, Massachusetts: Allyn and Bacon, Inc., 1960.

JONES, VINCENT, and BAILEY, BERTHA W., *Exploring Music.* Evanston, Illinois: Summy-Birchard Co., 1941.

LEEDER, JOSEPH A., and HAYNIE, WILLIAM S., *Music Education in the High School.* Englewood Cliffs, New Jersey: Prentice-Hall, Inc., 1958.

LEONHARD, CHARLES, *Recreation through Music.* New York: The Ronald Press Company, 1952.

LEONHARD, CHARLES, and HOUSE, ROBERT W., *Foundations and Principles of Music Education.* New York: McGraw-Hill Book Company, Inc., 1959.

MORGAN, HAZEL N. (ed.), *Music in American Education.* Washington, D.C.: Music Educators National Conference, 1955.

MURSELL, JAMES L., *Education for Musical Growth.* Morristown, New Jersey: Silver Burdett Company, 1948.

MURSELL, JAMES L., *Music Education Principles and Programs.* Morristown, New Jersey: Silver Burdett Company, 1956.

Music Buildings, Rooms and Equipment. Prepared by an MENC committee, Elwyn Carter, chairman. Washington, D.C.: Music Educators National Conference, 1955.

The Music Curriculum in Secondary Schools. Prepared by an MENC committee, Frances M. Andrews, chairman. Washington, D.C.: Music Educators National Conference, 1959.

Music in the Senior High School. Prepared by an MENC committee, Wayne S. Hertz, Chairman. Washington, D.C.: Music Educators National Conference, 1959.

The Music Teacher and Public Relations. Prepared by the MENC Committee on Public Relations in Music Education, Edward J. Hermann, chairman. Washington, D.C.: Music Educators National Conference, 1958.

NORDHOLM, HARRIET, and BAKEWELL, RUTH V., *Keys to Teaching Junior High School Music.* Minneapolis, Minnesota: Schmitt, Hall & McCreary Company, 1953.

Selective Music Lists for Band, Orchestra, String Orchestra, Choral Groups. Washington, D.C.: Music Educators National Conference, 1961.

Selective Music Lists for Instrumental and Vocal Solos, Instrumental and Vocal Ensembles. Washington, D.C.: Music Educators National Conference, 1961.

SHETLER, DONALD J., *Film Guide for Music Educators.* Washington, D.C.: Music Educators National Conference, 1961.

SNYDER, KEITH D., *School Music Administration and Supervision.* Boston: Allyn and Bacon, Inc., 1959.

SQUIRE, RUSSELL N., *Introduction to Music Education.* New York: The Ronald Press Company, 1952.

SUR, WILLIAM, and SCHULLER, CHARLES F., *Music Education for Teen-Agers.* New York: Harper and Brothers, 1958.

SWIFT, FREDERIC FAY, *Fundamentals of Conducting*. Rockville Center, Long Island, New York: Belwin, Inc., 1961.

WEYLAND, RUDOLPH H., *A Guide to Effective Music Supervision*. Dubuque, Iowa: Wm. C. Brown Company, 1960.

WHYBREW, WILLIAM E., *Measurement and Evaluation in Music*. Dubuque, Iowa: Wm. C. Brown Company, 1962.

* * * * * * * * * * *

Part II. Reference materials pertinent to choral programs in junior and senior high schools.

COOPER, IRVIN, *Letters to Pat Concerning Junior High School Vocal Problems*. New York: Carl Fischer, Inc., 1953.

FINN, WILLIAM J., *The Art of the Choral Conductor*. Evanston, Illinois: Summy-Birchard Company, 1960.

GARRETSON, ROBERT L., *Conducting Choral Music*. Boston: Allyn and Bacon, Inc., 1961.

HOGGARD, LARA, *Improving Music Reading in the Choral Rehearsal*. Delaware Water Gap, Pennsylvania: Shawnee Press, 1947.

HOWERTON, GEORGE, *Technique and Style in Choral Singing*. New York: Carl Fischer, Inc., 1957.

JONES, ARCHIE N., *Techniques of Choral Conducting*. New York: Carl Fischer, Inc., 1948.

JONES, ARCHIE N., and RHEA, LOIS and RAYMOND, *First Steps to Choral Music*. New York: Bourne, Inc., 1957.

KORTKAMP, IVAN, *100 Things a Choir Member Should Know*. Belmond, Iowa: Mohawk Publishing Co., 1949.

KRONE, MAX T., *The Chorus and Its Conductor*. Park Ridge, Illinois: Neil A. Kjos Music Co., 1945.

MCKENZIE, DUNCAN, *Training the Boy's Changing Voice*. New Brunswick, New Jersey: Rutgers University Press, 1956.

RORKE, GENEVIEVE A., *Choral Teaching at the Junior High School Level*. Minneapolis, Minnesota: Schmitt, Hall & McCreary Company, 1947.

SUNDERMAN, LLOYD F., *Choral Organization and Administration*. Rockville Center, Long Island, New York: Belwin, Inc., 1954.

SUNDERMAN, LLOYD F., *Some Techniques for Choral Success.* Rockville Center, Long Island, New York: Belwin, Inc., 1952.

WESTERMAN, KENNETH N., *Emergent Voice*, 2nd ed. Privately published. Box 62, Ann Arbor, Michigan, 1955.

WILSON, HARRY ROBERT, *Artistic Choral Singing.* New York: G. Schirmer, Inc., 1959.

* * * * * * * * * *

Part III. Reference materials pertinent to instrumental programs in junior and senior high schools.

BRAND, ERICK D., *Selmer Band Instrument Repairing Manual.* Boston: E. C. Schirmer, 1946.

DUVALL, W. CLYDE, *The High School Band Director's Handbook.* Englewood Cliffs, New Jersey: Prentice-Hall, Inc., 1960.

GOLDMAN, RICHARD FRANKO, *The Wind Band.* Boston: Allyn and Bacon, Inc., 1962.

HENDRICKSON, CLARENCE V., *Instrumentalists' Handy Reference Manual.* New York: Carl Fischer, Inc., 1957.

HJELMERVICK, KENNETH, and BERG, RICHARD, *Marching Bands: How to Organize and Develop Them.* New York: The Ronald Press Co., 1953.

HOVEY, NILO W., *The Administration of School Instrumental Music.* Rockville Center, Long Island, New York: Belwin, Inc., 1952.

JOHNSTON, LAWRENCE, *Parade Technique.* Rockville Center, Long Island, New York: Belwin, Inc., 1944.

KUHN, WOLFGANG E., *Instrumental Music: Principles and Methods of Instruction.* Boston: Allyn and Bacon, Inc., 1962.

LEE, JACK, *Modern Marching Band Techniques.* Winona, Minnesota: H. Leonard Music Co., 1955.

LOKEN, NEWT, and DYPWICK, OTIS, *Cheerleading and Marching Bands.* New York: The Ronald Press Co., 1956.

LONG, A. H., *Marching to the Yard Lines.* Ponca City, Oklahoma: Luther Music Co., 1952.

MARCOUILLER, DON R., *Marching for Marching Bands.* Dubuque, Iowa: Wm. C. Brown Co., 1958.

Materials for Miscellaneous Instrumental Ensembles. Prepared by an MENC committee, George Waln, chairman. Washington, D.C.: Music Educators National Conference, 1960.

NORMANN, THEODORE F., *Instrumental Music in the Public Schools.* Philadelphia, Pennsylvania: Oliver Ditson Company, 1939.

PRESCOTT, GERALD R., and CHIDESTER, LAWRENCE W., *Getting Results with School Bands.* New York: Carl Fischer, Inc., 1938.

RIGHTER, CHARLES BOARDMANN, *Success in Teaching School Orchestras and Bands.* Minneapolis, Minnesota: Schmitt, Hall & McCreary, 1945.

ROBERTS, BOB, and SCOTT, CHARLES, *Art of Drum Majoring.* Rockville Center, Long Island, New York: Belwin, Inc., 1958.

The String Instruction Program in Music Education. Prepared by an MENC committee, Gilbert Waller, chairman. Washington, D.C.: Music Educators National Conference, 1957.

TIEDE, CLAYTON H., *Practical Band Instrument Repair Manual.* Dubuque, Iowa: Wm. C. Brown Co., 1962.

WETTLAUFER, J. MAYNARD, *Building a Show Band.* Rockville Center, Long Island, New York: Belwin, Inc., 1948.

WHISTLER, HARVEY, *Watch Your Step.* Chicago: Rubank Publishing Co., 1952.

index

Ability grouping, 42
Accompaniment, choral, 265
Acoustics, concert hall, 354
Active listening, 115
Activities, general music, 150, 151
Adolescence, characteristics of:
  emotional, 30
  individual differences, 36
  intellectual, 32, 36
  interests, 30, 35, 393
  physical, 29, 34, 35
  social, 31, 33, 96
  vocal, 58, 63
Adolescent voices, testing, 68
Aesthetic response to music, 103
Aesthetic satisfaction, 95
Alto-tenor, 59
Alumni chorus, 178
Appreciation, music, 47, 95, 391
Assistants, student, 315
  choral groups, 197, 203, 205
  general music, 159
  instrumental groups, 351
Audio-visual aids, 54
Aural skill, 48, 53, 92, 94, 96, 132, 137, 244, 390
Autoharp, 120, 134, 138
Awards, music, 315, 319, 378

Balance:
  band, 322
  choral, 197, 202
Bass, adolescent, 60
Boys, voice-change among, 59
Breath control, 82, 214
Budget:
  choral, 172
  instrumental, 357

Cambiata, 72
Carnegie units, 380
Choir, choral rehearsal, 212
Changing voice, 26, 35
Chants, 77
Chart, instrumental progress, 318
Checklist, music appreciation, 107
Choral concerts, scheduling, 255
Choral groups:
  administrative support, 171, 173
  alumni, 178
  balance, 197, 202
  breathing, 214
  budgets, 172
  choral speaking, 236, 241
  committees, 205
  conducting, 232
  costume, 266
  credit, 186
  director's qualifications, 206
  diction, 234
  ensembles, 181, 184
  exercises, 209, 222, 224, 228, 229, 233, 239
  intonation, 202, 227
  music form, teaching, 244
  music history, teaching, 243
  music reading, teaching, 237
  officers, 205
  parents association, 176
  posture, 211, 232
  public relations, 168, 172, 250
  recruiting, 173
  rehearsal room, 186

Choral groups (*continued*)
resonance, 218
rhythmic activity, 239, 241
rote teaching, 241
scheduling, 172, 185
seating, 201
sectional rehearsals, 187
student assistants, 203, 205
tone quality, 218, 222
tone support, 214, 232
tone thinking, 231
voice ranges, 188
voice testing, 192
Choral rehearsal:
lesson plan, 246
motivation, 245, 249
sectional, 187
Choral speaking, 130, 236, 241, 267
Classroom, general music, 41
Class instruction, instrumental, 304, 314
Clinic, music teachers', 375
Combined songs, 76
Committees:
choral group, 205
choral program, 256
choral steering, 255
Concert band instrumentation, 323
Conducting:
choral, 232
general music, 129
instrumental, 348
Contract, instrument loan, 369
Cooper, Irvin, 72
Correlation, 49, 50, 116, 139, 155
Credit:
choral groups, 186
general music, 42
music activities, 380
Criteria:
instrumental class method books, 315
music recordings, 113
Curriculum:
high school music, 10
junior high school music, 6

Dance band, 334
Dancing, folk, 128
Demonstrations, instrument, 278
Depreciation, instrument, 360, 369
Descants, 76
Diction, choral, 234
Drill:
music reading, 238, 240
song teaching, 87

Elective music, 40
Elementary school, music in the, 4
Emotional response to music, 100
Ensembles:
instrumental, 280, 311, 331
vocal, 51, 178, 181, 184
Ensemble skills, instrumental, 306
Equipment:
caring for, 368
instrumental, 356
music library, 372
Exercises, choral, 84, 209, 222, 224, 228, 229, 233, 239
Extra duties, teachers', 16

Fee teachers, instrumental, 340, 341
Field trips, general music, 54
Folk dancing, 128
Form, teaching music, 89, 244
Forms:
instrument inventory, 368, 369
music library, 371
personnel, 370
uniform inventory, 370
Fund raising, 361, 379

General music:
activities, 150, 151
appreciation, music, 95
audio-visual aids, 54
aural skill, 92, 94, 96, 132, 137
choral speaking, 130
classroom, 41
conducting, 129
correlation, 139, 155
credit for, 42
ensembles, vocal, 51
field trips, 54
folk dancing, 128
guest performers, 54
motivation, 148, 149
music form, teaching, 87, 89, 117, 120
music history, teaching, 54, 97
music reading, teaching, 74, 84, 120, 137
music theory, teaching, 53, 89, 91, 97, 116, 119, 134, 135
notebooks, 123
out-of-tune singer, 83
participation, 110, 150
popular music, 109, 142
qualifications of teacher, 55
rhythm instruments, 131

rhythmic activity, 52, 74, 91, 116, 119, 127
rote teaching, 87
scheduling, 40
seating, 72, 83, 159
taste, improving music, 98
tone quality, vocal, 81
unit teaching, 111, 123, 140, 141
voice testing, 61
voice training, 52
Girls, voice-change among, 60
Goals, instrumental rehearsal, 343
Grouping, ability, 42
Guest performers, 54, 226

Heterogeneous classes, 308, 309, 310, 338
High school, music in the, 8
Homogeneous classes, 305, 307, 338

Imaginative response to music, 101, 115, 143
Instrumentation:
band, 301, 321
orchestra, 327
stage band, 335
Instruments:
pre-band, 281
purchasing, 358
rhythm, 131
selection of, 364
Intellectual response to music, 102
Intonation, choral, 202, 227
Inventory, music instrument, 368

Junior high school, music in the, 5

Lesson plan:
choral rehearsal, 246
general music, 151
instrumental class, 316, 339, 344
Library, instrumental music, 360, 371
Listening:
active, 115
motivation for, 115
Load, teaching, 307
Loan plans, music instrument, 298

Maddy, Joseph E., 21
Manipulative desire, adolescent, 35
Marching band, 274, 323
Mason, Lowell, 20
Mason, Luther Whiting, 20
Motivation:
choral rehearsal, 245, 249
general music, 148, 149
instrumental rehearsal, 346
listening, 115
Music appreciation, 47, 95, 391
Music Educators National Conference, 23
Music form, teaching, 87, 89, 117, 120, 244
Music history, teaching, 54, 97, 243
Music reading, teaching, 74, 84, 120, 137, 237, 240
Music Supervisors National Conference, 23
Music Teachers National Association, 23
Music theory, teaching, 53, 89, 91, 97, 116, 119, 134, 135, 335

Notebooks:
choral groups, 247
general music, 123

Officers in choral groups, 205
Orchestra, 326
Out-of-tune singer, 83

Parents association, 176, 362, 376, 379
Part-songs, teaching, 75, 78, 79
Participation, 48, 110, 150
Philosophy of music education, 161, 168, 243, 273
Physical response to music, 99
Popular music, 109, 142
Posture, choral, 211, 232
Pre-band instruments, 281
Private instruction, 304, 312, 338, 340
Program committee, 256
Program, printed concert, 270
Public relations, 168, 172, 250, 275, 332, 376, 379
Purchasing instruments, 358

Qualifications:
choral director, 206
general music teacher, 55, 162
high school music teacher, 9, 11
junior high school music teacher, 7

Ranges, voice, 63, 188
Reading, teaching music, 74, 84, 120, 137, 237, 240
Recordings, criteria for, 113
Recruiting, 170, 173, 277
Rehearsal, 244, 336
Required music, 40
Resonance, vocal, 82, 218
Response to music:

Response to music (*continued*)
aesthetic, 103
emotional, 100
imaginative, 101, 115, 143
intellectual, 102
physical, 99
Rhythmic activity, 52, 74, 91, 116, 119, 127, 239, 241
Richards, James E., 224
Room, choral rehearsal, 186
Rotating schedule, 338
Rote teaching, 73, 87, 241
Rounds, 76

Schedules, teachers', 12, 13, 14
Scheduling:
choral concerts, 255
choral rehearsals, 172, 185
general music, 40
heterogeneous classes, 309
high school music classes, 10
homogeneous classes, 307
instrumental activities, 336, 338, 350
Seating:
band, 323
choral, 201, 265
general music, 72, 83, 159
orchestra, 328
Sectional rehearsals, 187, 336
Stage band, 334
Standardized tests, 290
Steering committee, 255
Student assistants, 159, 197, 203, 205, 315, 351
Summer band school, 297, 342
Supervision, music, 12, 374

Talent tests, 283, 290
Taste, improving music, 98, 249, 386
Teaching:
part-songs, 75, 78, 79
unison songs, 73
Teaching load, 307
Technique classes, instrumental, 337
Tessitura, 190, 225
Testing:
music talent, 283
voices, 61, 68, 192
Tone quality:
band, 322, 323
vocal, 81, 218, 222
Tone support, 214, 232
Tone thinking, 231
Tuning, band, 348

Unit teaching, 111, 123, 140, 141

Visual aids, 145
Vocal exercises, 84, 209, 222, 224, 228, 229, 233, 239
Vocal resonance, 82, 218
Voice-change:
boys, 59
girls, 60
Voice ranges, 63, 188
Voice testing, 61, 68, 192